Collaboration
— for —
Diverse
Learners

Viewpoints and Practices

Editors

Victoria J. Risko
Peabody College of Vanderbilt University
Nashville, Tennessee, USA

Karen Bromley
State University of New York at Binghamton
Binghamton, New York, USA

INTERNATIONAL
Reading
Association

800 Barksdale Road, PO Box 8139
Newark, Delaware 19714-8139, USA
www.reading.org

The International Reading Association attempts, through its publications, to provide a forum for a wide spectrum of opinions on reading. This policy permits divergent viewpoints without implying the endorsement of the Association.

Director of Publications   Joan M. Irwin
Editorial Director, Books and Special Projects   Matthew W. Baker
Special Projects Editor   Tori Mello Bachman
Permissions Editor   Janet S. Parrack
Associate Editor   Jeanine K. McGann
Production Editor   Shannon Benner
Editorial Assistant   Pamela McComas
Publications Coordinator   Beth Doughty
Production Department Manager   Iona Sauscermen
Art Director   Boni Nash
Senior Electronic Publishing Specialist   Anette Schütz-Ruff
Electronic Publishing Specialist   Cheryl J. Strum
Electronic Publishing Assistant   John W. Cain

Project Editor   Shannon Benner

Photo Credits
Cover: Clockwise from top: Adobe Image Library, PhotoDisc, Adobe Image Library, Comstock Stock Photography, Comstock Stock Photography, Adobe Image Library.

Inside: Robert Finken, p. 7; Image Productions, p. 103; Michael Siluk, p. 391.

Library of Congress Cataloging-in-Publication Data

Risko, Victoria.
  Collaboration for diverse learners : viewpoints and practices / Victoria J. Risko, Karen Bromley.
    p.   cm.
Includes bibliographical references (p.   ) and index.
  ISBN 0-87207-283-5
    1. Teaching teams—United States.   2. Inclusive education—United States.   3. Language arts—United States.   I. Bromley, Karen D'Angelo, 1944– .   II. Title.
LB1029.T4 R57   2000
372.6—dc21   00-011158

DEDICATION

In memory of Ruby Wheeler Martin (1931–1999)—a reading teacher and college professor, a department chair, a rosarian, a mother and friend—whose quest for collaborations that respect equity and honor differences enriched the lives of everyone involved.

CONTENTS

SECTION 1

WAYS TO THINK ABOUT COLLABORATION

SECTION 2

MULTIPLE PATHWAYS TO COLLABORATION

SECTION 3

CONCLUSIONS

FOREWORD

Upon establishment of the Urban Diversity Initiatives Commission by International Reading Association President Carmelita K. Williams, one of the early discussions centered around defining the word *diversity*. Commission cochairs David Hernandez and Phyllis Hunter and I wanted to ensure comprehensive inclusion of all learners in the definition. The importance of this was supported by the changes in population outlined by Cushner, McClelland, and Safford (1992):

- 1976—24% of total school enrollment in U.S. public schools was minority students
- 1984—that percentage increased to 29%
- 2020 projection—46% minority enrollment, with greater diversity in linguistic backgrounds and family patterns

Collaboration for Diverse Learners: Viewpoints and Practices embraces the same inclusive philosophy as the Commission. The book sets out to describe collaborations with varied regional representations, from urban to rural, ranging from individually focused projects to home-, university-, and technology-based ones. The contributing authors with divergent styles draw from their own teaching, research, and experience. The use of vignettes further explicates ways of implementing curriculum and providing effective instruction for diverse students. A most useful guide for extended research is the annotated bibliography included at the end of Chapter 4.

Each project described in this volume is built on a strong rationale for working together to effect positive change for diverse learners. The evidence of results, both formative and summative, was expressed as data, but also was used as feedback to inform the processes of reformatting and revising the projects to increase the desired results.

Collaboration for Diverse Learners also provides recognition of what does not work, as you will find in reading about the dissolution of a co-teaching situation between a special education and general education teacher (Chapter 4) and about the difficulty a teacher had in implementing a Read-at-Home project because of cultural misunderstandings (Chapter 16).

There have been many debates about practices for reaching *all* our students (diverse learners), but the common threads across the chapters in this book seem to touch on all of the components essential for success:

- support of all groups involved, particularly administrative support
- formal time for preparation, co-planning, and practice
- setting of expectations
- time to implement
- inservicing/professional development
- communication
- involvement of multiple stakeholders
- sharing of strategies
- assessment component
- openness
- commitment

Editors Victoria J. Risko and Karen Bromley state, "We believe this book is about more than collaboration" (p. 6), and I agree. It is about *best practice* to ensure quality education for all students.

Dolores B. Malcolm
St. Louis Public Schools
St. Louis, Missouri, USA
Chair, IRA Urban Diversity Initiatives Commission

Reference

Cushner, K., McClelland, A., & Safford, P.L. (1992). *Human diversity in education: An integrative approach.* New York: McGraw-Hill.

ACKNOWLEDGMENTS

On our way to completing this book, we learned how important collaboration is to our own professional development. As the concept for the book emerged, we enjoyed a rich exchange of ideas that deepened our understanding of the collaborative efforts that afford multiple pathways to successful literacy development for all students. As the book began to take form, we collaborated with a talented group of researchers who are involved in varied kinds of collaborative projects. We thank the contributors for sharing their knowledge and enthusiasm for collaboration and for being clear about challenges that confront those who collaborate. And we thank Dana Thomas, receptionist and secretary at Vanderbilt University, who took great care to manage the files and facilitate collaborative conversations with our authors. In completing the book, we collaborated with Joan Irwin, Matt Baker, and Shannon Benner at the International Reading Association, who we thank for their commitment and professionalism. And throughout, we appreciate the love and support of our families, Marino and Christopher Alvarez and Robert Bromley.

CONTRIBUTORS

Connie Spencer Ackerman
Coordinator of Ohio's Family, School,
and Community Partnership
Initiative
Ohio Department of Education
Columbus, Ohio, USA

Maria Elena Arguelles
Visiting Associate Professor of
Teaching and Learning
University of Miami
Coral Gables, Florida, USA

Rita M. Bean
Professor of Education
University of Pittsburgh
Pittsburgh, Pennsylvania, USA

Karen Bromley
Professor of Language and Literacy
State University of New York at
Binghamton
Binghamton, New York, USA

Sean P. Brophy
Assistant Research Professor
of Biomedical Engineering
Learning Technology Center
Peabody College of Vanderbilt
University
Nashville, Tennessee, USA

George F. Canney
Professor of Reading Education
College of Education
University of Idaho
Moscow, Idaho, USA

Jennifer C. Danridge
MSU Spencer Fellow/Graduate
Assistant
Center for the Improvement of Early
Reading Achievement
Michigan State University
East Lansing, Michigan, USA

Patricia Douville
Assistant Professor of Reading
Education
University of North Carolina at
Charlotte
Charlotte, North Carolina, USA

Patricia A. Edwards
Professor of Teacher Education and
Senior Researcher at the Center for
the Improvement of Early Reading
Achievement
Michigan State University
East Lansing, Michigan, USA

Jill L. England
Inclusive Education Specialist
Developmental Disabilities Institute
Wayne State University
Detroit, Michigan, USA

Gisela Ernst-Slavit
Associate Professor of Education
Washington State University,
Vancouver
Vancouver, Washington, USA

Mary Ann Fitzgerald
Consulting Teacher
Milwaukee Public Schools
Milwaukee, Wisconsin, USA

Ellen Fogelberg
Curriculum Coordinator, Reading and
    Language
Evanston School District #65
Evanston, Illinois, USA

Jofen Wu Han
Assistant Professor of Education
Western Michigan University
Kalamazoo, Michigan, USA

Marie Tejero Hughes
Research Assistant Professor of
    Teaching and Learning
University of Miami
Coral Gables, Florida, USA

Teresa J. Kennedy
Assistant Professor of Foreign
    Language Education
College of Education
University of Idaho
Moscow, Idaho, USA

Carol A. Lyons
Professor of Literacy Education
The Ohio State University
Columbus, Ohio, USA

Marjorie Montague
Professor of Special Education
University of Miami
Coral Gables, Florida, USA

Donna Ogle
Professor of Reading and Language
College of Education
National-Louis University
Evanston, Illinois, USA

Susan S. Osborne
Associate Professor and Coordinator,
    Graduate Program in Special
    Education
North Carolina State University
Raleigh, North Carolina, USA

Nancy D. Padak
Professor of Curriculum and
    Instruction and Director of the
    Reading and Writing Center
Kent State University
Kent, Ohio, USA

Jacqueline K. Peck
Project Director of Preparing
    Tomorrow's Teachers to Use
    Technology
Kent State University
Kent, Ohio, USA

Bertha Pérez
Professor of Education and Bicultural
    Bilingual Studies
University of Texas San Antonio
San Antonio, Texas, USA

Marleen C. Pugach
Professor of Teacher Education
Department of Curriculum and
    Instruction
University of Wisconsin - Milwaukee
Milwaukee, Wisconsin, USA

Beverly Rainforth
Professor of Special Education
State University of New York at
    Binghamton
Binghamton, New York, USA

Victoria J. Risko
Professor of Language and Literacy
Peabody College of Vanderbilt
    University
Nashville, Tennessee, USA

Flora V. Rodríguez-Brown
Professor of Bilingual Education and
    Crosscultural Studies
University of Illinois at Chicago
Chicago, Illinois, USA

Connie Sapin
Assistant Director of Ohio Literacy
    Resource Center
Kent State University
Kent, Ohio, USA

Ronald J. Scherry
Educational Consultant
Ballantine, Montana, USA

Patricia Ruggiano Schmidt
Associate Professor of Elementary
    and Literacy Education
LeMoyne College
Syracuse, New York, USA

Ann C. Schulte
Associate Professor of Special
    Education
Department of Psychology
North Carolina State University
Raleigh, North Carolina, USA

Jeanne Shay Schumm
Professor of Teaching and Learning,
    and Chair
Department of Teaching and Learning
University of Miami
Coral Gables, Florida, USA

Barbara J. Walker
Professor of Reading Education
Oklahoma State University
Stillwater, Oklahoma, USA

Cynthia Warger
Educational Consultant
Warger, Eavy, & Associates
Reston, Virginia, USA

Kerri J. Wenger
Assistant Professor of Education
Eastern Oregon University - Ontario
    Branch
Ontario, Oregon, USA

Karen D. Wood
Professor of Reading Education
University of North Carolina at
    Charlotte
Charlotte, North Carolina, USA

COLLABORATION FOR DIVERSE LEARNERS
A Beginning

This book addresses one of the most complex challenges confronting the literacy community: the building of collaborative relationships to support diverse learners. Such relationships involve a partnership between individuals whose goal is to improve the literacy development and learning of all students through the generation of shared decisions about literacy curriculum and instruction. Common to such partnerships is the belief that diversity is a rich resource for all involved; thus, the participants are guided by respect for diverse capabilities, perspectives, and cultural practices.

Authors of the following chapters describe collaborative projects that are characterized not by traditional views that often equate differences with deficits, but by forward-looking visions that allow explanations for alternative literacy practices and ways to view literacy achievement. These authors are engaged in inquiry directed at generating new knowledge and theory about ways to foster meaningful collaborations. Their goal is to increase "equitable and high quality" (Nieto, 2000, p. 10) literacy instruction for students who are often marginalized or excluded from the instructional mainstream. They describe connections made within classrooms and schools and within and across communities outside of schools, they analyze their communication and collaborative practices, and they scrutinize and redesign their curriculum—activities fundamental to creating "more inclusive literacy practices for children in our schools" (Rogers, Tyson, & Marshall, 2000, p. 2). The settings (representing every region in the continental United States) and participants vary widely across projects, but a common goal transcends each project—the goal of enhancing the literacy development and learning of all students.

Is this goal for collaboration a possible reality? Can all students in today's widely diverse classrooms—whether they differ in language, learning style, culture, ethnicity, race, socioeconomic background, ability, or age—achieve literacy goals that will allow them to become contributing, satisfied citizens? To both questions, we would answer yes.

During this last year, we studied carefully the collaborative projects described by the contributors to this book. We believe such projects hold great promise for helping literacy educators understand the dilemmas and insights of individuals involved in collaborations meant to benefit widely diverse student populations. Their projects are situated in schools and communities around the United States. Included here are the voices of teachers, reading specialists, special education teachers, ESL teachers, students, parents, administrators, community members, university faculty, and researchers. They have learned that sustaining communication among groups who have different literacy practices and expectations, and who often have no power in educational decision making, is quite a challenge for those involved. And they have learned, as Delpit (1995) argues, that solutions to problems "lie not in a proliferation of new reform programs, but in some basic understanding of who we are and how we are connected or disconnected to one another" (p. xv).

As You Read This Book

We have organized the material in this book into three sections. In the first section, "Ways to Think About Collaboration," six chapters provide alternate ways to conceptualize collaboration: as a shared partnership, as a problem-solving process, as a curriculum, and as a schoolwide or statewide initiative. This section also presents methods for engaging and sustaining collaborative involvement, ways to rethink curriculum within collaborative programs, and strategies for building and enhancing communication among collaborators. The second section, "Multiple Pathways to Collaboration," contains 14 chapters in which the authors describe their collaborative projects. These chapters are organized around two themes: classroom and school-based collaborative projects (five chapters), and school and home- and community-based collaborative projects (nine chapters). The third section, "Conclusions," summarizes the book with a discussion of practical implications and future challenges we envision for collaborative practices.

Ways to Think About Collaboration

In Chapter 1, we present our rationale for this book. In Chapter 2, Marjorie Montague and Cynthia Warger define collaboration as a shared partnership and explain its different purposes, discuss enabling strategies, and delineate potential barriers. Chapter 3, written by Barbara J. Walker, Ronald J. Scherry, and Christine Gransbery, provides a discussion of different problem-solving models and the application of one model to a school-based collaborative project. In Chapter 4, Jeanne Shay Schumm, Marie Tejero Hughes, and Maria Elena Arguelles describe their study of teachers involved in three different collaboration models for special education students. Interviews with over 200 K–12 regular and special education teachers who co-teach are used to guide recommendations for ways to engage and sustain collaboration in the classroom. Marleen C. Pugach and Mary Ann Fitzgerald in Chapter 5 discuss issues related to teaching in urban classrooms and classrooms with culturally diverse students who have special needs. The chapter explores ways in which collaborative teaching and team arrangements between classroom and special education teachers impact deliberate curriculum decision making. In Chapter 6, Nancy D. Padak, Connie Sapin, and Connie Spencer Ackerman describe a statewide Even Start program and discuss implications for fostering communication among educators and families to promote literacy.

Multiple Pathways to Collaboration

CLASSROOM AND SCHOOL-BASED PROJECTS. In Chapter 7, Jacqueline K. Peck describes an inquiry project developed in a classroom to support peer teaching and student-teacher collaboration. The author discusses the roles and responsibilities for both teachers and students and provides suggestions for promoting collaboration through inquiry-oriented instruction. Patricia Douville and Karen D. Wood, in Chapter 8, describe various literacy strategies that invite student collaboration and learning in K–8 classrooms with students who are culturally diverse and have special needs. Chapter 9, by Donna Ogle and Ellen Fogelberg, describes the shared decision making required when reading specialists and classroom teachers collaborate to adjust reading and writing instruction and provide supportive environments for literacy and learning. Carol A. Lyons, in Chapter 10, focuses on collaboration between classroom and reading recovery instruction. In Chapter 11, Beverly Rainforth and Jill L. England examine a schoolwide collaborative team approach designed to provide literacy support for students identified for special education.

SCHOOL AND HOME- AND COMMUNITY-BASED PROJECTS. Chapter 12, by Patricia Ruggiano Schmidt, profiles an urban project designed to strengthen home-school connections for building classroom community and literacy development. Methods for developing collaborative autobiographies, shared reflections, and communication are explored. In Chapter 13, Bertha Pérez discusses strategies for communicating with linguistically diverse communities and building a home-school shared curriculum. Patricia A. Edwards and Jennifer C. Danridge in Chapter 14 discuss nontraditional strategies for fostering communication with parents. The authors provide specific recommendations for engaging parents and teachers in meaningful activities that benefit the student and acknowledge the rich contributions of the home in children's literacy development. Flora V. Rodríguez-Brown in Chapter 15 describes a home-school program, Project FLAME, that benefits from the participation of Mexican American immigrant parents to support their children's literacy learning and the families' daily literacy practices. Gisela Ernst-Slavit,

Jofen Wu Han, and Kerri J. Wenger in Chapter 16 describe a home reading project and a teacher's response to conflict and miscommunication with parents.

In Chapter 17, Teresa J. Kennedy and George F. Canney describe methods for using technology as a tool for integrating content across the curriculum to support K–12 second-language learners. In Chapter 18, Susan S. Osborne and Ann C. Schulte describe a school-university collaboration/consultation project and teacher decision making about students with learning disabilities. Rita M. Bean in Chapter 19 discusses her professional development project aimed at preparing reading specialists for collaborative teaching. In Chapter 20, Sean P. Brophy describes collaborative projects enhanced by technology designed for teacher preparation and K–12 classrooms.

Conclusions

The final chapter, Chapter 21, provides a synthesis of the issues identified throughout this book. We discuss recommendations that affect literacy development; student learning and achievement; curriculum and instruction; parent, school, and community relationships; and professional development. We conclude with a discussion of future challenges we envision for individuals involved in collaborative practices.

Summary

The chapters in this volume provide a glimpse of the diversity represented in U.S. classrooms. The students live in rural communities in the Southeast and Northwest; they are inner-city children who live in the Northeast, Midwest, and Northwest; they are Hispanic children who live in urban areas in the Northeast or desert areas in the Southwest; they are Asian American and African American children who live in Northwest, Midwest, or Northeast communities. Some children are designated for special education placements, while others receive ESL instruction. Their families include parents with widely different educational backgrounds; some are recent immigrants to the United States. The projects provide "opportunities for telling all the diverse stories, for interpreting membership as well as ethnicity, for making inescapable the braids of experience woven into the fabric of America's plurality" (Greene, 1993, p. 17). The projects provide a picture of what can be attained through the forming of collaborative partnerships.

Although this book is about collaboration and describes classrooms, schools, and communities where collaborative projects operate, it can and should be read by teachers and other educators who may not be ready yet for collaboration, or who may not yet be in a position to implement these ideas in their entirety. *We believe this book is about more than collaboration.* It includes innovative and creative ways that teachers have adapted curriculum to support the literacy development and learning of students who have diverse backgrounds, strengths, and needs. It includes ideas for modifying curriculum, adjusting teaching arrangements, grouping students for instruction, and adapting teaching strategies to better meet the literacy needs of all students. It builds understandings about the importance of language, family, culture, and social interactions as they affect student learning in the classroom.

—*VJR and KB*

References

Delpit, L. (1995). *Other people's children: Cultural conflicts in the classroom.* New York: The New Press.

Greene, M. (1993). The passion of pluralism: Multiculturalism and the expanding community. *Educational Researcher, 22*(1), 17.

Nieto, S. (2000). *Affirming diversity* (3rd ed.). New York: Longman.

Rogers, T., Tyson, C., & Marshall, E. (2000). Living dialogues in one neighborhood: Moving toward understanding across discourses and practices of literacy and schooling. *Journal of Literacy Research, 32*(1), 1–24.

SECTION

WAYS TO THINK ABOUT COLLABORATION

NEW VISIONS
OF COLLABORATION

Victoria J. Risko and Karon Bromley

> To love, to cherish, to set an example, to respect.
>
> —from "To be a Teacher," a poem by Angel Nieto Romero (Nieto, 2000)

Few schools have developed comprehensive plans for accommodating the multiple problems associated with instruction for diverse learners (Allington & Walmsley, 1995). Many programs currently in place are underfunded, fragmented, and less than desirable (Allington, 1995; Fafard, 1995; Fuchs & Fuchs, 1995; Zigmond et al., 1995). Fafard (1995) and others suggest that programs will remain ineffectual until there is a substantial redesign of instructional programs and a reinvestment not only in educational funding but in professional resources and development—and serious networking across professionals, children, and families. Unfortunately, most school structures (e.g., curriculum plans, class schedules, testing programs, role expectations) separate teachers, teachers and families, even administrators and teachers in ways that prevent them from building communities in which communication and professional exchanges are valued (Barth, 1990; Bolman & Deal, 1994; Brubaker, Case, & Reagan, 1994; Goodlad, 1984; Lieberman, 1988; Lieberman & Miller, 1991; Nowicki & Meehan, 1997).

Calls for Change

During the last three decades, the U.S. Congress has required public schools and educational agencies to develop and sustain programs that support diversity. Since the passage of the Elementary and Secondary Education Act in the United States in 1965 and during the last three decades, schools have been required to hire professionals across different disciplines to collaborate on the design and implementation of instruction for students designated for special services (e.g., special education placements, Title I literacy classes, second language acquisition programs). Recent legislation aims to diminish role differences among professionals such as reading specialists and special education teachers, involve a broader base of experts and representation, provide integrative and cohesive curriculum that builds on students' strengths and history, and respond to demographic and budgetary factors that affect local schools. Additionally, this legislation is aimed directly at strengthening educational support for linguistically and culturally diverse children (Garcia, 1999) and away from the "labeling" and "sorting" of students that typically follow legislative mandates (Hoffman, 2000). This change has come about as a result of the reauthorization of Titles I and VII in 1998, the reauthorization of IDEA (1998), the authorization of America 2000 (1991) and Goals 2000 (1994), the passage of the Reading Excellence Act (1999), and changes in state regulations. For example, regulations changed in New York (1997) allowing reading specialists to take active roles in designing curriculum and providing literacy instruction to students who have been identified with learning disabilities that involve literacy problems.

Such legislation also makes prominent the importance of developing *shared responsibilities* among classroom teachers, specialists, school administrators, families, and communities. Similarly, international forums such as the International Special Education Congress (1995), UNESCO task force groups (1994), and the World Conference on Education for All (1990) have called for educational reforms that bring professionals, policy makers, and families together to ensure improved education for all students—especially for those who are denied education because of their learning differences. The message conveyed widely by these groups is that high quality literacy instruction for all learners will remain less than optimal until we re-think the roles of classroom teachers and instructional support professionals, and their relationships with families and the communities in which schools are located.

Yet, as Garcia (1999) and others warn, legislation, policy makers, and educational forums have not been able to afford the far-reaching curriculum changes that are needed to support linguistically and culturally diverse students. Even with national mandates in place, we as literacy professionals need to examine ways to build shared knowledge and shared responsibilities about literacy learning among professionals, families, and communities, and we need to invite communication that encourages mediation, negotiation, and respect for differences (Allington & Cunningham, 1996; Friend & Cook, 1996; Garcia, 1999; Griffin, 1995; Ladson-Billings, 2000; Nieto, 2000; Pugach, 1995). Further, we need to advance our understanding of how different and alternative models of collaboration can promote programs in which classroom teachers, specialists, families, administrators, and other educators are actively engaged in a process that ensures successful literacy learning for all students.

> *We need to advance our understanding of how different and alternative models of collaboration can promote programs in which classroom teachers, specialists, families, administrators, and other educators are actively engaged in a process that ensures successful literacy learning for all students.*

Why Collaboration?

Among the many reasons for collaboration, we identify those that we believe are the most compelling. We believe that collaboration

- ◆ aims for the success of all literacy learners;
- ◆ acknowledges many pathways to achieve optimal literacy practices for diverse students;
- ◆ moves professionals and families from a deficit model to one that affirms and is responsive to students' strengths, backgrounds, beliefs, and values;

- reduces role differentiation among teachers and specialists, resulting in shared expertise for problem solving that yields multiple solutions to dilemmas about literacy and learning;

- provides a way to respond to complex problems that holds power for its members by allowing all to contribute and take leadership roles so that all are committed to the same goals;

- allows for social and intellectual interactions among families, communities, and schools that can promote the establishment of cultural understandings and connections;

- provides avenues for curricular change and nontraditional approaches that make visible students' capabilities and out-of-school experiences and literacy practices;

- creates the potential for family literacy development and invites parents to become partners in the education of their children; and

- holds promise for developing an informed citizenry that can build strong local communities and a stronger nation.

Persistent Problems That Deter Successful Collaborations

Collaborative efforts are difficult to achieve for several reasons. First, too often collaborative agendas are motivated by outside forces (e.g., legislators, state education agencies, educational policy makers, researchers, and/or curriculum experts) that are too far removed from the children, teachers, families, and communities they intend to support. Decision making is not situated in the broad context of students' school lives and home lives. Often the culture of the local school and out-of-school community is not represented.

Also, literacy educators and researchers have made little progress in developing a notion of collaboration that is inspired by theory and research, has practical implications for constructing curriculum that is based on students' life experiences, and engages participants in meaningful collaborative exchanges.

Teachers, administrators, and families are typically unprepared for the multiple and complex roles they are asked to assume. Even when these individuals want to work together and are given opportunities to do so, such desires and opportunities can be insufficient for building and sustaining meaningful working relationships. Efforts to bring groups together around common goals are often stymied because of limited knowledge of what contributes to effective collaborations, limited time allocation, and a lack of mediation strategies. Difficult issues such as inability to communicate effectively, a teacher's preference for autonomy, or scheduling and curriculum demands imposed on instruction are not easily resolved, and even subtle differences in beliefs, background, and preferences are not always recognized.

Often changes that are accomplished are superficial, temporary, or "peripheral" (Marks & Gersten, 1998, p. 53) and directed toward adjustments in routine rather than deep curriculum changes. Trying to resolve complex problems with simple solutions leads to teacher disillusionment and disengagement, and ineffectual practices.

> *Efforts to bring groups together around common goals are often ineffectual because of limited knowledge of what contributes to effective collaborations, limited time allocation, and a lack of mediation strategies.*

Finally, insufficient planning and involvement of only a few participants can produce a lack of congruence in goals and expectations (Marks & Gersten, 1998). Without a mechanism for empowering the participants and sustaining participation, the benefits that can be derived from collective or "shared expertise" (Graden & Bauer, 1992, p. 95) and shared expectations for outcomes are lost. Curriculum restructuring efforts, teacher practices, and parent and community involvement become fragmented, resulting in a lack of congruence between goals and outcomes.

Given these concerns, the following questions may be helpful for analyzing the design and implementation efforts of collaborative programs. We will return to these questions in the final chapter of this volume, which discusses the collaboration projects described in the book.

- Is there meaningful improvement in the literacy development and learning opportunities for all students?

- Does collaboration serve as a catalyst for restructuring curriculum and instruction, and as an invitation for participant involvement?

◆ Do participants assume new roles and take ownership for their contributions, the implementation of programs, and students' literacy development and learning?

◆ Does collaboration allow for continuous and dynamic interactions both inside and outside classrooms and schools?

A New Framework for Collaboration

The organizational culture of the school and the procedures and policies involved in decision-making processes can either facilitate or inhibit successful collaboration (see Bolman & Deal, 1994; Brubaker, Case, & Reagan, 1994; Rossman, Corbett, & Firestone, 1988). For too long, collaboration has been a puzzle with pieces that simply failed to fit. Our vision of a new framework for collaboration pulls these pieces together. Within this framework, we acknowledge that collaboration takes place in various settings (within the classroom, across the school setting, and within the larger community) and involves many different people (students, teachers, specialists, administrators, families, university faculty and researchers, and other community members) who come together in pairs, teams, and large groups. The expected outcomes are many.

For too long, collaboration has been a puzzle with pieces that simply failed to fit. Our vision of a new framework for collaboration pulls these pieces together.

One set of outcomes relates to shared problem solving and decision making, enhanced communication, and restructured curriculum and instruction. Another set points to the importance of distinguishing expectations for collaborators' roles. Rather than expecting all participants to contribute equally or with the same expertise, we would agree with Erickson (1989), who describes collaborative work as the "exchange [of] mutual help" (p. 431), and we would add, the exchange of different forms of expertise. As Clark et al. (1996) and others indicate, joint ownership is the desired outcome. A third set of outcomes relates to developing inter- and intracultural competence—the ability to communicate effectively with people across communities who have different beliefs, histories, communicative styles, and literacy practices and to understand individual variation within communities (Garcia, 1999). A fourth set relates to building understandings of fluid roles members can assume and different models of collaboration that can develop (John-Steiner, Weber, & Minnis, 1998).

Underlying Assumptions

Our vision of collaboration is guided by four assumptions, represented in Figure 1. First, *collaboration is a problem-solving process*. It should

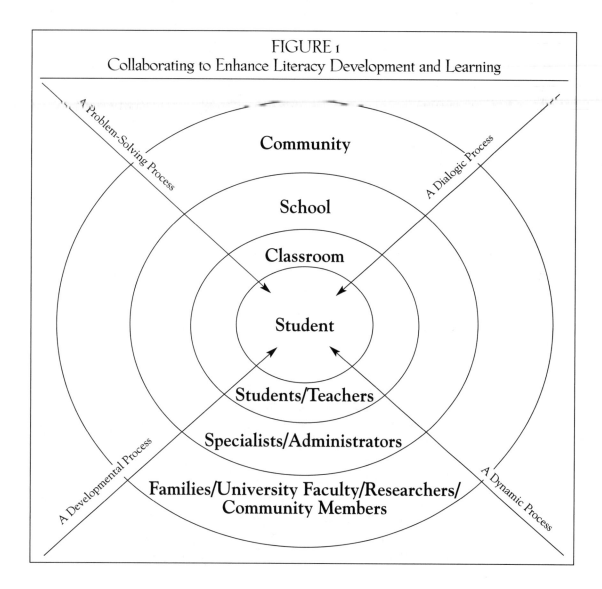

FIGURE 1
Collaborating to Enhance Literacy Development and Learning

be guided not by tradition but by visions of restructuring curriculum to meet the needs of all students and notions of instruction that are guided by ongoing assessment. This process should establish meaningful ways for individuals to participate so that they are all committed to its goals and outcomes. Second, *collaboration is a developmental process.* It occurs over time as individuals generate questions, identify goals, make plans, implement these plans, and revise them when necessary. The collaboration process is often recursive as individuals recognize the need to revisit goal setting or planning, or as they find a need to revisit and improve the ways they communicate or share decision making. Members are transformed and common understandings that develop represent more than a sum of individual perspectives (Buber, 1970). Third, *collaboration is a dynamic process.* Collaborative arrangements, if effective, are not static. They serve as a catalyst for restructuring schools, confirming identities of individuals and cultures, and responding to diversity in order to improve learning opportunities and achievement for all students. And fourth, *collaboration is a dialogic process.* It affords discussions that encourage deep thinking about differences and the development of shared values and expectations.

We agree with many educators (e.g., Bolman & Deal, 1994; Putnam, Spiegel, & Bruininks, 1995) who believe that an emphasis on collaboration will increase in the 21st century. Initiating opportunities to understand and take advantage of multiple perspectives can only enhance our effectiveness as informed literacy professionals and curriculum leaders.

Summary

In this opening chapter we discussed a rationale and goals for collaborative efforts that we believe can make a difference in how literacy instruction is conceptualized and developed. At the heart of our vision for collaboration is respect for differences and a belief that every child can be a successful literacy learner. And, we argue, it is this fundamental belief in the success of every child that provides a catalyst for forming and maintaining collaboration among teachers, students, parents, community members, researchers, teacher educators, and all others. The collaborative efforts we envision involve complex relationships among complex individuals who are trying to tackle difficult challenges and issues. These efforts require careful thought and planning, a sensitivity to competing goals and values, and a recognition that there are many different pathways for achieving progress. Collaboration is not attained easily, but it may be one of our best hopes for creating dynamic learning environments that are responsive to students' diverse learning characteristics and powerful out-of-school learning experiences. Thus, we believe that the merging of multiple talents and perspectives to redesign literacy teaching practices holds great promise for changing radically the schools of the 21st century and meeting the challenge of ensuring literacy success for all students.

> *At the heart of our vision for collaboration is respect for differences and a belief that every child can be a successful literacy learner.*

References

Allington, R.L. (1995). Literacy lessons in the elementary schools: Yesterday, today, and tomorrow. In R.L. Allington & S.A. Walmsley (Eds.), *No quick fix: Rethinking literacy programs in America's elementary schools* (pp. 1–15). New York: Teachers College Press; Newark, DE: International Reading Association.

Allington, R.L., & Cunningham, P.A. (1996). *Schools that work: Where all children read and write.* New York: HarperCollins.

Allington, R.L., & Walmsley, S.A. (1995). No quick fix: Where do we go from here? In R.L. Allington & S.A. Walmsley (Eds.), *No quick fix: Rethinking literacy programs in America's elementary schools* (pp. 253–264). New York: Teachers College Press; Newark, DE: International Reading Association.

Barth, R.S. (1990). *Improving schools from within.* San Francisco: Jossey-Bass.

Bolman, L.G., & Deal, T.E. (1994). *Becoming a teacher leader: From isolation to collaboration.* Thousand Oaks, CA: Corwin Press.

Brubaker, J.W., Case, C.W., & Reagan, T.G. (1994). *Becoming a reflective educator: How to build a culture of inquiry in the schools.* Thousand Oaks, CA: Corwin Press.

Buber, M. (1970). *I and thou* (Walter Kaufman, Trans.). New York: Charles Scribner's Sons.

Clark, C., Moss, P.J., Goering, S., Herter, R., Lamar, B., Leonard, D., Robbins, S., Russell, M., Templin, M., & Wascha, K. (1996). Collaboration as dialogue: Teachers and researchers engaged in conversation and professional development. *American Educational Research Journal, 33*(1), 193–231.

Erickson, F.D. (1989). Learning and collaboration in teaching (research currents). *Language Arts, 66*(4), 430–441.

Fafard, M.B. (1995). Twenty years after Chapter 766: The backlash against special education in Massachusetts. *Phi Delta Kappan, 76*(7), 536–537.

Friend, M., & Cook, L. (1996). *Interactions: Collaboration skills for school professionals.* New York: Longman.

Fuchs, D., & Fuchs, L.S. (1995). What's "special" about special education? *Phi Delta Kappan, 76*(7), 522–530.

Garcia, E. (1999). *Student cultural diversity.* Boston: Houghton Mifflin.

Goodlad, J.I. (1984). *A place called school: Prospects for the future.* New York: McGraw-Hill.

Graden, J.L., & Bauer, A.M. (1992). Using a collaborative approach to support students and teachers in inclusive classrooms. In S. Stainback & W. Stainback (Eds.), *Curriculum considerations in inclusive classrooms: Facilitating learning for all students* (pp. 85–100). Baltimore: Paul H. Brookes.

Griffin, G.A. (1995). Influence of shared decision making on school and classroom activity: Conversations with five teachers. *The Elementary School Journal, 96*(1), 29–45.

Hoffman, J.V. (2000). The de-democratization of schools and literacy in America. *The Reading Teacher, 53*(8), 616–623.

John-Steiner, V., Weber, R.J., & Minnis, M. (1998). The challenge of studying collaboration. *American Educational Research Journal, 35*(4), 773–783.

Ladson-Billings, G. (2000). *In pursuit of equity or sameness? The challenge to define equitable education.* Paper presented at the Spring Lecture Series: Issues of Cultural Diversity and Equity in Education, Peabody College of Vanderbilt University, Nashville, TN.

Lieberman, A. (1988). *Building a professional culture in schools.* New York: Teachers College Press.

Lieberman, A., & Miller, L., (Eds.). (1991). *Staff development for education in the 90's: New demands, new realities, new perspectives.* New York: Teachers College Press.

Marks, S., & Gersten, R. (1998). Engagement and disengagement between special and general education: An application of Miles and Huberman's cross-case analysis. *Learning Disability Quarterly, 21*(1), 34–56.

Nieto, S. (2000). *Affirming diversity* (3rd ed.). New York: Longman.

Nowicki, J.J., & Meehan, K.F. (1997). *Interdisciplinary strategies for English and social studies classrooms: Toward collaborative middle and secondary teaching.* Boston: Allyn & Bacon.

Pugach, M.C. (1995). On the failure of imagination in inclusive schooling. *Journal of Special Education, 29,* 212–223.

Putnam, J.W., Spiegel, A.N., & Bruininks, R.H. (1995). Future directions in education and inclusion of students with disabilities: A Delphi investigation. *Exceptional Children, 61,* 553–576.

Regulations of the Commissioner (1997, May). *Provision of specially designed reading instruction to students with disabilities* (Amendment 200.6). Albany, NY: New York State Education Department.

Rossman, G.B., Corbett, H.O., & Firestone, W.A. (1988). *Change and effectiveness in schools: A cultural perspective.* Albany, NY: SUNY Press.

U.S. Congress. (1994). *Goals 2000: Educate America Act* (103rd Congress, H.R. 1804). Washington, DC: U.S. Government Printing Office.

U.S. Department of Education (1991). *America 2000: An education strategy.* Washington, DC: U.S. Government Printing Office.

U.S. Department of Education (1994). *Sixteenth annual report to Congress on the implementation of the Individuals with Disabilities Education Act (IDEA).* Washington, DC: U.S. Government Printing Office.

Zigmond, N., Jenkins, J.R., Fuchs, L.S., Deno, S.L., Fuchs, D., Baker, J.N., Jenkins, L.M., & Couthino, M. (1995). Special education in restructured schools: Findings from three multi year studies. *Phi Delta Kappan, 76*(7), 531–510.

Getting Started With Collaboration

Marjorie Montague and Cynthia Warger

Fourth-grade teacher Ms. Williams has been teaching for 3 years. Due to redistricting efforts and a districtwide policy to include all students in general education, Ms. Williams has a very diverse group of students in her class this year. Although she considers most of her students to be within the average range, there are a few students who will require special attention. For example, Tony has been identified as having attention-deficit hyperactivity disorder (ADHD) and has a special accommodation plan, and three students—Malyn, Danny, and Pedro—were placed in special education programs for learning disabilities and have individualized educational programs (IEPs). Todd has emotional problems and is seeing the school counselor three times per week. About one-third of the class is reading below grade level, and several students are in English as a Second Language (ESL) programs.

The district has discontinued most of the pullout programs. Instead, the reading, learning disabilities, ESL, and other specialists schedule time to work with the students in the context of their general education classes. Consequently, Ms. Williams must work collaboratively with these teachers to plan appropriate instruction for her students. The administration also expects her to collaborate regularly with her grade-level team to make decisions about curriculum and other issues that arise. Although Ms. Williams values the expertise of colleagues who have more training or experience in teaching students with special needs and varying abilities, she is apprehensive about the expectations others will have of her, what role she will play as a member of these collaborative partnerships, her responsibilities as a team member, and the type of support she will receive.

As schools and classrooms become more diverse, more specialized services and supports are needed to ensure that students learn and progress to their full potential. Increasingly, these services and supports are being offered in the context of collaborative partnerships—that is, classroom teachers are being required to participate as a member of a team or group that includes other teachers, specialists, and often family members in planning instruction that addresses the strengths and needs of their students.

Although teachers have always worked with others to improve teaching and learning, there is a current trend in schools with diverse student populations to rely on collaborative relationships when addressing learning and behavioral issues. School reform efforts have heightened awareness of the value of collaboration as both a process of interacting as well as a service delivery model. This trend to view collaboration as a key element in addressing the diverse learning and behavioral needs of students has led many practitioners to reflect on the nature and practice of collaboration.

Many of us say that we are collaborating, but are we really? Over the years, teachers have tended to work in isolation from one another, which has limited their experience with collaborative partnerships. Specialists such as school psychologists, social workers, and reading specialists have also had limited experiences working outside of the expert role. Family members as well have not typically been invited as full partners in planning for their children's success. However, professionals and family members are finding ways to form collaborative partnerships that respect the contributions of all parties.

This chapter discusses the concept of collaboration in the context of teaching in diverse classrooms. It begins by defining the concept and then briefly describes how to enhance implementation of collaborative approaches by ensuring that all parties have collaborative skills, developing a sanctioned collaboration program, and providing administrative support.

What Is Collaboration?

There is no universally accepted definition for collaboration in the context of educating diverse groups of learners, but most view collaboration as a shared partnership among all parties on behalf of students. At its core, collaboration is a style of interaction. It is a reciprocal, mutual activity in which problems are shared and solutions developed. The defining elements of collaboration are (Aldinger, Warger, & Eavy, 1992; Warger & Rutherford, 1996)

- collaborators have equal roles,

- the collaborative partnership is voluntary,

- there is an emphasis on problem solving or planning, and

- the emphasis is usually on long-term outcomes.

Over the years, the term *collaboration* has been used loosely in the educational context. It sometimes is used interchangeably with consultation and with expert-based models (e.g., behavior assistance teams, teacher consultation approaches) in which specialists share their expertise with others. These consultation and expert-based approaches often differ from collaborative partnerships with regard to parity—that is, one party is viewed as having the expertise or answers and the other party is viewed as in need of help. There is generally a hierarchy inherent in such relationships as well, with the consultee having limited autonomy and being expected to follow through and act on the advice. Although there may be collaborative aspects of these expert-based approaches (see Aldinger, Warger, & Eavy, 1992; Idol & West, 1987; Pugach, 1987), they generally are designed to provide specialized information to the consultee, who is expected to implement the suggestions with the client.

True collaboration differs from expert-based approaches in its emphasis on egalitarianism and cooperation among team members, whose contributions are equally valued and respected. Teams may need training in effective collaboration and problem-solving skills.

Ensuring Collaboration Skills

Collaboration relies on positive interpersonal interactions and an understanding of the problem-solving process. Because collaboration requires direct interaction between at least two individuals who set common goals and work cooperatively to make decisions as they move toward the goals (Aldinger, Warger, & Eavy, 1992), it is often necessary to provide workshops in effective communication, problem solving, and meeting management skills for everyone—teachers, specialists, family members, and administrators. Just as we cannot make assumptions about what children know, we also cannot assume that adults communicate effectively and are good problem solvers.

Sound communication skills are at the heart of collaboration. Principles underlying effective communication among members of collaborative teams include acceptance of team members, an encouraging and positive attitude toward others, maintaining direction and commitment to goal attainment, and establishment of an alliance among team members (Montague & Warger, 1998). All members must accept differences within the group and demonstrate respect for each person's knowledge, skills, beliefs, culture, background, and language.

Effective collaboration occurs when all individuals willingly participate, identify problems and establish mutually acceptable goals, respect the contributions of all participants, and share in making decisions. Responsibilities are divided equitably among participants, who work together to identify resources, understand the expertise of the others, assign tasks, take responsibility for task completion, and evaluate outcomes.

Skills in problem solving and planning are also central to effective collaboration. Having a process in place helps individuals stay focused on the task and ensures input from all parties. It essentially sets the norm for equity in participation and provides a framework for gathering everyone's ideas and solutions. For example, problem solving is a process that requires team members to identify and describe the problem, understand the influences that might contribute to the problem, make suggestions or brainstorm

Effective collaboration occurs when all individuals willingly participate, identify problems and establish mutually acceptable goals, respect the contributions of all participants, and share in making decisions.

about solution strategies, formulate a plan to solve the problem, implement the plan, and evaluate the outcomes. Collaborators, whether working as a partnership or team, should select a problem-solving process that works for them. Consider one of the problems faced by Ms. Williams, our fourth-grade teacher introduced at the beginning of this chapter.

Ms. Williams is very concerned about Todd, one of the children who is seeing the school counselor for emotional problems. During silent reading time, Todd fidgets with objects, whistles under his breath, and leaves his seat without permission. Similar behaviors are evident during reading group, when he wiggles around in his seat and interrupts other students who are reading. He refuses to read aloud and rarely completes his reading assignments.

Although Ms. Williams has been working with the school counselor to establish a positive behavior management program for Todd, she is concerned about his lack of progress in reading. During one of her regular meetings with Mr. Webber, the reading specialist, she raises concerns about Todd. Mr. Webber asks Ms. Williams what she thinks Todd's problem is. Ms. Williams tentatively identifies the problem as off-task behavior that prevents him from completing his work during reading group, and, as a result, he is falling further and further behind. Together they explore this problem statement. Mr. Webber asks questions such as whether she observes these same behaviors during other assignments that require reading. As Ms. Williams reflects, it becomes apparent that Todd primarily exhibits these behaviors during reading-based assignments. For example, he typically finishes math computation assignments. They decide to collect additional information to help with problem identification. Mr. Webber agrees to observe Todd and conduct some informal reading diagnostics. Ms. Williams keeps track of Todd's behaviors throughout the day during various activities. The following week Ms. Williams and Mr. Webber share the data with one another and decide that perhaps Todd's behavior may be related to his poor reading skills. They hypothesize that Todd may be compensating for his skill deficit through inappropriate behaviors.

Then they talk about solutions. Ms. Williams thinks that Todd may need a referral for special education assessment. Mr. Webber suggests that other strategies be implemented prior to referral and that they involve the school counselor, who has a very good relationship with Todd. Ms. Williams then identifies several strategies she would like to try, including reading aloud all assignment directions, audiotaping stories for Todd to follow in his book during silent reading, allowing Todd to practice reading the story before small-group activities, and providing Todd with a reading buddy.

After discussing these and other ideas, they decide to proceed slowly. Mr. Webber will talk with Todd's third-grade teacher and also will assess and interview Todd. Ms. Williams agrees to make sure that all directions are read aloud and that Todd has the opportunity to listen and follow along to stories. She will also talk with the school counselor and invite her to the next meeting. A schedule is made for the next 2 weeks and another meeting is arranged.

The Planning Process

Having an established planning process enhances collaborative planning. To illustrate, Pugach and Warger (1996) devised a model for curriculum-centered collaborative planning that is intended to facilitate access to the curriculum for students with disabilities who are included in general education classes. The model has four stages:

1. In stage one, participants meet to establish rapport and negotiate a contract in which expectations for collaboration are outlined.

2. In stage two, problem identification, the group collaborates to identify curriculum goals as well as instructional strategies and assessment techniques to meet the goals developed for students with special needs. New relationships among students, teachers, the curriculum, and peers may be discussed. Relevant data are introduced to help collaborators identify areas of difficulty and potential mismatches between student characteristics and the instructional program.

3. Stage three focuses on intervention. This is when the collaborative members brainstorm suggestions for adjusting the curriculum, instruction, and assessment; select strategies; and identify support practices for students and teachers.

4. During stage four, collaborators come together to evaluate the implementation and reach some closure.

Shifting the focus of collaboration to the curriculum and away from student and teacher problems has a positive impact on classroom instruction and generally improves the school's educational program.

Pugach and Warger (1996) found that shifting the focus of collaboration to the curriculum and away from student and teacher problems has a positive impact on classroom instruction and generally improves the school's educational program.

Consider how this approach might be used in the following vignette:

Ms. Williams likes to engage students in many hands-on activities during reading groups. For example, students act out stories, use puppets to tell stories, perform choral readings, and interview one another. She is launching a new unit on personification in literature, in which the students will be expected to listen and respond appropriately. She collaborates with Mr. Webber, the reading specialist, to plan and implement this unit. They decide to use the collaborative curriculum planning process. Ms. Williams begins by stating her goals for the unit. Together they identify all the cognitive, social, and independent learning prerequisites. As they think about the group of students, it becomes clear there will be a mismatch between instructional requirements and student abilities. Specifically, students have not mastered good listening skills such as using listening manners, acknowledging the speaker, and giving appropriate responses. They recognize that a problem exists because the curriculum requires students to listen and respond, but many students have not mastered these prerequisite skills.

Ms. Williams and Mr. Webber begin brainstorming solutions and decide that they will integrate a mini-unit on listening skills into the literature unit and will co-teach the mini-unit. During sessions with small groups of students, Ms. Williams and Mr. Webber explicitly teach listening skills and provide opportunities for practice. Then, during the literature lessons, Ms. Williams prompts the students to use the listening skills they have learned and gives positive feedback to students when they do. They also implement a reinforcement system in which students keep their own social skills point cards.

Meeting Management Skills

Meeting management skills are needed to enhance communication and collaboration, especially when working with one or more people. Meetings should always begin and end on a genuinely positive note. They should be structured and goal-focused with an agenda that allows for participation by everyone. During meetings collaborators should strive to understand points of view within the group, trust and respect one another, be prepared and on time, maintain a relaxed but professional demeanor, be sensitive to differences of opinion, and have skill in resolving differences.

Ms. Williams schedules a meeting with Todd's parents, who are concerned about Todd's progress. Both she and Mr. Webber meet with the parents before school begins, because the parents work and this is the most convenient time. Ms. Williams has an agenda for the meeting. First, introductions are made, and, to set a positive note, Ms. Williams tells the parents that Todd's behavior and reading have improved and shows them his social skills point card. Then she asks the parents how Todd is doing at home and if the homework presents any problems. After getting their input, Mr. Webber explains the results of his informal testing and discusses some strategies they are using to address Todd's reading difficulties. He gives the parents a list of strategies that they can use at home to improve Todd's reading. Both Ms. Williams and Mr. Webber emphasize the importance of everyone working together to help Todd. The parents express their appreciation and agree to work with Todd at home. The meeting ends on a positive note.

In sum, meetings should be held on time at a convenient location, and team members should arrive on time. A member should be appointed to serve as the designated facilitator so that meetings are efficient and accomplish the established goals. The facilitator should introduce team members who do not know one another, have an agenda, and make sure the meeting moves along at an appropriate pace. This individual is responsible for guiding the problem-solving process, so it is essential that these important skills have been acquired. Another team member may take notes and manage the paperwork if forms must be completed. At the end of the meeting, the facilitator should summarize the meeting, restating the goals and outcomes. Any decisions should be reviewed and future meetings planned, if necessary.

Developing a Sanctioned Program for Promoting Collaboration

A variety of educators and specialists, along with parents, may be involved in a collaborative effort to ensure that the needs of students are met. In addition to classroom teachers and parents, collaborative partnerships can include school administrators, reading specialists, counselors, psychologists, social workers, nurses, speech and language therapists, bilingual education teachers, special education personnel, community agency representatives, and other individuals as required. Collaboration works best when all participants sanction the process. Sanctioning may take the form of any or all of the following:

- specific time allotted during the day for meetings,
- formal recognition within an individual's performance plan or scope of work, and
- discussion at a school and/or district level regarding collaborative processes.

Each collaborative effort must have a specified purpose that is clearly understood by all team members. For example, schools typically have in place pre-referral or child study teams to process referrals for students for possible evaluation and placement in special education programs. These teams often consist of general and special education teachers, counselors, social workers, and administrators. The purpose of the team is to review all information about a student and make suggestions to the classroom teacher about strategies to improve the student's learning or behavior in the classroom. Another meeting is then scheduled to review the child's progress and make a recommendation regarding referral to the special education evaluation team. The collaborators on this team clearly understand their roles and have a systematic, collaborative plan to fulfill their responsibilities.

Other examples of collaboration for specific purposes include

- grade-level planning teams in which teachers review curriculum issues and help one another with implementation and evaluation of the curriculum;

- team-teaching arrangements in which teachers agree to teach together to achieve a common goal;
- professional problem-solving groups that could include educators, parents, and students who work together to identify and solve problems that arise in the school;
- consortia consisting of school and community persons who meet regularly for a specific purpose such as developing and maintaining an after-school program for students; and
- school improvement teams that are responsible for developing long-range plans for the school.

Providing Administrative Support

From an administrative level, collaboration is enhanced when a number of supports are in place.

First, time for adequate planning and implementing the decisions must be provided. For example, collaborative teams cannot be expected to meet before or after school without compensation. Collaboration needs to be perceived by everyone, including administrators, as valuable. This will not happen unless steps are taken to make sure that groups have regular meeting times and that time is not usurped by other activities.

Also, incentives for participating in collaborative activities should be provided. For instance, the principal might hire a permanent substitute teacher to support teachers who need to be away temporarily from their class for collaborative activities. Provisions for child care and transportation must be made if family members are expected to participate in collaborative activities. Releasing teachers from time-consuming duties such as recess and cafeteria duty may provide additional incentive for teachers to participate.

Collaboration plans need to be part of the school's mission statement and vision. Most schools have school improvement plans that consist of both short- and long-term goals. The individuals responsible for these plans collaborate in the overall design for the school program. They should become knowledgeable about the additional collaborative groups in the school and incorporate the plans and activities of these groups into the overall plan for the school.

Supervision ensures that there is parity among members of collaborative partnerships. Equity among members of collaborative groups and between collaborative groups is essential within a school. Administrators must ensure that groups have equal status. Furthermore, training in collaboration skills such as communication, problem solving, and meeting management should be provided on an ongoing basis so participants develop and use these skills effectively within the context of their collaborative activities.

Finally, the collaborative team must be given the authority to follow through with plans, decisions, and solutions. This includes making sure that the problem should and can be solved collaboratively. Collaborators will experience frustration and failure if they are asked to solve problems over which they have no control.

What Makes Collaboration Difficult

Although the above elements can be addressed within an administrative context, collaboration may still be difficult to achieve. Sometimes difficulties arise from intangible factors such as role confusion, power struggles, and hidden agendas. Certain interpersonal issues may arise that, if unattended, will undermine the best collaborative efforts. At each stage of problem solving, these issues may block successful progress. Resistance may be in the form of reluctance to change, but it also may be a result of an individual feeling a loss of ownership in the partnership, which occurs when an element of collaboration has been violated. For example, individuals in a group may try to take on the "expert" role and give advice, blame someone in the group for the problem, take over and limit the input of others, or refuse to take responsibility or be involved in the group effort (Aldinger, Warger, & Eavy, 1992).

The source of resistance will vary across individuals. An individual's own behavior may be part of the problem. Many solutions to problems require people to change, but frequently people are resistant to change and do not perceive their behaviors as problematic. Depending on the nature of the problem, an individual may feel vulnerable or sensitive and may lack the confidence to be a contributing member of the group. New teachers often are unsure of the "territory" and are less likely to become involved in groups. Also, some teachers may lack knowledge and skills to make curricular and instructional adjustments for their students. Training and other types of support may be necessary to help these teachers make appropriate accommodations.

Some professionals are reluctant to give up control. These individuals find sharing responsibility for instruction difficult and often fail to see the value of new strategies or approaches to instruction. Individuals often have very different perceptions of the source of the problem and have a difficult time identifying the problem itself. Impasses may occur and need to be dealt with in a professional manner.

Conclusion

With planning and commitment, collaboration can and does work. In our work with practitioners we have seen that if the collaboration process is valued and the necessary supports and resources are provided, professionals and families can work together to achieve common goals. Ms. Williams is just one example of a committed teacher who has been willing to work with colleagues and to involve parents in the educational process for children. With planning and cooperation, she knows that collaboration can facilitate her teaching and her students' learning.

> *If the collaboration process is valued and the necessary supports and resources are provided, professionals and families can work together to achieve common goals.*

References

Aldinger, L., Warger, C.L., & Eavy, P. (1992). *Strategies for teacher collaboration.* Ann Arbor, MI: Exceptional Innovations.

Idol, L., & West, J.F. (1987). Consultation in special education (Part II): Training and practice. *Journal of Learning Disabilities, 20,* 474–494.

Montague, M., & Warger, C.L. (1998). *Attention deficit hyperactivity disorder: Knowledge & skills.* Reston, VA: Exceptional Innovations.

Pugach, M.C. (1987). The national education reports and special education: Implications for teacher preparation. *Exceptional Children, 53,* 308–314.

Pugach, M.C., & Warger, C.L. (1996). Challenges for the special education–curriculum reform partnership. In M.C. Pugach & C.L. Warger (Eds.), *Curriculum trends, special education, and reform: Refocusing the conversation.* New York: Teachers College Press.

Warger, C.L., & Rutherford, R. (1996). *Social skills instruction: A collaborative approach.* Reston, VA: The Foundation for Exceptional Innovations.

CHAPTER 3

COLLABORATION IN THE SCHOOLS
A Theoretical and Practical View

Barbara J. Walker, Ronald J. Scherry, and Christine Gransbery

Maureen:	The next unit focuses on the digestive system.
Christine:	What is it that all students should know when they finish this unit?
Maureen:	Let's see, one aspect that I think is very important is the knowledge of the stomach.
Christine:	Yes! We might also want to focus on the role that teeth play in digestion. That is very important information for the students who need some reinforcement for hygiene.
Maureen:	You know, I have a worksheet that walks the students through assembling the digestive system. Would making a model be something all students could do?
Christine:	Yes, for Jerry, we might make the lines bolder so he can cut out easier. Let's do that after we discuss teeth because teeth are more familiar to the students. When we do the digestion model, you can teach, and I will circulate to support students who need extra help. Does anyone else need special adaptations?
Maureen:	On the day we introduce the unit, let's team-teach using the K-W-L format. I can lead the discussion of what students' know.
Christine:	I will take notes on the board and try to organize the information. What would you think about using a semantic map for that part? Later, we can have the stu-

	dents write what they know from the map in the "What I Know" column on their sheet.
Maureen:	That's a good idea, but what about Betty and Jerry who have such trouble with writing and spelling?
Christine:	Let's do this activity in pairs; therefore, one of each pair can do the writing. Do we need to use the chalkboard or should we use the word wall?
Maureen:	Let's use the word wall so we can have the information posted in the classroom during the whole unit. I am sure that Jerry, Betty, A.J., and Kamal will need some review of the information.
Christine:	So on the last day, you can do an extension activity while I will take a small group to review the information using the semantic map from the beginning of the unit.
Maureen:	The new information is very detailed. After we do the model, why don't we split the class and each of us teach the information about the functions of the stomach. Since each student will have a model of the digestive system, they will be able to keep track of how the information fits together.
Christine:	Good idea. This will make each group smaller so that we can spend more time with individual students as they write what they learned....

The previous dialogue represents a typical planning session that teachers who collaborate have each week as they develop lessons. They think not only about the content, but how they will co-teach and how they will account for individual student differences. Our journey toward a more collaborative, inclusive school began when this chapter's second author started his principalship at Huntley Project Elementary School (HPES) in Worden, Montana, USA. What he feared would be an overwhelming task proved to be a challenging yet rewarding experience.

Initially, HPES's new principal spent time getting to know the staff and trying to become a part of the community. HPES is a K–6 targeted Title I school with an enrollment of approximately 400 students. It is a consolidated school district that serves the communities of Worden, Huntley, Ballantine, and Pompeys Pillar in Montana. The school has a 30% mobility rate and about the same number of students qualify for Title I services. As he made classroom visits, he noticed three things in particular: (1) the school seemed to be serving a large number of students, both Title I and special education, in a pull-out setting; (2) there seemed to be a lot of duplication in the instruction the students were receiving (e.g., a small group of pull-out special education students would be working on the same skill and at the same level as another pull-out group of Title I students); and (3) the services of paraeducators in both programs were being used for things other than improving student learning, and the paraeducators were not very well prepared for their positions. These were issues we wanted to address.

The first author was working in one of the second-grade classrooms with some struggling readers, so she became a resource for collaboration. The third author was working at Lockwood Intermediate School, Billings, Montana, USA, and helped us select co-teaching models. As we began we discussed ideas about how we could better meet the needs of all students. As the discussions progressed, we focused on the best setting for student instruction, and how we could better utilize all the staff members. Also, we began discussing some possible goals. This led to the formation of our Building Improvement Team, which eventually led to our implementing a Collaborative Teaming Model at HPES. This model is depicted as a limited, modified pull-out program that uses a learning lab setting and collaborative planning and instruction to better involve all members of our educational team. This also resulted in our paraeducators becoming better prepared and more involved in student instruction under the supervision of our certified teachers, including classroom, Title I, and special education teachers. We were also able to include our counselor and other specialists as important parts of the team. We will discuss this model further when we look at the attributes of collaboration later in this chapter.

Usually, teachers work in isolation, implementing the approved curriculum in their own classroom. HPES was no different when we began. The teachers entered their classrooms each day alone and isolated. However, as we came to know, collaboration is the inverse. It is by definition a social interaction that requires teachers to continually share rationales and create options for teaching. In fact, teachers count on their colleagues to present alternative perspectives to troubling issues and to work with them to find insightful solutions.

According to Friend and Cook (1997), collaboration is a process of interacting among a group of individuals who share decision making and problem solving, working toward a common goal. In this process, the group members share their expertise and unique perspectives on problems. Individuals who are willing to work together in an open and honest atmosphere are integral to collaboration. Through mutual respect, they become comfortable moving between giving advice and accepting suggestions from others. For example, we readily followed the recommendations of the Title I teacher when implementing a tutoring session for a struggling reader because the team had thoroughly reviewed the instructional profile of the child. Yet the next day, we advised the Title I teacher on the behavioral plan for a different student. When collaboration becomes an integral part of a school, teachers, specialists, and administrators accept suggestions from all team members to meet the instructional needs within the school. Parents along with teachers, administrators, and specialists work to reach a wise solution that all those involved view positively.

> *Individuals who are willing to work together in an open and honest atmosphere are integral to collaboration. Through mutual respect, they become comfortable moving between giving advice and accepting suggestions from others.*

Attributes of Collaboration

Collaboration is characterized by certain attributes among the learning community. *First, each member of the collaborative team or school holds a personal belief that collaboration adds value to the community.* Team members believe that the group decision-making process is better for the community than every member making and implementing individual decisions. For instance, at HPES, we began our collaborative team effort with the formation of a Building Improvement Team. The team, made up of staff members, school board members, and parents, was given the task of identifying ways in which we might better meet the needs of our students, school, and community. One of the major areas addressed by the team was how we could better meet the needs of the at-risk students in our system. We worked from the premise that children do not fail because they cannot read and write but because they have difficulty adjusting to the classroom activities and maintaining attention. We also held the premise that all children should be educated in the least restrictive environment and that that environment often is the regular classroom. For us, collaborative teaming meant working together to solve problems, invent, create, build models, and produce results as a team. As we began to work together, we realized that we valued this team approach to problem solving and the results it produced.

Second, group members are willing to share emerging perspectives. The power of collaboration is that all perspectives are valued and shared. This individual perspective sharing is important in understanding the problem because each perspective adds to a shared understanding of the problem. As team members "try on" each perspective, they suspend judgment and try honestly to understand each individual perspective. This means that each individual actively listens to the views of each member of the collaborative team. Along with this, the group comes to accept each individual's unique personality. This respect for individual perspectives and unique personalities is the cornerstone of being able to disagree on individual points but agree on common solutions. Along with active listening, group members respect the confidentiality of their discussions. As conversations occur, ideas become dynamic and are molded by other group members. The collaborative team recognizes that within the group process individuals will grow and change their ideas about children, learning, and schooling. One thing we found at HPES as we held our weekly planning meetings was that we were indeed coming together as a team, and we had new-found respect for each team member's point of view. This greatly improved communication. Thus, confidentiality and respect for each individual perspective as growing and changing is essential.

The third attribute of collaborative groups is that all members of the group are treated as equals, regardless of the position held within the school community (e.g., teacher, principal, aide, parent). Each individual is viewed as having expertise to contribute to the collaborative process (Pugach & Johnson, 1995). Interestingly, educators readily understand individual differences in students, but often forget that these differences also exist in adults. In order for collaboration to work, it is essential to remember that all views from various members of the collaborative team must be considered thoughtfully with the same amount of care. This characteristic means that group members learn how to communicate their perspectives. Stating a perspective concisely and following up on the statement with a concrete example help develop a common understanding of the situation in question.

A fourth trait is that group members work toward a common goal. Although groups of teachers have always worked together, they have not had to use each other's ideas. What makes collaborative teams different is that they are committed to the joint decision and implement it together to achieve the common goal. For example, in the Huntley collaborative team, we felt that there was a more effective way to utilize the special education teachers, the Title I teacher, the aides, and the classroom teachers. We believed that an alternative to the pull-out approach might be more appropriate. After sharing our perspectives, we decided that collaborative teams working within the regular classroom would provide the most appropriate education for all students in the least restrictive setting. This goal developed as we discussed students taking ownership for their own learning and working independently. We also felt it was important that all students develop a sense of belonging within their classroom. Therefore, we decided on the goal of serving students from Title I and special education programs within the regular classroom setting.

A fifth aspect of collaborative groups is that decisions are made through consensus. Each group member must agree to the plan of action. As options are considered, the group asks each individual if the proposed solution meets his or her concerns. Each member discusses options by using each other's suggestions to meet children's needs. Through discussion, options are redesigned until each individual finds the solution acceptable. At this point, the group decides on the plan of action. In HPES, we decided to form subgroups at each grade level that would work with one classroom to include the students with special needs. This classroom would be rotated every 2 years so that all teachers would eventually have a collaborative teaming experience.

The final attribute is shared recognition. Because the entire group contributes to the shared solution, the members also must share in the recognition of their accomplishments; such sharing is foreign to the competitiveness that dominates many of our interactions. The collaborative group rather than individual members must learn to share the recognition for their efforts. For example, the entire Huntley Project team has presented at school board meetings, state and national Title I conferences, and PTA meetings.

As collaboration at HPES began, it was beneficial to involve the entire school and community in the Building Planning team. Later we formed subgroups of the Building Planning team called the collaborative teams. These teams of teachers were involved in delivery of services. Even if individuals are not involved in delivery of services, each individual does influence the collaborative, problem-solving climate in the school. Too often, however, schools try to start collaboration with only those teachers who volunteer or who happen to have children that need collaborative structures. These efforts are frequently unsuccessful because the entire school is not working toward the goal of collaboration. All members of the school staff can participate in staff development related to effective communication, problem solving, decision making, resolution of differences, self-assertion, integration, and self-control. One model that can embed many of these areas is a problem-solving model based on shared interests. When collaborating, we are looking for common goals we all share as we work with children. Using a problem-solving model can facilitate decision making and consensus building.

A Problem-Solving Model

Whether the overall goal is schoolwide reform or providing inclusive services, most teams will follow a problem-solving format. Although these formats may vary according to the type of collaborative group, several procedures can help move the collaborative process successfully toward its goal: (1) problem setting, (2) problem describing, (3) problem alternatives, and (4) problem solution and implementation. These four steps form a basis for collaboration.

Problem Setting: Identify and Focus on the Problem

The first step in collaboration is to identify and name the joint problem that needs to be solved. This step encourages individuals to clarify their understanding of the substance of the problem. According to Friend and Cook (1997), the problem should be stated clearly enough so that the disparity between the current circumstances and the ideal conditions are apparent to all group members. A product of this step is a "brief statement that articulates in general terms the problem area to be examined" (Pugach & Johnson, 1995, p. 145). Stating the problem helps individuals keep their focus on the common issues rather than diverging on personal perspectives. For example, John transferred to HPES in the third grade. He had difficulty reading stories like *Frog and Toad Are Friends* (Lobel, 1979), which places him between first and second grade in his reading performance. A collaborative team began discussing John's academic performance and began to share perspectives related to an academic plan for John. This process helped team members state the problem and identify the common issues related to the problem.

Stating the problem in plain language helps group members sensibly and honestly review each member's point of view and not entangle the perspective with the individual's personal concerns. Likewise, this initial step does not include strategies or solution statements that might compromise a collaborative solution (Friend & Cook, 1997). By avoiding making solutions part of the problem statement, it will be more likely that all participants' perspectives will be enhanced during the problem-solving process. As individuals discuss the problem and its parameters, the group members develop a greater understanding of the problem. In the case of John, the group members often shared their perspectives on why John was not reading; however, other group members would redirect the discussion to focus on the academic perspective related to meeting John's needs within the current instructional program. The final problem statement was brief: John, a third-grade student, needs instruction to develop his sense of belonging within the school and also needs to enhance his reading performance.

Problem Describing: Focus on Shared Interests

Although it would seem that all teachers, specialists, parents, and administrators would have the same interests, this is not always the case. Making decisions about how a student's needs will be addressed within the current academic situation involves considering a complex framework of variables. By sharing observations related to the problem, the entire group can begin to look at the problem from multiple analytical viewpoints (Friend & Cook, 1997), which vary according to people's points of view, the interactions they have on a daily basis, and the responsibilities of their present position.

As members of the collaborative group state their interests and concerns, the group creates a list (Fisher, Ury, & Patton, 1991). To do this, each individual needs to describe his or her interests, concerns, issues, and needs. Interests are those hopes for children we have as teachers. Some of us are more interested in the social aspects related to children's interactions with their peers, while others are more interested in the reading progress of the students. As group members look at the child's or class's profile, they identify their interests or hopes for the child or the school. The same thing happens when members consider the student's concerns, needs, and issues, which are not always as positive, but are essential to understanding the problem. For instance, a concern for specialists might be the amount of time they can spend in the classroom, while a concern for the classroom teacher might be a disruption in the classroom schedule. Using the framework of shared interests puts the description in more positive terms. Furthermore, framing these in specific terms with concrete examples helps all group members identify individual perspectives and, thus, shared interests can be developed. Group members can actually write their interests, needs, issues, and concerns on chart paper or in a grid like the one developed for John's case (see Figure 1).

After individual interests are shared, group members look for common interests and concerns. In this example, everyone agreed that (a) John could profit from an inclusive instructional environment with support in the classroom from the reading specialists, and (b) John could benefit from seatwork and instruction that is adapted to meet his instructional performance level. Overlapping ideas helps

---

FIGURE 1
Chart for Stating Interests, Needs, Issues, and Concerns

Interests
John needs to participate in third grade
Using John's strength of discussion
John having a learning partner

Needs
Support for adapting instruction
John to complete some work other students do

Issues
Meeting all students' needs
Phonics needs to be addressed
Extra support for John's reading
Reading material too difficult

Concerns
John's reading development (more like a first-grade
  reader)
Behavior problems when John's seatwork is too hard
John's penmanship is OK, but spelling is a concern
Including John in classroom reading

---

individuals consolidate their concerns and issues, which results in shared interests of the entire group. Later this list of interests, needs, issues, and concerns serves as criteria to evaluate options.

Problem Alternatives: Generate a Variety of Options

Solutions that are quickly decided on often do not involve all members in generating options. A key element in collaboration is to involve all group members in suggesting alternative solutions to the identified problem. The collaborative group tries to generate a wide number of options without judging them (Pugach & Johnson, 1995) until it has numerous possibilities. The process of brainstorming (Friend & Cook, 1997) facilitates generating numerous solutions because, in brainstorming, all responses are accepted without evaluation as the group focuses on the quantity of ideas. In fact, someone's wild idea may prompt a creative solution from another group member. In John's case, the team generated many options. Some of them included using unison poetry reading at the beginning of each day; doing a class Readers Theatre with John taking shorter parts; using literature discussion groups and having John listen to the book recorded on

Too often people believe there is only one way to solve a problem; however, in a collaborative group, multiple perspectives give rise to many solutions.

audiotape before the discussion; having John and others write their own versions of easy predictable stories and read them to kindergarten students; and having the specialists help John read a short book each day during writers' workshop and then help him write his version. Too often people believe there is only one way to solve a problem; however, in a collaborative group, multiple perspectives give rise to many solutions.

Problem Solution and Implementation: Use Agreed-Upon Criteria

After various solutions have been generated, the group goes back and evaluates the options based on the members' shared interests. The interests and needs that were generated previously become the criteria to evaluate solutions (Fisher, Ury, & Patton, 1991). A common question in this step is "Does this meet your interests (concerns/needs/issues) as a teacher/specialist/parent?" The individual can answer "yes" or "no," but there is an invitation to follow with an explanation. Because the question is prefaced with the word *interests* (*concerns/needs/issues*), the individual assumes that a rationale is needed. It is up to all group members to present and accept personal justification and views that are consistent with the shared interests discussed previously.

Using the shared interests as criteria, some of the solutions will be stronger because they will meet more of the concerns and issues of every individual in the collaborative group. These are put forth as reasonable solutions, and the group decides on a course of action. Those solutions that meet *most* individuals' interests become back-up plans. In John's case, the group decided that the reading specialist would work on the side of the class with John and a partner during writers' workshop. Each week they would read a predictable book, write their own version of the book, and then publish it. They would read both books to the kindergarten students. John would also listen to the story or chapter being read in literature discussion group, make a character or story map, and then be included in the discussion group. This plan met the interests and concerns of the most individuals in the group.

Because these decisions are constructed among a group of individuals, it becomes a group effort to make sure the shared decisions are implemented. This is a difficult process. Daily implementation may be the responsibility of only a few individuals, but implementation is usually a shared responsibility. As in the problem setting, problem describing, and problem alternative phases, the problem solution and implementation phase is a shared process. Because a collaborative group made a commitment to a plan, it is more cumbersome to modify that plan. Thus, during the implementation stage, the collaborative group needs to agree on alternative or back-up strategies if the first option is not working.

Models of Collaborative Problem Solving

There are many models for collaboration that use variations of the model of problem solving presented in this chapter. Besides using a model for problem solving, collaboration also brings together teachers with other specialists to focus on the common goal of improving the instructional opportunities for at-risk learners. This section will present three frameworks that reflect the various models currently used in schools: (1) collaborative consultation, which uses specialists and consultants; (2) classroom teacher teams, which utilize the expertise of classroom teachers; and (3) schoolwide collaborative teams, which are an ongoing collaboration for all children in the school and include specialists as well as classroom teachers.

Collaborative Consultation

Beginning with the Education of All Handicapped Children Act of 1975, teams of U.S. teachers began discussing at-risk learners. Rather than simply identifying children who were at risk and pulling them out of the classroom for services, teachers began to work in multidisciplinary teams to identify the placement and strategies to use with at-risk students. The collaborative team was composed of the school psychologist, administrator, special education teachers, reading specialists, classroom teachers, parents, and other specialists as necessary.

In this method of collaboration, the specialists often served as consultants who gave information about the student profile and recommended placement. Collaborative consultation viewed all members as equal with varying forms of expertise and information to contribute to the problem-solving process. One example of this approach is the mainstream assistance team (Fuchs, Fuchs, & Bahr, 1990), which involves specialists as consultants who direct the problem solving. Each team member describes the issues related to the instruction of a particular at-risk student. After the problem is described using information from all team members, teachers choose interventions from a specifically designed list. Teachers rely on the specialists to recommend and guide instructional decision making, yet the student remains in the classroom. The specialists monitor the implementation and evaluation of the plan chosen. This approach was developed out of the stated need for efficiency.

Interagency collaboration with schools also follows a model of collaborative consultation (Fishbaugh, 1997) in which consultants join the collaborative team to support decision making by offering their expertise. For instance, in secondary schools, often a parole officer becomes part of the collaborative team to offer assistance in identifying instructional situations that will benefit the students under their supervision. Rehabilitation counselors who work with school-to-work issues, psychiatrists who work with children with emotional problems, and physicians who work with children with attention-deficit disorders can also become part of the interagency collaborative team. This type of collaborative team needs to be cognizant of reciprocity among the members' expertise and must describe their ideas with concrete examples because they may not share a common language. For example, the teacher-researcher movement involved university professors who became part of the collaborative interactions to restructure schools (Fishbaugh, 1997). Initial interactions often involved establishing a common language for discussing issues, which was followed by honing the focus on the problem in concrete terms.

In one elementary school, the first- and second-grade teachers, the Title I aides, the principal, and the first author of this chapter collaborated on an early intervention program. Each week, teachers and aides met and discussed student progress, while each month the principal and college faculty met with the team. During these meetings, we reviewed the information on the children and the program. Using this information, we modified the original plan and created ways to monitor performance. In this situation, everyone's expertise was valued. All members of the team made contributions to the design of the program and to the success of the Title I students in the regular classroom. The continuous team meetings contributed to this program's success. In this situation, as in all collaborative interactions, it was imperative that the consultants probe for understanding and reflect the team members' intentions.

Teacher to Teacher Collaboration

As teachers became part of the referral process, they began to assert more control in the pre-referral process. Teacher assistant teams (Chalfant & Pysh, 1989) and peer collaboration (Johnson & Pugach, 1991) serve as forms of collaborative problem solving in which classroom teachers share observations and data about a child and collaborate to generate options to try before further referral. Teacher assistant teams began as a response to the increasing referrals to special education programs (Chalfant & Pysh, 1989). In this model, expert classroom teachers are selected or elected to be part of an ongoing problem-solving team that helps classroom teachers review information about a child who is experiencing academic difficulty. This changed the focus of identification and curriculum planning by putting classroom teachers at the heart of the collaborative process. Similar to teacher assistant teams, peer collaboration focuses on using pairs of classroom teachers who use their expertise to collaboratively reflect on a child's learning difficulty in all its intricacies. In this approach, classroom teachers use their strengths to work together to construct instructional options. The initiator describes the problem and related issues while the facilitator guides reflection by asking clarifying questions and assisting in generating more than one solution.

Teacher assistant teams and peer collaboration are important models of collaborative planning because the classroom teacher is at the focus of the planning and is a full participant in the problem-solving process.

Schoolwide Collaboration

In schoolwide collaborative planning, the entire school staff is involved in collaboration, deciding the nature of the curriculum and specific methods it will use as well as the philosophical stance it will adopt toward instructing at-risk learners. Rather than simply pulling at-risk children out of classrooms, teachers team together to identify strategies to use with these students. This often leads to restructuring the delivery of reading and writing instruction. After the HPES project established goals, we set about learning what it meant to collaborate in a regular classroom setting. As a school, we attended training sessions on collaborative teaching. We decided on a schoolwide restructuring of reading and writing instruction that involves inclusive practices as much as possible. These decisions were followed with collaborative planning sessions in which teachers worked through how collaboration might look in their classrooms. As collaborative teams were formed, time was set aside for planning and implementing the common goal. Thus, when schools decide to include at-risk students in the regular classroom, teachers must experiment and adapt their instruction. This draws on the creativity of teachers, team building, and schoolwide discussions. Through using shared plans and building consensus, teachers work in subgroups and smaller teams to meet individual classroom and student needs. As they collaborate, teachers become more willing to take risks and try new approaches. At the core of schoolwide collaboration is an environment that supports shared decision making, shared teaching, and shared experimentation.

Various models have been developed to assist in collaborative problem solving. Some are fairly structured and directed by specialists, as in the mainstream assistance teams, while others are more open-ended and directed by the strengths of group members and the needs of the school, as in schoolwide collaboration.

Collaborative Teaching

The concept of classroom teachers and specialists teaching together has grown in its implementation during the last 10 years. An increasing number of plans have been developed that involve the inclusion of students with special needs in the regular classroom. In many of these classrooms, specialists work alongside regular classroom teachers collaboratively planning and implementing curricular adaptations. For instance, at HPES one of our collaborative teams involved a regular classroom teacher and a special education teacher. The two teachers not only collaborated on planning and implementing individual education plans for special education students in the room, but they also collaborated on lessons that they team taught for the entire classroom. This process involved making adaptations for individual students and deciding which role each teacher would take in implementing and evaluating the lessons. Ways that teachers can collaborate during instruction vary, and teachers decide which method best meets the needs of the children and the instructional purposes. The more common structures for collaborative teams in the classroom are described in the following section.

Leader and Teacher-Observer Dyad

One way to collaborate is to have one teacher deliver the lesson to the entire class while the other teacher moves around the room helping and observing students, making notes and monitoring how at-risk students are learning. The teacher-observer may also participate in instruction by helping students who are at-risk. The teacher-observer circulates around the room paraphrasing and clarifying information presented by the lead teacher (Gransbery, 1998). Many beginning efforts at teaming use this approach. Often the specialist is the one supporting the lesson delivered by the regular classroom teacher. However, as the team begins to work together, members become more comfortable in all roles. Some days, the specialist may lead a lesson while the classroom teacher circulates around the room offering support when needed. This allows the classroom teacher to observe the learning and engagement of all students in the classroom.

Two Teachers—Divided Class

Another way to offer support for at-risk students is to divide the class in two groups. This is effective for various reasons. The class can be divided in half to decrease the instructional size of the group. In this approach, the teachers are like twins because they have planned the lesson activities together, but they deliver it to only one-half the class (Gransbery, 1998). This approach helps at-risk students because they may more readily participate in small groups. In another model, the class can be divided in half as in the twinning model, but each teacher prepares part of the overall lesson, and the teachers rotate to each half of the class. As they teach their specialized lesson on a particular part of the content, they can increase depth of knowledge because of their familiarity with the topic. Another way to divide the class is between those students who need more experience with the new concept and those students who can readily extend the learning to new situations. In this plan, one teacher re-teaches the concepts with new examples while another creates activities to extend learning.

Team Teaching

Another way to implement collaboration is for both teachers to plan and deliver a lesson together. For example, one teacher may demonstrate a science activity while the other teacher writes students' observations on the chalkboard. In this model, one teacher may readily offer information about the topic and another may demonstrate how that information helps to increase understanding. The students observe two teachers combining their own knowledge and expertise to construct meaning about a particular topic. As they circulate the room, demonstrating the information and discussing with the children and the other teacher, the class as a whole observes how students help each other understand information.

Varying Co-Teaching Models

Teachers can use a variety of co-teaching models (Gransbery, 1998). In one elementary science class, teachers planned together. They selected materials and concepts, and they selected the types of collaborative teaching that would be used. In their unit, they used various co-teaching models. The first day of the unit, they used team teaching to provide an introduction to the unit with lecture, notes, and models. On the second day, they divided the class into two groups, and each teacher taught a different concept then exchanged places halfway through the time. On the third day, they used the leader/teacher-observer structure because explicit directions were needed to assist students in putting a science model together. This allowed one teacher to move around the class to assess students' needs while the other continued to give the class directions. The fourth day they used the team teaching model similar to the first day while on the fifth day one teacher re-taught the students who were struggling and the other provided an alternative lesson.

At Huntley Project, we developed our collaborative teams by utilizing our regular classroom, special education, and Title I personnel. This model ensured that we were able to serve the needs of all students in the least restrictive setting, which most often was the regular classroom. In addition, this model allowed us to create teams of teachers and support staff who could meet on a regular basis and devise the best instruction for all students in their classrooms. Through this model, we saw gains in all students' learning; as importantly, we saw higher teacher morale and satisfaction.

Summary

The collaborative climate developed within a school community is an evolutionary process. Collaborating is something individuals come to know. It is constructed within each community. Long-term change begins to take place because there is a change in the school culture, including the way one thinks about how students learn and how adults work together to support that learning. Together the adults gather authentic data about children's learning and discuss their observations to establish common patterns among learners. As they collect data about how their instruction works, they begin to realize what students need to know and need to be able to do at each grade level. When this happens, teachers develop a shared responsibility for every child's learning.

The collaborative climate developed within a school community is an evolutionary process. Collaborating is something individuals come to know.

Of course, collaboration does not just happen. Strong support from the school board and the administration—as well as from parents, staff, and community—are essential if effective collaboration is to take place. Thus, all individuals continually work toward creating a collaborative community where everyone can engage in a multidimensional range of collaborative interactions (Pugach & Johnson, 1995). Collaboration occurs smoothly when all teachers are involved in making a shift toward a more collaborative context in the school. Because this process is more dynamic, it depends on constant communication. Through their interactions, teachers, administrators, and parents begin to discuss children in new ways. All teachers begin to believe they are responsible for all the children in the school rather than only those students in their classes. Those teachers who are not directly involved in collaborative structures offer support to those who are. In other words, the bond of collaboration creates a community in which an ethic of care (Noddings, 1992) prevails.

NOTE

Christine Gransbery died of cancer during the writing of this chapter. She was a special education teacher who designed co-teaching models to use with classroom teachers in content areas. She shared her experience in a graduate seminar while finishing her master's degree in special education. We dedicate this chapter to the memory of her unyielding commitment to at-risk learners and to collaborative interactions to enhance their learning.

References

Chalfant, J., & Pysh, M. (1989). Teacher assistance teams: Five descriptive studies on 96 teams. *Remedial and Special Education, 10*(6), 49–58.

Education for All Handicapped Children Act of 1975, Pub. L. No. 94-142.

Fishbaugh, M.S. (1997). *Models of collaboration*. Boston: Allyn & Bacon.

Fisher, R., Ury, W., & Patton, B. (1991). *Getting to yes: Negotiating agreement without giving in* (2nd ed.). New York: Penguin Books.

Friend, M., & Cook, L. (1997). *Interactions: Collaboration skills for school professionals* (2nd ed.). White Plains, NY: Longman.

Fuchs, D., Fuchs, L.S., & Bahr, M.W. (1990). Mainstream assistance teams: A scientific basis for the art of consultation. *Exceptional Children, 57*(2), 128–139.

Gransbery, C. (1998). *The 1,2,3's of co-teaching*. Unpublished paper, Montana State University—Billings, Billings, MT.

Johnson, L.J., & Pugach, M.C. (1991). Peer collaboration: Accommodating the needs of students with mild learning and behavior problems. *Exceptional Children, 57*(5), 454–461.

Lobel, A. (1979). *Frog and Toad are friends.* New York: HarperCollins.

Noddings, N. (1992). *The challenge to care in schools: An alternative approach to education.* New York: Teachers College Press.

Pugach, M.C., & Johnson, L.J. (1995). *Collaborative practitioners, Collaborative schools.* Denver, CO: Love Publishing.

CHAPTER 4

Co-Teaching
It Takes More Than ESP

Jeanne Shay Schumm, Marie Tejero Hughes, and Maria Elena Arguelles

Barbara, a special education teacher, and Anita, a general education teacher, were assigned to co-teach in a fourth-grade inclusion class. Their principal explained that there would be approximately 35 students in their class, 15 of whom were district-identified as learning disabled (LD). Because of the number of students with learning disabilities assigned to the class, Barbara was assigned to co-teach full-time in the general education classroom.

Barbara was new to the school, so the teachers did not know each other nor had they ever worked together. To help Barbara and Anita get acquainted, the principal offered to pay their registration fees to attend a workshop on writing across the curriculum. The week-long workshop (held 2 weeks before school started) proved to be a "bonding" experience for Barbara and Anita. At the end of the workshop Barbara commented, "We make a perfect pair. I know what Anita is thinking before she says a word. We have ESP."

The school year started off with a bang. Barbara and Anita put their best effort into co-planning. Their goal was to develop an accepting classroom atmosphere in which all students could learn. Unfortunately, before the first grading period was over, trouble began brewing. Barbara and Anita had very different ideas about reading instruction, grouping during math and reading, and the use of textbooks during content area instruction. Moreover, their classroom management styles were divergent. Students sensed the tension and began to play one teacher against the other. At a conference with the principal toward the end of the school year, the partnership was dissolved.

Barbara and Anita are among thousands of teachers throughout the United States who are being invited to engage in co-teaching partnerships. For years, pull-out resource programs for special education and Title I services have been criticized for their inefficiency and incongruence with general education instruction (see Allington & Johnston, 1989). As more schools move away from pull-out resource rooms for special education and Title I services, teachers are being asked to work collaboratively in the general education setting either full or part time.

As a result of the movement toward inclusion of students with disabilities in the general education classroom, collaborative models of teaching between special and general educators have steadily grown in popularity during recent years. Correspondingly, research regarding these new types of collaborations has followed suit (Bauwens, Hourcade, & Friend, 1989; Cook & Friend, 1995; Reinhiller, 1996). Positive outcomes for both students and teachers have been reported in several studies (Adams & Cessna, 1993; Friend & Cook, 1992; Harris et al., 1987). Indeed, co-teaching in general education settings offers the promise of coordinated instruction and provides the support general education teachers need to accommodate the needs of students with disabilities.

However, many general education teachers report they lack the knowledge, skills, confidence, and time they need to make instructional adaptations for students with special needs (Bauwens & Hourcade, 1995; Pugach & Wesson, 1995; Schumm & Vaughn, 1992). The benefit of on-the-spot, in-class support from a trained special education teacher is overshadowed by the reality that many general and special education teachers have not been prepared to co-teach in either preservice or inservice teacher education programs. Like Barbara and Anita, many teachers are beginning to realize that creating successful co-teaching experiences necessitates more than extrasensory perception—it takes more than ESP.

> *Many general education teachers report they lack the knowledge, skills, confidence, and time they need to make instructional adaptations for students with special needs (Bauwens & Hourcade, 1995; Pugach & Wesson, 1995; Schumm & Vaughn, 1992).*

This chapter will share what we have learned from our conversations with more than 200 general and special education teachers engaged in co-teaching partnerships in elementary and secondary schools. The chapter will begin with an overview of our investigation and a summary of key findings related to teachers' perceptions of the impact of co-teaching on their own roles and responsibilities, as well as the impact of co-teaching on their students. The chapter continues with a description of recommendations that emerged from our conversations with teachers about key components of successful co-teaching. We titled these suggestions ESP Plus. This chapter also includes an annotated bibliography of resources for co-teaching.

Overview of Data Sources

As part of a statewide pilot program, the Florida Department of Education encouraged schools to identify and implement instructional delivery strategies that would result in more inclusion of exceptional students into the mainstream, special assistance and consultation for exceptional students in general education environments, partnerships and collaboration between special and general education teachers, and a broader scope of instructional services provided to all students. During the second year of this program, 69 schools across the state of Florida participated in this restructuring initiative (see Arguelles, Schumm, & Vaughn, 1996, for a technical report). We conducted extensive observations and interviews in these schools (43 elementary, 23 secondary, and 3 combination). Participants in this study included at least one general education teacher, one special education teacher, and one support personnel (e.g., occupational therapist) from each of the 69 schools.

Schools varied considerably in terms of the service delivery models used for special education. Some schools used a collaboration model in which the special education teacher served as a consultant, assisting general education teachers during planning and making adaptations to tests and assignments. Under the collaboration model, the special education teacher did not actually co-teach, but did help with co-planning. Other schools used a part-time co-teaching model in which special and general education teachers worked in the same classroom during certain subjects such as language arts and math. In this model, the special education teacher worked with two or three general education teachers, spending a few hours per day with each. Still other schools used a full-time co-teaching model with special and general education teachers working together the entire school day. What the schools did have in common was a higher level of collaboration than in previous years between general and special educators in the general education classroom—either part or full time.

Multiple data sources were used to cross-validate findings (Strauss & Corbin, 1990) and data were drawn from both qualitative and quantitative sources (Yin, 1989). Individual interviews were conducted with participants, as were focus group interviews with key personnel at each site. Focus group interviews consisted of an average of five staff members, including general and special education teachers and support personnel. Procedures for focus group interviews described by Vaughn, Schumm, and Sinagub (1996) were followed. In addition, personnel at each site completed surveys designed to elicit participants' perceptions of the pilot program and its impact on their roles and responsibilities.

Quotes from the individual interviews, focus group interviews, and open-ended survey items were transcribed into one document. The information was then categorized to summarize the findings in meaningful ways. The guidelines for data reduction and analysis were suggested by Miles and Huberman (1994). Using the transcriptions, categories for analysis were generated and defined by two researchers who independently conducted examinations of one randomly selected data set. For each issue, they searched the responses for common ideas and themes (Strauss & Corbin, 1990), which they then used to develop an initial list of categories. The researchers then met to negotiate a mutual set of categories, with examples for each.

The data were coded using coder-determined "chunks" of discourse (Evertson & Green, 1986). A chunk of discourse is defined as a sentence, paragraph, or larger segment of discourse that provides evidence of a particular category or theme. After coding subsamples of data sets using the defined categories, the two researchers conferred to compare responses, further revise, and resolve differences in coding (Vaughn, Schumm, Klingner, & Saumell, 1995). Themes were subdivided or collapsed as required during the process (adapted from Lincoln & Guba, 1985). Two independent researchers who were experienced in developing coding systems reviewed the final coding scheme.

Teachers' Perceptions of the Impact of Co-Teaching

Impact on Teachers' Roles and Responsibilities

Regardless of the variety of service delivery models found, teachers were mostly positive about co-teaching and endorsed this instructional arrangement. Therefore, data were collapsed and findings will be presented as a whole. Teachers used words such as "exciting," "exhilarating," and "enjoyable" to describe their experiences. As one special education teacher stated, "It's fun to have someone to plan with and share duties. It's rejuvenating." Two major reasons cited were increased collegiality and shared responsibility.

Teachers felt that they were now part of a team and enjoyed that feeling of camaraderie. This feeling of being part of a group was especially prevalent among special education teachers. Teachers made remarks such as these: "I feel included now," "I feel like an equal partner," and "When I was self-contained nobody knew what I was doing, but now we all have to work together. Now I am part of the school."

Teachers also felt good about co-teaching because they could now share their responsibilities. Many teachers made statements similar to this general education teacher's: "I feel less frustrated at the end of the day because I'm sharing responsibilities for meeting students' needs."

Although most teachers perceived co-teaching as a positive experience, teachers did vocalize some concerns, including lack of clarity about roles and responsibilities, need for increased flexibility, and for increased planning and preparation time. The concern that was most commonly expressed dealt with understanding and defining the roles of teachers within the classroom. Many teachers, particularly special education teachers, felt that their role in the classroom had become secondary and that they were seen as aides or assistants. One special education teacher expressed it this way: "It's tough changing professional roles. There are times when it's not my class-room. I feel that these are her materials and her grading system. I sometimes feel like an aide." This lack of clearly defined roles made many teachers feel uncomfortable and for many others it is the reason that co-teaching arrangements caused stress and anxiety.

Another frequently cited concern was that teachers had to "give and take" more than when teaching on their own. Teachers needed to learn how to compromise and see things from a different perspec-tive. They told us repeatedly that co-teaching required flexibility from all those involved. This flexibility was seen by many as the essential component in successful co-teaching arrangements, but not always easy to do. One special ed-ucation teacher said, "I co-teach with two different teachers—teachers with very different styles. I have had to learn how and when to give in and how and when to hold my own when thinking about what is best for the exceptional education students."

Although teachers enjoyed the opportunity to teach and share responsibilities with other professionals, co-teaching did not reduce the amount of work required to prepare and plan for lessons. In actuality, many teach-ers increased the amount of time they spent preparing for daily lessons. Teachers made comments such as, "I work twice as hard." Working with another teacher made their jobs even more de-manding because teachers needed to spend time planning together.

> *[Teachers] told us repeatedly that co-teaching required flexibility from all those involved. This flexibility was seen by many as the essential component in successful co-teaching arrangements, but not always easy to do.*

Impact on Students

Overall, school staff surveys and interviews indicated that, as a re-sult of the changes in service delivery models (i.e., more general and special education cooperation), academic outcomes of special stu-dents were stronger or better than in the past. Moreover, teachers and administrators also overwhelmingly reported that the academic achievement of general education students was stronger or better than in the past. Teachers were enthusiastic about the positive so-cial outcomes that evolved as a consequence of co-teaching. They felt that students were able to work together more and with a wider range of peers. Many teachers made statements such as these by special education teachers: "I have seen the self-esteem and social skills of the students increase," and "The students are thriving in the environment of acceptance and the celebration of diversity."

These positive outcomes were attributed to three primary reasons. First, teachers saw co-teaching as a *union of strengths* and, because of this union, students were provided with better instruction. Teachers made statements such as, "There is a marriage between the special education teacher's skills and the general education teacher's knowledge of the academic areas," and "The special education teacher is able to teach the whole class if needed. She provides other teachers with strategies to use with all students."

Second, teachers reported that co-teaching had *broadened their instructional repertoire*. General education teachers indicated that they learned more about instructional strategies: "I have learned many skills from my special education co-teacher which help me meet the needs of my students better," and "I have learned so much from having the gifted teacher coming into the classroom. Now I use those strategies with all my students." Special education teachers said they learned more about content: "I never had to really teach social studies before—I've learned so much!"

Third, teachers felt that co-teaching had *changed the way they viewed students in the class*, and that now they felt more accountable for meeting the needs of all students. Students were no longer thought of as "yours" or "mine," but rather as "ours."

Teachers' Recommendations: ESP Plus

In this section we share the nine most commonly voiced recommendations for making co-teaching successful. Recommendations are organized around the abbreviation E (engagement, expectations, elasticity), S (skills, support, structure), P (planning, preparation, and parity).

E = Engagement, Expectations, Elasticity

ENGAGEMENT. To ensure a successful match, particularly in full-time co-teaching arrangements, teachers recommend that self-selection of partners is imperative. Having the choice to participate in co-teaching and having input in choosing a partner was endorsed by many of the general and special educators with whom we spoke. Although administrators indicated that allowing teachers to choose their partners was desirable, they also cautioned that it is not always practical to implement.

Nonetheless, teachers endorsed the idea of providing choice in participation, but more so in choice of their partner. One special education teacher put it this way: "The keys to successful co-teaching are a match between the teachers' styles and philosophies." Another special education teacher cautioned, "Inclusion can be a great thing, but forcing it on two teachers who don't work well together is not a good idea."

Because co-teaching necessitates collaboration between teachers who have very different professional training and experiences, teachers told us that it is imperative that they have the opportunity to have input in selecting a partner. One special education teacher told us, "GE teachers should choose the special education teacher to work with. It's hard to admit they don't know what they're doing—harder to admit it to someone they don't care for. It must be someone they like and trust."

When successful partnerships occur, news spreads quickly. When we interviewed individuals who were having a good experience as co-teachers, they could hardly contain their enthusiasm. The opportunities for learning from and with each other and to think collaboratively about meeting the needs of all students brought unexpected satisfaction to their lives. As one teacher explained, "It's very important to have teachers who volunteer. Successful partnerships spawn others by example."

EXPECTATIONS. Because of differential training and experiences, general and special education teachers can have very different expectations about what students can and cannot accomplish. One principal recommended that for co-teaching to be successful, "teachers must have a clear understanding of the goal for each individual child because of the pressure of accountability for student achievement. They need to know what parents, administration, etc., expect that child to learn." Another principal cautioned, "General education teachers need to understand that special education students learn in a different way and get away from the 'one size fits all' mentality." The opportunity to learn about different needs proved an eye-opener for many general education teachers: "I didn't know the needs of special education students before—this has been a great year for my growth."

While general education teachers learned about individual differences, special education teachers learned more about the realities of the general education classroom. One special education teacher told us, "I was not prepared for the pace at which general education moves." Another special educator said, "Special education teachers have little professional training in content. I am learning more about content and what students are expected to do in the general education classroom." Many special education teachers made comments such as, "The special education students surpassed my expectations," and "I didn't realize that special education students could do as much as they could in the regular classroom!"

Perhaps differences in expectations became most tangible in the form of grades. The question about whether or not special education students should be evaluated in the same way became an issue for some partners. Some general education teachers were willing to adopt different grading policies: "I look at the grading system differently now. I used to have a problem with grading special education students as compared to the general education students. Now I grade on the basis of each child individually."

Issues related to expectations for completing work, pacing of instruction, and grading require ongoing discussion and negotiation. There are no simple answers to these issues; however, for successful partnerships to occur channels of communication must be open and operational.

ELASTICITY. One of the most frequently cited recommendations teachers offered was *be flexible*. Teachers are often accustomed to having the classroom as their own domain. Sharing that domain can be challenging and demands elasticity. One principal cautioned, "As soon as you welcome someone else into your world, there must be an ongoing dialogue to make it work. The teachers must have the philosophy of making the room big enough for everyone."

Flexibility is necessary to adapt to different teachers' styles. This becomes particularly imperative for special educators who co-teach with more than one general education partner. One special education teacher working with multiple partners told us, "We are all learning to be more flexible. We try to create a team spirit without hierarchy. Everyone has important information to share."

S = Skills, Support, Structure

SKILLS. Teachers need to recognize the skills and talents of their teaching partners and build on those to enrich the learning experience for all students. General education teachers are the content specialists and are skilled in working with large groups of students; special education teachers are the specialists in identifying individual needs and are skilled in making adaptations to meet those needs.

General and special educators also need to develop some mutual skills to enhance co-teaching. Communication and interpersonal skills, in particular, are imperative to ensure a smooth working relationship. One special education teacher commented, "It's not easy for some teachers to find themselves without 'their kids' and 'their classroom' and it takes a special skill to be a facilitator—to consult with another teacher. It takes a different mind-set, it takes a certain amount of interpersonal skill."

SUPPORT. Co-teaching cannot succeed without administrative support. Teachers have specific suggestions about what types of support they need. First, more personnel are needed. This comment was typical: "I think the impression is that full inclusion equals less teachers, but in reality the opposite is true. For it to work well we need more teachers, not less. Ideally having one special education teacher for only two classes would work best."

Second, small class sizes are imperative. Many teachers lamented that, "We're spread too thin." One general educator observed, "I feel like I am exhausted. There are way too many kids in my class. Had I known there would be 38 kids involved, I would not have volunteered."

Third, administrative support from an emotional perspective seemed to be particularly important. When exploring new collaborative efforts, having the backing of administration is viewed as vital. One special education teacher reported, "Our administration has been very supportive. The assistant principal has been wonderful and positive. She sees problems as just another part of the process."

STRUCTURE. Our classroom observations and discussions with teachers have taught us that disagreements occur more frequently regarding classroom management than philosophy of instruction. Therefore, the structure of the classroom and ongoing routines need to be determined from the start and revised on an ongoing basis.

Teachers who have managed to resolve issues related to classroom management note the benefits: "With two teachers in the room it makes it easier to handle a conflict. I can remove students who are acting out, and she can continue teaching without stopping the flow of the lesson. Sometimes having just an extra eye on the students helps," and "With two teachers in the classroom you can support each other. When a child is being difficult you can say, 'Take him—I can't deal with it today.'"

P = Planning, Preparation, Parity

PLANNING. Second only to the need for flexibility is the need for joint planning time. As one special education teacher put it, "We need extra planning time because we need to plan for so many levels. With 37 children it is impossible to give individual attention to the students who you can see would benefit from it." A general education teacher informed us, "I agree with my colleagues that we need constructive planning time—not just for planning lessons, but to assess problems with learning styles so that we can help them!"

Successful co-teaching partners have told us that they consider their planning time as "sacred." But many find that they need more planning time: "My partner and I plan together on a daily basis. We talk about what didn't work that day and what we will do tomorrow. We are always here past the time we should be; we both agree that this is necessary. It is our nature to stay after school and plan, but it would help us if we had more time to plan during the day." Finding the time to plan is challenging and teachers have found that they need to be creative. Many teachers continue to lobby for administrative support in finding planning time: "We need mutual planning time and a better way to plan. We write notes, talk in the hallway. We need something more effective." Lack of planning time can be deadly. One of the teachers of gifted students told us, "Co-teaching without planning is like diving into a pool of cold water. We struggled."

PREPARATION. Ongoing professional development is needed—particularly when most teachers have little training and experience with co-teaching. One general education teacher warned, "Don't throw a program at teachers. They threw it at us, and it was sink or swim. First train and then get the program." Teachers and administrators have informed us that inservice teacher education should include (1) specific multilevel practices for implementation in diverse classrooms, (2) strategies and models for co-teaching with emphasis on roles and responsibilities, and (3) opportunities to visit and converse with teachers who have had successful co-teaching experiences.

This chapter includes an annotated bibliography of books and articles related to co-teaching. Ongoing professional development includes attending classes and workshops. It also includes reading the professional literature. The bibliography at the end of this chapter can serve as an initial reading list.

PARITY. Parity is another component for successful co-teaching. A clear understanding of roles and responsibilities and recognition that there are *two professionals in the classroom* are imperative. The consequences of lack of parity are expressed in the following comments from special education teachers: "Sometimes I feel like an aide. I have to raise my hand to say something, just like the students," and "When my input is put in at the last minute and then my ideas are ignored, I do feel like the aide." General education teachers have expressed concerns as well: "I feel intimidated by the special education teacher. She knows more than I do about exceptionalities. I always feel that I'm missing something I should know."

> *A clear understanding of roles and responsibilities and recognition that there are* two *professionals in the* classroom *are imperative.*

Simple steps can be taken to ensure parity:

- Provide both teachers with "space" in the classroom that says to students, "We are both your teachers."
- Communicate to students that they have two teachers.
- Share responsibilities for taking the lead in teaching lessons using a variety of formats (see Vaughn, Schumm, & Arguelles, 1997, for suggestions).
- Send joint letters home to parents and hold joint parent conferences.
- Develop a checklist to divide responsibilities.

These simple steps go a long way. Eventually, parents, students, and others will learn that there are two professionals in the classrooms. One teacher told this story: "A substitute teacher walked in one day and she looked at me and said, 'Oh, you're the aide.' And you know I took offense to it and I said, 'Absolutely not.' Of course, as time went on she saw my relationship with the children and my role in the classroom was definitely not as an aide."

A Final Word

At the beginning of this chapter, we shared the story of Barbara and Anita, who showed that successful co-teaching takes more than ESP. Intuition alone is not enough to teach in collaborative ways. Many teachers have not been trained to work collaboratively. Even when teachers have such training, the day-to-day challenges of working as partners can be daunting.

As part of a larger investigation of the restructuring of special education in Florida, we had the opportunity to learn from the experiences of more than 200 school-based professionals. Findings from our investigation informed us about the promises and pitfalls of co-teaching. The promises are increased collegiality and shared responsibility among professionals. More significant promises are improved student academic and social progress due to a union of strengths, broadening of instructional repertoires, and changed views about the potential of students. Pitfalls include lack of clarity about roles and responsibilities, need for increased flexibility, and necessity of increased planning and preparation time.

We also learned from our conversations with scores of teachers and administrators that it takes engagement, expectations, elasticity, skills, support, structure, planning, preparation, and parity to have a successful co-teaching experience. Obviously, all these components will not fall into place overnight. Successful partnerships take time to emerge and strengthen. But keeping recommendations from experienced co-teachers in mind (ESP Plus) can help new co-teachers get started on the right foot. The ultimate goal is to provide quality instruction for *all* students in highly diverse classrooms. Two prepared, collaborative professionals can work to make that goal a reality.

References

Adams, L., & Cessna, K. (1993). Metaphors of the co-taught classroom. *Preventing School Failure, 37*(4), 28–31.

Allington, R.L., & Johnston, P.A. (1989). Coordination, collaboration, and consistency: The redesigning of compensatory and special education intervention. In R. Slavin, N. Karweit, & N. Madden (Eds.). *Effective programs for students at risk* (pp. 320–354). Boston: Allyn & Bacon.

Arguelles, M.E., Schumm, J.S., & Vaughn, S. (1996). *Executive summaries for ESE/FEFP Pilot Program.* Report submitted to the Florida Department of Education.

Bauwens, J., & Hourcade, J.J. (1995). *Cooperative teaching: Rebuilding the schoolhouse.* Austin, TX: PRO-ED.

Bauwens, J., Hourcade, J.J., & Friend, M. (1989). Cooperative teaching: A model for general and special education integration. *Remedial and Special Education, 10*(2), 17–22.

Cook, L., & Friend, M. (1995). Co-teaching: Guidelines for creating effective practices. *Focus on Exceptional Children, 29*(3), 1–16.

Evertson, C.M., & Green, J.L. (1986). Observation as inquiry and method. In M.C. Wittrock (Ed.), *Handbook of research on teaching* (3rd ed., pp. 162–213). New York: Macmillan.

Friend, M., & Cook, L. (1992). The new mainstreaming. *Instructor, 101*(7), 30–36.

Harris, K., Harvey, P., Garcia, L., Innes, D., Lynn, P., Munoz, D., Sexton, K., & Stoica, R. (1987). Meeting the needs of special high school students in regular education classrooms. *Teacher Education and Special Education, 10,* 143–152.

Lincoln, Y.S., & Guba, E.G. (1985). *Naturalistic inquiry.* Beverly Hills, CA: Sage.

Miles, M.B., & Huberman, A.M. (1994). *Qualitative data analysis.* Thousand Oaks, CA: Sage.

Pugach, M.C., & Wesson, C.L. (1995). Teachers' and students' views of team teaching of general education and learning-disabled students in two fifth-grade classes. *The Elementary School Journal, 95*(3), 279–295.

Reinhiller, N. (1996). Co-teaching: New variations on a not-so-new practice. *Teacher Education and Special Education, 19*(1), 34–48.

Schumm, J.S., & Vaughn, S. (1992). Planning for mainstreamed special education students: Perceptions of classroom teachers. *Exceptionality, 3*, 81–98.

Strauss, A., & Corbin, J. (1990). *Basics of qualitative research.* Newbury Park, CA: Sage.

Vaughn, S., Schumm, J.S., & Arguelles, M.E. (1997). The ABCDEs of co-teaching. *Exceptional Children, 30*(2), 4–10.

Vaughn, S., Schumm, J.S., Klingner, J., & Saumell, L. (1995). Students' views of instructional practices: Implications for inclusion. *Learning Disability Quarterly, 18*, 236–248.

Vaughn, S., Schumm, J.S., & Sinagub, J.M. (1996). *Focus group interviews: Use and application in education and psychology.* Newbury Park, CA: Sage.

Yin, R.K. (1989). *Case study research: Design and methods.* Beverly Hills, CA: Sage.

Annotated Bibliography of Co-Teaching Resources

Angle, B. (1996). 5 steps to collaborative teaching and enrichment remediation. *Teaching Exceptional Children, 29*(1), 8–10.

The strategies presented in this article are designed to encourage the collaboration between general and special education teachers. In addition, these strategies use students' interests as a source of motivation to increase their participation and academic growth.

Braaten, B., Mennes, M.B., & Samuels, H. (1992). A model of collaborative service for middle school students. *Preventing School Failure, 36*(3), 10–15.

A collaborative service model for students with disabilities at the middle school level is described. It involves provision of special education services in general education classrooms through curricula that are adapted, complemented, and modified. The roles of the collaborating teachers are explored.

Cook, L., & Friend, M. (1995). Co-teaching: Guidelines for creating effective practice. *Focus on Exceptional Children, 28*(3), 1–16.

The issues and concerns related to co-teaching are discussed to try to ensure that educators planning to co-teach can make deliberate and thoughtful choices concerning this service delivery model.

Cramer, S.F. (1998). *Collaboration: A successful strategy for special educators.* Boston: Allyn & Bacon.

This book is especially designed for undergraduate and graduate special education teachers-in-training. It provides readers with the necessary skills to examine and improve collaborative relationships and the opportunity to practice these skills by developing an individualized collaboration project.

Dieker, L.A., & Barnett, C.A. (1996). Effective co-teaching. *Teaching Exceptional Children, 29*(1), 5–7.

Dieker and Barnett address questions that usually come up when educators consider co-teaching. They suggest and discuss three answers: planning, communication, and more planning.

Donaldson, G.A., & Sanderson, D.R. (1996). *Working together in schools: A guide for educators.* Thousand Oaks, CA: Corwin Press.

Using an informal and friendly tone, Donaldson and Sanderson explore several forms of collaboration in schools. Teachers can use this volume to examine and discuss their own relationships with other school professionals. Each chapter begins with a scenario that illustrates the difficulties and opportunities inherent in collaborative relationships. Commonly used techniques, sample agendas, and reminders of information covered are also included in each chapter.

Friend, M. (1984). Consultation skills for resource teachers. *Learning Disabilities Quarterly, 7,* 246–250.

The perceptions of special education teachers who consult with general education teachers and the skills special educators should possess are examined in this article. The authors also describe how proficiently special educators are judged to perform in their role as consultants.

Friend, M., & Cook, L. (1992). *Interactions: Collaboration skills for school professionals.* White Plains, NY: Longman.

Interactions can be used as a class text, a small-group inservice training manual, or a self-teaching skills book. It offers a comprehensive treatment of collaboration in schools and shows school professional collaboration, including team meetings, conferences with parents, co-teaching, and problem solving with colleagues. The book contains many case studies and sample interactions, and it is written for a broad audience, including preservice and inservice special and general education teachers and related service providers.

Gersten, R. (1990). Enemies real and imagined: Implications of "teachers' thinking about instruction" for collaboration between special and general education. *Remedial and Special Education, 11,* 50–53.

The implications of collaborative efforts between special and general education teachers are examined in this article. The evolution of a shared language between special and general education, the nature of expertise and methods for sharing expertise, and the nature of the change process are discussed. Potential problems in collaborative approaches and guidelines for sensible, sensitive collaboration are provided.

Hewit, J.S., & Whittier, K.S. (1997). *Teaching methods for today's schools: Collaboration and inclusion.* Boston: Allyn & Bacon.

Frequently used instructional strategies for K–12 classrooms are brought together with innovative concepts such as collaboration, inclusion, community involvement, and reflective teaching. This volume includes reflections on related research as well as discussions about the social and environmental influences affecting students. In addition, each chapter includes activities that can be applied to everyday classroom situations.

Idol, L. (1988). A rationale and guidelines for establishing a special education consultation program. *Remedial and Special Education, 9*(6), 48–62.

This article provides a comprehensive definition of consultation and a rationale for the use of such a program. Guidelines for establishing a teacher consultation program are outlined.

Idol, L., Paolucci-Whitcomb, P., & Nevin, A. (1986). *Collaborative consultation.* Rockville, MD: Aspen Publishers.

A good resource for university professors who are interested in familiarizing preservice teachers with the collaborative consultation model. The book is intended to stimulate collaboration between general and special education teachers who are working with students with disabilities in the regular classroom.

Orkwis, R. (Ed.). (1999). *ERIC/OSEP Mini-Library* (Vols. 1–3). Reston, VA: The Council for Exceptional Children.

This three-volume series is a minilibrary on adapting curricular materials for inclusion classrooms. The series was funded by the Office of Special Education Programs and the Office of Educational Research and Improvement, U.S. Department of Education. Each volume contains multiple instructional resources for general and special educators to aid in co-planning and co-teaching.

Pugach, M.C., & Johnson, L.J. (1995). *Collaborative practitioners, collaborative schools.* Denver, CO: Love Publishing.

In addition to discussing special and general education collaboration, the authors have tied together the similarities across collaboration as it occurs in all its varying contexts in schools. This book has a strong focus on teamwork and also shows rationale and framework behind collaboration; it includes communication skills, group solving, and team teaching.

Schumm, J.S., Vaughn, S., & Harris, J. (1997). Pyramid power for collaborative planning for content area instruction. *Teaching Exceptional Children, 29*(6), 62–66.

This article describes a framework for co-planning in general education classrooms, the Planning Pyramid. This framework helps general and special educators work collaboratively to identify key concepts and skills to be taught and to consider the needs of individual students when teaching key concepts and skills.

Sugai, G.M., & Tindal, G.A. (1993). *Effective school consultation: An interactive approach.* Pacific Grove, CA: Brooks/Cole.

Practical collaborative strategies designed to deal with academic and behavior difficulties are presented. The authors view consultation as a problem-solving strategy and outline the necessary skills to forming a successful partnership. Some of the topics covered include identifying and analyzing problems, choosing appropriate interventions, and collecting useful assessment data.

Vaughn, S., Bos, C.S., & Schumm, J.S. (1999). *Teaching mainstreamed, diverse, and at-risk students in the general education classroom* (2nd ed.). Boston: Allyn & Bacon.

This book addresses a general education teacher audience. It includes chapters on collaboration with other professionals. It also includes practical instructional strategies for teaching in classrooms that include students with exceptionalities and students who are English language learners.

Vaughn, S., Schumm, J.S., & Arguelles, M.E. (1997). The ABCDEs of co-teaching. *Teaching Exceptional Children, 30*(2), 4–10.

This article provides an overview of models of co-teaching and common co-teaching issues. The authors provide the example of two teachers, one general education and one special education, engaged in a positive co-teaching relationship.

West, J.F., & Idol, L. (1990). Collaborative consultation in the education of mildly handicapped and at-risk students. *Remedial and Special Education, 11*(1), 22–31.

In this paper the authors describe collaborative consultation as a professional problem-solving process, as well as a service delivery option for educating mildly handicapped and at-risk students. Critical issues in developing collaborative consultation models in the context of school reform are discussed.

COLLABORATION AS DELIBERATE CURRICULUM DECISION MAKING

Marleen C. Pugach and Mary Ann Fitzgerald

Marleen: So what have we learned since 1987 when we began working together on collaboration?

Mary Ann: Well, we know there are three important parts to a good collaborative relationship. There's the personal relationship between the teachers, the organizational structures that allow them to work together, and then there's the "Now what?"

Marleen: And the "now what" is what we have always talked about, what teachers actually do with children, the curriculum and how it is taught.

Mary Ann: And if this piece is missing, the collaboration fails the kids.

The emergence of collaboration as a viable form of professional interaction in schools signifies a fundamental change in the way the teaching profession is conceptualized. With the advent of collaboration, teachers have moved away from the classic, isolated model of teaching toward having multiple adult professionals share instructional responsibility for groups of students, often in the same classroom. Collaboration is now common to the vocabulary—albeit not necessarily to the practice—of teachers nationwide (Hargreaves, 1994). Today teachers who are considering how best to practice collaboration face a second generation of challenges, namely those that follow from initial efforts in the early 1980s to begin breaking down longstanding traditions that separated special and general education teachers and students in schools. Beyond special education, the practice of professional collaboration has been extended to reading teachers and bilingual and ESL teachers working with general education teachers.

In short, collaboration has redefined the way most specialists and general education teachers conduct their work—as well as the places in which students who require the help of specialists receive support. In the initial renegotiation of these relationships, efforts to collaborate often focused on questions of process: How do we get together? How do we overcome the existing hierarchies among school-based professionals? How do we share responsibility? In this chapter we have chosen to move the conversation beyond these concerns and address what has been identified as one of the most important of the second generation challenges—the challenge of linking collaboration to the quality of the curriculum itself.

Rethinking the Purpose of Collaboration

One of the first questions one might ask about collaboration is, "Why do it?" It is easy to get caught up in the rhetoric of collaborating because it is the "in" thing to do or because "it's the way special education or Title I reading is done today." From our perspective, the sole purpose of collaboration is to provide equitable, meaningful, and effective learning environments for all students—wherever they attend school and whatever their backgrounds—so that they can achieve success. Collaboration is about creating and implementing the best learning situations possible for all students; after all, that is what schools are for. Consistent with a definition of collaboration as a means of improving teaching and learning, when teachers decide to work together what is most important is that they set their students' learning at the center of the collaborative endeavor. This, of course, means setting the

From our perspective, the sole purpose of collaboration is to provide equitable, meaningful, and effective learning environments for all students—wherever they attend school and whatever their backgrounds—so that they can achieve success.

quality of their own teaching at the center of collaboration as well. Defining collaboration in this way immediately takes it beyond simply creating new ways for how special education or designated reading supports are delivered. Instead, we are automatically focused on the overall quality of classrooms, schools, and teaching.

In other words, collaboration is not merely a process to be mastered; it is a process to be mastered in the service of the deliberate goal that drives it. Clarifying this goal is essential in order for collaboration to be worthwhile. Further, everyone who participates in collaborative teaching must be clear, vocal, and assertive about the reasons that drive their joint work. "How well are our efforts helping to improve our students' learning?" should be the guiding question. If the answer is, "They are not," a fundamental rethinking of the purpose of the collaboration will be required.

Collaboration in schools can take many forms, including periodic consultation between a specialist and a classroom teacher; regularly scheduled teaching by various specialists in general education classrooms; informal meetings to solve targeted problems; ad hoc work teams for temporary, well-defined tasks; or team teaching for part or all of the day. Some forms of collaboration are more prescriptive than others, depending on the situation for which professionals are engaged in joint work. From a theoretical perspective, multiple forms of and purposes for collaboration are legitimate (Pugach & Johnson, 1995) and provide those who have specialized expertise with various avenues for interaction. However, no matter who is on a given team, or whether it is a periodic collaboration or a situation in which a specialist and a general education teacher work together daily in the same classroom from 8:00 a.m. until 3:00 p.m., the quality of professional collaboration is only as good as the questions teachers raise about how their practice might need to change to meet the needs of a particular student—or, for that matter, for a whole class of students. Another way to think about this is to ask this question: In the context of collaboration, what kinds of issues do we consider appropriate targets for changing our own practice?

Situating collaboration within these essential questions about what goes on in schools and classrooms inevitably moves us into a consideration of the curriculum. Pugach and Warger (1996) note that it is usually when students come into contact with the standard, general education curriculum in school that their learning difficulties most often arise in the first place. As a result, they argue further, teachers who collaborate must always be ready to ask significant questions about the curriculum itself. Otherwise, teachers run the risk of approaching the difficulties their students are encountering from the often misguided assumption that the entire problem rests within the student and that the curriculum has nothing to do with it—instead of questioning the essential worth of what we are asking students to do in the first place (Pugach & Warger, 1996). If collaboration fails to take the quality of the curriculum into account, the greatest source of difficulty may never be addressed at all. Teachers who are committed to practicing as part of collaborative teams need to begin with the premise that curriculum should always be part of, and is in fact central to, the collaborative conversation (Pugach & Warger, 1996; Warger & Pugach, 1993).

Furthermore, if collaborating teachers fail to ask questions about how meaningful the standard curriculum is, their attention can be diverted from addressing underlying systemic difficulties that surface in the context of curriculum. For example, by failing to address curriculum in general as a primary source of students' difficulties, teachers lose the opportunity to question the cultural relevance of the curriculum for students of color who may be experiencing difficulty learning.

In urban schools, the context of our own work, what most often interferes with student learning are four things: (1) low teacher expectations based on race, culture, and class (Irvine, 1991); (2) lack of cultural congruence between primarily white teachers and primarily minority students (Irvine, 1991; Ladson-Billings, 1994); (3) conditions of schooling that are not conducive to learning—for example, large class sizes or inflexible approaches to curriculum or inadequate physical and curricular resources (Irvine, 1991); and (4) complicated bureaucracies (often including large, separate special education bureaucracies) that can regularly distract teachers and administrators from the students and their educational needs (Haberman, 1996). In combination, these interferences often result in the overrepresentation of students of color in special education and their underrepresentation in programs of academic acceleration (Artiles & Trent, 1994; Harry & Anderson, 1994). Teachers in urban schools who engage in professional collaboration need to keep all these barriers in mind as they strive to develop plans to improve the educational experience they offer their students.

Further, not only in urban schools, but in any school that educates students of color and students from low socioeconomic levels, all teachers need to keep in mind the first two sources of interference with success (i.e., low teacher expectations and the absence of cultural congruity). If these issues are not kept in the forefront and if collaboration does not take them into account, then it is likely that whatever collaborative processes are adopted will not fully address all the institutional, structural sources of students' problems. And when students of color or students from low socioeconomic levels do have real disabilities that require special accommodations as well as flexibility on the part of the teacher and the system, meeting their needs is undoubtedly made more complex by the teacher's obligation first to address these four overriding sources of interference overtly. In other words, the learning problems students experience in school always exist within a broader sociocultural context (Pugach & Seidl, 1998) and collaboration will be successful only insofar as the full context of schooling is part of the deliberations.

In summary, a complex view of curriculum in its full context must be part of teachers' initial understanding of the purpose of collaboration if it is to be successful. And this view must take into account all aspects of curriculum in relationship to the students about whom teachers are collaborating.

A Personal View on Collaboration

We began working together to build support structures for collaborative teaching in Milwaukee, Wisconsin, USA, in 1987 through the creation of the district's consulting teacher program. In Milwaukee Public Schools, consulting teachers have provided technical assistance to any school or teacher team that is striving to build capacity to serve all students in inclusive settings. Our own professional collaborative relationship, as well as our personal friendship, grew out of our mutual commitment to build a collaborative culture in Milwaukee's schools and represents the joint perspectives of the university and the school district. The vignettes we offer here represent a cross section of issues we have addressed as our own collaboration has developed through the years.

Missing the Point With Spelling

Consider the case of these two teachers whose collaboration, though apparently successful, never took into account this question: How worthwhile is what we are asking students to do each week in spelling?

Randi and Maria, special and general education teachers respectively, had developed many exciting social studies and science units that met the needs and interests of a wide variety of learners in their classroom. They supplemented the basal reader required at their school with engaging trade books and they encouraged writing across the curriculum. Yet what Randi and Maria were eager to showcase for visitors to their team-taught collaborative classroom was how they had adapted spelling for a wide range of students—that is, typical fifth graders and those with cognitive disabilities. Following is a brief glimpse of one aspect of the adapted spelling program.

It is Friday, 11:00 a.m., and all the students seem to know what time it is: spelling time! Teachers distribute papers and, after a few minutes, one teacher begins calling out the spelling words. Each word is spoken, used in a sentence, and repeated. In response to the teacher, all students busily write their answers. Randi encourages any visitors who are present to walk among the students to see what is so unique about their participation in the spelling activity. In doing so, visitors notice that the student responses are actually as varied as the papers the teacher distributed. Some students have spelling sheets with words printed on them; students who have received these papers are expected only to circle the correct response. Other papers are numbered, with blank lines next to each number. For others, some blanks are highlighted, which means that the student has to supply only the beginning and ending letter. The teacher continues until all the words have been read and everyone has completed his or her work, then collects the students' papers.

This "adapted spelling" routine reflected individualized expectations and assessments, clearly an indication that the two teachers had worked together and shared information about what seemed appropriate for various groups of students. What was missing, however, was any indication that Randi and Maria had questioned the relevance of teaching spelling as an isolated subject, or the worth of asking their students to learn a new group of words each week that had nothing to do with the rest of their curriculum—or their lives. They were more comfortable with the notion of how to adapt the existing spelling curriculum than they were with what the curriculum stood for in the first place. Had a consideration of the entire language arts curriculum been the departure point for collaboration prior to any adaptations of existing curriculum, their decisions about spelling might have been different. For example, they may have selected spelling words from books the students were reading, still adapting for individual students.

Failing to Promote a Culturally Relevant Approach to Literacy

Often it is the teachers' reluctance to consider the cultural mismatch among the students, the teacher, and the curriculum that gets in the way of student success, which results in the persistent, inappropriate marginalization of some students in school.

To promote inclusive education, Hawkins Elementary School had recently assigned two teachers to each primary classroom and capped enrollment at 30 students. As teachers involved in this initiative, Sharonda Carter, a special education teacher who is African American, and Kelly Stevens, a White general education teacher, were extremely comfortable with their new co-teaching assignment in third grade. They divided students into flexible groups for many instructional activities and were particularly pleased with their literacy program. They relied on a balanced reading approach that embedded basic skills instruction within a larger framework of comprehension. Each teacher retained some autonomy in the selection of books and materials she used.

It became evident that things were not perfect under the surface when Kelly began to encounter a problem in her reading group. André, a capable student in this group, was becoming increasingly disruptive and challenging. Kelly could not wait until the end of the day to express her frustration with André to Sharonda, whom she knew would understand.

As Kelly described the morning's latest incident, Sharonda began to wonder about the books Kelly had been using. She recalled that in social studies, André was eager to share and participated actively in discussions about the continent of Africa. André's father was a professor of African American history, and André's knowledge of this subject enlightened his classmates. In Kelly's reading group, however, Kelly's limited scope in her choice of books did not enable André to demonstrate this knowledge or life experience. André blurted out "This is boring!," fell off his chair, teased his classmates, and frustrated his teacher.

Sharonda listened to her partner vent her frustration and wondered whether she should bring up some issues that might be "touchy." Was Kelly taking into account André's knowledge and experiences? Were the books she was using culturally relevant? Did André have a voice in the discussion of the books? Perhaps it was best not to address these issues; instead she could just volunteer to have André join her group. After all, Sharonda and Kelly got along well despite their cultural differences. Their collaboration was considered a great success and addressing concerns about race and diversity might rock the boat.

Had Sharonda and Kelly begun their planning for collaboration based on a curriculum perspective that included a shared view of a classroom community whose curriculum is sensitive to all the students, raising the question of cultural relevance (Ladson-Billings, 1994) would not have been a new issue. Instead, because it was not part of their original shared agenda, when and how to bring it up was a delicate decision for Sharonda.

Guarding Against Collaboration's Seductive Nature

Some schools that practice collaboration do so with the idea that as long as specialists and general education teachers work in the same room, the solution to the problem of how to deliver special services to children has been addressed adequately. Consider the case of the following school.

The principal at Spring Street Elementary School was eager to have university teacher education faculty and their students observe in his inclusive school. The teachers frequently co-taught in the regular classroom with the support of the special educators, and the principal knew that students and staff were happy with this arrangement. The teachers were, he was sure, ahead of many other schools in the district, and he was proud of them for their forward-thinking practices.

Professors Smith and Parsons decided to spend the day in several classrooms before arranging for teacher education students to observe. They agreed to take observational notes that would then be shared in a meeting at the end of the day with the school's teachers and administrators.

However, at the end of the day, the two university staff members scrambled to find a constructive way to share what they had observed. In the majority of classrooms, they saw instruction that followed an all too familiar approach: all students sat in rows; students with special needs typically sat around the edges or in the back of the class with a paraprofessional or special education teacher next to them; teachers always presented instruction from the front of the room followed by small-group instruction provided in what appeared to be homogeneous groups; and, finally, students worked independently on worksheet assignments. All students used the same materials and were assigned the same worksheets. A special education paraprofessional or teacher helped students with special education needs by providing adapted directions. No individualization was observed.

Clearly, what the teachers and administrators at Spring Street were proud of was the fact that general and special education teachers, paraprofessionals, and general and special education students were present together in typical classrooms. Despite the new undertaking that paired special and general education staff, what they had failed to grasp was that presence alone does not mean that meaningful instruction—or meaningful involvement—is taking place. The teachers, it seems, had never questioned the status quo in terms of curriculum and instruction, what was important for students to learn, or how they could best demonstrate their knowledge. Thus, they were not really addressing the needs of students who already may have been identified as having special needs. Nor, we would suspect, were the teachers and administrators asking important questions about whether their standard approach was meeting the needs of all the other students in their classrooms.

As Pugach and Wesson (1995) note, if teachers are feeling good about collaborating but are not addressing curriculum change, the sum effect of collaboration may be to make teachers feel better about helping more students achieve well in a poorly designed curriculum. As such, collaboration can be a seductive undertaking—and it is this that must be guarded against. If teachers share teaching responsibilities, a fundamental commitment ought to be sharing the work of changing teaching practice for the better; a built-in expectation for professional interaction and for discourse around the quality and aims of teaching should drive the collaborative work.

One of the most powerful arguments for teaming is that it provides the built-in capacity to engage in professional peer coaching as teachers work together on a daily basis to change their curricular and instructional approaches to improve all their students' learning (Pugach & Wesson, 1995). This capacity can only be maximized if, as an essential part of collaboration, teachers are willing to identify new directions in which they wish to take their work.

> *If teachers share teaching responsibilities, a fundamental commitment ought to be sharing the work of changing teaching practice for the better; a built-in expectation for professional interaction and for discourse around the quality and aims of teaching should drive the collaborative work.*

Collaboration to Meet Individual Literacy Needs and to Broaden Collaborative Practices

In the following case, meeting Tyrone's literacy needs necessitated a serious, multifaceted conversation about the teachers' beliefs about literacy teaching and about overt changes in how literacy instruction is delivered.

When the third-grade teacher at Stratton School, Cindy Barreto, questioned whether Tyrone's individual needs were being met within her reading program, she spoke to the special education teacher with whom she shared instructional responsibility, Ellie Morgan. Tyrone had been fully included within general education since kindergarten, and he had blossomed socially and grown academically. However, now the reading gap was widening, and the latest reading book was clearly above his instructional level. Still, Tyrone's mother did not want him to receive academic instruction in a separate special education setting. The two teachers planned to meet with everyone involved in Tyrone's instruction, including the speech pathologist and Tyrone's mother. The special education support person for the district was present to facilitate the meeting.

The critical question posed to all at the meeting was, Is Tyrone's current literacy program meeting his individual needs? The group began by sharing information about Tyrone, highlighting his strengths and addressing his unique needs. Next, they discussed each professional's beliefs about literacy instruction. The special educator was a strong proponent of phonics and small-group instruction, but she had shaped her practice around the belief that children learn to read by having access to and opportunity for reading "real" books. Tyrone's mother believed her son was learning a great deal about the book the class was currently reading even if he could not read it himself. The speech pathologist believed that Tyrone's language skills were greatly enhanced by his participation in whole-group class discussions. Following this sharing, they began to examine the existing structures and instructional opportunities for Tyrone. It became clear that sufficient plans for individualization were not in place, and even clearer was the fact that although they each had Tyrone's well-being at heart in terms of literacy, collaboration among these staff members was not really occurring.

At this point in the meeting, some heated conversation took place and the facilitator guided the team toward deciding what modifications and supplemental instruction could be provided. It was determined that Tyrone would maintain his involvement in the regular third-grade reading program. He would use a related book for shared reading; while the students were reading *Mr. Popper's Penguins*, Tyrone would read from a book at his level titled *I Like Penguins*. Instead of partner reading Tyrone would be a part of a triad. He would also have the class book read to him nightly by his mother, and he would continue to be involved in whole-group discussions of the book as well as related projects. Language lessons provided by the speech pathologist within the regular classroom would incorporate information from his books. Finally, it was agreed that Tyrone would participate in a heterogeneous skill group taught by the special education teacher focusing on the acquisition of phonics. This would take place during independent reading time in the multipurpose resource room. Tyrone's mother agreed to this plan, aware that at this point in time, one-to-one support was temporarily a more immediate need than was independent reading time.

Collaboration between educators would take place in a weekly meeting and also through regular mailbox communication. Tyrone's mother relied on e-mail communication, which facilitated the home-school connection.

As it turned out, this simple concern about one student was the impetus for Stratton School to develop a much stronger collaborative culture. The team decisions that helped strengthen Tyrone's learning provided a template for what collaboration could look like in other situations at Stratton. In terms of curriculum, the decisions this group of professionals made retained Tyrone's connection with real books and real stories rather than limiting his literacy experiences to skill practice alone as the means of supporting his literacy growth.

The important thing in Tyrone's case is that all the professionals involved showed a willingness to participate actively in developing new working relationships that had the potential to make a significant difference in the quality of Tyrone's education. The classroom teacher, the special education teacher, the speech pathologist, and Tyrone's mother all pulled together to figure out what had to change for Tyrone's literacy learning to be more successful. And Tyrone was relieved to be actively participating in a small group and acquiring the skills that would finally let him read independently.

Collaboration: Only as Good as the Questions We Ask or the Problems We Try to Solve

The four examples presented so far demonstrate the importance of asking good, hard questions about the curricular basis of teaching and learning that drives the school experiences of children on whose behalf we collaborate. They also illustrate how critical it is that as a part of their preparation for entering into collaborative teaching arrangements, specialists and general education teachers place the curriculum and all its implications at the center of their deliberations in relation to the problems students are experiencing. In the absence of asking questions about the basic educational program as a fundamental part of collaboration, problems that stem from curricular inadequacies may never be addressed adequately.

For Randi and Maria, the important question was, What kind of spelling program was most tied to the curriculum and to students' lives? For Sharonda and Kelly, the question was, Did their collaborative relationship extend to the delicate issues of race, class, and culture as they related to the curriculum? For the teachers and principal at Spring Street School, the question was, What is the responsibility of teachers who collaborate to ensure they are providing meaningful instruction? And for the professional teaching staff at Stratton School, the question was, What changes in the delivery of services and instructional approaches need to be explored together to meet every child's needs across curricular areas?

Although what affects students most directly occurs at the level of classroom interaction and day-to-day teacher decisions, these decisions are disciplined by the curriculum that a given school or district adopts. So in addition to the classroom-based, micro-level examples of collaboration offered here, we must also attend to what it means to collaborate at the school level. Consider the following snapshots of a school, 20 years apart.

1978. Martha Bell, the principal at Martin Luther King Elementary School, casually stops by Phyllis Carter's room to inform her that it won't be necessary for her to attend the faculty meeting scheduled immediately after school. Phyllis is the special education teacher in room 212, responsible solely for 10 learning disabled students. The purpose of that afternoon's faculty meeting is to discuss and select a new reading series. Clearly, according to the principal, there would be no need for Phyllis to participate because the decision will not involve her students; Martha is sure she has plenty of paper work to do, anyway. Who is involved in curriculum decision making? Everyone, it seems, except the special educator.

2000. George Vincent, school principal, makes a point of stopping to talk with Claire Lonne, the special education teacher, before school to remind her of the important curriculum committee meeting after school. A new math series is soon to be adopted, and George values Claire's views about the appropriateness of the program for a wide variety of learners. He checks with her to see if the parent representative, who will also be able to attend this first of several meetings, has contacted her. George is confident that this representative group of educators, staff, and parents working together will be able to select the series that will be most effective in reaching all learners. Who is involved in curriculum decision making? Everyone involved in the instruction of students.

It seems almost simplistic to think that a decision as significant as the adoption of literacy or mathematics series, which in large part defines the curriculum, would exclude certain teachers. However, the first scenario is not that far-fetched, and the authors have witnessed the exclusion of special education teachers from such deliberations as recently as a year ago. Although this kind of exclusion from a curriculum decision would not be the case with specialists in reading or mathematics who would always be involved (and in fact might lead the effort), a serious consideration of the degree to which a given series is able to meet wide-ranging student needs is critical. For this reason, special educators must be involved in these kinds of decisions. Otherwise the practice of collaboration as a means of making a poor curriculum more palatable might persist.

That is not to say that any curriculum is foolproof and will not require adjustments for the full range of students who are part of general education classroom communities. In particular, curricula must be relevant to the cultures and communities of the students in any given school. However, the quality of the basic program in place— whether commercial or locally developed—represents an important foundation upon which collaboration is based and how a particular student's experience will or will not depart from it.

Further, how teachers decide to group students when engaging in collaboration also has implications for how they consider the curriculum in relation to those students. Downtown Middle School in the year 2000 is a good example.

Downtown Middle School, a large urban school, has developed a collaborative teaching model that provides for the assignment of one special education teacher to a "family unit" consisting of four general education teachers and approximately 120 students. The school houses four of these families. Of the 120 students in each family, 16 to 20 of them are identified as having disabilities that range in category and severity. Student assignments to family units are arranged carefully by a student assignment team consisting of all the special educators, the school psychologist, and several general education teachers. This team reviews the individual education plans of all students already identified as needing special education, as well as the basic profiles of new incoming students and those from the prior year. The assignment team then determines which family is the best match for each student.

Special and general education teachers assigned to each family unit collaboratively determine the schedules and grouping for all students in the unit. The roles and responsibilities of all educators are discussed and clearly defined. Weekly unit planning to address curriculum, students, and family concerns is an important part of this collaborative structure. In addition to family meetings, all special educators meet together weekly to address common issues of concern as well as to discuss individual education plans and assessments for specific students. During this weekly planning, the teachers rely on one another to provide strategies for dealing with specific behavioral or academic challenges across academic areas.

What is unique about this arrangement is that Downtown Middle School has resisted the temptation to create teams that include students with only one kind of categorical disability. As a result, they are encouraged to consider each student as an individual in relation to the curriculum, rather than making the assumption that a particular curriculum adaptation is required to meet the needs of all students with, for example, cognitive disabilities. Further, by refusing to group students labeled as having behavior disorders (among other disability categories), the teachers at Downtown have the opportunity to break out of the pattern of persistent overrepresentation of male students of color in this category and to attempt to meet student needs as defined by the students and teachers themselves, rather than by a disability label.

A Final Note

Together we are unabashed supporters of a collaborative approach to teaching. We believe in the power of pooled expertise and the role of collaboration in increasing a teacher's sense of accountability. We have seen collaborative relationships among teachers result in the highest levels of commitment to improving children's learning. We believe that collaboration takes place in many forms and that there is not one right way to construct a collaborative relationship.

> *Collaboration can only be as good as the questions teachers ask each other—and themselves—about the quality of their work and the curriculum basis for their collaboration.*

However, as we have made clear in this chapter, it has also been our collective experience that collaboration can only be as good as the questions teachers ask each other—and themselves—about the quality of their work and the curriculum basis for their collaboration. The vignettes we offer in this chapter portray some important dimensions of these questions. Placing deliberate decisions about curriculum at the center of collaboration redefines the goals of the joint enterprise (Pugach & Warger, 1996). It holds the potential for raising the level of discourse about the kinds of changes that need to be made for all students, and then what in addition might need to occur to assure success for students who are having persistent problems learning in school. If collaboration is to be a meaningful form of professional interaction, it must go well beyond process to the heart of the matter of schooling—namely, the curriculum itself and what it is we expect students to learn as a result of being in school.

References

Artiles, A., & Trent, S. (1994). Over representation of minority students in special education: A continuing debate. *The Journal of Special Education, 27*, 410–437.

Haberman, M. (1996). Selecting and preparing culturally competent teachers for urban schools. In J.P. Sikula, T.J. Buttery, & E. Guyton (Eds.), *Handbook of research on teacher education: A project of the Association of Teacher Educators* (2nd ed., pp. 747–760). New York: Macmillan.

Hargreaves, A. (1994). *Changing teachers, changing times.* New York: Teachers College Press.

Harry, B., & Anderson, M.G. (1994). The disproportionate placement of African-

American males in special education programs: A critique of the process. *Journal of Negro Education, 63,* 602–619.

Irvine, J.J. (1991). *Black students and school failure: Policies, practices, and prescriptions.* New York: Praeger.

Ladson-Billings, G. (1994). *The dreamkeepers: Successful teachers of African-American children.* San Francisco: Jossey-Bass.

Pugach, M.C., & Johnson, L.J. (1995). *Collaborative practitioners, collaborative schools.* Denver, CO: Love Publishing.

Pugach, M.C., & Seidl, B.L. (1998). Responsible linkages between diversity and disability: A challenge for special education. *Teacher Education and Special Education, 21,* 391–333.

Pugach, M.C., & Warger, C.L. (1996). *Curriculum trends, special education, and reform: Refocusing the conversation.* New York: Teachers College Press.

Pugach, M.C., & Wesson, C.L. (1995). Teachers' and students' views of team teaching of general and learning disabled students in two fifth-grade classes. *The Elementary School Journal, 95*(3), 279–295.

Warger, C.L., & Pugach, M.C. (1993). A curriculum focus for collaboration. *LD Forum, 18*(4), 26–30.

"TITLE I BOUGHT THAT COFFEE POT!"
Family Literacy Professionals Learn to Collaborate

Nancy D. Padak, Connie Sapin, and Connie Spencer Ackerman

The newly hired Even Start staff was touring the school district offices where the program would be housed. "Oh, good," one Even Start professional commented, "a coffee pot. That will really help for meetings."

"No, no!" replied their tour guide, a Title I professional in the district. "You can't use that. Title I bought that coffee pot!"

The 2-day family literacy planning retreat for state-level policy makers was nearing conclusion. Small groups were prioritizing plans for enhancing family literacy programs and services at state and local levels. One group member, a representative from a health services agency, began to chuckle. "I just got it," she said. "It's not just mothers and children reading stories together. I've been sitting here for 2 days wondering what all the fuss was about!"

These are both true stories that illustrate some of the challenges surrounding collaboration in family literacy programs. Some of these challenges are fairly abstract, such as the need for collaborators to develop shared understandings of concepts like "family literacy." More concrete challenges, such as deciding if and how to share resources—even coffee pots—seem mundane, but can prevent the growth of effective collaborations.

We know about both collaboration and family literacy through the direct experience of having worked together in a variety of roles on a variety of family literacy initiatives for more than a decade. In this chapter we first define family literacy and describe the multiple collaborations necessary for successful family literacy education. Next we illustrate these collaborations from the perspective of local family literacy programs and through the example of a statewide initiative designed to build awareness of family literacy. We conclude the chapter with comments about the lessons we have learned about successful family literacy collaborations.

Family Literacy: Collaboration Is Natural

Although a relatively new concept, family literacy education has received enormous attention from policy makers and educators alike, probably because of its potential to support the educational achievements of parents and children and to improve families' economic self-sufficiency. Policy makers' support is evidenced in legislation, such as Even Start (a federally funded, state-administered family literacy demonstration project) and legislative mandates in Head Start and Title I to offer family literacy services for families of participating children. Educators are drawn to family literacy because of longstanding research about the influence of parental education level and parents' involvement in school on children's achievement (see Henderson & Berla, 1994; Sticht, 1995; Van Fossen & Sticht, 1991). Adult educators see promise in family literacy because undereducated parents persist in family literacy programs to a greater extent than they do in more "generic" adult education programs, thus providing more opportunity to learn (see Nickse, 1990; Paratore, 1993; Tracey, 1995). Moreover, research syntheses (see Padak & Rasinski, 2000) have documented that participation in family literacy programs greatly benefits children, adults, families, and society as a whole.

By definition, family literacy involves collaboration on several different levels. State-adopted definitions of family literacy reflect multiple layers of collaboration:

By definition, family literacy involves collaboration on several different levels.

- Family—"Family literacy is coordinated learning among different generations in the same family which helps both adults and children reach their full personal, social, and economic potential" (Massachusetts Family Literacy Consortium, in Sapin & Padak, 1998, p. 5);

- Program—"Family literacy provides instruction to enrich the home environment through interactive, intergenerational learning that models, supports, values, and promotes literacy and lifelong learning skills" (Office of Adult Education, Colorado Department of Education, in Sapin & Padak, 1998, p. 5); and

- Community—"Family literacy programs are unique to each community. Using existing resources, local organizations collaborate to provide integrated learning and support services that promote literacy and lifelong learning skills for family success" (Ohio Family Literacy Task Force, in Sapin & Padak, 1998, p. 4).

These definitions point toward a current trend in publicly funded programs for families, whether their missions are primarily educational, health-related, or human service-related: to view the family as a unit. Agencies that serve similar populations with similar client needs are being urged to collaborate in order to provide integrated services to entire families. Ideally, this approach is more efficient and therefore effective for families.

Those who desire to establish partnerships must determine who their collaborators might be. Sometimes this question is answered by regulations or the legislation authorizing the program. For example, the revised standards for Head Start stipulate that programs "provide, either directly or through referrals to other local agencies, opportunities for...assisting parents as adult learners to recognize and address their own literacy goals." In other words, by law, Head Start programs must offer adult education opportunities or work closely with adult education programs in their communities. Other times, programs have more latitude in creating collaborations. And because of the comprehensive nature of family literacy programs, the list of possible collaborators is quite long, as seen in Table 1.

TABLE 1
Possible Collaborators for Family Literacy

Adult education programs
Bookstores
Boy Scouts, Girl Scouts, other
  youth organizations (e.g., 4-H,
  Camp Fire Girls)
City recreation programs, Parks
  and Recreation departments
Civic groups (e.g., Altrusa,
  Kiwanis, Rotary, Zonta)
Community colleges, colleges,
  and universities
Corporations
Corrections facilities
Courts
Day-care centers
Employment services
Even Start programs
Head Start programs

Health and mental health
  services, hospitals, clinics
Housing authorities
Humanities councils
Job/vocational training programs
Libraries
Literacy coalitions
Newspapers, radio and television
  stations
Organizations to serve or support
  immigrants
Public transportation
Reading councils, other teachers'
  groups
Religious groups
Retired Senior Volunteer
  Program
School districts

Senior citizen centers
Service organizations (e.g., Junior
  League, Jaycees)
Social service agencies (e.g.,
  TANF; Women, Infants, and
  Children [WIC] programs)
Substance abuse treatment pro-
  grams
Title I
Unions
United Way
Veterans' organizations (e.g.,
  American Legion, VFW)
Volunteer centers, voluntary
  action agencies
Women's shelters
Workplaces, local businesses
YMCAs, YWCAs

Adapted from a list distributed by the Literacy Volunteers of America and developed by the Southwest Ohio Regional Team Mock Grant Writing Activity.

Collaboration has become a recommended first step in family literacy program planning. However, each of the potential partners in a collaboration has its own regulations, reporting requirements, forms, and funding sources. Moreover, each agency representative has his or her own values and desired leadership role. How do the many possible stakeholders arrive at a shared vision, common goals, shared fiscal responsibilities, and a plan of action? Our experiences have taught us that considerable time and energy must be devoted to successful collaborations and that partners must often be willing to relinquish some autonomy. But we have also learned that these are small prices to pay. Successful collaborations result in more targeted, effective services than a single agency could accomplish alone. In the next two sections of the chapter, we describe two collaborative efforts that demonstrate this potential.

A Local Perspective: Establishing an Even Start Family Literacy Program

Even Start (ES) legislation encourages family literacy programming within communities. ES programs must build on existing community resources to provide adult education and parenting education for undereducated parents, developmentally appropriate early literacy experiences for their children, and opportunities for parents and children to interact around educational issues.

Applying for an ES family literacy grant is a daunting process that requires collaboration. Partnerships are required, and the grant funds are meant to support coordination of services. Moreover, ES funding decreases over the 4 years of support because communities are expected to strive for fiscal self-sufficiency for their ES projects. Before actually writing a successful proposal, people have been meeting for months, sometimes years, to assess the literacy needs of undereducated families in their communities and to invite leaders from organizations who can meet these needs to plan together. One result is that planners frequently develop such a commitment to family literacy and to each other that they implement a program whether or not they receive ES funding. Another result is that no two ES programs look alike.

After receiving funding, these partners often continue to be involved in the operation of the program as members of advisory councils or management teams; as recruiters and referrers; and as providers of instruction, classroom space, child care, home visits, and transportation. Cleveland Public Schools, for example, partnered with Parents as Teachers (PAT) and the County Board of Mental Retardation and Developmental Delay (MRDD), both publicly funded agencies in Ohio. PAT contributed home visits, a joint advisory board, and a teacher for parent-child activities; MRDD provided classroom space, transportation for parents, and a wealth of agency resources. PAT gained easy transition to ES for participants whose children had turned 3, and MRDD acquired program support for their parents.

Unfortunately, some groups assemble just prior to writing the grant and short-circuit the process of consensus building and shared responsibility that comes with time and effort. For example, very different views of participants are implied in the terms *client, patient,* and *recipient.* Even deciding on common vocabulary can take time, especially when uncovering underlying values and assumptions is part of the process. But such an expenditure of time pays off in program continuity.

The second collaborative effort begins when partnering agencies receive ES funding. Questions of authority on decision making—both day-to-day and long-term—and hiring, supervision, and strategies for conflict resolution must be answered in ways that allow enough autonomy for the program to operate smoothly. Many ES programs are staffed by part-time teachers, case managers, and administrators who also work in other programs at other locations, which makes program scheduling, staff planning time, and program loyalty difficult to navigate. Within large bureaucracies, programs may not have choices about hiring, disparity of salaries, and budget control. Some staff may work under union contract, while others do not; this affects salaries, working hours, and stability of support staff. To complicate the picture further, programs must often diplomatically share space with others—a lunchroom, a community center room, or, in one case, a bingo room. Equipment and materials must be moved in and out of rooms, depending on whose use is scheduled next. And people can become very protective of their belongings and their exact placement in a room, as our opening story of the Title I coffee pot demonstrates.

State and federal policies can permit or even encourage collaboration. Sometimes collaboration is influenced by traditions within the partnering agencies. For example, confidentiality is a huge issue between human service providers, whose tradition is to guard information, and educators, whose tradition is to share information. To resolve this issue, staff from all partnering agencies must develop shared understandings of the law and of reasons for their differing practices. Collaboration can also be affected by the degree of communication within an agency. More than once, Connie Spencer Ackerman (who was then Ohio's state Even Start coordinator) attended national meetings to learn about possibilities for collabora-

> *State and federal policies can permit or even encourage collaboration.*

tion, such as between family literacy programs and Department of Agriculture food programs to provide meals for families. She found it difficult to encourage these collaborations in Ohio. When federal leaders commit to a change in practice and promote flexibility, it takes time for this new perspective to trickle down to state and local program managers. But the fact remains that the degree of collaboration encouraged by state and federal program leaders can influence collaboration at the program level.

Additionally, collaboration at the program level involves the relationships among staff members, among staff and program participants, and between the program itself and the larger community. Adequate staff training and protected staff planning time are necessary to assess program activities and to develop consensus about mission, view of participants, teaching methodology, type and understanding of assessment, and confidentiality concerns in reporting. Staff in one Ohio program spent weeks of planning time ostensibly creating intake, goal-setting, and lesson plan forms that, in actuality, permitted the staff to air their differences about how they would work with the participants and with each other. Staff in another program found it helpful to invite non-teaching staff from partnering agencies to attend professional development activities so that the noneducators could understand the value of a learner-based curriculum rather than a workbook-based General Equivalency Diploma (GED) preparation program.

Team teaching can promote staff collaboration. One Ohio program paired a social worker who was responsible for leading discussions around goal-setting, discipline, sexuality, and other psychosocial issues with a teacher who was responsible for basic skills content. Their joint planning and teaching blurred their roles, and an outside evaluator observed that the team accomplished more as models for social interaction, tolerance of racial differences, and congenial disagreement than they realized. New family literacy staff routinely visited this program to see excellence in curriculum development and classroom practice. On the other hand, teachers, in particular, must learn to rely on the expertise of their partners. Teachers who take on all the roles that other professionals can provide, especially when concerns of spousal or child abuse arise, can succumb to emotional exhaustion.

In many family literacy programs, parents collaborate in determining topics for study. Whether teachers brainstorm with participants about topics of interest or incorporate concerns that students voice, the result is content that is anchored in real-life application, from understanding the diagnosis of a father's need for coronary surgery to determining how much carpet a student needs to buy at a sale. In one class, young mothers who did not have high school diplomas and were all on welfare proudly shared their research on child development topics. This example is the norm rather than the exception in mature family literacy programs in which staff value participants as collaborators.

Of course, parents and children work together in many ways in family literacy programs, from reading books or playing games that encourage learning and language development to taking field trips together to explore community resources such as a farm, park, library, or candy factory. This particular form of collaboration can be surprisingly difficult to achieve. Many family literacy participants lead relatively isolated lives. They may respond so positively to the social interaction with other parents that they initially show little interest in (or even real resistance to) being with their children. Staff, surprised that the natural and immediate pleasure that parents can learn to take in their children does not occur, must patiently model play with children. In some programs, parents study child development to learn about the importance of playing with young children. One Ohio program bases its project-centered adult curriculum on constructing wooden learning games for parents to use at home with their children. As a consequence of a curriculum that addresses parents' needs and interests, family literacy programs show higher retention rates than other programs for undereducated adults. And, invariably, participants will tell others that their group of classmates is like a family.

> *As a consequence of a curriculum that addresses parents' needs and interests, family literacy programs show higher retention rates than other programs for undereducated adults.*

A Statewide Perspective: The Ohio Family Literacy Initiative

Because of our previous collaborations, working primarily with adult education in Ohio (Adult Basic and Literacy Education or ABLE in

Ohio) and Ohio's Even Start programs, we believed that we understood the nature and needs of these programs fairly well. In 1997, however, Ohio received an Even Start Family Literacy Statewide Initiative Grant that was intended to broaden discussions about family literacy programs to include personnel from ABLE, Even Start, Head Start, library literacy programs, public school preschools, and Title I. Prior to this, although much federal legislation encouraged or mandated family literacy, it was the exception that Even Start programs were truly comprehensive family literacy programs. Usually, because of lack of some key partnerships, something was missing. So the statewide project focused on ways to begin to remedy this situation.

We quickly realized that we had no systematic information about the nature of family literacy efforts within all these programs or the professional development needs of personnel who worked in these programs. So we collaborated to develop a mail survey to collect some of this information. The planning team for this effort included Tim Rasinski at Kent State University and Cathy Oriole at the Ohio Department of Education, in addition to the three of us.

The survey's three sections sought general demographic information about responding programs and asked open-ended questions about professional development needs. In addition, respondents (usually program directors) were asked to assess themselves on 12 "best practice" statements, once to indicate how they perceived their programs actually operated and again to indicate desired operations. The "best practice" statements (see Table 2) reflected findings from two nationwide efforts to define high quality family literacy programs: the RMC publication *Guide to Quality: Even Start Family Literacy Programs* (1995) and the National Center for Family Literacy's System Reform Project (no date), which was part of the National Institute for Literacy's ongoing Equipped for the Future Project.

Nearly 1,700 surveys were distributed in early 1997. Return rates ranged from 3% (libraries, subsequently excluded from analysis) to 100% by program type, with an overall return rate of 46%. Among the most interesting conclusions from analysis of returned surveys are the following:

- There were more similarities among programs than differences. Statistical analyses of responses showed very few differences by type of program (e.g., Head Start, ABLE), region of the state, or type of community. Much to our surprise, we found no statistically significant differences between urban and rural programs, for example. This helped us see that a statewide plan to address professional development needs within all these programs made sense.

◆ Except for Even Start, most programs served relatively few families (although many programs worked with parents only or children only), which pointed to considerable room for growth in family literacy offerings throughout the state.

◆ Very few programs focused on family literacy in their professional development sessions, yet several issues seemed to concern a majority of programs: understanding the family literacy concept, recruitment, retention, inter-agency collaboration, and development of integrated curricula. These became our professional development goals for subsequent collaborative activities. (The complete report of the survey is available at http://literacy.kent.edu.)

Survey results provided some, but not all, answers to our questions about the nature and needs of family literacy programs throughout Ohio. Accordingly, we held four regional focus group meetings in late

---

TABLE 2
"Best Practices" From the Ohio Family Literacy Survey

Activities focus on families (including other family members) and family development.

Programs emphasize social interaction among parents, children, families, and staff.

Curriculum is thematically organized and reflects integration of content and skills.

The program is carefully evaluated.

Planning is based on participants' input (both adults and children), program evaluation results, and current "best practices."

Recruitment is planned, comprehensive, and successful.

Parents and children have multiple, guided opportunities to solve problems.

Program activities support and encourage home-school involvement.

Educational experiences are based on parents' goals, children's choices, and family interests.

Education for parents, children, and families accommodates a range of learner levels and stresses knowledge and skills needed for daily life.

The overall administration of the program supports program goals (e.g., use of staff time, choosing staff, planning time, materials, integration and collaboration with other family-oriented programs in the community).

Families participate in programs long enough to meet their goals. In addition to making referrals, program staff facilitate family members' transitions into other educational or employment institutions/organizations.

spring 1997, with key regional leaders from all the agencies surveyed, and later a day-long meeting with statewide leaders. The agenda for these meetings included an overview of survey results, small-group discussions about the results, and whole-group summarizing and consensus building. Additionally, these meetings provided a setting for people from various agencies to begin to learn about one another as individuals and as agency representatives. At each meeting, two issues emerged as major focal points for needed professional development activity: (1) developing shared understandings about the concept of family literacy and (2) finding ways to promote communication and collaboration among various programs and agencies with interest in family literacy.

All groups spoke to the need to develop and disseminate a concept of family literacy that emphasized the family as the "unit" for focus. Groups suggested that mission or vision statements be developed collaboratively and disseminated to all within the state who were (or wished to be) involved in family literacy programming. All programs needed to see families as central to all educational efforts, they contended; everyone needed to learn to be "family friendly." Other groups suggested that this shared philosophy should be based on a "strengths" model of family functioning and family education; the notion of true partnerships, which might involve programs and agencies "looking outside the box" for ways to work together; and an expanded definition of *family literacy*—one that went beyond "just mothers and children reading stories together," as the representative from the health services agency in our opening vignette discovered. The entire group agreed on the concept of a continuum of family literacy activities, from library storybook hours with parent involvement to comprehensive efforts such as Even Start.

Groups shared several ideas for developing and promoting this shared concept of family literacy. Mentoring, modeling, shadowing, and program visitations were suggested, as was the development and dissemination of family literacy "best practices." Regionally developed family literacy resource fairs were suggested as a means for local professionals and community members to learn about family literacy offerings. Electronic resources, such as an electronic list dedicated to family literacy issues and electronic access to resource information, also were requested.

Groups saw the development of collaborative relationships as time consuming and possibly frustrating, but well worth the effort. Many family literacy programs seem isolated from one another, they commented; programs supported by one state agency seldom know what is happening in programs supported by other state agencies. A worthy goal of statewide efforts might be to help build self-perpetuating, community-based systems so that programs could communicate with and support one another.

In summer 1997, a statewide group of family literacy leaders began developing suggestions for state, regional, and local activity to address professional development needs. Groups worked with a planning grid that identified four broad goals for professional development support, which were synthesized from previous activities:

1. Develop and promote the concept of family literacy.
2. Enhance communication among programs.
3. Provide resources for programs.
4. Provide staff development for family literacy professionals.

State, regional, and local activities were developed for each of these goals. State-level suggestions generated at this meeting called for several types of activity, all of which required collaboration and some of which we subsequently accomplished:

- An electronic list was developed for Ohio family literacy practitioners as a way to share resources and ideas.
- With support from the Honda Corporation, the Ohio Literacy Network (a statewide adult literacy advocacy group) collaborated with personnel from the Department of Education's Division of Early Childhood Education to develop public service announcements and boilerplate ads about family literacy to be run in local newspapers. A family literacy logo was also developed, and bookmarks and posters were printed and distributed throughout the state with artwork contributed by several Ohio cartoonists.
- The coordinator of the Ohio Family Literacy Statewide Initiative arranged a 2-day policy makers' seminar attended by agency heads,

legislators, and other state leaders, which was designed to foster understanding about family literacy and to build cross-agency partnerships.

- A family literacy strand was added to the annual statewide Early Childhood Conference.
- A cross-agency resource guide was requested, which would include general resources, statistics about family literacy, contact information for family literacy programs throughout the state, funding ideas, curriculum suggestions, and so forth.

We did not begin this project with the intention to assemble a 1,200-page resource guide, but after the survey was analyzed and the various stakeholder groups had met, we realized that Ohio agencies attempting to support family literacy had a problem: Everybody needed more information about ways to develop and expand family literacy programs and especially about each other. Consequently, we assembled the *Family Literacy Resource Notebook* (FLRN) (Sapin & Padak, 1998), which was subsequently distributed to key personnel representing all the agencies surveyed and made available electronically at the Web site of the Ohio Literacy Resource Center (http://literacy.kent.edu). Conceptualizing the FLRN was no small feat. We thought of our audiences—community members, teachers, program directors, policy makers—and aimed to select topics and develop information that all would find useful. The FLRN's 12 chapters provide definitions and case studies of various types of family literacy programs; resources such as curriculum suggestions and booklists; and concrete suggestions about such issues as staffing, finding resources, program public relations, and evaluation.

Family Literacy Professionals Learn to Collaborate

Our experiences, both at the local level and statewide, have taught us some valuable lessons about collaboration. We comment on several of the most important here:

◆ *Collaboration is not easy, even among willing partners.* It takes time to develop trust. It even takes time to develop shared understandings of issues that are central to the purpose of the partnership, in our case family literacy. In this regard, we agree with Bruner's (1991) caution that interagency collaboration is time consuming and process intensive and should only be used when the benefits are expected to be substantial. In the case of family literacy programming, persistence pays off.

◆ *Institutions do not collaborate; people do.* Formal partnership agreements may result from collaborative activity, but the success of any collaborative effort rests in large part on the willingness of the people involved to work together. People will work together if they believe strongly in the importance of the collaborative effort. Those who are committed to family literacy as a promising practice are more likely to "hang in" when the inevitable partnership difficulties arise.

◆ *Effective collaborators have the ability to view situations from perspectives other than their own.* They respect others' perspectives on issues. Often effective collaborations have different people playing different roles. Someone may be the "policy person" in a discussion about family literacy programs, for example, while another may be "family advocate" and still another "fiscally prudent" or "researcher/evaluator." If partners respect each other and trust in others' abilities, then many areas of expertise can be tapped collectively, even though no one person has all that expertise individually.

◆ *A collaborative approach among leaders within agencies and organizations creates a positive mindset for collaboration.* Often this mindset even addresses such issues as work habits and personal relationships. All partners must be willing to pitch in, to spend time doing their share to see a project through to completion. Those more interested in abdicating responsibility for their share of the work will soon find themselves unwelcome partners.

◆ *Friendships among partners are not necessary, but they lead to long-term collaborations.* The three of us, for example, have held seven jobs over the past decade, yet we always stay in contact and look for ways to work together because we share a passion for common ideas and because we are friends.

One of a set of Even Start Family Literacy Focus Papers (RMC, no date) makes the point that "after one year of operation Even Start project directors reported the establishment of working relationships with partner agencies as the number one barrier to project success." Instead of aiming at "what's in it for me," effective family literacy collaborations focus on "what's in it for families." The most successful family literacy programs in Ohio cobble together adult basic education, early childhood education, vocational education, child care, meals, transportation services, and more. Their collaborations succeed thanks to committed, passionate, hard-working individuals who persist in overcoming longstanding barriers to families' success.

References

Bruner, C. (1991). *Thinking collaboratively: Ten questions and answers to help policy makers improve children's services.* Washington, DC: The Education and Human Services Consortium.

Henderson, A., & Berla, N. (Eds.). (1994). *A new generation of evidence: The family is critical to student achievement.* Washington, DC: National Committee for Citizens in Education. (ERIC Document Reproduction Service No. ED 375 968)

National Center for Family Literacy. *System reform project.* Louisville, KY: Author.

Nickse, R. (1990). *Family and intergenerational literacy programs.* Columbus, OH: ERIC Clearinghouse on Adult, Career, and Vocational Education.

Padak, N., & Rasinski, T. (2000). *Family literacy programs: Who benefits?* Kent, OH: Ohio Literacy Resource Center. (Available online at http://literacy.kent.edu)

Paratore, J.R. (1993). An intergenerational approach to literacy: Effects on the literacy learning of adults and on the practice of family literacy. In D.J. Leu & C.K. Kinzer (Eds.), *Examining central issues in literacy research, theory, and practice: Forty-second yearbook of the National Reading Conference* (pp. 83–92). Chicago: National Reading Conference.

RMC. *Even Start family literacy focus papers.* Portsmouth, NH: Author.

RMC. (1995). *Guide to quality: Even Start family literacy programs.* Portsmouth, NH: Author.

Sapin, C., & Padak, N. (Comp.) (1998). *The family literacy resource notebook.* Kent, OH: Ohio Literacy Resource Center. (Available online at http://literacy.kent.edu).

Sticht, T. (1995, November/December). Adult education for family literacy. *Adult Learning, 23–24.*

Tracey, D. (1995). Family literacy: Overview and synthesis of an ERIC search. In K.A. Hinchman, D.J. Leu, & C.K. Kinzer (Eds.), *Perspectives on literacy research and practice: Forty-fourth yearbook of the National Reading Conference* (pp. 280–288). Chicago: National Reading Conference.

Van Fossen, S., & Sticht, T.G. (1991). *Teach the mother and reach the child: Results of the intergenerational literacy action research project.* Washington, DC: Wider Opportunities for Women.

SECTION

MULTIPLE PATHWAYS
TO COLLABORATION

COLLABORATION IN A FIRST-GRADE CLASSROOM
Shared Inquiry Supports Diverse Learners' Literacy Development

Jacqueline K. Peck

It is the middle of November, a few weeks before the U.S. celebration of Thanksgiving, and Sharon Hughes's first-grade classroom is studying early American culture. Sharon provides a variety of materials to support the classroom inquiry. A film presents many facts and vocabulary associated with early America. Sharon contends, "Material should be a little sophisticated." Then Sharon describes a most exciting outcome of using this "sophisticated" material: "I planned that we would look at the books, watch this movie, and then make a display for the hallway bulletin board. But after watching the movie the children said, 'Oh no, Ms. Hughes. We need to know more about the games they played. And how did other canoes look?' The children wanted to know more about how the people dressed. So now I'm trying to gather all this additional material!"

From the time I first began doing collaborative research with Sharon Hughes almost 7 years ago, I knew she was an exemplary teacher-researcher whose insights held the power to make schools places where all children become literate, participatory members of their community. Over the years as we developed a deep mutual respect for each other's thinking, we realized that we share key understandings that affirm our beliefs about literacy learning and teaching.

This chapter describes how Sharon's inquiry-oriented pedagogy supports the literacy development of the diverse learners in her classroom. Sharon's comments and the classroom vignettes presented in this chapter were collected as part of a naturalistic case study of her literacy instruction (Peck, 1995). Data for the study were collected during the first 10 weeks of the school year. Although I formally analyzed the corpus of data collected for the case study using the constant-comparative method (Glaser & Strauss, 1967), ongoing collaborative analysis occurred informally as Sharon and I interacted in her classroom, viewed videotapes of the children at work, and dialogued about the classroom literacy events.

The rich dimensions of collaboration in this classroom (see Figure 1) were particularly significant. The classroom vignettes that follow invite you, the reader, to consider these questions: What is the nature of collaboration in this first-grade classroom? More specifically, how does it promote literacy development? The chapter closes with a dis-

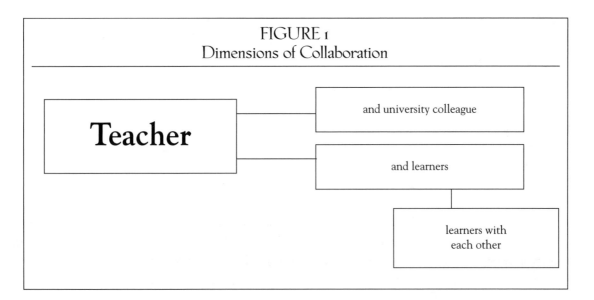

FIGURE 1
Dimensions of Collaboration

Teacher

and university colleague

and learners

learners with each other

cussion of the impact of the collaboration and my conclusions. But first, meet Sharon and her classroom.

Teacher and Learners Inquire Together

This inquiry-oriented urban first-grade classroom was labeled a "regular" classroom because the learners identified as "gifted" were placed in another first-grade classroom in the building. Sharon holds a graduate degree in education and at the time of the study had 7 years of experience teaching 6- to 8-year-olds. She holds leadership roles in her district by serving on curriculum committees; she is a frequent provider of professional development in local, state, and national venues; and she participates in statewide policy making efforts. Her work has been widely recognized and documented (see Peck, 1997; Peck & Hughes, 1994; Peck & Hughes, 1996; Peck & Hughes, 1997).

Sharon told me the children in this first grade "all come from diverse backgrounds." Their various kindergarten experiences ranged from traditional half-day to whole-day sessions of learning and involvement, "but for the most part they're just a group of children." And, like most groups of children, they were quite diverse in ways other than their kindergarten experience. Here are some examples: Tanya and Tyrone, although eager learners, had language delays, were introverted, and lacked confidence. Dionne and Sonya were strong readers who were extroverted and competed with each other. Matt and Nathan were self-assured and helpful; Sharon referred to them as "encouragers." David's parents wanted him tested for ADHD, and Joey's parent put forth medical excuses to limit his participation in challenging material. Miles was "immature" and did not appear to be interested in reading. Donte and Mary were repeating first grade due to literacy difficulties; Donte had been with another teacher the previous year, but Mary had been with Sharon. This was a relatively typical group of diverse learners, including several who would likely be labeled as "at-risk" or "disabled" in some classrooms but whose literacy blossomed in Sharon's. She did not attribute the success of her inquiry pedagogy to the particular children in her class in any one year, because she noticed "this happens every year with each group of children. It isn't specific to any year or any group."

From Sharon's perspective, inquiry-oriented curriculum is not teacher directed, with the teacher posing questions that the children research. In Sharon's classroom, the children pose questions to each other and then look for answers. Sharon's perspective also involves inquiry into the learning process itself. Both she, the teacher, and the learners engage in shared inquiry—teacher as learner and learner as teacher and all as inquirers. Learning is perceived as a meaning-making process; the learners and the teacher are recognized as legitimate knowledge-producers, and the learners are authentic collaborators in inquiry (Davydov, 1995; Dewey, 1910).

The case study simultaneously emerged from our prior collaborative projects (see Peck & Hughes, 1994) and nurtured ongoing collaboration that occurred in multiple dimensions. For Sharon and I, collaboration helped us find our voices by listening to each other (McDonald, 1987), and our collaborative research helped us examine our own beliefs and practices (Kagan, 1993).

The distinguishing feature of shared inquiry in Sharon's classroom is that the process is fully shared by the teacher and the learners, as the opening vignette vividly portrays. Sharon expects the learners to become teachers and requires herself to again become a learner. This expectation is held by other inquiry-oriented teachers (see Condon, Graft, Jensen, & Tuell, 1996; Tower, 2000; Visovatti, 1994). Sharing the inquiry process with the learners also supports their mutual collaboration. Teachers who share roles with the learners and encourage development of a classroom community are creating culturally relevant classrooms (Ladson-Billings, 1994) in which learners are expected to learn with and from each other.

Being a "Collaborator in Inquiry"

What does it mean to be a "collaborator in inquiry" in Sharon's classroom? Often the children collaborate with a partner to create a product. Sometimes this occurs during the opening time of the day as the children prepare for a shared book experience. In other instances the partners or small groups work to create a culminating piece for a literacy theme study. Early in the school year, Sharon clearly explains to the children that "you don't have to do [your work] the same way as your partner." Reflecting on one of her literacy lessons, she said, "I want them to know that when we work as partners, it doesn't mean that we give up our individuality. We still make choices for ourselves, but the end result has to be cooperative or collaborative."

Sharon intentionally establishes conditions that support collaboration. For example, on the first day of the school year, she read a story to the class about a cartoon-like character who could not get along well in school because he did not follow the rules. As the class brainstormed helpful and appropriate behaviors the cartoon character might try, Sharon wrote their ideas on a chart. Then she guided their reading of the chart and asked them to decide which ideas they wanted to use to formulate their classroom rules. Sharon planned this initial literacy event to serve multiple purposes: It engaged the learners in authentic reading and writing on the first day of school, it demonstrated that their ideas are legitimate and valued, and it gave her important insight into the learners' expectations about school.

"I want [the children] to know that when we work as partners, it doesn't mean that we give up our individuality. We still make choices for ourselves, but the end result has to be cooperative or collaborative."

The quality of the interaction of the learners in Sharon's classroom is noteworthy. She works to help them do more than just share their ideas. "The real point of that time is for them to listen to each other and provide feedback to and for each other," she explained. Sharon plans for partner sharing because everyone cannot be heard in a whole-class setting: "If the lesson is important enough for them to do it, they should have the opportunity to share those ideas." Another important outcome of this interaction is that it helps the class develop mutual respect for each other and their ideas. Sharon said,

> Sometimes, particularly because of the environment that many of these children live in, some of the ideas are pretty grizzly. And I want them to feel free enough to share those experiences so that other children can see how the world isn't only the way it is at your house. Some of us live in less than ideal circumstances, but that doesn't mean that they're less than ideal persons.

In addition to working with partners, the use of multiple and flexible groupings provides further opportunities for these diverse learners to collaborate. For example, daily whole-class groupings, like shared book readings, give this diverse classroom of learners a chance to be on the same learning level: "No child at that point sees himself as the genius or less than the genius of the group," said Sharon. Other times the children work in mixed ability groups. Sharon made the following comments about one particular instance:

> The children were grouped using mixed ability, and it worked out perfectly. The stronger student was there to support and assist the less able students. But on the other hand, the less able student was there to provide many, many, many concepts for the student with greater abilities. And this is how it should be. We begin to see each other as resources. I want this always, because I want children to see the ability within them and the ability within others.

In this way, working in mixed ability groups supports the development of mutual respect that Sharon expects to occur through meaningful collaborative interactions. She asserted,

> When I have them working in groups and consciously making an effort to respect others, they take into account those individual differences. No one ever says, "Well why is it that Terrell can do it and I can't?" I've never heard that—not one time—because they know that the time will come when they'll have a need or a pressing desire that we have to make allowances for.

The learners in this class respect differences because they know and trust that the same respect will be extended to them.

Sharon uses ability groups at times; however, membership in these groups is not fixed and stable for the entire school year. "Highs, mediums, and lows" do not remain in these categories forever. Sharon groups learners based on the strategies they need to develop or the materials most likely to bring them success, which is demonstrated in the "Culminating 'The Little Red Hen' Study" vignette later in this chapter.

Random groupings are yet another pattern Sharon uses to provide a variety of opportunities to interact and collaborate. Sometimes the benefits are unexpected, as Sharon explains in this example from early in the school year:

Jose is bilingual. He speaks little English in the household where Spanish predominates. It was interesting to watch him because he was so very engrossed in the dialogue with the members of his group, as if he was not just listening to the ideas but also hearing English spoken and being able to talk actively with children using English. It will be real important for me to provide him with a lot of opportunities to hear the sounds of language and for him to participate in those language experiences. It will be necessary for me to expose him to a lot of different pieces of material and give him an opportunity to talk in front of the children and make sure that he is involved in a group that does a lot of active exchanging.

Sharon's intentional planning for collaboration—with partners and with multiple and flexible groupings—beautifully supports her goals for learners like Jose. I selected the following classroom vignettes to demonstrate how this kind of collaboration supports the literacy development of the diverse learners in Sharon's classroom.

"Friends Help Each Other Inside the House and Outside the House"

It is Wednesday morning, the third week of school. The children are drawing about a time they have been a good friend and a time they have not been a good friend. At 10:30, Sharon asks them to share their drawings with a partner.

At 10:40, the class gathers on the carpeted area for shared book reading. They have been reading various versions of the folktale "The Little Red Hen," and they have talked about the friends' roles. Now today, after they sing some warm-up songs and identify the characters in "The Little Red Hen," they read the story again and talk about how the characters in the story helped or did not help the little red hen. Sharon writes what they say on a chart: "Friends didn't help cut the wheat, didn't help her bake it, didn't help grind it, didn't help make it, didn't help cook it." They read the chart together, and Sharon asks which things happened outside the house and which things happened inside the house. The children say "pick wheat, find wheat" happened outside, and "cook, bake" happened inside.

Sharon then explains that they are going to work in small groups to create a poster showing ways friends can help each other inside the house and ways they can help each other outside. She

explains that they will need to talk in their groups first, and then create a poster to show all their ideas. She tells them that they will
share their finished posters with the class. At 11:00 the groups begin to work together.

The children collaborated in several ways to complete their posters.
They needed to talk about their concepts of sharing inside and outside the house. Sharon also planned for them to collaborate on use
of materials; each group had only one box of crayons and one poster,
although they each had their own pencil and eraser. She wanted
them to share the crayons and draw on one poster because she wanted it "to be a composite of all of their ideas." At one point Sharon observed that several groups were unclear about what to do. She
completed a sample on the chalkboard to demonstrate and model the
project for them.

The finished posters showed a variety of ideas, such as watering
the garden as a way to help a friend outside and washing dishes as a
way to help inside. Many of the children drew the red hen and other
animal characters from the story to illustrate how they could help
their friends. They used the story characters but showed ways to help
that went beyond the text of the story. One group of particular interest included Jose, Charlie, and Joey, who were relatively new to the
classroom, and two other children. Although Jose and Charlie initially hit at each other in a playful way, their finished poster did show
that all members of the group had contributed ideas. On the side of
the poster showing ways to help inside, they had drawn a track; Jose
and Charlie talked about playing together using a train track. It
pleased Sharon that they showed "one of the ways of helping a friend
inside was playing with them." She carefully structured this literacy
lesson around concepts of friendship because

> one of my major concerns with teaching my children is that they take the
> concepts that we cover in the classroom and apply them to their lives out-
> side the classroom. Many of these children live in environments...that in-
> volve a lot of gang activity...are less than friendly. So I'm expecting them
> to, as we talk about this, figure out ways that they can be better people in
> how they treat each other.... And as a result, that'll encourage others to
> perceive them as friends.

Sharon's initial goals for collaboration were met in this literacy event in which the children

◆ contributed individual ideas but incorporated them into their joint project,

◆ began to develop mutual respect for each other through joint exploration of the concept of friendship,

◆ developed a supportive relationship (e.g., as developed when Terrell and Tyrone, both described as introverted, were grouped together and expected to open up to each other), and

◆ began to evaluate their own participation in the collaborative processes.

Sharon began to establish the groundwork for this literacy event the first day of the school year when she engaged the class in co-construction of classroom rules. School supplies—crayons, scissors, glue—are community owned and shared. Using these materials tangibly supported the learners' collaboration. Sharon's reflections tell how it happens:

> The partnerships were randomly assigned, and the children had to share materials. It was interesting to listen to some of the conversations that developed. One of the things that Sam talked about in his group was, "What happens if you can't share the materials?" I told him that within the group they would figure out a way to share and that they will share. And it was funny; that's exactly what happened. They did share!

Trusting that their individual ideas will be respected as they create a joint product intellectually supports the learners' collaboration. Sharon reflected on how the groups shared responsibility. One of her concerns was that the person who recorded ideas on paper was "actually recording ideas others in the group have shared and not changing those ideas to fit her or his own perceptions." To ease this concern, Sharon decided to be sure the learners did daily journal writing to "spark everyone's interest in text."

"Community" is inherent in all aspects of Sharon's classroom. Cooperation, not competition, is recognized and valued. Sharon frequently designs literacy events that result in products with both collective and individual input; this prompts the collaborative talk so characteristic of her classroom. Sharon plans for learner interaction throughout the school day, particularly in partner format. The learners become comfortable talking through their ideas with each other, and they learn to honor and respect each other's thinking. Sharon does not immediately intervene when disagreements arise; she encourages her students to work out solutions and becomes involved only when she determines they need her guidance. Sharon recognizes "there is a point at which they should come to me, but I should not be the first attempt made by them to resolve their conflict. They must remember to try to work it out within the group before they come to me."

"Community" is inherent in all aspects of Sharon's classroom. Cooperation, not competition, is recognized and valued.... The learners become comfortable talking through their ideas with each other, and they learn to honor and respect each other's thinking.

The collaboration Sharon and I experienced helped us articulate our developing insights. For example, I asked Sharon if some observers, upon seeing the learners in her classroom spread out on the floor in groups talking to each other, might say her classroom lacked "structure." She thought some might; but she feels if the class events were structured every time "so that one child speaks at a time, raising her hand, and waiting to be called on, too much would go unspoken." I agreed with Sharon and affirmed that she effectively structured a student-centered collaborative environment: "These videotapes are documentation that there is structure. The learners knew what the task was—they maybe needed clarification—but they knew," she pointed out.

Culminating "The Little Red Hen" Study

It is the fourth week of school, and Sharon's class is concluding a study of "The Little Red Hen." For their first activity of the morning, as they settle in the classroom and Sharon takes care of attendance, lunch arrangements, and notes from parents, the children are drawing in response to the question, "What do you see on a farm?" to connect to their study of the setting of the story. At 10:30 they gather on the carpeted area and sing "Six Little Ducks" and "Old MacDonald Had a Farm."

Sharon then asks the children to use pictures from "The Little Red Hen" to retell the story. Then together they read the repetitive sentences from the story that Sharon has written on strips. After reading the key vocabulary words in the context of the sentences, Sharon asks the students to look at individual words on cards and put them in the order they appear in the sentences; they read the sentences again. Children indicate if the words are in the correct order by using thumbs up or thumbs down, and then they read the key words individually from the cards.

Sharon explains to the class that today they will finish their study of "The Little Red Hen" by writing their own "Little Red Hen" books. They will work in three groups of approximately 10 students each. Each group reads its sentence strips together; then the students read the individual sentence strips they have chosen. At 11:00 each group moves to a specific part of the classroom, and the children begin to illustrate their sentences of the story. When their illustrations are finished, they put their sentence strips underneath their pictures and decide as a group how to sequence them to tell the story. They read their story several times in their group and then share it with the whole class.

For this lesson, Sharon decided to have the children work in ability groups. She prepared sentences on strips for three different tellings of the folktale—one for each of the three groups. She wanted to be sure the sentences used the vocabulary from the story so each group would be able to read its book. She also planned for them to collaboratively decide how to sequence the pictures because

> I'm not sure where each child is in this area [sequencing], and I want to make sure that this entire book-making project, this culminating activity, is successful for all children. If I had them sequence the books before we've had an opportunity to work on that skill, I'm concerned that many of the children won't be able to do that and the other children will tell them how to do it. And at this point, I want each child to have some input as to where their page fits into the total story.

Sharon explained that as the school year progressed, the children would provide their own sentences because she expects them to become more independent and see themselves as authors. But she said that because "building self-esteem and encouraging success...is a primary concern with the culminating activity of these early lessons, I'll provide the text for them."

The collaboration of one group was particularly interesting. Those readers with the least print experience worked with very minimal "sentences" to tell the story—"The hen. The dog. The pig. The duck. The cat. The wheat. The bread. Yum, yum!" Because there was no obvious order to these sentences, the students needed to figure out how they wanted to sequence their pages. This is how Sharon later described their process:

> [It] was pretty interesting because they all had opinions on where their picture should go. And of course, everybody wanted their picture to be the first one.... One of the children decided that the hen should be first since she was the main character. And then the other thing was where they were going to put the bread and wheat. I was curious to watch that. And it didn't take any discussion; everybody felt that the wheat should go first, and then the bread would come last, and then "yum, yum." And then Sonya said, "Now Ms. Hughes, I want to make the hen, but how should I have her say 'yum, yum'? Do you think I should make her say 'yum, yum' by having her rub her stomach or do you think I should make her say 'yum, yum' by having the words inside of her stomach like she'd already eaten the bread?" I said, "Well Sonya, I don't know. You have to think about it for yourself, and you know whatever you decide I think will be fine because either of those suggestions are good ones." She didn't know how to make a hen so that's when I got some other book that we'd been reading that had blacklined illustrations.... So she used that, and she put "yum, yum" inside her tummy.

When the groups read their books to the class, each child received credit for his or her individual picture. One of the things that surprised Sharon as she considered their readings was how well the children in all the groups knew the key words: "I was really amazed with how much of the vocabulary, the individual words, the children learned from context.... I would not have expected them to know very many of the words."

Sharon was very pleased with this culmination of "The Little Red Hen," and she was able to evaluate the children's developing sense of story. She observed, "The children really have a sense of sequencing what happens at the beginning, in the middle, and at the end of the stories."

This literacy event also met Sharon's high expectations regarding the children's collaboration. Individual contributions were integrated into a satisfying whole piece. And in this project, working in ability groups enabled all children to be successful and to meaningfully collaborate with each other to create a text they could read proudly and confidently.

Sharon and I frequently talked about the negative effects of ability grouping and conditions under which it is appropriate. Sharon uses ability grouping primarily for skill development, "but also to give children an opportunity to interact with people who think similarly to the way they do or who have similar intellectual levels." She also uses mixed ability grouping, usually based on the children's choice, "because they have a common interest, or want to research a particular topic, or want to read a particular book." Partner grouping may involve children of similar academic abilities or a higher achieving student with a lower achieving student who often is able to take an "expert" role because of specific knowledge about a topic or a talent in traditionally nonacademic areas such as the arts or interpersonal intelligence. Partners may also choose to work together or be randomly paired. Through our dialogue about groupings, it became apparent that Sharon's success with these multiple grouping patterns is rooted in the respect she extends to the learners—and her expectation that they respect each other—and in her belief in their ability to produce knowledge (Ladson-Billings, 1994).

Evaluating the Impact of Collaboration

I chose the vignettes in this chapter to illustrate richly how the diverse learners in Sharon's classroom collaborated in ways that supported their literacy development. One of the most striking outcomes of their collaboration is that the *children maintained ownership of their individual ideas and thinking, yet were able to create products that represented their combined understandings.* Through talking, sharing materials, and making decisions together they were able to develop mutual respect for each other. Also, through Sharon's intentional establishment of a classroom community, curricular planning that invites learner input, and design of authentic literacy events that include time to interact, the learners supported each other's learning.

Through Sharon's intentional establishment of a classroom community, curricular planning that invites learner input, and design of authentic literacy events that include time to interact, the learners supported each other's learning.

Moreover, these vignettes clearly show that Sharon views diversity as a support for learning. *She creates an environment and plans for situations in which differences are used to promote learning, not seen as obstacles to overcome.* Jose's small-group interaction with spoken English is an excellent example. Because Sharon fully shares her inquiry orientation with the learners in her classroom, they also think positively of their differences. In an earlier collaborative study (Peck & Hughes, 1994), Sharon commented that mixed ability groups are often initiated by the learners, and they often have very successful outcomes:

> They [students] didn't automatically go connect with people in a group that had similar academic levels or similar learning styles. Some of the children in the group would be much more artistic, some would be much more verbal, some would be a lot better at listening and offering ideas that way, and they would automatically develop the groups that would meet their needs.

All the positive outcomes Sharon and others have observed when diverse learners collaborate in inquiry do not go unquestioned by others or by Sharon herself. Learners in shared inquiry classrooms take responsibility for their own learning and ultimately for their own lives, but Sharon regularly asks, "Am I doing those children a service or a disservice in having them so involved in curricular decisions and in being responsible for their own learning?" This question grows out of her concerns about how they will fare if their next teacher is very traditional and bases instruction solely on the manual.

Another perhaps even more difficult issue is the disbelief other teachers have expressed to Sharon and, regrettably, even to the children at times. The disbelief is often couched in a question about mechanics, such as, "How is it that children who are only in first grade could do...." But Sharon understands, "They're not interested in the mechanics to replicate the process in their own classroom. The real purpose is to almost verbalize the fact that you couldn't have done it." Sharon laminated the culminating "Little Red Hen" books and knew the children would read them in their classroom, to their parents at Open House, and to their principal, who was very supportive of their work. Yet she spoke hesitantly about placing them in the school library because of the doubting comments they were likely to draw from those who do not believe first graders could do this much.

But the evidence is undeniably present—in the vignettes, in the learners' joint productions, and in their changed actions. Sharon shares all aspects of her inquiry process with the learners, including the evaluation of the information they gain, and this promotes the rich collaboration that occurs in her classroom:

> When you talk about creating this inquiry-based environment where you have got children asking questions, doing the research, and answering those questions, they have to be a part of evaluating the quality of their answers and also the impact that those answers have.... If they're not carrying that same questioning, seeking out the answers to solve problems, and self-evaluation over into their personal or social lives, as far as I'm concerned the learning has been nominal. My whole perception of learning has to do with the knowledge we acquire and how we use that knowledge to make ourselves different, how we're changed by that knowledge, and how we impact the world around us.

"If [the children are] not carrying that same questioning, seeking out the answers to solve problems, and self-evaluation over into their personal or social lives, as far as I'm concerned the learning has been nominal."

This is why the collaboration described in this chapter promotes literacy development to the extent it does.

Concluding Thoughts

The rich dimensions of collaboration in shared inquiry described in this chapter and the ensuing benefits offer hope and insight to those desiring to improve literacy practice. Sharon and I have learned, however, that for some, the outcomes are not believable—for others the process is just too difficult. But to those who do believe in the ability of children to learn, to teach, and to inquire, and who believe the rewards more than outweigh the labor, I offer these suggestions and recommendations:

◆ Intentionally plan for collaboration and expect it to occur. Expect the learners to talk to each other and provide time for them to get comfortable with it. Expect the learners to make decisions about who they work with, how they work together, and what they produce; then design authentic literacy events that invite their input. Use curricular planning that is global enough to accommodate learner ideas and suggestions. Expect the learners to create joint products and then construct group projects that require incorporation of the ideas of all group members.

◆ Develop comfort with the process. Shared inquiry is messy and full of ambiguity, so discomfort is to be expected; but "when you plan open-ended lessons that the learners can take in different directions, you really get an opportunity to see how they are developing, how they're thinking, the 'why' behind their actions. And it forces you to rethink how you plan."

◆ Trust the learners, and trust yourself. Let go of control of the literacy events and recognize the learners as teachers too. Communicate your expectations of collaboration and question-asking. An inquiry-oriented teacher must be a risk-taker who is comfortable with asking questions and who encourages the learners to do the same. Observe the learners and how they work together and with you and other adults in your classroom. Then let your observations lead to authentic questions and guide the decisions you make.

The collaboration Sharon and I experienced, and continue to experience, has nurtured our professional and personal growth. Several years ago another university colleague and I asked Sharon if she would be interested in working with us to create video materials to use in our literacy courses. We wanted to provide our preservice teachers with "kidwatching" (Goodman, 1978) experiences using authentic literacy classroom contexts. Sharon participated in the process of designing the literacy event to be videotaped and later in editing the footage. Adding another important dimension to our collaboration (see Figure 2), when our students viewed the materials Sharon also visited our university classroom to answer questions about her learners and her teaching.

What have we learned through our collaboration in shared inquiry? We have learned to see ourselves as learners and the learners in our classrooms as co-constructors of the curriculum. We understand the need to establish culturally relevant university classrooms so preservice teachers will carry a vision of collaboration into their classrooms of the future. Together we have affirmed our longstanding beliefs that literacy is a complex social process that can only be served with complex social thought and action, such as the collaboration

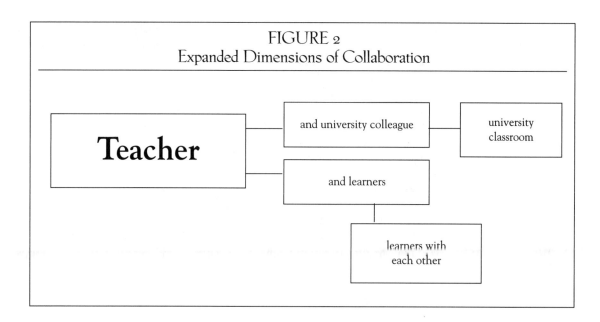

FIGURE 2
Expanded Dimensions of Collaboration

Teacher — and university colleague — university classroom

Teacher — and learners — learners with each other

in shared inquiry presented in this chapter. It is a powerful vision of teachers and learners collaborating to develop literacy to the fullest extent and to forge more positive relationships in the world.

Note

Sharon Hughes has continued to inquire into her literacy practice and to collaborate in other settings within her district. She served 1 year as a primary reading teacher in another elementary building; she then moved into a district level leadership role in which she provides professional development in literacy for classroom teachers.

Sharon has my steadfast respect and gratitude for opening her remarkable inquiry process to me. Without her this chapter could not have been written.

References

Condon, M.W.F., Graft, L., Jensen, T., & Tuell, J. (1996). Learners as teachers, teachers as learners: The blurring of roles through collaboration. *Primary Voices K–6, 4,* 32–38.

Davydov, V.V. (1995). The influence of L.S. Vygotsky on education theory, research, and practice. *Educational Researcher, 24,* 12–21.

Dewey, J. (1910). *How we think*. Lexington, MA: D.C. Heath.

Glaser, B., & Strauss, A. (1967). *The discovery of grounded theory*. Chicago: Aldine.

Goodman, Y. (1978). Kidwatching: An alternative to testing. *National Elementary School Principal, 57*, 41–45.

Kagan, D.M. (1993). Contexts for the use of classroom cases. *American Educational Research Journal, 30*, 703–723.

Ladson-Billings, G. (1994). *The dreamkeepers: Successful teachers of African-American children*. San Francisco: Jossey-Bass.

McDonald, J.P. (1987). Raising the teacher's voice and the ironic role of theory. In M. Okazawa-Rey, J. Anderson, & R. Traver (Eds.), *Teachers, teaching, & teaching education* (pp. 26–49). Cambridge, MA: Harvard Educational Review.

Peck, J.K. (1995). *Inquiry pedagogy: A case study of a first grade teacher's literacy instruction*. Unpublished doctoral dissertation, Kent State University, Kent, OH.

Peck, J.K. (1997). Redefining reflective practice: Thinking forward about conditions that support literacy learning. In W.M. Linek & E.G. Sturtevant (Eds.), *Exploring literacy* (pp. 245–255). Platteville, WI: College Reading Association.

Peck, J.K., & Hughes, S.V. (1994, April). *The impact of an inquiry approach to learning in a technology-rich environment*. Paper presented at the annual meeting of the American Educational Research Association, New Orleans, LA.

Peck, J.K., & Hughes, S.V. (1996, April). *Inquiry pedagogy: Maximizing literacy learning and teaching through shared inquiry*. Paper presented at the annual meeting of the American Educational Research Association, New York, NY.

Peck, J.K., & Hughes, S.V. (1997). So much success...from a first-grade database project! *Computers in the Schools, 13*, 109–116.

Tower, C. (2000). Questions that matter: Preparing elementary students for the inquiry process. *The Reading Teacher, 53*, 550–557.

Visovatti, K. (1994). Developing primary voices. *Primary Voices K–6, 2*, 8–19.

Collaborative Learning Strategies in Diverse Classrooms

Patricia Douville and Karen D. Wood

Rick Hernandez is a first-year second-grade teacher. Last year Rick had a successful student teaching semester that reflected consistent applications of the contemporary practices in which he was trained in his university courses. In his first year as a full-time elementary teacher he is confident in his knowledge of what constitutes effective instructional strategies, but he feels overwhelmed by the demands of externally imposed mandates related to end-of-grade test scores. He expresses particular concerns for his second graders for whom English is a second language (ESL) or who possess limited English proficiency (LEP). Although he is aware of the importance of making these culturally and linguistically diverse students feel secure and accepted, Rick never feels he has the time to meet their myriad needs.

Doris Spears is a fifth-grade teacher with more than 20 years of elementary teaching experience. Doris has a clear sense of curricular mandates and her responsibility for what should be taught. Although some of her students complete assignments and projects and appear to master most targeted concepts, Doris is dismayed by the lack of progress she sees in other students. She is particularly concerned with the low reading and writing abilities of the six students in her class who were identified as having learning disabilities by the special education teacher. Even though Doris has tried to instill motivation in these students by implementing a rewards incentive system for completing assignments and doing at-home reading, she continues to perceive in them a sense of learned helplessness and academic disinterest.

In our work assisting preservice student teachers and experienced inservice teachers in translating research into effective practice, we frequently hear the same concern expressed: "How do I meet all these students' learning needs when their needs are so different?" For teachers like Rick Hernandez and Doris Spears who are challenged by the unique needs of an increasingly diverse student population, collaborative learning activities represent promising instructional alternatives. Academic collaboration provides students with opportunities to observe and engage in peer modeling, to dialogue about learning process and product, and to engage in learning that is rich in social interactions that are motivating as well as informative. Most importantly for many students, collaborative learning is just more fun.

What Theory and Research Tell About the Effectiveness of Collaborative Learning Strategies

Mankind's inherent need to communicate and socialize can be seen in classrooms on a daily basis as students take advantage of every available moment to interact with one another. Educators can capitalize on this inherent need by incorporating more group activities with regular classroom instruction.

Providing students with opportunities to learn and problem solve together has been discussed as many topics in the professional literature including cooperative learning, collaborative learning, and flexible grouping. Researchers such as David Johnson and Roger Johnson (1991), Spencer Kagan (1994), and Robert Slavin (1995) are most often associated with the term *cooperative learning* and have titled their publications accordingly. Collaborative learning models are said to focus on the creation of meaning through dialogue and discussion and tend not to break tasks into specific, rewardable component parts. According to Davidson (1994), advocates of cooperative learning models, for the most part, tend to be more structured with an emphasis on specific, rewardable behaviors.

Because we believe that students must be able to cooperate (get along well with others) in order to collaborate (work together toward a common goal), we use the term *collaborative learning* because it tends to be all-inclusive. We also recommend flexible grouping as a means of collaborative learning because it is not static or rigid, but instead involves forming many varied grouping arrangements to coordinate with classroom objectives (Wood, McCormack, Lapp, & Flood, 1997).

The value of having students interact with one another has theoretical roots in the social constructivist perspective of Vygotsky (1978), who maintained that the way students talk and interact with one another helps them to internalize new information and shapes the way they think and learn. Similarly, Rosenblatt (1976) advocates the need for a social exchange of ideas as a means to broaden readers' perspectives as they construct personal responses to reading. Much research has been conducted to determine what goes on during these peer interactions (Paratore & McCormack, 1997; Teasley, 1995; Webb, 1982). Apparently, students engaged in peer conversations about learning topics are motivated to establish mutual knowledge; that is, they implicitly attempt to monitor each other's understanding, request explanations, and offer clarification (Cazden, 1988; Cullinan, 1993; Wathen & Resnick, 1997). Peer-assisted learning strategies have been shown to improve the achievement of diverse learners as well (Fuchs, Fuchs, Mathes, & Simmons, 1997; Maheady, Mallette, Harper, Sacca, & Pomerantz, 1994).

> *The value of having students interact with one another has theoretical roots in the social constructivist perspective of Vygotsky (1978), who maintained that the way students talk and interact with one another helps them to internalize new information and shapes the way they think and learn.*

From a social constructivist point of view, it can be said that little is learned in an atmosphere that is constricted with silence. Stated another way, "learning is noisy" (Kasten, 1997, p. 88), particularly if that noise represents students retelling a story to one another, discussing a concept in their own words, whisper-reading with a buddy, or sharing their favorite part in a book. With that said, we present strategies for promoting "meaningful noise" as a means of including students of all ability levels within the classroom community. We begin with a snapshot of two students—one from Rick Hernandez's class and one from Doris Spears's class. Each of these students reflects diverse learning needs. Rick's student, Tuan, entered his classroom with little ability to communicate in English. Doris's student, Lily, diagnosed with a learning disability by the school's special education teacher, has difficulty staying on task and recasting learned material when tested. The experiences of these two teachers and their students illustrate how collaborative strategies have been incorporated successfully into actual classrooms as a means of engaging all types of students in the learning process.

Cultural and Linguistic Diversity: Tuan's Story

Tuan's family recently came to the United States from Southeast Asia. Both his mother and father, as well as his grandparents, speak only their native language at home. Like Tuan, his younger sisters and older brother speak very little English. In his second-grade classroom Tuan has few opportunities to use the limited English he does possess. His heavily accented pronunciations and nonstandard syntax sound strange to his classmates. They have little patience when he searches for an "American" word to express his thoughts. Although his teacher, Rick Hernandez, works with Tuan whenever he can, Rick's responsibilities to the other students and their varied needs do not afford him the time with Tuan that he knows he needs.

Tuan characterizes a growing group of culturally and linguistically diverse learners who are frequently denied entrance into the literacy culture of the classroom (Lewis, 1998). The barriers that are constructed by Tuan's noncommand of English isolate him, not only from the social community of his peers, but also from the learning community of his classroom. In order to provide Tuan and students like him a viable academic voice, we worked with Rick to investigate activities that would invite Tuan into the instructional environment.

The large body of research in language development demonstrates that language is learned through authentic and purposeful use (Cox & Boyd-Batstone, 1997; Tompkins, 1998). For ESL and LEP students like Tuan, collaborative reading and learning activities provide both an established purpose for engaging in meaningful discussions of what has been learned and the opportunity to hear language spoken by more capable peer models. Ensuring that learning tasks, within the framework of collaborative activities, are specifically tailored to meet individual needs and abilities provides culturally and linguistically diverse students with the essential voice that will assist them in achieving academic success.

Collaborative Activities Designed to Give Diverse Learners a "Voice" in Classroom Cultures

A number of collaborative grouping and instructional activities have been developed within the last 25 years. In spite of the fact that a large body of research supports the efficacy of integrating collaborative strategies into the instructional environment (Echevarria & Graves, 1998; Franklin & Thompson, 1994; Heath & Mangiola, 1991; King, 1990), we find that many teachers continue to relegate their culturally and linguistically diverse students to learning in isolation. Because collaboration provides students with the opportunity to problem solve within a supportive social context, collaborative activities are especially beneficial for diverse learners. We worked with Rick to incorporate Language Experience Approach, Jigsaw, and Readers Theatre into his classroom instruction because these particular activities provided him with the ability to customize student participatory roles in ways that would give all his students a voice to facilitate entrance into the culture of the classroom. This is especially crucial for ESL and LEP students like Tuan who do not benefit from more traditional learning approaches that isolate them from their peers.

Language Experience Approach

Language Experience Approach (LEA) activities use children's actual spoken ideas about real or vicarious experiences as the source of text used in reading and language skills instruction (Stauffer, 1970). For emergent readers, as well as their older counterparts, LEA provides the essential connection between the concept that what is thought can be spoken, what is spoken can be written, and what is written can be read. In this manner a direct and meaningful transfer from oral language to written language is provided. LEA also provides numerous opportunities for purposeful social interaction as students exchange ideas. We believe these instructional characteristics make LEA especially beneficial for culturally and linguistically diverse students like Tuan.

HOW CAN TEACHERS DESIGN COLLABORATIVE LEA ACTIVITIES FOR DIVERSE LEARNERS? LEA begins with a small- or whole-group discussion of a shared experience such as a field trip, a classroom visit by a special pet, a science experiment or project, or even reactions to the "lunchroom special" of the day. As ideas emerge from the group, teachers may elect to write students' sentences directly on chart paper or the chalkboard, or word process the sentences using a classroom monitor to ensure visibility for all students. (LEA procedures are shown in Figure 1.)

To provide Rick with an authentic model of how LEA activities are structured, we suggested that he observe a kindergarten teacher in his school who routinely and successfully incorporated LEA into her instruction. The lesson Rick observed began with a teacher-led stu-

---

FIGURE 1
Language Experience Approach (LEA) Procedures

Step 1: A group experience is provided to all members of the class (e.g., trip to the zoo).

Step 2: Teachers lead a group discussion of the experience. Ideas may be organized in a cluster or web.

Step 3: Students form collaborative groups in which story ideas are dictated to a capable group member.

Step 4: The resultant story/text becomes the source of subsequent reading and language skills instruction over a number of days.

Step 5: (Optional) Teachers may laminate and bind completed stories into books that become a permanent part of the classroom library.

dent discussion of the new classroom hamster. As students dictated ideas, the teacher wrote the sentences on chart paper. For example, one kindergarten student offered the idea, "Our new hamster is cute." As more ideas were offered by other students, the teacher added them to the story. When the story was completed, it was read chorally by all the students in the group. Figure 2 shows the completed kindergarten class story.

FIGURE 2
Completed Kindergarten LEA Story

Our new hamster is cute.

She likes her cage.

She gets her seeds on the floor.

She gets in trouble when she chews up the computer.

To modify the LEA activity Rick observed, we suggested he use an upcoming field trip to the zoo as a story topic with Tuan and his classmates. Instead of directly writing down completed sentences as they were offered during the class discussion of the trip, Rick decided to represent students' ideas with key words and phrases in a cluster format organizing students' initial ideas into categories. Using a cluster strategy in this manner enabled Rick to model a prewriting organizational strategy. Figure 3 shows the completed cluster in which Rick organized students' ideas about how the trip began, followed by ideas about what students saw and what they learned at the zoo, and con-

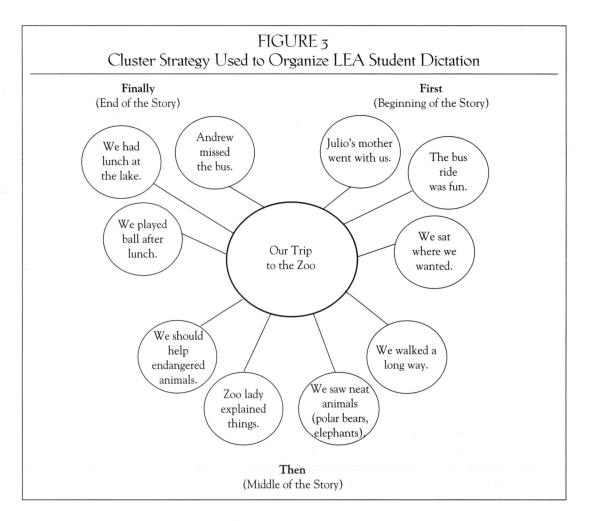

FIGURE 3
Cluster Strategy Used to Organize LEA Student Dictation

Finally
(End of the Story)

First
(Beginning of the Story)

We had lunch at the lake.

Andrew missed the bus.

Julio's mother went with us.

The bus ride was fun.

We played ball after lunch.

Our Trip to the Zoo

We sat where we wanted.

We should help endangered animals.

Zoo lady explained things.

We saw neat animals (polar bears, elephants).

We walked a long way.

Then
(Middle of the Story)

cluding with ideas about how the trip ended. Rick's use of a cluster strategy in this particular LEA lesson provided instructional scaffolding that assisted all his students in constructing a cohesive story that flowed from beginning, to middle, to end.

To give his students the opportunity to collaboratively construct their "zoo stories," Rick grouped his second graders into dyads, pairing lower and higher achieving students. This ensured that all his students had the chance either to contribute sentences to the story based on the prewriting cluster ideas or to contribute additional story ideas. Tuan was able to work with Ryan, a more capable second-grade peer, who provided both modeling and support for him. Although Ryan and Tuan collaborated on ideas for the story, Ryan assumed most of the responsibility for writing the sentences with Tuan sometimes providing spelling information. Rick believes that the cultural or language barriers that could serve to deny Tuan an active voice within a whole-class LEA were circumvented by the more supportive dyad group. Rather than working in isolation, a collaborative LEA provided Tuan with the opportunity to complete a purposeful literacy activity with the support of his more capable classmate, Ryan.

What are the advantages of collaborative LEA activities for diverse learners? Rick found LEA effective for a number of reasons. Because Tuan had created the story with his partner, he was motivated to revisit it throughout the week. Capitalizing on this motivation, Rick used the completed LEA story with Tuan in subsequent lessons that included rereadings and integrated skills instruction in which Tuan and Ryan corrected misspellings, identified "doing words," and added "describing words" to their story. Rick also found LEA to be an invaluable approach because it enabled Tuan to observe and to make purposeful connections between reading, writing, speaking, and listening within a supportive social environment. Although Rick did not feel comfortable using LEA stories as the sole source of text for reading and language skills instruction for Tuan and his classmates, he found the approach effective and used it in conjunction with basals and literature selections as well as with content area expository texts. Rick also discovered that collaborative LEA stories make wonderful additions to classroom libraries because his students were motivated to read them again and again. This makes LEA texts effective resources for readers like Tuan for whom repeated readings are essential (Dowhower, 1987). Although Rick found the amount of time devoted to taking multiple LEA stories to a "publication stage" somewhat daunting, he believes the advantages are worth the time investment. Working collaboratively with a capable peer or with a small group of classmates enabled Tuan to become an active participant in the culture in the classroom.

Jigsaw

We also suggested that Rick investigate the Jigsaw approach as a way to support Tuan as an active member of his classroom learning environment. Jigsaw is a team learning approach designed to assist students in completing learning tasks collaboratively (Slavin, 1986). Each member of the team becomes responsible for assuming a portion of the assignment, and individual "expert" students teach the other members of their team. Because team members become experts in specific areas, Rick was able to customize Tuan's participatory role in order to ensure his academic success. That is, Tuan's responsibility to his group was tailored to meet his individual capabilities as well as his individual academic needs.

HOW CAN TEACHERS USE JIGSAW ACTIVITIES TO ASSIST DIVERSE LEARNERS? Slavin's description of the Jigsaw strategy reflects two distinct phases of the activity—preparation and implementation. (See Figure 4 for Jigsaw procedures.) In the preparatory phase, teachers

---

FIGURE 4
Jigsaw Procedures

Step 1: Home teams are formed with four or five students who reflect a range of academic or reading abilities.

Step 2: A reading selection is assigned to all students.

Step 3: Students from each home team with the same topic or postreading question(s) form an "expert" group. Together, students decide how to complete the task or answer the question(s), as well as the best way to teach their home team peers.

Step 4: Each student expert teaches what he or she has learned to the other home team members.

Step 5: Teachers assess student performance and assign a team grade based on academic or cooperative performance.

form home teams of four or five students that reflect a range of individual academic abilities. In order to help promote a climate of solidarity and collaboration in which all students work together to seek ways to achieve group goals, Rick had each home team group choose a home team name; Tuan's group named itself the "Pokémon" team. Another component of the preparatory phase includes the assignment of a reading selection to all members of the class. Tuan's class read the story *Ira Sleeps Over* by Bernard Waber (1972). Rick assigned parts of the story to be read across 4 days with a specific purpose for reading provided for each assignment. Although some of his students read the story independently, Rick provided support for Tuan by pairing him with a more capable reader from his home team with whom he whisper-read each of the assignments.

During the implementation phase of the Jigsaw activity, each student in the home team is assigned a separate question or problem. On the fifth day, after the entire story had been read, Rick assigned each member of the home team groups one of five questions about the *Ira* story. Rick assigned Tuan a literal-level, right-there-in-the-book question (Raphael, 1986): "Tell the story that scared Ira and Reggie." Tuan met with other classmates who had been assigned the same question. In this manner, Tuan and the other students formed an "expert group" for the ghost story question. The expert group members worked together and decided how to correctly answer the question and how they were going to "teach the answer" to their respective home team peers. Tuan then returned to the Pokémon group as an expert in his question. He taught his home team members the answer to his question and, in return, was taught the answer to additional questions by other experts who had been responsible for different questions.

In order to promote group goals rather than individual goals, Slavin (1986) recommends administering individual quizzes to the members of each home team group. Individual scores may then be averaged into a single home team score, with the highest scoring team receiving some sort of recognition. Rick was uncomfortable assigning grades on the basis of home team quiz averages. Instead, he used collaborative team self-assessments as an alternative assessment procedure. Figure 5 shows the collaborative team self-assessment rubric

---

FIGURE 5
Collaborative Assessment Rubric

How Did Your Team Work Together?

Team Name: _____

Assignment: _____

1. We all read the story.	Yes.	No. Why not? _____
2. Our team took turns sharing ideas.	Yes.	No. Why not? _____
3. We helped each other.	Yes.	No. Why not? _____
4. We each did our job.	Yes.	No. Why not? _____

We did a good job _____

_____.

Next time we'll do a better job _____

_____.

Rick used with his students. Because he is concerned with helping each of his students learn essential teamwork behaviors and strategies, the information gleaned from this collaborative assessment instrument provided Rick with valuable information.

WHAT ARE THE ADVANTAGES OF JIGSAW ACTIVITIES FOR DIVERSE LEARNERS? Holding Tuan responsible for reading the story and answering the five postreading questions in isolation from his peers might have overwhelmed him. Instead, Rick constructed a learning environment in which Tuan gained peer support in both the home team and expert groups. In these lessons Tuan was also able to observe the effective reading and problem-solving strategies of more capable students. Perhaps most importantly, when Tuan was afforded the opportunity to act as an "expert," his contributions to the group became valuable. Although the students had often shown impatience with Tuan's accented English, in this particular lesson Rick constructed a learning environment in which his peers depended on Tuan for information. Tuan's status as an expert ensured not only his peers' attention when he spoke, but also his place as an essential member of the learning community. Because Tuan had seldom experienced academic success, becoming an expert with his classmates was both a novel and exciting experience for him. Observing Tuan make the transformation to being in control of his learning in this lesson was exciting for all of us to see.

Readers Theatre

Readers Theatre is an activity designed to develop oral language skills and oral reading fluency by providing students opportunities to read a scripted selection aloud to a targeted audience (Hill, 1990; Sloyer, 1982). With individual students reading the dialogue of various characters, Readers Theatre represents an ideal instructional vehicle for culturally and linguistically diverse students like Tuan who benefit from the support of rehearsed or repeated group oral reading activities.

HOW CAN TEACHERS USE READERS THEATRE TO BENEFIT DIVERSE LEARNERS? Preparation for a Readers Theatre activity begins by choosing a reading selection from which a script can be developed. (See Figure 6 for Readers Theatre procedures.) We suggest that teachers investigate a number of criteria when selecting a text for Readers Theatre. Certainly, potential for student interest should always be considered. Selections rich in dialogue as well as stories that reveal characters' inner thoughts and emotions are also important text characteristics of appropriate sources for Readers Theatre scripts. Novel

---

FIGURE 6
Readers Theatre Procedures

Step 1: The teacher first selects an appropriate source for script development (*Ira Sleeps Over*).

Step 2: A script is adapted from the selection by the teacher, or collaboratively by students, and parts are developed for a narrator and multiple characters.

Step 3: Rehearsals are scheduled to address issues of fluency and interpretation as well as other presentation strategies such as the use of props or simple costumes.

Step 4: The script is presented to a selected audience in a Readers Theatre format.

excerpts, short stories, poems, and even picture books that can be translated into verbal interpretations are all excellent sources. As a way of integrating reading, writing, and oral language development across the curriculum, intermediate and middle-grade teachers with diverse student populations might also consider developing scripts that recreate historical events such as the establishment of the Underground Railroad or the Wright brothers' first flight at Kitty Hawk, North Carolina. Even historical paintings can be used as sources for Readers Theatre scripts (Wood, Finke, & Douville, 1999).

Rick selected the *Ira Sleeps Over* (Waber, 1972) story because it met all the criteria above, and the students were already familiar with it. He explained to his students that they would be "acting out" the story for the kindergarten classes in their school because they had done such a good job reading it, and the "little kids" would enjoy hearing and seeing this story "come to life."

Once the source is selected, written scripts are adapted from the text. Although teachers may decide to begin Readers Theatre in their classrooms with scripts that initially are provided *for* the students, we believe the best scripts are those written collaboratively *by* students (Douville & Finke, 2000). Rick decided he would create the script for his students because this would be his first Readers Theatre lesson and he felt his second graders were not yet independent enough to collaboratively adapt a script from text. Creating parts for five characters and a narrator, Rick simply pulled characters' dialogue directly from the selection. He also converted narrative portions of the selection to create additional character dialogue. Story information that was *not* revealed to the audience through the various characters' voices—such as prologues, epilogues, and descriptions of setting—was also provided through the narrator's role.

Although Reutzel and Cooter (2000) suggest that teachers allow students to list their top three character preferences as a means of making character assignments based on student interests, Rick preferred to make assignment decisions based on his students' instructional needs and abilities. Because the role of the Father was an important one, yet not as lengthy as some of the others, Rick believed it was the best one for Tuan. During rehearsals, Tuan's team collaboratively decided how to use their voices and gestures most effectively. The team also collaborated on how to use simple props and bits of costume for the final audience presentation. One of Tuan's team members, Ryan, made him a father-like paper mustache that the boys unfortunately decided would best stay in place with white glue.

WHAT ARE THE ADVANTAGES OF READERS THEATRE FOR DIVERSE LEARNERS? Although the collaborative level of decision making for his students was limited to presentation strategies, Rick found Readers Theatre to be a truly effective and purposeful way for Tuan to improve his speaking and reading of English. Tuan's place in the group was also strengthened as he exchanged ideas with other members of his team. Rick also believes that Tuan's sight reading vocabulary was extended through his repeated exposures to the *Ira* story. Additionally, Rick had the opportunity to address oral language skills of pitch, stress, and fluency that he often neglected, although he realizes these represent an essential instructional focus when working with culturally and linguistically diverse students. Although Rick found the task of developing the script for his students somewhat time consuming, he believes it was time that was well spent. He hopes that as the students gain experience, he will be able to release more responsibility to them for collaborating on script development in future Readers Theatre activities. Tuan's positive experience with Readers Theatre has encouraged Rick to develop similar activities that bring stories to life for both the actors and the audience in ways that invite all his students to collaboratively step into the world of the text (Langer, 1990).

Academic Diversity: Lily's Story

Eleven-year-old Lily is well liked by her classmates and is always one of the first to be included in peer social activities, such as recess games and after-school play. Her parents are both professionals and Lily and her siblings have been exposed to travel and varied experiences. Lily's parents report that they have consistently modeled a love of leisure reading and have always provided their children with a variety of at-home reading materials such as books and children's magazines. In spite of what appears to be a home environment designed to nurture literacy development, Lily avoids reading whenever possible. Diagnosed this year with attention-deficit hyperactivity disorder (ADHD), Lily's academic performance is inconsistent. Her teacher, Doris Spears, reports that at times Lily appears to have mastered and understood skills and concepts reflected in daily homework and in-class assignments when questioned orally, only to "fall apart" when formally assessed in testing situations. In spite of her parents' providing after-school tutoring, Doris says that Lily's academic performance continues to deteriorate and her learned avoidance of reading increases yearly.

Lily's profile is a familiar one to many teachers. Seemingly she has the environmental advantages and home support that facilitate academic success. Nevertheless, Doris finds that Lily exhibits a learned helplessness and avoidance of learning tasks, particularly those associated with reading, that relegate her to an academic at-risk status. Although the traditional instructional approaches Doris usually employs serve the needs of her more capable students, these methods only continue to alienate Lily further from the learning process. We encouraged Doris to investigate activities and strategies designed to provide a motivating and stimulating purpose for learning in order to facilitate Lily's becoming an active member of her classroom learning environment.

Collaborative Activities Designed to Motivate and Support Learning Disabled Students

Lily's learned helplessness and avoidance of academic tasks are behaviors that many students with learning disabilities exhibit (Good & Brophy, 1991). Unfortunately, many of these students' needs have been addressed in the past with a reduced academic task load. That is, instead of being held responsible for spelling 20 words correctly on the weekly spelling test, students identified as having learning disabilities have been held responsible for only 10 words.

Instead of simply tasking students with learning disabilities with fewer academic responsibilities, these students must be taught how to use a variety of effective learning tools. As workers in any endeavor use particular tools to complete jobs or projects, students, especially those diagnosed with learning disabilities, also must have a repertoire of learning tools at their disposal. Rather than communicating lower expectations for students with learning disabilities, teachers must focus on giving them more effective strategies that will enable them to succeed in the same academic tasks their peers are expected to perform.

Just as research has demonstrated the benefits of incorporating collaborative learning activities into the instructional context for students who reflect cultural and linguistic diversity, research also supports the positive effects of collaborative activities for students diagnosed with learning disabilities (Pressley, Brown, El-Dinary, & Afflerbach, 1995). Collaboration provides academically diverse students not only with the opportunity to act as both teacher and student, but also with the invaluable opportunity to observe the academic tools and strategies used by their more capable counterparts. Another advantage of incorporating collaborative activities into classroom instruction is found in the motivational aspect of providing students the chance to work together within the type of social context they most enjoy. For these reasons, we assisted Doris in implementing Collaborative Strategic Reading and Think-Pair-Share Response Discussion because we find these to be effective approaches that can benefit academically diverse students like Lily. Each of these activities provides students the opportunity to work and learn with peers, as well as a purpose for learning. Establishing a specific purpose for learning is essential if Doris is to be successful in engaging Lily academically and reversing her developing patterns of avoidance and learned helplessness.

> *Rather than communicating lower expectations for students with learning disabilities, teachers must focus on giving them more effective strategies that will enable them to succeed in the same academic tasks their peers are expected to perform.*

Collaborative Strategic Reading

Developed by Klingner and Vaughn (1999), Collaborative Strategic Reading (CSR) combines collaborative learning with four reading comprehension strategies: "preview" before reading to facilitate the activation of prior knowledge and predictions, "click and clunk" to self-monitor comprehension during reading, "get the gist" to focus on main ideas, and "wrap-up" after reading to summarize important ideas and predict possible future test questions. By applying well-established reading strategies within a framework of social interactions, we believe CSR provides students like Lily with reading and problem-solving tools within a motivational environment of peer support.

HOW CAN TEACHERS USE CSR TO BENEFIT ACADEMICALLY DIVERSE LEARNERS? CSR begins with teachers' providing students with a clear rationale of how the activity will help them become better and more efficient readers. This explanation is followed by teacher modeling of each of the four reading strategies using a think-aloud procedure. (CSR procedures are listed in Figure 7.)

Students are taught to use the "preview" strategy by scanning the targeted reading selection, focusing on headings and subheadings as well as illustrations and graphics, in order to activate and build background knowledge. What, who, when, and where questions are also constructed to serve as an established purpose for reading.

"Click and clunk" gives students a specific tool for self-monitoring comprehension during reading. When meaning and ideas are smoothly constructed during reading, students are said to be clicking through the text. When students "clunk" on an unknown or difficult word, however, they are instructed to use context clues, prefixes and suffixes, or structural analysis (breaking the unknown word apart to look for smaller embedded words) as strategic tools. Klingner and Vaughn (1999) suggest that teachers write the procedures for using context clues, prefixes and suffixes, and structural analysis on "clunk cards" as

---

FIGURE 7
Collaborative Strategic Reading (CSR) Procedures

Step 1: The teacher models the preview, click and clunk, get the gist, and wrap-up strategies using a think-aloud procedure.
Step 2: Students form collaborative groups to apply the four strategies with a targeted reading assignment.
Step 3: Reading and learning is supported within the group with students assuming the roles of leader, starter expert, clunk expert, gist expert, or rubric expert.

a means of cueing students about how to surmount comprehension blocking "clunks" in order to resume "clicking" through the text.

The "get the gist" strategy gives students the opportunity not only to identify the most important story or text ideas, but also the opportunity to articulate ideas in their own words. A student's ability to explain concepts in his or her own words is indicative of conceptual understanding. Prereading questions supplied by the teacher provide instructional scaffolding that helps students "get the gist" of a story. Other instructional strategies such as story frames or story maps also provide students with a specific structure for getting the gist of a story or passage.

Finally in "wrap-up" students think about possible high level thinking questions that a teacher might ask on a test. Klingner and Vaughn (1999) advocate that students write the questions on one side of an index card and store corresponding answers on the other side of the card.

On the first day of CSR instruction, Doris divided her students into five heterogeneous collaborative groups. She explained that each member of the group had a specific job, but that everyone in the group would understand all the jobs because they were all important. Doris then provided the students with a rationale for CSR and followed with teacher modeling of the preview strategy with a social studies text selection on "Westward Expansion in the U.S." Doris demonstrated for her students how she first focused on the headings and subheadings and how she was able to turn this information into questions that could be used to focus her reading. She then released partial responsibility to the groups to help her find other information to preview. Finally she released all responsibility to the groups to find independently one additional piece of previewing information that would provide another important purpose for reading. Lily received modeling and support for the previewing strategy, first from Doris, then from her group members as her team collaborated to use the previewing strategy independently.

On the second day of instruction, Doris reviewed the previewing strategy with the grouped students and followed the same instructional procedure she had on the first day to instruct her students in the "click and clunk" strategy. Days three and four mirrored the same approach with the "get the gist" and "wrap-up" strategies, so by the fourth day the students had received instruction in all four strategies.

On the fifth day of instruction, Doris explained that each group member would be assigned a special job or role designed to help everyone in the group do a good job with the four strategies. Klingner and Vaughn describe five different group roles designed to facilitate student collaboration. Individual students may serve as a leader who guides the reading and ensures the strategies are applied; as a "clunk expert" who provides guidance in following the clunk strategy; as a "gist expert" who determines that the most important ideas in the reading selection have been targeted; as an announcer who ensures that all group members share participation equally; or as an encourager who assesses group behavior and provides praise. We suggested that Doris adapt the roles by merging the announcer role with that of the encourager. Although Klingner and Vaughn do not specifically advocate the use of a collaborative rubric for the announcer or encourager, we worked with Doris to develop an assessment instrument to provide specificity and guidance for what we came to call the "rubric expert." Collaborating with the other members of the group, the rubric expert was responsible for completing a group-assessment rubric at the conclusion of each CSR lesson. An additional role for a "starter," who would be responsible for guiding the preview strategy, was also developed.

Doris found that Lily not only used the previewing strategy successfully, but she also liked to review key text ideas with her peers using the "wrap-up" cards. However, Lily continued to display reading avoidance behaviors by skipping over text passages she found difficult rather than using the "click and clunk" strategy. Therefore, Doris decided to pair Lily with her group's clunk expert during reading in order to provide her with more viable comprehension monitoring and repair support.

Because Lily did not yet appear ready to act as an expert in any of the four strategies, Doris decided to appoint her as the group's rubric expert. This collaborative role provided Lily with the opportunity to observe all her group members as models in their expert roles as she assessed the group's strategy application and as she provided praise for well-accomplished tasks. Acting as the rubric expert also allowed Lily to use her strong social skills to academic benefit. Because she was well liked by her peers, Lily's group members were already predisposed to work with her in completing the collaborative rubric. Additionally, the rubric expert role served as a constant reminder to Lily of the importance of completing academic tasks.

WHAT ARE THE ADVANTAGES OF CSR FOR ACADEMICALLY DIVERSE LEARNERS? CSR provides all students with instruction in effective reading strategies. As students complete each step of the CSR activity, reading is reflected as an active, meaning-making experience. Doris found this approach effective because she was able to address both reading process and product in an instructional framework of meaningful integration. Her students reported that they enjoyed CSR because they were able to read and solve problems together.

Although the four reading strategies are labeled in a student-friendly fashion such as "clicking and clunking" or "wrap-up," these particular strategies do not represent new approaches to reading instruction. What makes CSR especially effective is the collaborative framework in which students apply the strategies to reading and learning. Working in a collaborative group, Lily was held responsible for completing an assignment using the four reading strategies in addition to performing her specific role for the group. By using the CSR approach, Doris created a learning environment in which Lily was unable to avoid reading as she often did with more traditional approaches in which she worked in isolation from her peers. Additionally, because she was held responsible for her participatory role in the group, Lily was unable to assume an attitude of academic helplessness. Each step of the CSR activity provided Lily with a specific purpose for reading and learning. Working within a small group, Lily was also able to observe other students using reading and study tools effectively. Although Lily has not yet mastered all the CSR strategies in a way that has facilitated reading independence, Doris has observed that Lily assumes more responsibility for reading and, most importantly, less avoidance of reading. Doris continues to use the CSR approach and eventually plans to rotate roles among the students in each group in order to provide Lily with the experiences of being a leader or expert in each of the roles.

Think-Pair-Share Response Discussion

The Think-Pair-Share Response Discussion is an approach based on McTighe and Lyman's (1988) Think-Pair-Share strategy. By collaboratively discussing text ideas with others, students are encouraged to develop an open attitude to listening that allows for multiple points of view. When the strategy is presented to students prior to reading, Think-Pair-Share Response Discussions constitute a purpose for reading and ensure continued engagement during reading. Collaborative postreading discussions of what was learned create important opportunities for students to share ideas within a supportive social context.

HOW CAN TEACHERS USE THINK-PAIR-SHARE RESPONSE DISCUSSIONS TO ASSIST ACADEMICALLY DIVERSE STUDENTS? Doris implemented Think-Pair-Share Response Discussions by first activating her students' prior knowledge of a literature selection they had been reading but had not yet completed, Mildred Taylor's *The Gold Cadillac* (1987). (See Figure 8 for Think-Pair-Share procedures.) She constructed a web that focused on the central question, "Do you agree with the mother or father character about the Cadillac at the end of the story? Why?"

Using the central question as a purpose for reading, Doris divided her students into pairs to read the story. Lily and her partner read the last part of the story together and then collaborated on a response to the central question. After all the students had read the last part of the story and answered the central question, Doris opened the dis-

---

FIGURE 8
Think-Pair-Share Response Discussion Procedures

Step 1: The teacher leads a whole-class discussion of text concepts to activate prior knowledge.

Step 2: A central question(s) is presented to the students that provides a purpose for reading.

Step 3: Pairs of students reflect on the question(s) as they read. Students may provide support for one another during reading as they collaborate to answer the central question.

Step 4: After reading, the pairs collaboratively discuss the question, with each student responsible for contributing at least one idea to the completed web or guide.

Step 5: After working in pairs, individual students are encouraged to elaborate on the guide with additional sentences or illustrations.

cussion to the whole class with selected pairs sharing their answers to the question. She provided important instructional support for her students through her use of the central question/web activity. This strategy facilitated the organization of individual students' ideas as they emerged from the whole-class discussion. Additional support was provided by the students themselves as they read and responded to the central question together.

Although Lily usually avoided most reading activities, Doris reported that content area and expository text reading assignments generally were more problematic for Lily than literature reading assignments. The specialized vocabulary and different text structures reflected in content area reading appeared to create obstacles to learning that Lily felt powerless to circumvent. Therefore, Doris was especially interested in investigating strategies that would provide Lily with content area reading support. We explained that most reading strategies could be adapted for use with either literature or content area text, and most could be used to support effective viewing of visually presented information.

Doris put these ideas to good use with a lesson she developed that included a video presentation on electricity, a science topic the students had been studying. With only minor adjustments, Doris used the Think-Pair-Share Response Discussion strategy as an approach to facilitate effective video viewing for Lily and her classmates. After dividing the students into pairs as she had with the *Gold Cadillac* lesson, Doris asked the students to share one idea with their partner about what they already knew about electricity. Figure 9 shows Lily's response, "Electricity can burn you and kill you." Lily's partner, Kunal, already knew, "Electricity deals with complex stuff like electromagnetic fields. Things like lights, video cameras, game boys [sic], and other things are powered by electricity." Hearing Kunal's ideas about electricity in this way served to elaborate the prior knowledge Lily took to the subsequent viewing of the video. Additionally, Kunal was able to validate Lily's idea.

After selected student pairs shared ideas with the whole class, Doris helped students brainstorm questions reflecting what they still wanted to learn about electricity. This brainstorm session helped to form the students' central question or purpose for viewing. After

FIGURE 9
Think-Pair-Share Responses Discussion Guide Used
With Video Text on Electricity

Video Viewing Guide

Name *Lily*

Name *Kunal*

The title of the video is *Elementary Electricity*

We already know that *Electricity can burn you and kill you. Electricity deals with complex stuff like electro magnetic fields. Things like lights, video games, game boys and other things are powered by electricity.*

We are watching to find out

How electricity was invented.

After watching the video we learned *Thomas Edison and other inventors made the first light bulb.*
Electricity has to have magnitiseam, current, and electrons. There is space craft going beyond our solar system.

watching the video, each student pair discussed what they had learned from the video. Kunal wrote, "Thomas Edison and other inventors made the first light bulb." Because Kunal's response reflected the pair's purpose for viewing, Lily wrote that she learned, "Electricity has to have magnetism, current and electrons. There is space craft going beyond our solar system."

WHAT ARE THE ADVANTAGES OF THINK-PAIR-SHARE RESPONSE DISCUSSIONS FOR ACADEMICALLY DIVERSE LEARNERS? Doris reported that pairing Lily with a more capable counterpart benefited Lily because she was able to observe how Kunal made connections between existing knowledge and new ideas. Lily also saw how Kunal followed through with an established purpose for reading or viewing. Although Think-Pair-Share Response Discussions help students learn the importance of accepting alternative points of view with literature selections, Doris found that students' alternative points of view were not always appropriate when forming responses to concepts reflected in content area topics. Nevertheless, Doris liked the strategy because it enabled Lily and the other disadvantaged learners in her class to benefit from the modeling more capable students provided. Also, it enabled her to evaluate and monitor each student's level of understanding. Doris also liked the flexibility that enabled her to use Think-Pair-Share Response Discussions with reading, listening, or viewing activities.

Conclusions

Facing the daily challenge of meeting the myriad academic needs reflected by the diverse student population in classrooms today can be daunting for even the most experienced teacher. Although traditional instruction that relegated students to isolated learning and problem solving was *de rigueur* in the past, 21st century social and educational needs dictate that teachers investigate instructional approaches that not only meet the diverse instructional needs of students but also utilize the vast network of support that students represent for one another. Collaborative activities provide students with a language-rich environment in which they teach one another and learn from one another within a social context that shapes

Although traditional instruction that relegated students to isolated learning and problem solving was de rigueur in the past, 21st century social and educational needs dictate that teachers investigate instructional approaches that not only meet the diverse instructional needs of students but also utilize the vast network of support that students represent for one another.

engagement. Even though the collaborative activities presented in this chapter were categorized by cultural/linguistic diversity and academic diversity, we believe that the very act of collaboration serves all at-risk learners through the development of self-assurance that comes from being part of a group.

The efficacy of incorporating collaborative instruction into the learning environment of classrooms has been observed. Why, then, do many teachers continue to ignore the value of collaboration in favor of approaches that fail to demonstrate the same degree of effectiveness? Long-established professional tendencies evolve into habits that entrench some educators in outmoded and ineffective instruction. For other teachers collaboration constitutes a threat to classroom control they believe is found in rows of desks occupied by isolated students completing worksheets and answering textbook questions.

Although both Rick and Doris found that Tuan and Lily, as well as their other students, benefited from collaborative reading and problem solving, these teachers experienced challenges in implementing new instructional approaches. First, Rick and Doris found that preparing the students to use different strategies was time consuming. Not only did they have to instruct their students in how to use strategies like Jigsaw and Collaborative Strategic Reading in ways that could help them become effective learners, but they also had to teach their students how to collaborate. This problem was addressed through the use of rubrics, which Rick and Doris found to be extremely valuable as concrete reminders of appropriate and expected group behaviors. These teachers also continue to struggle with balancing instructional support with academic independence. That is, Rick and Doris know it is essential to provide peer modeling and support for their diverse learners, but they worry that the students will use instructional support as a crutch rather than as a springboard to academic independence.

Rick and Doris have only begun to investigate collaborative approaches. In time, with consistent yet flexible use, we believe these teachers will observe Tuan and Lily learning within social contexts in ways that will result in academic achievement and independence.

References

Cazden, C.B. (1988). *Classroom discourse: The language of teaching and learning.* Portsmouth, NH: Heinemann.

Cox, C., & Boyd-Batstone, P. (1997). *Crossroads: Literature in culturally and linguistically diverse classrooms.* Upper Saddle River, NJ: Merrill.

Cullinan, B.E. (Ed.). (1993). *Children's voices: Talk in the classroom.* Newark, DE: International Reading Association.

Davidson, N. (1994). Cooperative and collaborative learning: An integrated perspective. In J. Thousand, R. Villa, & A. Nevin (Eds.), *Creativity and collaborative learning: A practical guide to empowering students and teachers* (pp. 13–30). Baltimore: Paul H. Brookes.

Douville, P., & Finke, J. (2000). Literacy as performance: The power of creative drama in the classroom. In K.D. Wood & T.S. Dickerson (Eds.), *Promoting literacy in the twenty-first century: A handbook for teachers and administrators in grades K–8.* Boston, MA: Allyn & Bacon.

Dowhower, S.L. (1987). Effects of repeated readings on second-grade transitional readers' fluency and comprehension. *Reading Research Quarterly, 22,* 389–406.

Echevarria, J., & Graves, A. (1998). *Sheltered content instruction: Teaching English-language learners with diverse abilities.* Boston: Allyn & Bacon.

Franklin, E., & Thompson, J. (1994). Describing students' collected works: Understanding American Indian children. *TESOL Quarterly, 28,* 489–506.

Fuchs, D., Fuchs, L.S., Mathes, P.G., & Simmons, D.C. (1997). Peer-assisted learning strategies: Making classrooms more responsive to diversity. *American Educational Research Journal, 32*(1), 174–206.

Good, T.L., & Brophy, J.E. (1991). *Looking in classrooms* (5th ed.). New York: HarperCollins.

Heath, S.B., & Mangiola, L. (1991). *Children of promise: Literate activity in linguistically and culturally diverse classrooms.* Washington, DC: National Education Association.

Hill, S. (1990). *Readers' Theatre: Performing the text.* Armadale, Victoria, Australia: Eleanor Curtain.

Johnson, D.W., & Johnson, R.T. (1991). *Learning together and alone* (3rd ed.). Boston: Allyn & Bacon.

Kagan, S. (1994). *Cooperative learning.* San Juan, CA: Kagan Cooperative Learning.

Kasten, W.C. (1997). Learning is noisy: The myth of silence in the reading-writing classroom. In J.R. Paratore & R.L. McCormack (Eds.), *Peer talk in the classroom: Learning from research.* Newark, DE: International Reading Association.

King, A. (1990). Enhancing peer interaction and learning in the classroom through reciprocal questioning. *American Educational Research Journal, 27*, 664–687.

Klingner, J.K., & Vaughn, S. (1999). Promoting reading comprehension, content learning, and English acquisition through Collaborative Strategic Reading (CSR). *The Reading Teacher, 52*(7), 738–747.

Langer, J.A. (1990). The purpose of understanding: Reading for informative purposes. *Research in the Teaching of English, 24*(3), 229–260.

Lewis, C. (1998). Literacy interpretation as a social act. *Journal of Adolescent & Adult Literacy, 42*(3), 168–177.

Maheady, L., Mallette, B., Harper, G.F., Sacca, K.C., & Pomerantz, D. (1994). Peer-mediated instruction for high-risk students. In K.D. Wood & B. Algozzine (Eds.), *Teaching reading to high-risk learners: A unified perspective* (pp. 269–290). Boston: Allyn & Bacon.

McTighe, J., & Lyman, F.T. (1988). Cueing thinking in the classroom: The promise of theory-embedded tools. *Educational Leadership, 45*(7), 18–24.

Paratore, J.R., & McCormack, R.L.(Eds.). (1997). *Peer talk in the classroom: Learning from research.* Newark, DE: International Reading Association.

Pressley, M., Brown, R., El-Dinary, P.B., & Afflerbach, P. (1995). The comprehension instruction that students need: Instruction fostering constructively responsive reading. *Learning Disabilities Research and Practice, 10*, 215–224.

Raphael, T.E. (1986). Teaching question answer relationships, revisited. *The Reading Teacher, 39*(6), 516–523.

Reutzel, D.R., & Cooter, R.B. (2000). *Teaching children to read: Putting the pieces together.* Upper Saddle River, NJ: Merrill.

Rosenblatt, L.M. (1976). *Literature as exploration.* New York: Modern Language Association of America. (Original work published 1938)

Slavin, R.E. (1986). *Using student team learning* (3rd ed.). Baltimore: Johns Hopkins University, Center for Research on Elementary and Middle Schools.

Slavin, R.E. (1995). *Cooperative learning* (2nd ed.). Boston: Allyn & Bacon.

Sloyer, S. (1982). *Readers Theatre: Story dramatization in the classroom.* Urbana, IL: National Council of Teachers of English.

Stauffer, R.G. (1970). *The language experience approach to the teaching of reading.* New York: Harper & Row.

Taylor, M. (1987). *The gold cadillac.* New York: Bantam Skylark.

Teasley, S.D. (1995). The role of talk in children's collaborations. *Developmental Psychology, 31*(2), 207–220.

Tompkins, G.E. (1998). *Language arts: Content and teaching strategies.* Upper Saddle River, NJ: Merrill.

Vygotsky, L.S. (1978). *Mind in society: The development of higher psychological processes* (M. Cole, V. John-Steiner, S. Scribner, & E. Sauberman, Eds. and Trans.). Cambridge, MA: Harvard University Press. (Original work published 1934)

Wathen, S.H., & Resnick, L.B. (1997, March). *Collaborative vs. individual learning and the role of explanations.* Paper presented at the annual meeting of the American Educational Research Association, Chicago, IL.

Webb, N.M. (1982). Peer interaction and learning in cooperative small groups. *Journal of Educational Psychology, 74*(5), 642–655.

Waber, B. (1972). *Ira sleeps over.* Boston: Houghton Mifflin.

Wood, K.D., McCormack, R.L., Lapp, D., & Flood, J. (1997). Improving young adolescent learning through collaborative learning. *Middle School Journal, 28*(3), 26–34.

Wood, K.D., Finke, J., & Douville, P. (1999). Literacy as self-expression: Interpreting the subject areas through the arts. *Middle School Journal, 30*(4), 68–72.

EXPANDING COLLABORATIVE ROLES OF READING SPECIALISTS
Developing an Intermediate Reading Support Program

Donna Ogle and Ellen Fogelberg

> Our best prepared and most competent reading teachers need to spread their expertise more broadly in our schools.
>
> —District Reading Coordinator

Moving from a pull-out model of remedial reading instruction to an in-class, collaborative team model requires an enormous transition of roles and responsibilities. This chapter summarizes what we learned about how to make that transition. We, a university professor and a district reading coordinator, worked together in two contexts. The first was at the local district level where we built an in-class reading support model for intermediate-grade students (1994–1995). The second was with a group of reading specialists who met monthly as part of an area-wide group of literacy leaders called the Reading Leadership Institute (RLI). The topic for the year 1995–1996 was providing more inclusive instruction. Because we were aware of difficulties reading specialists encounter in their shift in roles, we decided to do some research on these experiences both in the district and in the broader metropolitan area. To learn from the experiences of those just shifting roles in the district as well as from the experience of others who had made similar transitions in roles, we developed a survey instrument and administered it to the whole group of RLI members. We followed this with seven in-depth interviews. The conclusions we have drawn from the surveys and interviews are presented here.

Background

Current efforts in education highlight the need for closer instructional collaboration among school professionals. First, research on pull-out programs that utilize either reading specialists or aides has not shown strong positive effects on student learning (Allington, 1983; Allington & McGill-Franzen, 1989; McGill-Franzen & Allington, 1991). The generally negative data from large-scale studies of Chapter 1 programs has led to less emphasis on taking children out of the classroom for added instruction, especially when that instruction often has not been connected with the classroom program and when time is wasted in transitions.

Given the lack of positive effects shown from pull-out programs for both reading and special education, there has been a significant movement to inclusion of special needs students within the regular education classroom. This direction within special education has certainly led many districts to consider also shifting reading support to the classroom (Allington & Walmsley, 1995).

Second, attention to student learning as represented by standards and high-stakes assessments has intensified attention to outcomes and classroom learning. The focus on measurable results has increased school-to-school comparisons and intensified efforts to improve achievement. Teachers and schools are being evaluated by how students perform on these publicly reported assessments. As part of this shift in interest to student performance outcomes, the standards movement has led to the creation of a much more demanding curriculum with specific outcomes clearly delineated. These two movements, performance accountability and specific standards, make the need for collaboration among school-based professionals clear. If all students, despite the diversity they represent as learners, are going to be able to meet the expectations enumerated in standards documents then differentiation of instruction is required and the involvement of all teachers is essential.

> *If all students, despite the diversity they represent as learners, are going to be able to meet the expectations enumerated in standards documents then differentiation of instruction is required and the involvement of all teachers is essential.*

Survey of Reading Specialists

Making the change from pull-out to in-class instruction was not easy for the reading specialists. Many issues surfaced. The year after we initiated the in-class reading program we were able to take our concerns to the larger RLI. While working with the reading specialists from our focus district who had shifted their role, it became clear to us that the design of the in-class model was critical to its success. However, we needed a clearer plan for how specialists would work in the buildings with the classroom teachers and a stronger statement of the support systems they needed in order to be effective. Therefore, we used the RLI group to help us crystallize our thinking. Because we knew other districts were engaged in similar shifts to in-class instruction, we decided to survey people serving in that role and to conduct personal interviews with some. Our purpose was to find out how the specialists were working with classroom teachers providing in-class instruction and support. Specifically, we wanted to know how the reading specialists who took part in our survey negotiated the sharing of classroom activities and what kinds of instructional support they provided.

The districts represented in this survey and interview process represent a range within a large metropolitan area. Most are what would be termed "first tier" suburbs; however, the other suburban districts were also experiencing changing populations.

Written interview forms were distributed to all the participants in the RLI network (20 responded), and we also interviewed seven specialists in person. We selected representatives from four of the school districts and three from our target district. We began the survey asking for examples of successful collaboration. (See Figure 1.) From there we probed to find out what made the collaboration successful—how specialists worked with teachers, how often they met and planned together, and what kind of activities the specialists engaged in while in classrooms.

We used this written survey as the basis of the oral interviews, too. The additional questions flowed from the conversations. We asked about planning time and communication, what supplemental reading programs were ongoing and how they dealt with them, the variety of ways they worked with teachers, the ways they understood the in-class model, and what they thought was important in working

---

FIGURE 1
Collaboration Among Teachers Survey

We are asking for your help. Part of the new effort to provide more flexible settings in which at-risk readers receive added instrumental support means that specialists, classroom teachers, and aides have to work together more closely than before. We are trying to find out how you are learning to work together as part of an IRA Commission on Diverse Learners project. What solutions to the problem inherent in such collaboration are evolving? What are the major problems that you have confronted? We would appreciate your responding to the questions below or any elaborated reflection you would provide. Thank you in advance for your insight and support of this effort.

1. Describe one example of how you and a classroom teacher have successfully worked out a collaboration for particular students. What is making it work for you? How do you and the teacher plan, instruct, and evaluate? How often do you work together with children?

2. How did you develop this working relationship? Did you have support from other school models? Did the special education inclusion effort have any impact?

3. What does the term *collaboration* mean to you?

4. How and when do you find time for talking, planning, and problem solving?

5. Have school team meetings been restructured since you began collaboration? If so, how?

6. Are there opportunities for teachers who are working together to reflect on/evaluate their efforts on an ongoing basis? How? What suggestions would you make to improve or change this?

7. Have other teachers or schools tried to replicate what you have already done? (Explain if yes.)

8. What is your role as a specialist in increasing understanding of the in-class model of support for students? What would you like to be able to do?

9. How have you changed in your own role perception? Does working with other adults shift your priorities?

10. How would you describe the various ways you work in classrooms with teachers? Is there a great deal of diversity depending on teachers, grades, and situations?

11. What else do you think is important to know about the potential and the pitfalls of working collaboratively with classroom teachers?

Thank you for your assistance with this survey.

in this kind of setting. Not only was the information enlightening, but there were clear patterns in responses across the four districts and the seven participants.

We have learned a great deal from both the in-district work and from the surveys and interviews with the RLI members. After careful analysis of the data, we consolidated our findings in the form of 10 essential conditions that promote effective collaborations. The remainder of this chapter elaborates on each of these conditions and provides specific examples and quotations from the surveys and interviews where appropriate.

Essential Conditions

Administrative Leadership

Support for the changing roles of reading specialists needs to come from all administrative levels—from the building principal to the curriculum coordinator to the superintendent—and must be articulated to staff and parents. School leaders must help build a climate of collaboration and trust to establish a team approach to meeting the reading needs of the range of students in a classroom. This is most basic; if the school is not a learning community where issues are addressed openly and everyone's input is valued, any change will be difficult. The principal and central office administrators communicate their values and respect in multiple ways.

One of the most obvious ways in which principals help support collaboration is in the careful assignment of students to classrooms. Classrooms must reflect the range of students in the school, yet with inclusion and in-class support for reading, some special considerations are required because specialists do not have time to work in all classrooms.

For example, some specialists reported that a cluster model facilitated their work within classrooms. Administrators changed the typical spread of at-risk students so that different teachers had groups of similar students with whom specialists could work. No one teacher was faced with the usual wide variety of needs. Thus, the ESL cluster was in one room while students needing support in reading were clustered in another room. This arrangement made it possible for specialists to reach children in need at each grade level without going into every classroom at every grade level. Building principals also worked side by side with the specialists in determining which teachers they worked with; some teachers are much more open to collaboration than others. When the in-class reading program began, the principal in one of the schools conferenced with the reading specialist to determine which teachers should be involved in the project the first year. Together they discussed with whom the specialist already had a good, open relationship and who seemed most likely to be flexible and interested in this new model.

Style of teaching became an important variable. If the teacher did mostly whole-group teaching then there would be little opportunity for the two teachers to function together. Learning new ways of organizing students at the same time as learning to work with another adult seemed too much to take on all at once. The principal realized that to implement the intermediate program throughout the school, he would need to provide staff development to help all teachers move to small-group activity for at least a portion of each content class. At other schools this factor also stood out as an essential first step. Until administrators helped change the grouping conditions, little valuable instruction was provided by the specialist.

Central office administrators are also critical in other ways. They set the context in which change is possible. They provide the time and money for change to occur. They also fund the needed positions, important materials, and other resources. One example of this, cited in the interviews, was when Ellen brought in outside consultant support for the reading specialists. Over the course of a full year the specialists met with Donna to design the in-class program. The specialists reported that they felt the district supported their new efforts and that they had been treated professionally in structuring these shared learning opportunities.

Predictable Schedules and Routines

Collaboration in our model requires that the specialist come into a classroom where students have flexibility to work in small groups and where a consistent schedule is followed. For two teachers to be in the room at the same time, scheduling and grouping arrangements are essential. The surveyed specialists reported how important it was for teachers to have a regular schedule so that when the specialists entered the room, the class was prepared—they would not be in the midst of an art project, away in the library, or listening to a videotape. Routines must be established that allow the reading teacher to work in the classroom when small-group instruction is occurring. Specialists reported that targeted students should be able to move into their small groups at the same time as all students are working in small groups. Without such structure, the classroom teacher would be unable to plan a schedule that did not interrupt whole-group direct instruction or read-aloud time or any other content instruction. Students also needed the structure of these routines to know what was expected of them on a daily basis.

We found a variety of ways in which accommodations were made. Some teachers who used literature had established predictable schedules so specialists could work easily in their classrooms. Others who used a published reading program also established regular routines so it was easy to arrange time for two or more teachers to be working side by side in a room.

One of our specialists reported that she worked very well with a fourth-grade teacher who scheduled units from her reading program on a 2-week cycle. The day before a new unit began the specialist met with the struggling readers and provided preparation for them. She "jump-started" their thinking about the theme or topic and prepared them for what was coming. Sometimes she did this by engaging them in brainstorming on the topic and writing key words they would need to know on take-home word cards. Then the specialist had students write the words in meaningful sentences and illustrate them. At other times she helped build background knowledge by showing a video, reading a book, or engaging students in reading from easier materials on the same topic. Because of the regular schedule of 2-week units and with the use of the published materials (so she could preview the units) the specialist could provide this preliminary support that helped students participate more fully in the class instructional activities. Then, during the unit the specialist and teacher both worked with small groups without calling attention to any particular children. If some children needed more support, either teacher could assist them.

Flexible Grouping

Flexible grouping within a reading program allows for whole-group, small-group, and individual instructional times. In addition, flexible grouping allows students to be grouped by instructional needs, interests, and choices. Thus, students are not placed in the same groups all the time. Teachers employ flexible grouping strategies to avoid tracking students and to allow students to move to different groups as their instructional level improves.

Flexible grouping provides the opportunity for reading specialists to be most productive. When students are in small, flexible groups, reading specialists can support the classroom teacher by working with one group of students while the teacher works with another group. Without this basic component of a collaborative teaching model, most differentiated instruction is impossible. If the entire class, except for the two or three students needing added support, are listening to the teacher and participating in a whole-class lesson, the stigma attached to being "special" is hard to overcome. If, on the other hand, everyone in the class is working in small groups and adults move among the groups, there is no stigma attached to getting support for learning. All classrooms need to have a mix of whole- and small-group opportunities in order for two adults to work in the room productively. If a teacher insists on whole-class instruction, there is no place for a second adult to become part of the learning experience. In one school the specialist reported that after one year she changed from working with fourth and fifth grades to working with third-grade teachers who used flexible grouping. In the upper grades she had been almost immobilized and felt her time was wasted.

> *All classrooms need to have a mix of whole- and small-group opportunities in order for two adults to work in the room productively.*

Grouping arrangements are fundamental. This was perhaps the area that received the strongest comments from our specialists. Without flexibility and small-group activity, collaboration was almost impossible; with it almost anything seemed possible.

New Reading Curriculum, Textbook Adoption, and State Standards

As districts invest in new reading curricula and materials, the opportunities for providing in-class support for the range of readers increase. Teachers often need help in using the new materials and adapting them to meet the needs of their students. Teachers struggle with managing the demands of grade-level anthologies and providing opportunities for students to read at their instructional levels. It is a natural time for reading specialists to provide demonstration lessons as well as in-class support for at-risk students.

One of our specialists explained that having a new reading program provided her an ideal opportunity to work side by side with classroom teachers; it leveled the playing field. Instead of being the "expert" she could be a novice along with the classroom teachers. She asked to teach some specific lessons to learn better what the series was like. When she came to teach a lesson she either asked the classroom teacher to co-teach with her or to observe her teaching and give feedback. It created what one specialist called a "beautiful opportunity" for shared teaching and learning.

In another school, classroom teachers and reading specialists collaborated to design activities and lessons to help students reach the state standards related to reading informational text. One of the standards for reading in Illinois requires students to "identify structure of nonfiction texts to improve comprehension." In this instance, the reading specialist helped the classroom teacher differentiate instruction using a variety of nonfiction materials. The reading specialist suggested easier texts on the topic of insects to prepare students to read the grade-level text that was part of the third-grade science unit on classification. She brought many materials to the classroom and involved the school librarian in helping find materials for the range of reading levels in the class.

Struggling students used the easier texts to discuss text structure and graphic aids before considering the same elements in the grade-level text on insects. This collaborative effort allowed the teachers to design activities that scaffolded the struggling students' reading and understanding of grade-level text to meet the standard. Because the standards were being monitored, even teachers reluctant to open their doors were utilizing and appreciating the support of the specialists more than in the past. The standards also opened the door to discussion about parts of the reading program some teachers had tended to ignore. Specialists reported having discussions with teachers who did not want to teach informational texts or exposition. These teachers needed individual professional development from specialists in what is important and then demonstration teaching from the specialists in how to make the reading of informational texts a part of their instruction. The standards reform movement requires all students to succeed and meet high levels of performance expectations. It has opened the doors of many classrooms to the specialists.

Clear Operating Plan

Teachers providing in-class support must have a clear plan of what they will do each day in the classroom. Whether they are team-teaching a lesson, providing a demonstration lesson, or working with small groups of students, everyone must know what to expect when the reading specialist comes into the room. Without such a plan, precious time is lost to inefficient use of the resources.

Working with our support, the reading specialists in Ellen's district designed a 5-day plan for an in-class model that addressed the students' instructional level needs and supported students as they read age-appropriate grade-level material. Reading specialists spent a day meeting with small groups of students to work on word analysis and word building, spent 2 days guiding students as they read instructional level text, and spent the last 2 days supporting students as they read grade-level material. This model presupposed that the classroom teacher included small-group work daily so the reading specialists could work with the struggling readers at a time when all students were working in small groups. If children needed more support, either teacher could assist them. The specialist and the classroom teachers periodically shifted the small groups with which they worked so both would know the children well as readers. Although this was the cycle that the reading specialists as a group had determined they would all try, only a few actually were able to work with the faculty in a productive way to implement this model. For some, however, it did provide a consistent, predictable way to collaborate in classrooms that has continued in those schools.

Choice in Teaming

In the spirit of collaboration, all teachers should be open to having reading teachers work in the classroom to support struggling readers. However, when collaboration is new to a school, classroom teachers as well as reading teachers should be given the choice of working together. Moving slowly and starting with teachers who want to work together may provide the necessary track record for additional staff members opening their doors to collaboration and teaming. It also gives the specialists time to develop their own style of working in the classroom with other teachers. Providing time for specialists to meet together and discuss how they work with other teachers is also valuable, we have found. Discussions about our personality differences can help us gain appreciation for behaviors in others that we have only seen as irritating before. As specialists share examples of how they have resolved conflicts in their buildings the range of possible working relationships becomes larger.

This is also an area in which support of the principals is important. The administration can open the way for collaboration and support variations in collaborative arrangements. As we shared earlier in this chapter, one specialist decided that the fourth- and fifth-grade teachers were not ready for real collaboration because they taught almost entirely to the whole class and did not have small-group periods when adults could freely move in a classroom. When she approached the principal he agreed that this was a dilemma for the specialist and arranged for a shift to the third-grade level for the next year while the school worked on grouping. This kind of flexibility that allows both teachers and specialists to have some choice was reported as being very important to three of our specialists. Others indicated the human relations were basic to all their successful efforts.

Variations, Adaptations, and Flexibility

Our specialists frequently noted that the closer they got to meeting individual needs of students and teachers, the more variety they seemed to adopt in their practices.

Although in-class support may be the recommended model, some students may have particular needs that can best be met in occasional pull-out sessions. For example, intermediate or middle school students who continue to have decoding issues may be more comfortable working on these strategies outside the classroom setting. However, when working on comprehension strategies, these same students can successfully work within the classroom setting if they are supported in their decoding of the text.

When there are very few students needing support in one classroom, they may join with a small group in another classroom for instructional level reading. The reading specialist may work in only one classroom or vary the room by semester. Individual circumstances and availability of adequate staff may dictate variation in and adaptation of the support program.

One specialist who had previously not liked working with parents found that when she was in classrooms where small-group work was common and the structure clear, she began involving more parents. They came in for particular projects and assisted teams of students in their work.

Although it is necessary for teachers to have a clear operating plan, sometimes the reading specialist needs to be flexible in providing the support program to assist the classroom teacher. In addition, the classroom teacher may need to be flexible in establishing a schedule to accommodate the specialist coming into the classroom. One of our specialists put it well: "Working with teachers is just like working with at-risk readers. You need to go into the classroom, assess the situation, find the teacher's strengths and weaknesses, work with the givens, and support the program they have in place." This kind of flexibility is a real asset in collaborative arrangements.

We also noted in our interviews that the specialists' schedules need to be open enough so that they can adjust to the shifting demands across the school year. In the fall there is a need to support the diagnosis and placement of students. This may mean that both classroom teachers and specialists engage in diagnostic testing, that the specialist teaches groups so classroom teachers can do testing, or that some arrangement with other personnel is also made. During state testing (usually February through March) it may be important for the specialist to change roles again. December is often a month with many special programs and collaboration may take new forms. Readers Theatre, plays, and musical programs provide good reading opportunities in which practice and rehearsal of text come easily for struggling readers. Taking account of these shifting needs is not easy, but some preplanning and discussion with all involved can make them pleasant changes rather than times for misunderstanding.

We were surprised in our interviews and survey results that the issue of time for conferences between classroom teachers and specialists did not emerge. When we probed specialists for how they arranged time to meet with teachers, they had a hard time articulating their systems of communication. *Flexibility* was our summary term for their practices. Most seem to meet "on the run" in those small places and during brief moments when teachers find each other. None described formal conference times as either needed or desirable. The most regular meetings were during grade-level team meetings, when all teachers gathered together to discuss programs and individual students. It seemed that once a good relationship was established among the adults working together, they could communicate without hassle, especially in arrangements in which teams did meet on a regular basis. This was a surprising and positive outcome of the surveys; we had anticipated that time would be a major communication issue. It was not. This certainly highlights the flexibility of all the educators involved in these collaborations.

Adequate Time Frame

Time did emerge as an issue, however, in other ways. Particularly, specialists voiced concern that there must be enough time in the reading program for the teachers to provide consistent support to struggling readers. This means either sufficient time during the day or sufficient time during the week is needed to actually make a difference in the students' progress. If the classroom reading program is too fragmented, the reading specialist and/or the classroom teacher—as well as the student—will be frustrated by inability to finish a lesson. Many students who struggle with reading need more time for reading than is available during the regular school schedule. It may be necessary to provide the support program outside the regular school day; the reading specialists along with the reading coordinator for the district suggested using time either before or after school to provide the extra support. For example, a before- and after-school extended day program could be established, and during this time specialists could work with struggling readers.

The reading specialists also provided support to the classroom teachers to adapt and scaffold the grade-level materials to make them accessible to the struggling readers. Thus, through collaboration and coordination of the reading programs, students received a rich and extended reading curriculum.

Open School Culture

Teachers need to be open to suggestion and willing to try different approaches to meet the needs of the struggling reader. In an open school culture, no one is perceived as an expert. Rather, the reading specialist and the classroom teacher both bring expertise to designing a program that meets the needs of struggling readers. No one is blamed, but all good suggestions and support are welcomed. In addition, all teachers support the collaboration. No one is made to feel inadequate for seeking support. This is the culture in which collaboration thrives and students learn. We found variations of this among the schools in our survey. In most cases schools had some openness, but frustrations were often expressed about individual teachers or teams.

Openness is developed in many ways. A story from our project may help make this point clear:

In an open school culture, no one is perceived as an expert. Rather, the reading specialist and the classroom teacher both bring expertise to designing a program that meets the needs of struggling readers.

One school has been very traditional in its way of grouping students; ability grouping for reading has been practiced for many years. When the superintendent mandated that students would not be grouped by ability in an effort to eliminate racial divisions, the teachers nearly rebelled. The reading coordinator knew it was time to take action and began to visit the school regularly to meet with the teachers. She offered to work in the classrooms of any teachers who were willing to change their reading instruction and not just group by ability. At first she had no takers. After a few weeks, one of the most well-respected teachers asked for her help. Others queried, "Why do you want help? You are a great teacher." But she did ask and the coordinator responded.

Over the weeks that the two worked together they developed a structure that permitted both mixed-ability grouping and attention to skill areas and needs of the individual students. Finally, it was the classroom teacher who was able to reach her colleagues. With her risk taking and openness as an example the others also began to look at alternatives to their long-term practices.

In this case it took an "outsider" to spur change because the reading specialist in the building and the principal had not found the right opening. Yet, one teacher who was willing to make changes and open her classroom door began a process that is now well under way for most of the other faculty. A combination of pushes from outside and support from the community can create a new openness.

Conclusion

Changing the practices that teachers feel comfortable using is not simple. The more the climate of the school encourages innovation and provides support for experimentation, the more likely it is that change will occur. Mistakes can be made without leaving lasting scars. However, we are concerned with the growing insistence of high-stakes assessments and performance outcomes. Unless there is a high level of professionalism and support in buildings, teachers are going to experience a growing sense of frustration. Already in some districts teachers are leaving rather than seeking the support of new levels of collaboration to meet increasing pressures. We have seen schools where teachers are valued, where specialists and teachers and administrators work closely together, and where change is viewed as a challenge and opportunity to meet these demands successfully.

Fullan (1994) and Senge (1990) are among the professionals who have admonished us to nurture our schools as learning communities that are open to the changing conditions of our times, yet are grounded in our own shared values and knowledge. Our work confirms these admonitions. As reading specialists reexamined their own roles and stepped out into new territory, the benefits of changing their ways of working became clear to them. One specialist stated it well: "I am not the teacher of the low kids. I am another teacher in the classroom. I love it!"

References

Allington, R.L. (1983). The reading instruction provided readers of differing abilities. *The Elementary School Journal, 83*, 548–559.

Allington, R.L., & McGill-Franzen, A. (1989). School response to reading failure: Chapter 1 and special education students in grades 2, 4, & 8. *The Elementary School Journal, 89*, 529–542.

Allington, R.L., & Walmsley, S.A. (1995) *No quick fix: Rethinking literacy programs in America's elementary schools*. New York: Teachers College Press; Newark, DE: International Reading Association.

Fullan, M. (1994). *Change forces: Probing the depths of educational reform*. New York: Falmer Press.

McGill-Franzen, A., & Allington, R.L. (1991). Every child's right: Literacy. *The Reading Teacher, 45*, 86–90.

Senge, P. (1990). *The fifth discipline: The art and practice of the learning organization*. New York: Doubleday.

10

Developing Successful Collaborative Literacy Teams
A Case Study

Carol A. Lyons

> When Kevin entered first grade, he could not read at all and could write three or four words. His classroom teacher said he should get one-to-one help from a special reading teacher. By the end of the year, his Reading Recovery teacher had him reading on level 18 [text level equivalent to second-grade basal material] and he could write many words. His classroom teacher and I worked with his Reading Recovery teacher every day to reinforce and support what Kevin learned in his Reading Recovery lessons. I have been very pleased with his progress. He changed from an unhappy child who hated school to a confident child who loves school. The Reading Recovery program should be taught to all first graders.

—Parent of a first-grade student

As his mother indicated, Kevin's first-grade experience was positive due in part to the collaborative efforts of his mother and the classroom and Reading Recovery (RR) teachers. Reading Recovery, a one-to-one tutorial program that has been implemented in the United States for more than 16 years (Lyons, 1998), is designed to help the lowest achieving readers in first grade make accelerated progress. A specially trained teacher provides daily 30-minute lessons that engage the child in reading, writing, and exploration of print, including letters, sounds, and words. Through intensive, one-to-one instruction received in RR, and additional support from his classroom teacher, Kevin made accelerated progress, caught up with his peers, and benefited from ongoing classroom instruction.

Administrators, classroom teachers, and parents often agree with Kevin's mother that all students would benefit if RR procedures and techniques were transplanted to classroom instruction. The instructional procedures, though, were originally designed for individual teaching, not for group or classroom instruction. As RR creator Marie M. Clay states, "Most children (80–90 percent) do not require these detailed, meticulous, and special Reading Recovery procedures or any modification of them. They will learn to read in classroom programs of many different kinds" (1993, p. iv).

During the last several years, however, principles, practices, and the theoretical foundation of the RR program have begun to influence classroom and small-group reading instruction. Primary children who were once "drilled" on a programmed set of commercial materials are now being immersed in reading and rereading books and composing, writing, and reading their own stories. In primary classrooms, *An Observation Survey of Early Literacy Achievement* (Clay, 1993) is used to assess what children know and need to know to become literate.

The Literacy Collaborative (LC) began in response to requests from educators to develop a literacy framework and a model of professional development for primary classroom teachers. In 1986 a collaborative effort between faculty and staff from The Ohio State University RR program and classroom teachers from Columbus (Ohio, USA) Public Schools began to develop the LC, which is grounded in research on effective schools, teacher change, learning theory, and effective instructional approaches to beginning reading and writing instruction (Adams, 1990; Clay, 1993). Schools that are members of the LC network make a commitment to a 5-year plan that involves professional development of an in-school teacher educator, called a literacy coordinator, who works to teach and support classroom teachers. A language arts block of $2^{1}/_{2}$ to 3 hours is devoted to a balanced range of instructional components—including reading, writing, and word study—that constitute the literacy framework. The goal of the program is to raise the level of reading and writing achievement of all students. Year-long initial education and ongoing professional development are requirements of the program, which can only be implemented in schools that are implementing the RR program.

Concepts learned in the RR professional development program (e.g., observation and analyses of student behavior to inform practice) were incorporated into the design of the professional development component of the LC. The theoretical base of the LC professional development program is grounded in the research and writings of Bruner (1983), Clay (1991), and Vygotsky (1978). These theorists focus on the important role teachers play in the learning process. Teachers are viewed as critical to helping students become independent readers and writers. Through close systematic observation, teachers analyze how individuals and groups of students process information while reading and writing text, and try to determine where the processing is breaking down. This information is used to inform and guide instruction. This scaffolding process (Bruner, 1983) is conducted within the zone of proximal development (Vygotsky, 1978). Clay and Cazden (1990) refer to this teaching/learning process as sensitive teaching within the zone of proximal development. Teachers who understand the concept of assisted performance postulated by Vygotsky (1978) and others (see Rogoff, 1990) and the theoretical base of the LC program can transfer and use these theories to inform classroom practice (Fountas & Pinnell, 1996).

Similar to RR, the LC professional development program involves an intensive year-long initial education of an in-school literacy coordinator that includes 6 weeks of instruction and focused experiences at his or her home site. After the initial preparation year, the literacy coordinator returns to his or her local school to provide weekly inservice sessions and ongoing professional development to classroom teachers. Currently the LC is being implemented in 263 schools representing 103 districts in 22 states (Pinnell & Williams, 2000).

Developing a strong collaborative team of individuals to guide the implementation of the RR and LC programs requires building a shared knowledge among teachers, administrators, support staff, and parents. Without a collaborative instructional support system, mechanisms to provide high quality instruction to all students, and ongoing professional development for teachers, schoolwide literacy programs fail (Allington & Cunningham, 1996). But how do educators build shared knowledge and shared responsibilities that engender open communication, negotiation, and shared commitment to educating every child in the school? In this chapter, faculty, administrators, support staff, and parents from five schools located in the heart of Ohio's Appalachian country provide some answers.

First, I present a case study to illustrate one school's literacy team approach to implement the RR and LC programs. This case study represents a comprehensive, systematic, and in-depth study of teachers, students, LC literacy coordinators, and university staff over a 5-year period. Second, I share information gathered from literacy team members in five schools that provide insights into the impact of the RR and LC collaborative programs on professional development, the development of teachers' knowledge and skills, and students' academic, social, and emotional development.

What Did We Learn?

During the summer of 1995, two central office administrators investigated classroom literacy instruction and students' achievement in kindergarten through fifth grade in five elementary schools. Proficiency test scores were extremely low districtwide, and leadership at the building level seemed stagnant; everyone seemed content with the status quo and was resistant to change. In an attempt to infuse new blood and ideas to improve instruction and student learning, building principals were reassigned and asked to work collaboratively with their staff to select and implement a comprehensive literacy program that would improve student achievement.

School C, one of the five schools in the district, served approximately 150 students. The multicultural diverse population had the highest number of children (95%) receiving free and reduced lunch in the district and one of the highest levels of poverty in the state (45% Aid for Dependent Children). Student achievement on standardized tests was the lowest in the district. For example, fifth-grade students scored at the 17th percentile on the spring 1995 California Achievement Test.

After receiving her new assignment, the principal asked district administrators to convert an unused storage room into a literacy center and to provide teacher stipends for a 3-day work session prior to the beginning of the school year. Both requests were approved. The literacy center was built to include a one-way observation glass for conducting RR preparation and a larger room to hold inservice sessions for teachers, parents, and community members. The entire staff met for 3 days prior to the start of the school year to develop a plan to raise the literacy achievement of students in the school.

The 3-day work sessions were very productive. Teachers and administrators discussed students' progress in reading and writing during the past several years. They noted that the district had responded to the needs of low achieving first-grade students by implementing RR, but no comprehensive literacy program was in place to raise the level of achievement of kindergarten, first-, and second-grade students. They examined various schoolwide approaches designed to improve primary students' achievement. After much research, discussion, and debate, the faculty decided to implement the LC program and initiate three actions immediately:

1. First, find someone to prepare as a literacy coordinator so that the following year he or she could return to the building and conduct inservice sessions to help kindergarten through second-grade classroom teachers gradually phase in the new approaches learned during LC preparation.

2. Second, learn how to assess students' literacy needs and analyze the growth of individual students over time. In response to this request, teachers were introduced to *An Observation Survey of Early Literacy Achievement* (Clay, 1993), a set of six assessments that revealed what students can do independently, and learned how this information is used to inform and target instruction.

3. Third, create a school-based literacy team to facilitate decision-making processes related to schoolwide implementation of the RR and LC programs. Members of the team included the RR teachers and teacher leader; literacy coordinator; kindergarten, first-, sec-

ond-, and third-grade classroom teachers; special education teachers; school psychologist; parents; and principal. Team members addressed issues related to planning, staffing, professional development, funding, evaluation, level of service to children in kindergarten through third-grade classrooms, RR and special education rooms, and the level of implementation.

Although these compelling goals were agreed on, advocates of the school-based literacy team soon realized that the ideas were not enthusiastically embraced by every team member. The principal discussed building a literacy team during the first year of implementation:

> It was painful to confront the "why" for change and reform. Literacy teams must first confirm the need. Then came role ambiguity and conflict. Teachers were expected to go from relative isolation of the closed classroom to a whole-school team. Teacher education in Reading Recovery and Literacy Collaborative not only promotes shared knowledge but a collaborative setting that helps build a team. "We are in this together" attitude is a must, but it does not happen easily. Focusing on a child's needs and strengths is a natural part of both the Literacy Collaborative and Reading Recovery programs and encouraged the team to collaborate. Involving parents takes more effort. Parents *must* be a part of the process of decision making to feel they can impact their child's learning.

Classroom Instruction

During their year-long professional development program led by the Literacy Collaborative coordinator, the classroom teachers learned how to effectively engage students in a variety of reading and writing activities on a daily basis. Teaching focused on four reading elements (reading aloud to children, shared reading, guided reading and reading workshop, and independent reading) and four writing elements (shared writing and language experience, interactive writing, guided writing and writing workshop, and independent writing). Within the shared reading and writing activities, special attention was given to letters, letter sounds, and words throughout all elements of the framework (Pinnell & Fountas, 1998).

Students' Progress

Student progress on Text Reading (TR) and Hearing and Recording Sounds in Words (HRSIW) on *An Observation Survey of Early Literacy Achievement* were analyzed according to published guidelines. (HRSIW is a measure of the child's knowledge of relationships between letters and sounds in words. The assessor reads a sentence to the child and then reads it again slowly, asking the child to write the words. Products are scored as to the number of phonemes accurately represented through sound analysis. Measures of TR level were obtained by constructing a gradient of difficulty for text drawn originally from a basal reading system. A child's text reading level indicates the highest level that he or she has read at 90% accuracy.) Stanine frequency distributions on both measures were calculated for first-grade students in the fall and spring of the 1996–1997 (see Figures 1 and 2) and 1997–1998 (see Figures 3 and 4) school years. (Stanines are standard scores in which the range of reading achievement is divided into nine equal units with a mean of 5 and a standard of 2. Stanines of 1, 2, and 3 are below average; 4, 5, and 6 are average; and 7, 8, and 9 are above average.)

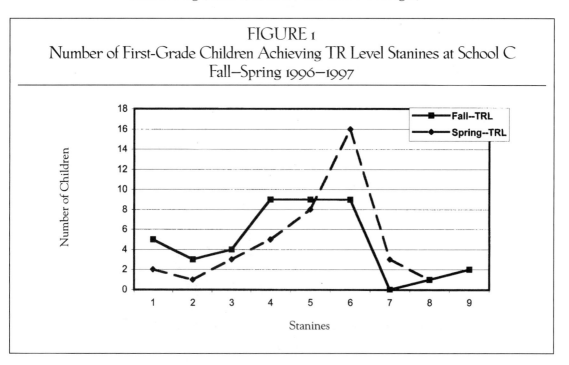

FIGURE 1
Number of First-Grade Children Achieving TR Level Stanines at School C
Fall–Spring 1996–1997

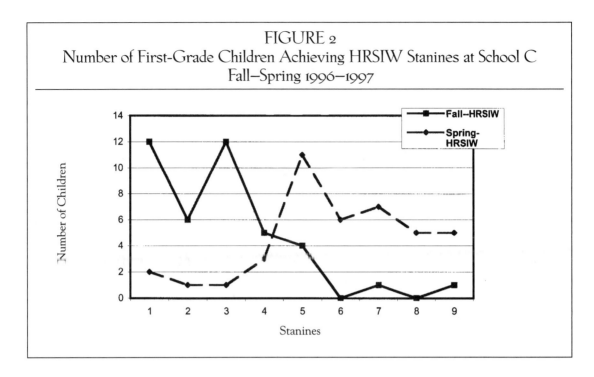

FIGURE 2
Number of First-Grade Children Achieving HRSIW Stanines at School C
Fall–Spring 1996–1997

In spring 1996, most Grade 1 students, including those who re-ceived RR, read at a higher level than expected for first graders. Frequency stanine distributions for first-grade students' results on TR and HRSIW are reported in Figures 1 and 2. These stanine shifts are impressive, especially for students from this low socioeconomic and transient population. First-grade students had the most noticeable sta-nine shifts in writing, demonstrated in the HRSIW assessment.

Frequency stanine distributions for Grade 1 students on TR level (see Figure 3) and HRSIW (see Figure 4) in 1997–1998 are more dra-matic than 1996–1997 figures. First-grade students produced the most noticeable shifts in writing. In fall of 1998 every child in first grade was reading at or above grade level—a remarkable achievement for students who entered Grade 1 with limited literacy knowledge and skill evidenced in very low achievement scores on *An Observation Survey of Early Literacy Achievement*. The impact of a comprehensive approach to instruction offered in the LC program with RR as the safety net for students who need more individualized support is evi-dent in shifts in student achievement.

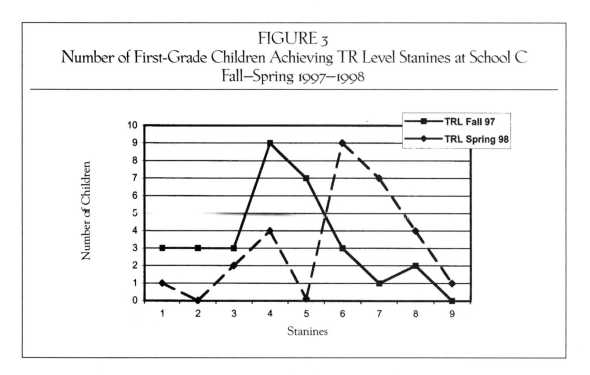

FIGURE 3
Number of First-Grade Children Achieving TR Level Stanines at School C
Fall–Spring 1997–1998

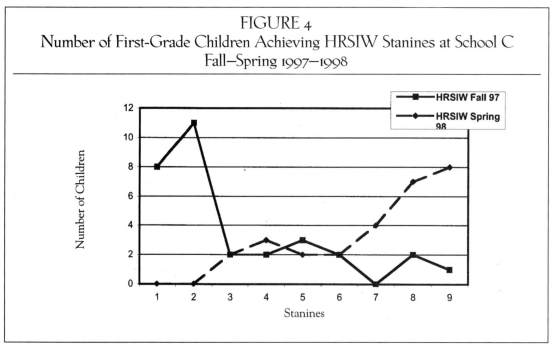

FIGURE 4
Number of First-Grade Children Achieving HRSIW Stanines at School C
Fall–Spring 1997–1998

TABLE 1

Percent of Second-Grade Students in School C at Each Quartile in Fall 1996, 1997, and 1998 on the Gates-MacGinitie Reading Test

Quartile	Fall 1996		Fall 1997		Fall 1998	
	Reading Comp PR	Total Reading PR	Reading Comp PR	Total Reading PR	Reading Comp PR	Total Reading PR
n	31	31	34	34	27	27
1st Quartile	61.3%	67.7%	50.0%	58.8%	29.6%	29.6%
2nd Quartile	22.6%	12.9%	26.5%	17.6%	25.9%	18.5%
3rd Quartile	3.2%	9.7%	11.8%	17.6%	22.2%	48.1%
4th Quartile	12.9%	9.7%	11.8%	5.9%	22.2%	3.7%

In fall of second grade, the total population of Grade 2 students was assessed on the Comprehension Subtest of the Gates-MacGinitie Reading Test (see MacGinitie & MacGinitie, 1989). As indicated in Table 1, second-grade students' Comprehension and Total Reading scores shifted from the lower 4th Quartile to the higher 1st Quartile every year with the most dramatic shifts in fall of 1996.

An NCE, Normal Curve Equivalent, is a statistical transformation of percentile ranks in which reading achievement is divided into 99 equal units with a mean of 50 and a standard deviation of 21.06. NCEs are generally considered to provide the truest indication of student growth in achievement because they provide comparative information in equal units of measurement. It should be kept in mind that NCEs are based on percentiles, which compare the student's performance in relation to the general population. An NCE of 50 represents where a student should be for his or her grade level. For a student's NCE score to remain the same at posttest as at pretest does not denote a lack of absolute progress; on the contrary, it means that the student has maintained the same relative position in terms of the general population. Even a small gain in NCEs indicates advancement from the student's original level of achievement. Standardized test results on the Gates-MacGinitie Reading Test (MacGinitie & MacGinitie, 1989), NCEs for second-grade students

TABLE 2
Standardized Test Results on Gates-MacGinitie Reading Subtests
for Second-Grade Students in School C

| | Fall 1996 | | | Fall 1997 | | | Fall 1998 | |
	Reading Comp.	Total Reading		Reading Comp.	Total Reading		Reading Comp.	Total Reading
n	*NCE*	*NCE*	*n*	*NCE*	*NCE*	*n*	*NCE*	*NCE*
31	31.3	27.9	34	35.8	33.1	27	44.8	45.0

in fall 1996 through fall 1998, are reported in Table 2. The results reveal an increase in NCE gain scores across each of the 3 years. This trend is impressive because it is much more difficult to demonstrate an upward trend in NCE scores when working with children from the bottom quartile (Pinnell & Williams, 2000).

Dramatic shifts were also noted in the number of students referred to special education. As indicated in Table 3, over a 3-year period, special education referrals in School C were significantly lower than referrals in four elementary schools in the district that chose not to implement the RR and LC programs. This trend suggests implementing the RR and LC programs is saving a substantial amount of money that otherwise would have been spent on testing and special education placement.

The special education teachers were very pleased that they had learned new observation and teaching techniques to help students learn how to read and write. A central office administrator commented that having special education teachers take RR and LC training was extremely successful and very worthwhile:

> Mary had been a special education teacher for more than 25 years. She frequently talked about how she now had new techniques to help her teach. She saw successes in children learning to read that she had not seen before. We [district central administrators] began to insist that any student in kindergarten or first grade being considered for referral for special education identification be first considered for Reading Recovery. There was a significant decline in identification of very young children for special education. All students including those with special learning needs can be taught to read and write if we just find the right way to teach them.

TABLE 3
Special Education Referrals in School C District 1996–1998

	1996–1997				
School	K	Gr 1	Gr 2	Gr 3	Total
A, B, D, E.*	4	11	15	11	41*
C	0	1	0	0	1
	1997–1998				
School	K	Gr 1	Gr 2	Gr 3	Total
A, B, D, E	3	17	13	3	36*
C	0	0	0	2	2
	1998–1999				
School	K	Gr 1	Gr 2	Gr 3	Total
A, B, D, E	4	16	26	10	56*
C	0	0	0	1	1

*Information not available for individual schools.

Reflections

When asked to reflect on their experiences over the 5-year period, respondents agreed that developing trust and collegial support among team members was not easy. During the first year, the literacy team had many challenges. Some classroom teachers were not as open to change. The LC and RR approach to literacy instruction required teachers to learn new observation techniques and to rethink their rationales for assessment and instructional techniques. For many teachers, however, ongoing weekly professional development sessions with live demonstration lessons and informal discussions about students' progress sustained and enhanced collaborative efforts and created more collegiality, teamwork, and support for one another. Materials and teaching techniques were

For many teachers...ongoing weekly professional development sessions with live demonstration lessons and informal discussions about students' progress sustained and enhanced collaborative efforts and created more collegiality, teamwork, and support for one another.

shared and demonstrated. These teachers developed a sense of community and feeling that many individuals were working together to support students' learning.

Teachers that had difficulty learning new approaches or were uncomfortable trying something new requested and received transfers to other buildings in the district. Classroom teacher vacancies were filled with teachers who requested instruction in the RR or LC programs. By fall of 1997–1998 every kindergarten through third-grade teacher had received either RR or LC instruction. Data reported in this chapter suggest that the LC comprehensive approach to literacy coupled with an RR safety net program for struggling first-grade students increases student learning and achievement.

A central office administrator, who in 1995 was responsible for reassigning principals and establishing site-based management, said,

> Problems, yes, many—unhappy staff members, a new Board of Education that didn't fully buy into the program—but during all the turmoil something wonderful was happening at [School C]. Students were becoming readers and writers. The old dingy building became alive and bright with classrooms and halls cluttered with student writing. Students were reading in "book nooks" with parent and community member volunteers. Children were asking to take books home to read to their parents; staff members were being asked to present at state and national meetings. One of my favorite stories of many was of the little boy who couldn't find paper at home to write his story on, but rather than not complete his assignment he used the paper out of a package of cigarettes. What you see and feel inside [School C] makes it all worthwhile.

Additional Feedback: Five Schools in Adams County

The feelings expressed by this central office administrator are supported by individuals involved in RR and LC programs in five other schools. Members of literacy teams in these schools responded to an open-ended questionnaire focusing on how to develop, support, and maintain collaborative schoolwide faculty partnerships.

As reported in Table 4, the most frequently mentioned obstacles individuals faced related to giving up old teaching techniques and learning new ones. More experienced teachers tended to try to fit new ap-

Questions	Categories	No.	% Responses
1a. Whar are major obstacles the literacy team faced in implementing RR/LC programs?	◆ Gaining K–5 teachers' support	15	27%
	◆ Gaining parents' support	12	22%
	◆ Establishing trust among team members	10	18%
	◆ Gaining central administration support	9	17%
	◆ Funding	6	10%
	◆ Other	3	5%
1b. What are major obstacles individuals faced in implementing RR/LC programs?	◆ Leaving old practices	17	30%
	◆ Learning new teaching techniques	15	26%
	◆ Managing time and organization	12	21%
	◆ Getting parents involved in child's work	10	18%
	◆ Other	3	5%
2a. How did the team resolve obstacles?	◆ Establishing regular team meetings	15	20%
	◆ Providing rationales and explanations for LC/RR teaching procedures	12	16%
	◆ Listening to concerns; developing a good problem-solving process	10	13%
	◆ Inviting teachers/administrators to observe demonstration lessons	10	13%
	◆ Organizing staff meetings so that different team members chair	10	13%
	◆ Inviting questions/concerns at every staff meeting	8	11%
	◆ Bringing in experts to explain how to resolve funding problems	5	7%
	◆ Creating a nonthreatening environment	4	6%
	◆ Other	2	2%
2b. How did you (individuals) resolve obstacles?	◆ Discussing concerns openly and getting help from others	17	38%
	◆ Meeting with parents regularly	10	22%
	◆ Sending home positive notes indicating child's progress regularly	8	18%
	◆ Supporting each other	8	18%
	◆ Other	2	4%

TABLE 4
Literacy Team Members' Responses About Developing Collaborative Partnerships

TABLE 5
Literacy Team Members' Advice and Lessons Learned
About the Collaborative Process

Questions	Categories	No.	% Responses
1. What is some advice to those thinking about developing collaborative teams to implement schoolwide programs?	◆ Allow time for buy in; go slowly	8	12%
	◆ Invite all faculty and administration to join team	7	10%
	◆ Train all faculty and administration in programs	7	10%
	◆ Involve parents; attend to their concerns	5	8%
	◆ Build in financial support at beginning	5	8%
	◆ Learn how to interpret and use data	5	8%
	◆ Select positive, respected individuals as leaders	5	8%
	◆ Select programs with compatible principles and practices	4	6%
	◆ Build in ongoing professional development	4	6%
	◆ Regularly inform school board and central administration	4	6%
	◆ Work together, not alone	4	6%
	◆ Schedule grade-level meetings to share	3	4%
	◆ Be flexible about scheduling	2	3%
	◆ Other	3	4%
2. What is the most important thing you (individuals) learned?	◆ All children can learn	14	25%
	◆ How to effectively teach reading	11	19%
	◆ How to become a community of learners	6	11%
	◆ Work together to resolve issues	5	9%
	◆ Select leaders with good communication and people skills	4	7%
	◆ Use on-site trainers/coaches to help resolve problems as they occur	4	7%
	◆ Ongoing professional development is critical	4	7%
	◆ Learning to read improves students' achievement in all academic areas	3	5%
	◆ Address problems fairly, openly, and in a supportive manner	2	3%
	◆ Other	4	7%

proaches to teaching reading and writing into traditional practices they had been using for years. For example, while introducing a book for the first time, they might have tried to introduce new vocabulary words on

TABLE 6
Parents' Advice to Teachers and Parents of Children Who Are Having Difficulty Learning to Read

Questions	Categories	No.	% Responses
1. What is some advice to teachers?	◆ Work collaboratively with every teacher who works with a specific child	4	36%
	◆ Talk with parents; let them know how to help	3	27%
	◆ Be patient; keep content challenging without pressure	3	27%
	◆ Other	1	9%
2. What is some advice to parents?	◆ Talk to the teacher regularly to see if your child has a problem	3	27%
	◆ Get help for your child as soon as you notice a problem	3	27%
	◆ Make time every night to listen to your child read	2	18%
	◆ Have patience; praise and encourage your child	2	18%
	◆ Other	1	9%

index cards rather than using the language structure and context of the story. Gaining support from other members of the faculty was also mentioned frequently as a major obstacle. These issues were resolved by team members in a proactive way by taking the time to listen to concerns and provide opportunities for observation, demonstration, questioning, rationale building, and problem solving with others.

Making attempts to be inclusive and allowing time for faculty, administrators, and parents to accept the programs were considered critical to long-term success. Table 5 represents lessons learned and provides advice to faculty and administrators who are thinking about a creating collaborative team approach to implement schoolwide literacy programs.

Table 6 reports parents' advice to teachers and parents of struggling readers. It is clear from their responses that parents want teachers to involve them in their children's education, and parents will continue to support their children's learning at home.

Issues were resolved by team members in a proactive way by taking the time to listen to concerns and provide opportunities for observation, demonstration, questioning, rationale building, and problem solving with others.

Two generalizations emerged from content analyses (Guba & Lincoln, 1981) of these open-ended questions. First, team members (including parents) are committed to establishing broad ownership and shared decision making to ensure that every child in the school becomes a reader and writer. Second, team members are actively involved and working toward establishing RR and LC programs as integral parts of the school's professional development and literacy education programs.

Final Comments

Researchers and practitioners are beginning to amass a body of knowledge about what it takes to ensure every child learns to read and write and what barriers get in the way of children's success. This research suggests that success depends on the knowledge and skills of the teachers and how well schools manage and implement literacy programs (Darling-Hammond, 1996). Implementation tends to be better, for example, when three factors are present: (1) school administrators and faculty have willingly chosen to implement a particular program(s); (2) theoretical principles underpinning the program(s) are compatible and support faculty members' philosophy of teaching and learning (Allington & Cunningham, 1996); and (3) ongoing high-level professional development focuses on systematic evaluation of teacher practices, contexts, and student outcomes (National Commission on Teaching and America's Future, 1996).

Characteristics of effective schools are revealed in this chapter and in the words of Brenda McClanahan, a kindergarten teacher from Adams County in Ohio:

> We have many opportunities for professional development through our district and school professional development programs. Working collaboratively with the other teachers in my building has been most beneficial to me. Sharing ideas, materials, hopes, and frustrations helped me not feel so isolated in my classroom. Seeing what the upper grades do to teach literacy has helped me see the bigger picture of a child's literacy program. Being able to brainstorm with others to come up with solutions and ideas of ways to help our children has greatly benefited our school. Most importantly, as teachers, parents, and the community see the results of our efforts as we collect data, there is much more of a trend to work toward our collabora-

tive efforts of improving the reading skills of every child in our school. We have learned that all children can learn to read and write.

The Commission on Teaching and America's Future (1996) recommends that teachers should be involved in collaborative planning and problem solving with school colleagues and networks of educators that include school-university partnerships. There should also be many opportunities for colleagues to work on common problems of practice that are directly linked to teachers' practice and student learning (Darling-Hammond, 1996). Goodlad (1984) discusses the value of establishing a network of peers to build a necessary support system in which to share information and constructively problem solve. Fullan (1993) argues that it takes the formation of collaborative literacy teams within schools to ensure effectiveness of the professional development effort, increase teachers' knowledge, improve teachers' skills, and raise student achievement.

Brenda's comments suggest that the recommendations made by the National Commission on Teaching and America's Future (1996) are taking place through the collaborative efforts of the RR and LC literacy teams in these five schools. Team members provide some insights into how to develop the capacity to create literacy teams of educators who have a shared vision and work collaboratively to ensure that all children learn to read and write.

Success in collaborative efforts such as the ones in the initial vignette and illustrated throughout this chapter cannot be simply a top-down administrative decision to adopt a comprehensive literacy program or transplant an existing program designed for the masses. As revealed in the voices of literacy team members and parents, successful collaborative efforts involve school faculty and support staff, administrators, and parents co-constructing literacy programs that have a shared vision and mission, as well as compatible theoretical orientations, goals, and principles of learning and teaching to meet the ever-changing needs of diverse student populations. These programs have a better chance of lasting success

Successful collaborative efforts involve school faculty and support staff, administrators, and parents co-constructing literacy programs that have a shared vision and mission, as well as compatible theoretical orientations, goals, and principles of learning and teaching to meet the ever-changing needs of diverse student populations.

because there are positive outcomes for students' academic, social, and emotional development and teachers' growth, satisfaction, and confidence.

References

Adams, M. (1990). *Beginning to read: Thinking and learning about print*. Cambridge, MA: MIT Press.

Allington, R.L., & Cunningham, P.A. (1996). *Schools that work: Where all children read and write*. New York: HarperCollins.

Bruner, J.S. (1983). *Beyond the information given: Studies in the psychology of knowing*. New York: Norton.

Clay, M.M. (1991). *Becoming literate: The construction of inner control*. Portsmouth, NH: Heinemann.

Clay, M.M. (1993). *An observation survey of early literacy achievement*. Portsmouth, NH: Heinemann.

Clay, M.M., & Cazden, C.B. (1990). A Vygotskian interpretation of Reading Recovery. In Luis Moll (Ed.), *Vygotsky and education* (pp. 206–222). New York: Cambridge University Press.

Darling-Hammond, L. (1996). What matters most: A competent teacher for every child. *Phi Delta Kappa, 78*, 193–200.

Fountas, I.C., & Pinnell, G.S. (1996). *Guided reading: Good first teaching for all children*. Portsmouth, NH: Heinemann.

Fullan, M. (1993). *Change forces: Probing the depths of educational reform*. New York: Falmer Press.

Goodlad, J.I. (1984). *A place called school*. New York: McGraw-Hill.

Guba, E.G., & Lincoln, Y.S. (1981). *Effective evaluation: Improving the usefulness of evaluation results through responsive and naturalistic approaches*. San Francisco: Jossey-Bass.

Lyons, C.A. (1998). Reading Recovery in the United States: More than a decade of data. *Literacy, Teaching, and Learning: An International Journal of Early Literacy, 1*, 110–119.

MacGinitie, W.H., & MacGinitie, R.K. (1989). *Gates MacGinitie Reading Test* (3rd ed.). Chicago: Riverside Publishing.

National Commission on Teaching and America's Future (1996). *What matters most: Teaching for America's future*. Woodbridge, VA: National Commission.

Pinnell, G.S., & Fountas, I.C. (1998). *Word matters*. Portsmouth, NH: Heinemann.

Pinnell, G.S., & Williams, E.J. (2000). *Literacy Collaborative 1999 research report*. Columbus, OH: The Ohio State University.

Rogoff, B. (1990). *Apprenticeship in thinking: Cognitive development in social context*. New York: Oxford University Press.

Vygotsky, L.S. (1978). *Mind in society: The development of higher psychological processes* (M. Cole, V. John-Steiner, S. Scribner, & E. Souberman, Eds. and Trans.). Cambridge, MA: Harvard University Press. (Original work published 1934)

EDUCATIONAL TEAMS FOR STUDENTS WITH DIVERSE NEEDS
Structures to Promote Collaboration and Impact

Beverly Rainforth and Jill L. England

Yesterday, a second-grade class read *Jack and the Beanstalk* as part of a unit on fairy tales. Today, the speech therapist introduces the language arts lesson and divides the class into three groups. In one group, children retell Jack's story, strengthening their comprehension of story elements and ability to sequence events, as well as building their oral language skills and confidence as public speakers. The classroom teacher checks their performance and progress as she writes their story on chart paper. The second group is led by a sign language interpreter, who records their story and interprets for a child who is deaf. The speech therapist leads the third group, which includes some children who receive speech and language services. As children in this group retell the story, the speech therapist writes each sentence in a different color, then emphasizes the beginning capitalization and ending punctuation. To strengthen language concepts, this group also signs key words and children take turns drawing a picture on the chart to illustrate the meaning of each sentence, strategies that are especially important for a child with severe cognitive and language disabilities.

his lesson occurred in a small school that made a commitment to inclusive education. Inclusion has been both criticized as ineffective (see Kauffman & Hallahan, 1995) and advocated as a philosophical and practical improvement over pullout services (see McGregor & Vogelsberg, 1998). Of particular relevance to language and literacy learning, pull-out programs have been criticized for failing to increase time spent in reading instruction, to provide more individualized intervention, to intersect with classroom instruction, to accelerate progress, or to graduate many students from special or remedial services (Allington & McGill-Franzen, 1989; Anderson & Pellicer, 1990; Espin, Deno, & Albayrak-Kaymak, 1998; U.S. Department of Education, 1995). Unfortunately, criticism of the "inclusion bandwagon" has also been valid, at least partially due to the practice of simply renaming existing service models. It is not surprising that adopting the *name* of an innovation without careful attention to the *features* of the innovation will not realize promised outcomes (Kovaleski, Gickling, Morrow, & Swank, 1999).

In this chapter, we will describe (a) inclusive education for children with a range of language and literacy needs, (b) a model of collaborative teamwork that supports classroom-based instruction, and (c) some of the organizational structures required to implement this model successfully. We identified these principles and practices through 15 years of teacher education and informal mentoring, as well as staff development and technical assistance to public schools. Our work with these schools has ranged from providing occasional workshops to providing long-term staff development and technical assistance through state and national projects to redesign special education systems. Our work to change systems began with the goal of developing inclusive education for students with special needs, but inevitably expanded to reforming educational communities to meet the needs of all students. These experiences have provided us with examples from a variety of rural, suburban, and urban schools, which we use throughout this chapter to illustrate our principles and practices.

> *Inclusive education is more than a philosophy or a new name for "mainstreaming."*

Inclusive Education Defined

Inclusive education is more than a philosophy or a new name for "mainstreaming." We assert that it is a specific model of service delivery, with the following characteristics:

- All children attend the same school and receive instruction in the same classroom that they would attend if they did not have special needs.
- Title I, special education, and related services are provided within general education, so specialists work closely with classroom teachers as they support students who need their services. (In this chapter, we use the term *specialists* to refer to professionals who specialize in language and literacy instruction, such as literacy specialists, special education teachers, speech/language pathologists, and teachers of English as a second language.)
- All students are provided the adaptations, specialized interventions, and personnel support needed to participate and learn in the context of the general education environment and curriculum. Accommodations are made in the general education curriculum, when needed, so all students learn skills appropriate to their chronological age and developmental needs.
- The curriculum is conceived to include academic, social-emotional, and other learning that is required for children to become contributing members of society.
- Classrooms are learning communities in which all children are valued members who support one another.

Educators adhering to more traditional models of remedial and special services may believe inclusive education does not allow for the individualized instruction required by children with language and literacy needs. In fact, the features of inclusive schools, as we define them, match well with practices Carbo and Kapinus (1995) recommend to accelerate reading achievement by students considered at risk for failure:

- literacy rich environments with good reading models, ample time for reading, and integration of language activities;
- emphasis on constructing, examining, and extending meaning;

◆ accommodation of learners' interests, abilities, and styles;

◆ explicit, systematic, and varied instruction;

◆ authentic purposes for learning and assessment;

◆ use of a variety of heterogeneous and homogeneous groups; and

◆ home-school partnerships.

Providing effective language and literacy instruction in inclusive schools requires a team approach that will ensure provision of appropriate supports within general education classrooms. Like the innovation of inclusive education, adopting a team approach requires more than a new name for old practices; simply calling a loose collection of people a team does not make it so. This collection of people must come together for planning, teaching, and problem solving—to provide their services in ways that produce greater impact than if they all work alone.

A Model of Collaborative Teamwork

Collaborative teamwork (Rainforth & York-Barr, 1997) has several features. There is an expectation that a classroom-based team will share responsibility for all members in the class. A small core team is chosen carefully to meet the needs of students in the classroom. Members of the core team have shared goals for the class, and plan together to achieve those goals. Team members engage in an intentional process of "role release" to expand their knowledge and skills, to enable them to meet the diverse needs of students in the classroom community. We describe each of these features by comparing the practices of a collaborative team with those of a loosely organized team.

Classroom-Based Teams Support All Students

Loosely organized teams work under the assumption that students can be grouped by unidimensional abilities or deficits, that specialists can correct deficits in isolation, and that students can and will apply isolated learning experiences to the regular education curriculum and routine. As children are labeled and divided, ownership for students is also divided, and many children become "educational orphans."

In contrast, collaborative teams understand that children have complex needs and believe that those needs can be met best in the context of general education classrooms, in the curricula and routines in which performance will be evaluated. Instruction is designed with individual needs in mind and is provided in whole-class, small-group, or individual formats. Groupings are heterogeneous, flexible, and change frequently (Cantrell, 1999; Carbo & Kapinus, 1995; Jenkins et al., 1994; Lenski, Wham, & Griffey, 1998; Tomlinson, 1999), based on recognition that every student has a range of academic and social needs and can also make a variety of contributions.

In the classroom scene described earlier, for example, some children with speech and language disabilities worked with the speech therapist, but they also needed the social and language models provided by other children. Many second graders needed to develop skills related to both writing sentences and retelling a story, which had different emphases in different groups. Each student derived certain benefits from the groupings in this lesson, and could benefit from being in other groups at other times. Just as groups are flexible, the location of instruction is flexible. Children may learn outside the classroom, but no specific group or staff member is always expected to stay or leave, and the classroom is understood to be everyone's home base. This flexibility both emanates from and contributes to the commitment that all members of the classroom team share responsibility for all students. Beyond this commitment, meeting the needs of all students in the general education classroom requires a strong team whose collective expertise holds solutions to classroom challenges.

The Classroom Team Is Compact

A loosely organized team has many members who independently try to address the needs of students on their "caseload." Every specialist works with students in several classes, and, in every class, several specialists may address similar needs for students with different labels. Team size and schedules become unwieldy, interfering with communication and coordination. Responsibility falls on teacher aides, parents, and the students who already face the greatest disadvantages to integrate what professionals have not.

Within a collaborative team, a small core group agrees to work cooperatively to address needs of all students in the classroom community. Members of the core team are selected by carefully considering the needs of students in a class as well as the abilities of available personnel, and then deciding whose expertise is really required to meet students' needs. Every effort is made to avoid gaps, duplication, and contradictions, so services are "only as special as necessary" (Giangreco, 1996, p. 37).

> *Within a collaborative team, a small core group agrees to work cooperatively to address needs of all students in the classroom community.... Services are "only as special as necessary" (Giangreco, 1996, p. 37).*

In the second-grade classroom described earlier, the classroom teacher had a strong background in reading and language arts and did not require the expertise of a literacy specialist. She did, however, need assistance from the speech therapist and the sign language interpreter to meet needs of certain students in her class. Another teacher might need support from a literacy specialist, a teacher of English as a second language (ESL), and/or a special educator. Depending on the needs of students assigned to each class and the expertise of the classroom teacher, the core team might include the classroom teacher and only one or two of the many professionals who specialize in language and literacy instruction. Keeping the core team as small as possible reduces the inherent challenges of communication and coordination among team members, enabling them to develop deeper and stronger relationships. While the total amount of service remains the same, every effort is made to reduce the number of specialists working with each class so each specialist can work with fewer classrooms for longer blocks of time, yielding a greater concentration of resources.

Paraprofessionals may also be assigned to support individual students and/or the class as a whole. Although a particular student may need additional support, we advocate assigning the paraprofessional to the classroom, which makes support available to the child without discouraging interactions with the teacher and other students (see Giangreco, Edelman, Luiselli, & McFarland, 1997).

This approach to allocating services may raise legal or ethical concerns for some teachers. U.S. federal laws increasingly encourage coordination among the various education entitlement programs, however, and allow "co-mingling" of funds to achieve common goals (see Individuals with Disabilities Education Act Amendments of 1997, 20 U.S.C. 1412 sec. 613[a][2][D]). States also have amended or interpreted regulations to increase flexibility, such as New York State's clarification that either special educators or literacy specialists may provide services to students with special reading needs (Waite, 1997). In addition, most states have a waiver system that allows deviations from regulations when the proposed practice is for the benefit of children. Strategies that improve service coordination and promote more comprehensive instruction meet this criterion.

Teams Plan Together to Achieve Shared Goals

In loosely organized teams, specialists establish their own goals and methods, which may duplicate, contradict, or lack relevance to classroom instruction. Without team planning, specialists who try to work in general education classrooms are usually dissatisfied with their roles. Some try to improvise and address personal goals during the classroom lesson, but usually tire of on-the-spot planning and see poor results. Some specialists plan and teach their own lessons in the regular classroom but, without connection to other classroom staff or activities, specialists rarely see results that justify the strains associated with providing itinerant services. Some try to support individual students while the classroom teacher provides whole-group instruction but, with few ways to contribute their expertise, specialists eventually feel like "glorified aides."

In collaborative teams, the small core group comes together to understand the demands and opportunities in the regular education classroom and curriculum, identify student strengths and needs, set goals, and determine instructional strategies that will enable every student to participate successfully and to achieve his or her goals. Team members plan instruction together, so each person knows the goals of a lesson, the methods to be used, and his or her role in the lesson. As lessons are planned, each member of the core team shares perspectives on how lessons could be adjusted to better meet needs of particular students while still keeping the needs of the whole class in mind.

Finding time to plan together can be a challenge. A principal or group of teachers may design a schoolwide plan for team meetings, or individual teams may find the time that best suits them. Schoolwide plans have involved designating one afternoon a week when no other meetings can be scheduled, devising a master schedule that coordinates planning periods of specialists with those of classroom teachers, and bringing in community mentors or substitutes to cover classes during planning periods. Clearly, plans of this type are easiest to institute at the start of a school year. During teaming workshops, we often assign teams the task of finding a time they can meet for planning. Even without a schoolwide plan, a small core team can usually find a time before school, after school, or even over lunch when members agree to meet. When a specialist belongs to several teams or works with teams in other buildings, planning meetings will need to be supplemented by other modes of communication, including e-mail, voicemail, fax, or "buddies" who stay in touch with absent team members.

Core Team Members Practice Role Release

Whether teams adopt a skills-based or more constructivist approach, language and literacy instruction is best provided throughout the day in thematic units, content area instruction, and the incidental instruction that permeates language-rich environments (Cantrell, 1999; Carbo & Kapinus, 1995; Lenski, Wham, & Griffey, 1998). In loosely organized teams, educators have few opportunities to share their expertise with one another, so students who most need effective instruction receive instead a series of disconnected services.

In collaborative teams, core team members intentionally share the knowledge and skills associated with their disciplines in a process known as *role release* (Lyon & Lyon, 1980). Role release can occur at many points during lesson planning and instruction. During planning, all team members expand their knowledge base when

In collaborative teams, core team members intentionally share the knowledge and skills associated with their disciplines in a process known as role release *(Lyon & Lyon, 1980).*

they share varied perspectives and explain specific strategies. During instruction, team members model and observe new strategies, both incidentally and in demonstration lessons. Exchanging roles and discussing methods, successes, and challenges extends knowledge and skill development. Role release enables all members of the team to plan and provide instruction that is comprehensive, thereby meeting the needs of more children. Research shows that classroom teachers expand their use of instructional strategies as they spend more time with specialists (deBettencourt, 1999), but that specialists still need to actively promote classroom implementation (Noell & Witt, 1999).

In the lesson described at the start of this chapter, responsibilities were divided to take advantage of the speech therapist's and the sign language interpreter's expertise. At the same time, the classroom teacher shared information about—and both specialists learned about—the second-grade curriculum and new strategies related to literacy instruction. In another lesson, the classroom teacher would incorporate strategies routinely used by these specialists. When another school or class includes a literacy specialist, ESL teacher, and/or special educator in the core team, these specialists would also engage in role release with the classroom teacher.

Scheduling for Collaborative Teamwork

The first part of this chapter alluded to several organizational supports for a model of collaborative teamwork, ranging from philosophical beliefs about students, teaching, and teamwork that make up the school culture, to practical arrangements such as team planning time that are part of the school structure. Another important structural support for collaborative teamwork is the way services are scheduled. As discussed previously, every effort should be made to identify a small core team and concentrate these resources within a classroom. We recommend three principles to guide scheduling of this classroom-based support:

1. *Class makeup reflects the same proportion of children with disabilities or differences in language and literacy learning as would be found in the school as a whole.* For example, a school district might have 12% of students receiving special education, 18% receiving Title I services,

and 10% receiving ESL services—a total of 40% of students who need special support. When all students are educated in regular education classrooms, natural proportions indicate that 10 students in a class of 25 require extra support. Looking at language and literacy needs collectively, students with similar needs can be clustered in general education classrooms to facilitate teaming with specialists who can best meet those students' needs. For example, one class might have a total of 10 students with special needs in reading, and the classroom teacher and a literacy specialist are the core team. In another class, five students might have learning or behavior disabilities, and five students might be learning English as a second language; the core team would consist of the classroom teacher, a special education teacher, and an ESL teacher. Bilingual teachers or teachers with dual certification (e.g., in elementary education and literacy, or in social studies and special education) would bring different strengths and require different supports.

Respect for natural proportions keeps general education classes from becoming de facto special classes, while thoughtful clustering (and keeping the classroom team small) allows specialists to concentrate their efforts in fewer classes. Usually specialists co-teach in no more than three classrooms at the elementary level. (We define "co-teaching" as a general education teacher and a specialist, together, teaching a heterogeneous group of students in a general education setting [see Bauwens & Hourcade, 1995].) A schedule illustrating this arrangement for an elementary school is discussed later in this section. In middle schools, specialists are usually assigned to a team and co-teach one section of each content area course: language arts, social studies, math, and science. Although this requires preparation for and teaching in four different classes, the middle school emphasis on the team and common planning time makes this workable. When two specialists support a team, they may divide responsibilities for course coverage; for example, one supports two sections of language arts and social studies while the other supports two sections of math and science.

2. Specialists and classroom teachers co-teach every day. For specialists to be effective members of the classroom team, they commit to be in the same class for the same time or subject every day. They spend a minimum of 60 minutes per day in each elementary classroom, or one period per day in a middle school classroom. During that time they may work with an individual child who needs their services, with heterogeneous small groups, or with the whole class. They plan instruction with the classroom teacher, so their respective responsibilities and roles are well coordinated. When few students require a service, such as occupational therapy for a child with a physical disability, the specialist works in the classroom less often (e.g., once a week) for the largest possible block of time (e.g., 2 hours). During that time, the specialist observes demands of the class routine, teaches the student to respond to those demands, develops adaptations for demands that exceed the student's current abilities, and engages in role release with other classroom staff who incorporate the specialist's strategies into ongoing instruction. The classroom teacher and specialist must also plan together if this time is to be used effectively.

3. *Every specialist is considered a potential co-teacher.* In an inclusive school, every child with special needs is educated in the regular education classroom. This includes children with behavior problems and those with multiple disabilities. The classroom team takes full ownership for every child and designs instruction and supports to meet students' individual needs. Because there are no resource rooms or special classes, teachers who were once confined to a class for a handful of children are now available to support those students in regular education classrooms. Some schools may lack the personnel resources to schedule sufficient classroom support; more often, available resources become compartmentalized in ways that make them unavailable. To implement this model, every specialist in the school must be available for co-teaching.

Some schools may lack the personnel resources to schedule sufficient classroom support; more often, available resources become compartmentalized in ways that make them unavailable.... Every specialist in the school must be available for co-teaching.

Table 1 shows part of the schedule of classroom-based support services for an inclusive elementary school. This school enrolls about 400 children; approximately 70% are bilingual, and about half of these have limited English proficiency. Students with disabilities make up 11% of the population. Effective literacy instruction is a major challenge for this school. The school structure, with several multi-age classes, facilitates an educational program based on differentiated curriculum and individualized instruc-

TABLE 1
Schedule for Classroom-Based Support

Time Block	Grade								
	K	1–2	1–2 (Bilingual)	2–3	2–3	3–4	3–4	4–5 (Bilingual)	4–5
9:00 a.m.	Speech	SpEd 1	BiPar	Para		SpPar1 Para	SpPar2	BiPar	SpEd2
10:00 a.m.		SpEd 1	BiPar	SpPar2	Para	SpPar1	Para	BiPar	SpEd2 Speech
11:00 a.m.	Lunch	Lunch	Lunch	SpEd1	Para	SpPar1 SpEd2	Para		BiPar
12:00 p.m.		BiPar	Speech	Lunch	Lunch	Lunch	Lunch	Lunch	Lunch
1:00 p.m.	BiPar	BiPar Speech		SpEd1	Para	SpPar1 Para	SpEd2	BiPar	SpPar2
2:00 p.m.	BiPar	SpEd 1	BiPar	Para	Speech	SpPar1 Para	SpEd2		SpPar2 BiPar

This example is abbreviated to keep the table to a manageable size, but it presents a representative sample of classes and staff.

Bilingual, bilingual classroom teacher; *SpEd 1*, special education teacher assigned to lower elementary grades; *SpEd 2*, special education teacher assigned to upper elementary grades; *Speech*, speech therapist (Tuesdays and Thursdays only); *Para*, paraprofessional (each shared between two classes); *BiPar*, bilingual paraprofessional; *SpPar1*, special education paraprofessional to support student with autism; *SpPar2*, special education paraprofessional to support students with mild disabilities.

tion. Students needing special education and/or bilingual education are clustered so appropriate supports can be provided in general education classrooms. Bilingual classroom teachers and paraprofessionals support students with limited English proficiency by providing instruction in both Spanish and English. Additional support comes from general education paraprofessionals shared between classrooms. For the classes shown in the schedule, two special education teachers, two special education paraprofessionals, and a part-time speech therapist provide support by co-teaching in the general education classroom. The speech therapist co-teaches in 1-hour blocks in five different classrooms, two times a week. The special education teachers each co-teach in two classrooms 2 hours or more daily. One special education teacher also works as a consultant teacher in a Grade 3–4 class, monitoring a student with autism and three children with mild disabilities, and practicing role release with the special education paraprofessional assigned to the class.

In this school, specialists and paraprofessionals are assigned to classes according to the needs of students clustered in general education classes and the instructional content for which classroom teachers desire support. The staffing schedule in Table 1 generally reflects the same type and number of specialists available in this school before adoption of the co-teaching model, but now specialists provide support in general education rather than working in separate therapy or resource rooms. Another school, with different needs and different resources, might have a different configuration of classroom-based support.

Providing an Individualized Education

With specialists scheduled to provide classroom-based supports, classroom teams can plan instruction that meets the unique learning needs of all students. Tables 2 and 3 show language arts units for a first-grade and a fifth-grade class, respectively, in another school where inclusive education is provided through a collaborative team approach. Many of the principles discussed in this chapter are illustrated in these two unit plans. Each example shows a thematic unit that addresses numerous language and literacy goals from the general education cur-

TABLE 2
Language Arts Plan for First-Grade Class
(Theme: Traditions; Topics: 1. Birthdays, 2. "Real" and "fantasy" as traditions in literature)

Activity	Goals from First-Grade Curriculum	Instructional Strategies	Individualization for Student With Speech/Language and Learning Disabilities[a]	Individualization for Students With Moderate Disability[b]	Integration of Support
Homework: collect birthdays of family members	Word recognition: months, days	Authentic learning: personal family birthday information will be used in activities	Produce "th" and "z" (e.g., Thursday)	Identify family members in pictures taken at birthday parties	Families: fostering the home-school partnership
Whole Class Reading: with Big Book *The Monster Party*	Word recognition: *what, can, do, little, this* Contractions: *can't, that's* Phonemic awareness: *w, m, j*	Activate prior knowledge: list kinds of parties (e.g, birthday) Choral reading: provides model Predictive literature: provides repetitive pattern	Learn patterns for "wh" questions	Identify (point to) pictures of cake, Jell-O, monster Press switch on Big Mac to play tape in choral reading ("What can this little monster do?")	Classroom teacher Paraprofessional
Journal Writing: What can people do?	Use punctuation: *?* Handwriting Beginning spelling skills Word recognition: verbs	Activate prior knowledge: talk about special talents that people have Provide models/ cues: write words children might use on blackboard (*teacher, doctor*)	Write sentences with "wh" question form Accommodation: use "label maker" to type words	Identify (point to) pictures of actions when named and paste on journal page Hold glue stick and rub on picture held by peer or teacher	Classroom teacher Paraprofessional

(continued)

TABLE 2 (continued)
Language Arts Plan for First-Grade Class
(Theme: Traditions; Topics: 1. Birthdays, 2. "Real" and "fantasy" as traditions in literature)

Activity	Goals from First-Grade Curriculum	Instructional Strategies	Individualization for Student With Speech/Language and Learning Disabilities[a]	Individualization for Students With Moderate Disability[b]	Integration of Support
Math Center: graph ages of family members, compute differences in ages	Addition and subtraction of two-digit numbers	Direct instruction	Accommodation: calculator and manipulatives available	Paste strips on chart to represent ages of family members. Learn concepts: *little, big* (chart materials premade by paraprofessional)	Paraprofessional
Language Arts Center: use context cues to read sentences with selected words covered	Strategies to improve comprehension. Phonemic awareness: *w, m, j* Word recognition: *this, little, do, what, can*	Direct instruction Reading Recovery strategy: using context cues	Conjoin verbs (e.g., "He can run and jump.")	Given a picture of the action, use two switches to answer yes/no questions (e.g., "Is the boy running?")	Classroom teacher
Listening Center: listen to related stories (e.g., "There's a Monster Under My Bed")	Word recognition	Good reading models	Book selected at individual level	Use switch to activate story on computer rather than do center activity (peer partner needed)	Peers
Role Play: retell story with different story elements (e.g., ending, character, verbs)	Oral language: rising intonation in questions Prediction: outcomes	Story retelling: increase comprehension and internalize story elements (e.g., characters, setting ending)	Conjoin verbs in sentences Improve articulation: "th" (birthday) "s" (monster, sing, dance)	Take turn in role play by pressing Big Mac switch (role selected based on concept to be reinforced)	Speech therapist

Activity	Goals from First-Grade Curriculum	Instructional Strategies	Individualization for Student With Speech/Language and Learning Disabilities[a]	Individualization for Students With Moderate Disability[b]	Integration of Support
Individual Work: paste words starting with M inside the monster's face, words starting with W outside the face	Phonemic awareness: *m, w*; Word recognition	Independent practice; 1:1 review with each student	Use correct pronunciation of "s" and "th" in words; Learn site words at his or her reading level: pre-first	Identify eyes, nose mouth, ears; Paste on monster's face	Classroom teacher
Class Discussion of Fear: discuss the feeling of "fear" or "afraid," and concepts of "real" and "pretend"	Understand concepts of dreams, nightmares, pretend and real	Graphic organizers used to enhance understanding of "pretend" and "real"	Ask "wh" questions	Introduce to concepts of happy, sad, afraid, and the pictures that represent them (to be used on augmentative communication device)	Social worker; Classroom teacher
Decorate Monster Muffins: children mix frosting of different colors, decorate monster muffins, and have a monster party	Take turns; Follow directions using measurement terms (e.g., 1 teaspoon, 1/2 cup)	Demonstration by teacher; Hands-on activity	Learn concepts of "first," "next"	Use (strengthen) grasp to mix and spread frosting; Identify eyes, nose, mouth	Classroom teacher; Paraprofessional; Peers

a These are IEP goals unique to this child. The child would still be expected to learn most of the goals in the first-grade curriculum.

b These IEP goals are alternatives to the regular education curriculum. This student would not be expected to learn goals from the general education curriculum, but would participate in the same activities.

TABLE 3
Language Arts Plan for Fifth-Grade Class
(Theme: Traditions; Topic: Mysteries and Clues)

Activity	Goals from Fifth-Grade Curriculum	Instructional Strategies	Individualization for Student With Learning Disability[a]	Individualization for Students With Severe Disability[b]	Integration of Support
Language Arts: after literature presentation of an Encyclopedia Brown mystery, students draw a map and write four clues to discover a treasure hidden in the school	Write directions using modifiers	Examples generated by class left on blackboard as cues	Generate and copy complete sentences Sequence four pieces of information Accommodation: dictate sentences to teacher	Identify symbols for rooms in school Accommodation: paste pictures of rooms on map of school (Boardmaker program)	Classroom teacher Special education teacher Paraprofessional (available for 1:1 support if needed)
Vocabulary: students work in cooperative groups to design a role play that uses a new vocabulary word and illustrates its meaning	Learn new vocabulary related to literature or content areas Practice oral language skills Cooperative group skill: everyone must participate	Active learning: visualization	Find word in dictionary	Wait for turn in group Press switch on Big Mac to participate in role play (play tape of part)	Classroom teacher Paraprofessional

Activity	Goals from Fifth-Grade Curriculum	Instructional Strategies	Individualization for Student With Learning Disability[a]	Individualization for Students With Severe Disability[b]	Integration of Support
Social Studies: Three Ancient Civilizations: Mound Builders, Aztecs, Olmecs Small-group discussions (one group/civilization)	Learn how artifacts can be clues to solving mysteries of ancient civilizations	Each group creates a graphic organizer to illustrate how artifacts were used as clues to learn about their ancient civilization	Learn sight words Learn to compare and contrast Accommodation: copy information from graphic organizer	Identify (point to when named) pictures of common items associated with civilizations (corn, tree) Paste on graphic organizer	Classroom teacher Special education teacher

[a] These are IEP goals unique to this child. The child would still be expected to learn most of the goals in the fifth-grade curriculum.

[b] These IEP goals are alternatives to the regular education curriculum. This student would not be expected to learn goals from the general education curriculum, but would participate in the same activities.

riculum using a variety of instructional strategies. Both examples incorporate all seven elements of effective literacy instruction outlined earlier in this chapter (as recommended by Carbo & Kapinus, 1995). Both examples also show goals and accommodations that have been individualized for students who require more support for their language and literacy development, as well as the staff who would support these students during each lesson. (See Tomlinson [1999] for guidance on individualization as a strategy to address the needs of all students in a class.)

Decisions about who will provide support and when are also individualized. For example, the fifth-grade team agreed that the special education teacher should co-teach during the portion of language arts that provided most opportunity to work on individualized education plan (IEP) goals and objectives for six students with special needs. During social studies, additional support was also needed due to the difficulty of concepts being taught, the high reading level of materials being used, and the very low reading levels of several students. Extra help would be needed to provide all students with access to the general education curriculum, as required by the Individuals with Disabilities Education Act (1997). Having the special education teacher co-teach social studies offered further opportunities to reinforce IEP goals and objectives, and to practice role release with the fifth-grade teacher and the paraprofessional assigned to a student with severe disabilities.

Outcomes

Although there is little published research on the efficacy of the models described in this chapter, there is an extensive pool of data from state Title I school improvement projects and special education statewide systems change projects. Some of these data do demonstrate efficacy of team approaches to educating children at risk for school failure and children with disabilities. These are not designed as controlled studies and, typically, the special education projects are not specifically designed to accelerate or evaluate progress in reading. Nonetheless, performance data show improvements that suggest growing competence in reading. One example comes from our work with a school district that adopted a collaborative team approach to support all students, including those with the greatest needs, in general education classes. This small district had approximately 920 students, with 32% eligible for Title I services and 7% receiving special education. Project evaluation data (England, 1997) showed the following:

- On state achievement tests, the general student body performed as well or better in inclusive education programs as when students were removed for special services. With appropriate supports, inclusive education had no negative impact.

- Title I teachers reported that the students they had previously pulled out for services made significant progress in reading and math achievement during co-teaching, benefited by not missing classroom activities, and showed increased self-esteem.

- Students with learning disabilities, whose IEP objectives related primarily to reading and writing, achieved an equal or greater proportion of their IEP objectives in inclusive education.

- The high school dropout rate declined from 25% to 35% during the last 2 years of pull-out services, to 7% to 12% in the first 2 years of inclusive education and collaborative teamwork.

Although none of these results specifically document accelerated reading, they do show overall improvements that are unlikely without growing competence in reading. Furthermore, these early data do suggest trends that are expected to continue as innovations become part of the school culture.

Conclusions

Adopting the changes outlined in this chapter requires professional collaboration that is planned, ongoing, and supported by both school culture and school structure. Some schools may lack the personnel resources to establish and maintain the kind of teaching partnerships described here but, more often, schools have defined neither a model of ongoing collaboration nor the organizational arrangements required to support collaboration among the education professionals concerned with language and literacy development. Without a clearly defined service delivery model, it is impossible to evaluate implementation or interpret results. Without scheduling that puts specialists in general education classrooms on a regular basis, classroom teachers and parents who support the concept of inclusion are often justified in their concerns about whether staffing is adequate to provide appropriate education for children with diverse needs within the general education classroom (Freeman, Alkin, & Kasari, 1999; Scruggs & Mastropieri, 1996).

We have described a model of collaboration that facilitates classroom-based support for students with special needs in language and literacy learning. Examples of staff schedules and unit plans illustrate how existing staff can be used more effectively to help design and deliver comprehensive instruction that meets the needs of all students. Although this model has not been studied in controlled research designs, analyses of extant data suggest positive trends in student achievement when schools adopt this model.

References

Allington, R.L., & McGill-Franzen, A. (1989). School response to reading failure: Instruction for Chapter 1 and special education students in grades 2, 4, and 8. *The Elementary School Journal, 89*(5), 529–543.

Anderson, L.W., & Pellicer, L.O. (1990). Synthesis of research in compensatory and remedial education. *Educational Leadership, 48*(1), 10–16.

Bauwens, J., & Hourcade, J.J. (1995). *Cooperative teaching: Rebuilding the schoolhouse for all students.* Austin, TX: Pro-Ed.

Cantrell, S.C. (1999). Effective teaching and literacy learning: A look inside primary classrooms. *The Reading Teacher, 52*(4), 370–378.

Carbo, M., & Kapinus, B. (1995). Strategies for increasing achievement in reading. In R. Cole (Ed.), *Educating everybody's children* (pp. 75–98). Alexandria, VA: Association for Supervision and Curriculum Development.

deBettencourt, L.U. (1999). General educators' attitudes toward students with mild disabilities and their use of instructional strategies: Implications for training. *Remedial and Special Education, 20*(1), 27–35.

England, J. (1997). *School change portfolio: Maries County R-II School District.* Pittsburgh, PA: Allegheny Singer Research Institute, Consortium on Inclusive Schooling.

Espin, C.A., Deno, S.L., & Albayrak-Kaymak, D. (1998). Individualized education programs in resource and inclusive settings: How "individualized" are they? *Journal of Special Education, 32*(3), 164–174.

Freeman, S.F.N., Alkin, M.C., & Kasari, C.L. (1999). Satisfaction and desire for change in educational placement for children with Down syndrome: Perceptions of parents. *Remedial and Special Education, 20*(3), 143–151.

Giangreco, M.F. (1996). *VISTA: Vermont interdependent services team approach: A guide to coordinating educational support services.* Baltimore: Paul H. Brookes.

Giangreco, M.F., Edelman, S.W., Luiselli, T.E., & McFarland, S.Z.C. (1997). Helping or hovering? Effects of instructional assistant proximity on students with disabilities. *Exceptional Children, 64*(1), 7–18.

Individuals with Disabilities Education Act Amendments of 1997. Pub. L. No. 105–117, 20 U.S.C. 1400 *et seq.* (1997).

Jenkins, J.R., Jewell, M., Leicester, N., O'Connor, R.E., Jenkins, L.M., & Troutner, N.M. (1994). Accommodations for individual differences without classroom ability groups: An experiment in school restructuring. *Exceptional Children, 60*(4), 344–358.

Kauffman, J.M., & Hallahan, D.P. (1995). *The illusion of full inclusion: A comprehensive critique of a current special education bandwagon.* Austin, TX: Pro-Ed.

Kovaleski, J.F., Gickling, E.E., Morrow, H., & Swank, P.R. (1999). High versus low implementation of instructional support teams. A case for maintaining program fidelity. *Remedial and Special Education, 20*(3), 170–183.

Lenski, S.D., Wham, M.A., & Griffey, D.C. (1998). Literacy orientation survey: A survey to clarify teachers' beliefs and practices. *Reading Research and Instruction, 37*(3), 217–236.

Lyon, S., & Lyon, G. (1980). Team functioning and staff development: A role release approach to providing integrated educational services for severely handicapped students. *Journal of the Association for the Severely Handicapped, 5*(3), 250–263.

McGregor, G., & Vogelsberg, R.T. (1998). *Inclusive schooling practices: Pedagogical and research foundations.* Baltimore: Paul H. Brookes.

Noell, G.H., & Witt, J.C. (1999). When does consultation lead to intervention implementation? Critical issues for research and practice. *Journal of Special Education, 33*(1), 29–35.

Rainforth, B., & York-Barr, J. (1997). *Collaborative teams for students with severe disabilities: Integrating therapy and educational services* (2nd ed.). Baltimore: Paul H. Brookes.

Scruggs, T.E., & Mastropieri, M.A. (1996). Teacher perceptions of mainstreaming/inclusion, 1958–1995: A research synthesis. *Exceptional Children, 63*(1), 59–74.

Tomlinson, C.A. (1999). *The differentiated classroom: Responding to the needs of all learners.* Alexandria, VA: Association for Supervision and Curriculum Development.

U.S. Department of Education. (1995). *Extending learning time for disadvantaged students: Vol. 1. Summary of promising practices.* Washington, DC: Author.

Waite, L.T. (1997, April). *Policy 97-03: Provision of specially designed reading instruction to students with disabilities.* Albany, NY: The State Education Department.

Emphasizing Differences to Build Cultural Understandings

Patricia Ruggiano Schmidt

"We are all so much alike in our little school, I wonder how an emphasis on diversity could build classroom community. I'm also skeptical about the link between an appreciation of diversity and literacy development." Johanna, a reading specialist in a rural, northeastern U.S. K–5 school, where 40% of the children receive free or reduced breakfasts and lunches, expressed her misgivings after designing a plan for connecting home and school as part of graduate work in education. However, she decided to implement the ideas when she realized that the school's push-in and pull-out programs gave her access to most classrooms. This fact allowed her opportunities for influencing many teachers and children.

Kelly, a teacher in an urban, northeastern U.S. pre-K–5 elementary school, where 90% of the children qualify for free or reduced breakfasts and lunches, also wondered about her own plan to connect home and school for literacy learning as part of her graduate work in education. She questioned, "The children in our classroom are from ethnically and culturally diverse backgrounds and many have special learning needs. How can emphasizing differences build classroom community?" But Kelly decided to go forward with the plan when the special education teacher and teaching assistant in the inclusive second- and third-grade classroom agreed to support her ideas.

oth Kelly and Johanna had been graduate students in my multicultural literacy learning course, in which the model known as the ABC's of Cultural Understanding and Communication (Schmidt, 1998b) was the focus of all assignments. They became involved in the following process:

- Autobiography is written with key life events related to education, family, religious tradition, recreation, victories, and defeats (Banks, 1994).

- Biography is written after interviewing a person who is culturally different. Information is gathered after several in-depth semi-structured interviews (Spradley, 1979).

- Cross-cultural analyses are charted of similarities and differences between the two life stories (Spindler & Spindler, 1987).

- Cultural differences are analyzed by writing about the differences that stimulate feelings of personal admiration and/or discomfort.

- Connections between home and school are designed for the classroom and school based on adaptations of autobiography, biography, cross-cultural analyses, and cultural differences.

Upon completing the autobiography, biography, cross-cultural analyses, and analysis of cultural differences, most teachers point to the importance of appreciating differences and thus the need for collaboration between home and school communities (Schmidt, 1998b; 1998c). "Know thyself and understand others" is a phrase often used to express their reflections on the process as they begin creating their own plans for connecting home and school. They soon see ways to adapt autobiography, biography, and the analysis of similarities and differences to encourage reading, writing, listening, and speaking activities in their classes to connect home and school.

After discussing Johanna's and Kelly's home-school connection designs, I urged both to execute their plans with a promise of my support through observations, journal entries, and consultations. What developed was a collegial relationship as I learned about their collaboration with teachers, families, administrators, community members, and children.

The ABC's Model and the Sociocultural Perspective

The ABC's Model was derived from the sociocultural perspective, a constructivist approach to literacy development (Heath, 1983; Rogoff, 1986; Vygotsky, 1978), and research aimed at preparing teachers for understanding and appreciating diverse groups of people (Banks, 1994; Cochran-Smith, 1995; Florio-Ruane, 1994; Noordhoff & Kleinfield, 1993; Sjoberg & Kuhn, 1989; Spindler & Spindler, 1987; Tatum, 1992; Zeichner, 1993). Often teachers in U.S. schools are from European American middle class backgrounds and have not been prepared to work with children and families who live in poverty or those from diverse ethnic and cultural backgrounds. Consequently, home-school connections may be weak, and the children's literacy development may suffer (Delpit, 1995; Edwards, 1999; Ladson-Billings, 1994; Schmidt, 1998a).

> *Often teachers in U.S. schools are from European American middle-class backgrounds and have not been prepared to work with children and families who live in poverty or those from diverse ethnic and cultural backgrounds.*

Similar to many literacy researchers (such as Bloome & Green, 1982; Green, Kantor & Rogers, 1990), teachers who have experienced the ABC's Model often realize that everyday life in the classroom is determined by social interactions that connect home and school knowledge. The children in their classrooms are comfortable bringing ideas and artifacts from home and see that their family literacies and cultures are valued. As a result the classroom environment becomes a strong community for literacy development (Dyson, 1993; Edwards, 1999).

The purpose of this chapter is to describe what occurred when Johanna and Kelly implemented their home-school collaborative plans based on the ABC's Model.

Johanna's and Kelly's Study

The study of Johanna's and Kelly's classrooms is reported following the qualitative tradition (Lincoln & Guba, 1985) and documents how two European American teachers collaborated to create literacy learning environments that benefited "typical" students and students with special needs in high poverty rural and urban schools. During the year, Johanna and Kelly kept personal journals of reflections, copies of lesson plans, and students' work. Kelly also tape recorded student discussions. Both teachers individually reported project progress to me through e-mail and personal interviews in their schools and my office. Furthermore, my field notes, recorded after participant observations in the schools, gave additional information and insights. This study was a collaborative effort.

Data analysis occurred from the beginning of Johanna's and Kelly's data collection. We coded and categorized data separately and together as it became available. Through inductive analysis (Bogdan & Biklen, 1994), patterns emerged and formed themes linked to collaboration that allowed all children, even those labeled as having special needs in oral and written expression, to experience success while completing the ABC's literacy activities.

Collaboration and Johanna's Plan

When this study began, Johanna was in her second year as a reading specialist in the northeastern United States, where higher standards for education and new testing instruments were being imposed simultaneously. Additionally, no extra education funds were allocated to assist in meeting the new standards. Needless to say, anxiety reigned in her school, as well as many other schools across the state, as teachers attempted to prepare students for the unknown. The fourth-grade teachers in Johanna's school were particularly interested in her knowledge of literacy development because sample questions from the state's new fourth-grade English language arts exam included reading, writing, listening, and speaking activities with an emphasis on process rather than product. Teachers in kindergarten through third grade also felt the pressure to prepare their students for fourth-grade language arts as they worked with student literacy learning.

Johanna's experiences with the autobiography, biography, and cultural analyses portions of the ABC's Model stimulated ideas for creating a plan in collaboration with the teachers and principal. Kindergarten through fourth-grade teachers and Johanna agreed to coordinate lesson planning before school, after school, and during lunch periods. It was established that she would meet with classes 2 days a week, introduce lessons, and bring them to closure. She and the classroom teachers would circulate and support all children during individual, paired, and small-group lesson activities. In the afternoons, when Johanna met with the children who were pulled out of classes for special literacy needs, she would follow individual remediation plans and reinforce what she was teaching in the classes.

Kindergarten and First-Grade ABC's Literacy Activities Study Differences

Johanna visited the K–1 classrooms and read literature related to differences—such as Archambault's *Grandmother's Garden* and Simon's *Why Am I Different?* and *All Kinds of Families*—to give children opportunities to talk about differences, become critical viewers and listeners, and relate their own experiences to stories. When Johanna read *All the Colors of the Earth* by Hamanaka, the children drew self-portraits using their crayons to study skin tones of classmates; shades of pink, peach, and tan, as well as albino white and Korean coffee skin colors, were examined and discussed. Then children shared other characteristics and charted their discoveries. (See the examples in Figure 1.)

Johanna heard the children tell about themselves and their families as they openly described their lives. She expressed her thoughts about children's opportunities to converse in the classroom: "It's amazing how many one-word answers I get from the children with special needs, but when I probe a little, they tell stories. Getting children with special needs in written and oral language to share verbally enables them to express themselves in writing as well as listening and reading."

The charts set the stage for students to create autobiographies that explained their stories through drawings and writing. These were read to each other throughout the next week. As the children became knowledgeable about their classmates, they discussed characteristics of each other's lives.

FIGURE 1
Characteristics Chart

How We Look	Food We Like	Our Homes
Red hair	Macaroni and cheese	Tents
Curly hair	Pizza	Apartments
Pointy ears	Plums	Farmhouse
Tall/short	Oranges	Cabin
Freckles	Doughnuts	Trailer
Tannish skin	Venison	Duplex

What We Can Do	Our Families	Parent's Work
Sword fight (imagine)	Mom, Dad, brother, animals	Carpenter
Swim in deep water	Mom, Dad, three brothers	Banker
Color	Dad	Cableman
Swim with no floaties	Mother, two brothers, Dad,	Handyman
Whistle	Mom	Veterinarian
Roller skate	Grandpa, Grandma	Teacher's aide
Ride dirt bike	Mother, two brothers, Dad,	Farmer
Ride Mom's bike for two	Aunt and our cat	Homemaker

Additionally, Johanna introduced the Venn diagram by using a large example on the chalkboard. She chose two children as models and drew pictures in the diagrams of their hair, eyes, mouth, freckles, moles, and birthmarks, showing similarities and differences. Then all the children worked in pairs filling in their own Venn diagrams. Each wrote his or her name over one circle and then drew their similarities in the intersecting portion. Individual differences were placed outside the intersection. From this experience, the children collaborated for the creation of class books titled *All the Colors of Our Class*, with one page devoted to each child's uniqueness. Furthermore, Venn diagrams became an integral part of future classroom activities as children begged to continue using them to demonstrate similar and different holidays, food portions, guests, distances from school, literature, and weather.

Finally, a study of famous women stimulated collaboration among families, teachers, and students. The teachers decided that children should become aware of the important contributions of women in their lives as well as women in history. Johanna read Hearne's *Seven Brave Women*, and at the same time introduced the contributions of other brave women in the United States. Then the children told stories about the special women in their lives, wrote or drew about them, and invited them to come to class and explain their work, hobbies, and interests. Cousins, aunts, grandmothers, mothers, sisters, and friends were celebrated in a booklet that was sent home to families.

Second- and Third-Grade ABC's Literacy Activities Develop Cultural Awareness

When Johanna began planning lessons in collaboration with the second- and third-grade teachers, curriculum objectives were related to cultures and geographic locations around the world. Again, Johanna followed adaptations of the ABC's model and began discussions around student lives and interests. Children practiced jotting notes on individual charts that included information concerning their environment, geography, homes, families, likes and dislikes, abilities, favorite entertainment, problems, fears, and responsibilities. They read their notes, created Venn diagrams, and recorded information in small groups and pairs. Additionally, Johanna read folktales from around the world as well as folklore from the northeastern United States. The children learned to compare and contrast the cultures and people of their region with others around the world. Maps and globes became a central focus in classrooms and, through charts and Venn diagrams, children began seeing relationships between where one lives and how one lives. The art teacher also collaborated by introducing examples and activities from various cultures, so children might copy designs and make reproductions.

Because the third-grade curriculum emphasized desert and rainforest studies, Johanna and the teachers chose to focus on these regions found on the African continent. Folktales and folklore were read as children investigated the African people's lives. They compared and contrasted their own lives with the desert and rainforest peoples by listing similarities and differences and writing compare-and-contrast paragraphs. As a final activity, the children composed letters to imaginary children in the United States from the perspectives of rainforest or desert peoples. The following is an example of an actual letter written by a third-grade student labeled with special needs (pseudonyms are used throughout this chapter), from the perspective of a young boy of the Ituri Tribe:

Dear Briant

Im form the Ituri tribe. Im nine yers old. Do you have any pets? I have two birds. Wat is the bes thing you lik to do? My home has trees, anumls and shelter. My hom has houses all arond, trees, weeds. My food is met, cadopilars, vegatibals. I have to hunt, fish, trad. For entertainment I dance, play insturments, play gams. Problemes are hunters, deforestatuon, poson foods. My job is to cary wood for the fre place and my favoit job is carin my baby sistr especely. I like that job

Sincerely, Efee (Thomas)

Efee (Thomas) and other students in the class shared letters with a partner and checked the accuracy of information in their nonfiction and realistic fiction centers.

During the year, teachers also read novels to their classes, such as *My Side of the Mountain* and *Dog Song*. The children researched information from references brought in by the school librarian to examine similarities and differences between their own life experiences and those of children from different geographic locations.

SCHOOLWIDE COLLABORATION. Finally, the third-grade study of Africa was reinforced by schoolwide events. During the spring, *The Soul of Africa* international art show came to a nearby urban center. Johanna, the art teacher, the librarian, third-grade classroom teachers, and the principal decided that this was a great opportunity for the entire school. As a result of their collaboration, many types of children's literature based on nations across the African continent were read. Children throughout the school learned Bantu and Swahili vocabulary and explored the artistic elements and style of basket weaving, jewelry making, painting, carving, and African home building. A popular family evening program of African cultures evolved with song and dance performances and displays of the children's art. Model homes of the desert and rainforest, as well as pictures of the many great cities and suburbs appeared in classrooms and hallways. A giant geographical and political map of the African continent produced by third-, fourth-, and fifth-grade children took center stage.

Fourth-Grade ABC's Literacy Activities Compare and Contrast Interviews

Similar to the second and third grades, the fourth grades began the year with locating and discussing the origins of folktales and folklore from around the world. These activities lead to paragraph writing that compared and contrasted similarities and differences between their lives and favorite stories and those of children from different parts of the world. Following these literacy activities, Johanna, the teachers, and students collaborated to bring parents to school for interviews. Students studied interview questions before the guests arrived and practiced appropriate introductions and courtesies. Several Native American parents from eastern and western regions in the United States shared Oneida, Otoe, and Ioway languages, dances, artifacts, and philosophies in third- through fifth-grade classrooms. Also, an Air Force captain and the principal were interviewed to give the children more perspectives for comparing and contrasting similarities and differences of people.

As a result of the fourth-grade study of the interview process, a collaborative assignment with adult family members emerged. First, children asked family members about likes and dislikes as well as descriptions of growing up in years past. During class, the children wrote discoveries and reported them in small groups. This evoked questions that led to more in-depth interviews and stimulated return visits by parents with new questions for the interviewees to answer.

Next, the children selected a culture from their own heritage, interviewed other family members, studied family artifacts, searched the Internet, and read magazines, maps, biographies, and encyclopedias. Upon sharing information in pairs and small groups, diversity of family heritages became apparent. Children then suggested that family members be invited to class to tell their stories.

A mother and father from the Cherokee Nation and mothers from Korea and England agreed to class visits and interviews. The class members took notes, wrote the interviewees' stories, and read them in class. Similarities and differences again were the focus of reports, but differences were accented as positive and interesting realities.

FAMILY STUDY GROUP. During the winter months, Johanna created a successful study group in collaboration with parents and teachers. On Wednesday evenings from 6:30 to 7:30, parents and teachers met to find ways for parents to help their children with reading, writing, speaking, and studying. At the meetings, parents of children who had a wide range of ability levels from kindergarten through fifth grade actually performed literacy activities and talked about their children's possible responses. From these experiences, discussions of home and school connections allowed parents and teachers to ask and answer questions that provided insights into the teaching and learning process. Johanna saw this collaborative attempt as the beginning of stronger communication between home and school.

Collaboration and Kelly's Plan

Kelly began her fourth year of teaching in an inclusive second/third-grade classroom, teaming with a special education teacher and teaching assistant. The principal appointed her because of past excellent teaching performance and ability to collaborate with others in the building. Kelly's team was expected to plan and execute lessons that supported the progress of not only the 10 children labeled with significant deficits in oral and written language, but also the other 14 students in the classroom. In this high-poverty urban setting, six children were from European American backgrounds, three children were from Latino backgrounds, and 15 children were from African American backgrounds. Furthermore, the pre-K–5 elementary school was experiencing anxiety about the new state education standards as well as the spring testing of English language arts.

Kelly completed the ABC's of Cultural Understanding and Communication 2 years before as part of her graduate studies and continued creating ABC's literacy activities each subsequent year. Now in her new setting, she had concerns about planning with two colleagues and about developing a classroom community with the large number of children labeled as having special literacy learning needs.

Kelly's ABC's Literacy Activities for Building Classroom Community

When Kelly discussed the purpose of the ABC's model with her colleagues, they agreed that the children needed a safe classroom environment where they could share authentic reading, writing, listening, and speaking activities on a daily basis. So, at the beginning of the school year, they initiated the community building process with children sharing stories about their likes and dislikes. Through Venn diagrams and charts, teachers and students, in pairs and small groups, talked and listened, and read and wrote about each other. These collaborative activities generated interest in individuals, helped children become acquainted, and began the community building process. At the same time, Kelly and her colleagues developed a home-school communication plan that included students' reflections on these literacy activities.

Home and School Connections

Weekly, the second/third-grade team sent reports home that highlighted each child's reflections on the week, reviewed portions of the school's mission statements, and explained upcoming class and school events. Families responded by recording their thoughts, suggestions, and recommendations. These seemed to stimulate the team's thinking about the frequency of communication and collaborative family and school activities.

The team then sent home Tuesday night reading activities. This scheduled family event emerged as a major topic in weekly progress reports. At the end of the school year, the team surveyed families about the year's communication. Statements were positive: "You made it easy to talk to you if I had a concern." "Much improvement over last year." "He's getting better and better." "Kept me up to date on my child's progress." "You supported my child and we helped her learn to read." "Reading night was a great idea!"

Literacy Activities for Exploring Similarities and Differences

Kelly and her colleagues focused on world geography and cultures in order to meet second/third-grade curriculum objectives. They decided that the accomplishments, contributions, values, beliefs, and traditions of people living on the plains of East Africa would be especially meaningful to students of color who sometimes are neglected in texts and other teaching materials. Kelly began by reading Kroll's *Masai and I* while the children listened for information. After the story, Kelly, the teachers, and the children collaborated in pairs and small groups to chart and categorize what they learned. Then they all contributed to a class chart. The next day children received individual charts to complete about themselves and the Masai. (See Figure 2.)

Each child noted many obvious differences and drew a picture showing similarities and differences between himself or herself and the Masai. When shared in class, teachers and students learned about each other as they compared and contrasted their own similarities and differences. From this experience, several children were inspired to write illustrated autobiographies.

Animated discussions about differences were typical for these literacy activities, and the work accomplished demonstrated ability levels above what was usual for the children. Kelly and her colleagues

---

FIGURE 2
Masai and I Chart

	Masai	I
Habitat	Huts in a circle	Brick townhouse
Water	Long distances to water hole	Faucet and refrigerator
Hygiene	Rub skin with cow fat and clay	Soap and water
Appearance	Smooth brown skin, black eyes	Smooth brown skin, black eyes
Dessert	Honey guide to beehive	Baked goods and ice cream
Chores	Milk cows	Wash dishes
Pets	Herd of cows	Cats and dogs
Footwear	Buffalo hide sandals	Sneakers, slippers
Transportation	Walk	Car, van, walk, bus

realized that comparing and contrasting similarities and differences is a valuable framework for practicing reading, writing, listening, and speaking, as well as a means for preparing children for the fourth-grade English language arts exams. Therefore, they decided that the next area of concentration would come from the children's own experiences as members of a diverse cultural and ethnic community.

Discovering Children's Perceptions of Similarities and Differences

To begin the project, the teaching team needed to discover what children knew about the major groups of people in the United States. They collected pictures from magazines and books showing African American, Asian American, Latino, and European American adults and children working, playing, studying, and sharing. The pictures of African Americans were introduced first. Each student in the class chose one picture from the group and wrote a story about the people pictured, which resulted in anecdotes that reflected the children's personal experiences. One African American child stated, "This picture only half family." When asked to explain, he clarified, "Cuz a whole family has five or six, like my family." All the children happily read their stories and responded to others with positive comments and questions.

Next Kelly gathered more specific ideas from the students about the different groups of people. The class was divided into small groups, composed of children from diverse cultural backgrounds and ability levels. The teaching team showed pictures and asked, "Tell us about these African American children. Who are these children?" Sample responses included,

> "They is Black kids, African American kids."
>
> "African Americans always wearing hats because they don't like the sun."
>
> "But, we love the sun."
>
> "They live in cities."
>
> "We live all over the place an' we like a lot of colors."

With a map of the African continent and the world, Kelly and the children discussed where African Americans originated and why they might travel and live around the world. When the group talked about similarities and differences, African American skin color was described as different shades of brown, black, and tan. They explained,

> "People think we all look alike."

> "We talk funny an' wear same clothes."

> "Other people think they different, but they want African Americans to be like them, but we don't have money."

Next, the pictures of Asian Americans were examined. The same group of children described the people as Chinese, Japanese, White, or mixed. Several in the group pulled skin back around their eyes and began making sounds mimicking Asian languages. Kelly asked the children to talk about why they were changing their eyes and making different sounds. As they shared information about their physical differences, she demonstrated the sounds made by speaking different languages. Again, she showed on a map of the world where many Asian people live and how they came to the United States. The children added that Asians are smart and know karate. One child commented, "They good fighters."

A few days later, Kelly introduced pictures of Latinos. Typical comments were,

> "They come from Puerto Rico."

> "They don't speak English."

> "They look like us, same skin."

> "They speak another language."

> "They live near my house."

> "Maria is in our class and she Puerto Rican."

> "Maria, tell us 'bout the place."

Kelly asked Maria, an ESL student, if she would like to be interviewed by the class. When Maria beamed and nodded, Kelly contacted Maria's family for permission. They happily obliged with stories and pictures.

The last group presented were the European Americans. The children referred to them simply as Americans. "The White people is jus' people. They is all Americans." When they talked about similarities and differences, they explained that there were other names for White people, such as crackers, Anglos, honkies, and red-necks:

"They honkies cuz they got long necks and red face."

"They crackers, square and white."

"They jealous and racist."

One African American child piped up, "Why we talking about White people? My mother is White." Other comments were,

"My father don't like them. White people don't like us."

"They lie 'bout us. This lady lied and said this Black guy beat her up."

"A White grandmother pick a flower out of her own garden and blame a Black person. She's a witch."

"They call us the 'N' word an' they took our land away."

"White people can't jump. We have more power."

"I play with White people. They fun and they can jump!"

During the days when the group discussions took place, most children tried to clarify or explain certain misconceptions. The six children from European American backgrounds appeared to listen intently and rarely added to the discussions. This was unusual because all six were high-profile participants in other class activities.

Kelly and her colleagues were also shocked by the honesty of children's conversations. They concluded that the children's open discussions and attentiveness to each other were enlightening, and were signs that all felt safe to express their ideas in the classroom community.

Appreciating Similarities and Differences

After Kelly's team gathered ideas about the children's perceptions of people of African American, European American, Asian American, and Latino origins, they decided to stimulate more discussions about similarities and differences. They gathered children's literature related to each group, invited people from the groups to be interviewed by the class, and gave the children opportunities to draw self-portraits using multicultural crayons, which contain skin tone colors from around the world. Tones can be blended and varying crayon pressure can achieve deeper or lighter skin tones. The same questions were repeated:

> How are we alike?
>
> How are we different?
>
> How do you feel about African American people?
>
> How do you feel about Asian American people?
>
> How do you feel about European American people?
>
> How do you feel about Latino people?

As the children read, wrote, listened, and spoke about similarities and differences among people in the community and world, they shared naturally with each other in thoughtful conversations. After several months of collaborative study in ability groups, special interest groups, and pairs, the questions raised and discussions held at whole-class meetings demonstrated a greater depth of understanding. All children participated in the literacy activities and freely expressed themselves. Excerpts from class conversations among eight students from diverse backgrounds and academic abilities follow:

> Student A: Why people mean to Black people?
>
> Student B: Why are people mean to White people?
>
> Student C: In old days people was prejudice. Some people don't respect.
>
> Student D: They try to boss people around.
>
> Student E: White people and Black people went to separate schools.
>
> Student C: In old days, Black people sat in back a the bus and White people was in front.
>
> Student F: Martin Luther King changed that!
>
> Student C: One little girl went ta school an' walk pass the White people. The White teacher help her.
>
> Student G: I think Black people have too many ribs in they heads. They rib an' tease them White people too much.
>
> Student H: I feel happy an' sad 'bout White people. I am happy that they is White an' sad that I Black. I feel mixed.

Student D: Yeah, I wish they's more White people where I live. The Black people crank up music an' I can't sleep.

Student F: Some Black people is good an' some not. Some White people is good an' some not. That the way it is.

All: Yup! Yaaaa!

The children actually carried on a discussion based on personal knowledge and they shared information in order to help each other understand that being different is not bad.

When the same group of children discussed Asian people, an appreciation of differences was revealed.

Student A: Chinese people come to our neighborhood an' some neighbor threw rocks at they house. That not right. I saw her baby an' it cute!

Student B: When people see Asian people, they think they look funny. It's the funny eyes.

Student C: They not funny, jes' different.

Student A: Do they eat roaches?

Student B: Nope, they eat Chinese food.

Student D: They play volleyball, but they can't play basketball.

Student F: Chinese play basketball. They put up a net in the parking lot near my house an' whole bunch of Chinese men come over an' play.

Student E: The Chinese know kung fu and karate. They fight good.

Student F: Who fights good? The Chinese or Japanese? How 'bout Black people an' White people? Some fight good too.

Student A: We all is different. That is good too!

The children began drawing conclusions that expressed an appreciation of differences that seemed to demonstrate more critical thinking.

Later, Puerto Rican children from the school, a third-grade classmate, and a father from Mexico were interviewed formally. The students composed and asked questions that added to their knowledge of people from Latino backgrounds. The following is another conversation among African American and European American children demonstrating the learning of new information:

Student B: They don't all come from Puerto Rico.

Student C: They come from Mexico too.

Student A: They like ta sing an' dance.

Student D: Not all.

Student E: Blacks and Whites sing and dance too.

Student F: Some Latino people speak English an' some don't.

Student B: I like Mr. Martinez. Maria got a smart father.

Student C: They come to this country for school an' weather.

Student D: They miss the beach an' family.

Student E: Some of us been to Puerto Rico.

Student A: I been to Buffalo an' Hawaii, jes' like Maria.

Kelly and her colleagues ended the unit of study by directing the children back to the original pictures about which they had chosen to write stories. They were then asked to write another story about the same pictured people. The resulting narratives were at least twice as long as the first and contained many more specific distinguishing details about the groups of people depicted. Additionally, spelling and grammar showed significant improvement for the children labeled as having special needs in oral and written language.

Conclusions: Communication With Students and Families Builds Classroom Communities

Johanna and Kelly not only collaborated with parents and teachers to create new family communication programs, but they also demonstrated how to get students to read, write, listen, and speak in ways that were directly related to the children's personal lives and experiences. The studies of differences stimulated Johanna's students to share their differences in great detail and generated powerful ideas through authentic dialogue in Kelly's children. Children in Johanna's and Kelly's schools easily shared their home and family stories. The teachers tapped into the homes and families, made them part of the classroom communities, and discovered their importance in school

The studies of differences stimulated Johanna's students to share their differences in great detail and generated powerful ideas through authentic dialogue in Kelly's children. Children in Johanna's and Kelly's schools easily shared their home and family stories.

programs. From the personal stories, teachers gained information that was not in the school files about the students and their families. This provided the teachers with a greater understanding of the children's families and lives outside of school and the confidence to talk to, write, and invite family members into the classroom to share knowledge and experiences as well as learn more about the school.

The teachers learned about collaborative relationships with families in an atmosphere of mutual respect. They discovered that educators may fear saying and doing the wrong things with people who are from different backgrounds, but because teachers are in a power position, they are the logical ones to reach out to the families (Edwards, 1999; Faltis, 1993; Goldenberg, 1987; McCaleb, 1994; Ogbu, 1983; Schmidt, 1999). Similarly, when communication between teachers and families becomes regular practice, families soon realize the significance of their involvement in their child's education (Faltis, 1993; Reyhner & Garcia, 1989). They become willing to share their time and their personal perspectives to enhance the school setting (Edwards, 1999; Goldenberg, 1987; McCaleb, 1994; Schmidt, 1999; Trueba, Jacobs, & Kirton, 1990).

Kelly's and Johanna's collaborative plans, adapted from "The ABC's of Cultural Understanding and Communication," connected home and school and assisted in the development of classroom communities for successful literacy learning in rural and urban settings. Children in these high-poverty areas had a wide range of literacy learning needs that appeared to be met with successful reading, writing, listening, and speaking activities associated with autobiography, biography, and the appreciation of similarities and differences.

Note

Special recognition is given to Johanna Shaw and Kelly Lape, educators who search continually for better ways to promote teaching and learning. Their collaboration benefits children, families, and schools.

References

Banks, J.A. (1994). *An introduction to multicultural education*. Boston: Allyn & Bacon.

Bloome, D., & Green, J.L. (1982). The social contexts of reading: A multidisciplinary perspective. In B.A. Hutson (Ed.), *Advances in reading language research* (Vol. 1, pp. 309–338). Greenwich, CT: JAI Press.

Bogdan, R.C., & Biklen, S.K. (1994). *Qualitative research for education: An introduction to theory and method* (2nd ed.). Boston: Allyn & Bacon.

Cochran-Smith, M. (1995). Uncertain allies: Understanding the boundaries of race and teaching. *Harvard Educational Review*, 65(4), 541–570.

Delpit, L. (1995). *Other people's children: Cultural conflict in the classroom*. New York: New Press.

Dyson, A.H. (1993). *Social worlds of children learning to write in an urban primary school*. New York: Teachers College Press.

Edwards, P.A. (1999). *A path to follow: Learning to listen to parents*. Portsmouth, NH: Heinemann.

Faltis, C.J. (1993). *Joinfostering: Adapting teaching strategies for the multilingual classroom*. New York: Maxwell Macmillan International.

Florio-Ruane, S. (1994). The future teachers' autobiography club: Preparing educators to support learning in culturally diverse classrooms. *English Education*, 26(1), 52–56.

Goldenberg, C.N. (1987). Low-income Hispanic parents' contributions to their first-grade children's word-recognition skills. *Anthropology and Education Quarterly, 18*, 149–179.

Green, J.L., Kantor, R., & Rogers, T. (1990). Exploring the complexity of language and learning in the classroom. In B. Jones & L. Idol (Eds.), *Educational values and cognitive instruction: Implications for reform* (Vol. 3, pp. 333–364). Hillsdale, NJ: Erlbaum.

Heath, S.B. (1983). *Ways with words: Language life and work in communities and classrooms*. Cambridge, UK: Cambridge University Press.

Ladson-Billings, G. (1994). *The dreamkeepers: Successful teachers of African-American children*. San Francisco: Jossey-Bass.

Lincoln, Y.S., & Guba, E.G. (1985). *Naturalistic inquiry*. Beverly Hills, CA: Sage.

McCaleb, S.P. (1994). *Building communities of learners*. New York: St. Martin's Press.

Noordhoff, K., & Kleinfield, J. (1993). Preparing teachers for multicultural classrooms. *Teaching and Teacher Education, 9*(1), 27–39.

Ogbu, J. (1983). Minority status and schooling in plural societies. *Comparative Education Review, 27*(2), 168–190.

Reyhner, J., & Garcia, R.L. (1989). Helping minorities read better: Problems and promises. *Reading Research and Instruction, 28*(3), 84–91.

Rogoff, B. (1986). Adult assistance of children's learning. In T.E. Raphael (Ed.), *Contexts of school-based literacy* (pp. 27–40). New York: Random House.

Schmidt, P.R. (1998a). *Cultural conflict and struggle: Literacy learning in a kinder-garten program.* New York: Peter Lang.

Schmidt, P.R. (1998b). The ABC's of cultural understanding and communication. *Equity and Excellence in Education, 31*(2), 28–38.

Schmidt, P.R. (1998c). The ABC's Model: Teachers connect home and school. In T. Shanahan & F.V. Rodriguez-Brown (Eds.), *National Reading Conference yearbook 47* (pp. 194–208). Chicago: National Reading Conference

Schmidt, P.R. (1999). Know thyself and understand others. *Language Arts, 76*(4), 332–340.

Sjoberg, G., & Kuhn, K. (1989). Autobiography and organizations: Theoretical and methodological issues. *The Journal of Applied Behavioral Science, 25*(4), 309–326.

Spindler, G., & Spindler, L. (1987). *The interpretive ethnography of education: At home and abroad.* Hillsdale, NJ: Erlbaum.

Spradley, J. (1979). *The ethnographic interview.* New York: Holt, Rinehart & Winston.

Tatum, B. (1992). Talking about race, learning about racism: The application of racial identity development theory in the classroom. *Harvard Educational Review, 62*(1), 1–24.

Trueba, H.T., Jacobs, L., & Kirton, E. (1990). *Cultural conflict and adaptation: The case of the Hmong children in American society.* New York: Falmer Press.

Vygotsky, L.S. (1978). *Mind in society: The development of higher psychological processes* (M. Cole, V. John-Steiner, S. Scribner, & E. Sauberman, Eds. and Trans.). Cambridge, MA: Harvard University Press. (Original work published 1934)

Zeichner, K.M. (1993). *Educating teachers for cultural diversity.* East Lansing, MI: National Center on Teacher Learning.

Children's Literature References

Archambault, J., Plummer, D., & Colon, R. (Illus.) (1997). *Grandmother's garden.* Parsippany, NJ: Silver Burdett Ginn.

George, J.C. (1988). *My side of the mountain.* New York: Penguin.

Hamanka, S. (1994). *All the colors of the earth.* New York: William Morrow & Co.

Hearne, B.G., & Andersen, B. (Illus.) (1997). *Seven brave women.* New York: Greenwillow.

Kroll, V., & Carpenter, N. (Illus.) (1992). *Masai and I.* New York: Simon & Schuster.

Paulsen, G. (1995). *Dog song.* New York: Simon & Schuster.

Simon, N., & Lasker, J. (Illus.) (1976). *All kinds of families.* Morton Grove, IL: Albert Whitman & Co.

Simon, N., & Leder, D. (Illus.) (1976). *Why am I different?.* Morton Grove, IL: Albert Whitman & Co.

Communicating and Collaborating With Linguistically Diverse Communities

Bertha Pérez

> Nos piden que vengamos a participar, pero yo no me he sentido a gus-
> to...pensaba que yo no tenía nada que hacer en la escuela...me daba
> vergüenza. Pero cuando Lita me hizo todas esas preguntas sobre las hierbas
> y cómo usarlas, me animé...pensé que quizás les podría ayudar. [You ask us
> to come and participate, but I have not felt comfortable...I thought that I
> did not have anything to do in the school...I was embarrassed. But when
> Lita asked me all those questions about herbs and how to use them, I got
> encouraged (motivated). I thought that maybe I could help you.]

—Mrs. J., parent of a Brewer Elementary student

Teachers often lament that parents of culturally and linguistically diverse students do not participate in school activities. Parents, such as the one quoted above, may not
feel comfortable in schools or may feel that they do not have knowledge that can contribute to school learning. The reluctance of culturally and linguistically diverse parents to take part in school
activities is sometimes misinterpreted by teachers and principals to
mean a lack of interest in their children's education. In order to

increase the participation of diverse parents, these parents need to feel that their participation is worthwhile for them and valuable for their children. Designing activities that engage parents and community members in sharing their knowledge and cultures is a meaningful way to value both parental involvement and true collaboration. This chapter describes a multilayered collaboration named Community Connections, and specifically focuses on the engagement of parents and the use of community resources as learning opportunities within culturally and linguistically diverse communities.

Building a Collaborative Culture

The collaborative project described here was an outgrowth of a professional development program between Brewer Elementary, San Antonio, Texas, USA, and the University of Texas at San Antonio. University teacher education students completed fieldwork and student teaching at the elementary school, and the school faculty and professors collaborated on research and other professional development activities. During a biannual planning meeting of the collaboration, teachers brought up recurring topics such as the lack of student motivation for learning in the upper grades, the need to get more parents involved, integrating literacy (reading and writing) across the curriculum, and the use of technology. After an animated discussion, the idea of an inquiry project to be conducted at the upper elementary grade levels evolved. The group decided to continue the discussion during the following week's professional development meeting and to invite all the fourth- and fifth-grade teachers to participate. During the next meeting, the idea of a community collaborative inquiry project emerged, and two fourth-grade and two fifth-grade teachers volunteered to participate. This inquiry project later became known as Community Connections.

The children and parents at Brewer Elementary reflect the population of many elementary schools and communities in the southwestern United States, which is comprised mainly of low socioeconomic status Mexican Americans and less than 5% of White and African American students. The participating teachers had an average of 6 years of teaching experience; three were Mexican

American and one was African American; two of the teachers were trained as bilingual (Spanish/English) teachers. The university students involved in the collaboration were approximately 75% White and 25% Mexican American. I am a Mexican American reading/bilingual professor, and my two university colleagues were White, one a reading professor and the other an elementary education professor.

From its inception, the collaborative sought to embrace Freeman and Johnson's (1998) recommendation for teachers of linguistically diverse students to construct new knowledge with a process that is a "socially negotiated one, because teachers' knowledge of teaching is constructed through experiences in and with students, parents, and administrators" (p. 401). Thus, we strove to understand how to improve learning and teaching within this community and how this could reform and inform teacher education. We reviewed recent research that examined literacy learning as sociocultural phenomena (Erickson, 1993; Moll, 1992), which suggested that teachers and learners are co-constructors of knowledge. And we adapted this perspective, for it supports the inherently cultural and socially mediated nature of learning and seeks to examine how school practices reflect a specific group's or community's perceptions and judgments (Pérez, 1998).

From this perspective, the teachers and professors saw this collaboration as an opportunity to synthesize what each group knew about the learning processes of culturally and linguistically diverse learners and how to teach these students. As we proceeded, we sought to expand the collaborative culture to include parents and children, as is described later in this chapter. We sought to nurture a collaborative culture by sharing responsibility for

- determining goals,
- planning activities,
- identifying resources and experts,
- building interdependence, and
- documenting the processes, interactions, and outcomes of the collaboration and the inquiry project.

Through mutually respectful collaboration we sought to create a learning community that expanded everyone's understanding, confidence, and effectiveness. For example, when the group decided we all needed additional technology education, a consultant was brought in to teach the children, and then the children taught the teachers, professors, and parents. This collaboration created robust zones of proximal development (Vygotsky, 1978); within these zones, more knowledgeable individuals shared their knowledge with others regardless of titles or pre-established roles. Thus, parents and children with more sophisticated community knowledge became teachers, and university researchers and teachers became learners. Learning was mediated across these zones of development in what Schustack, King, Gallego, and Vasquez (1994) define as "multiple sites of learning" (p. 37), where the community (e.g., housing projects, community gardens, clinics, branch public libraries) became the learning environment.

Through mutually respectful collaboration we sought to create a learning community that expanded everyone's understanding, confidence, and effectiveness

As Figure 1 illustrates, each child's cultural community was central to the dynamic interaction that guided the collaboration. The Community Connections collaboration consciously challenged its participants to use community resources for learning. It sought to utilize the community culture, members, and spaces as integral to the social organization of learning. The social organization was central, for as Cole (1996) argues, "It is insufficient to describe the artifacts of the culture without saying something about the social relations they mediate" (p. 297).

Community Connections Inquiry: Getting Started

The initial goals for the inquiry project identified by the teachers and professors evolved with the participation of the children and the parents. These goals were to (a) consciously promote inquiry and problem solving; (b) integrate literacy across the curriculum and across languages (Spanish/English); (c) integrate technology; and (d) create a community of learners among children (working in a variety of group settings) and among children, teachers, administrators, parents, community, and university personnel.

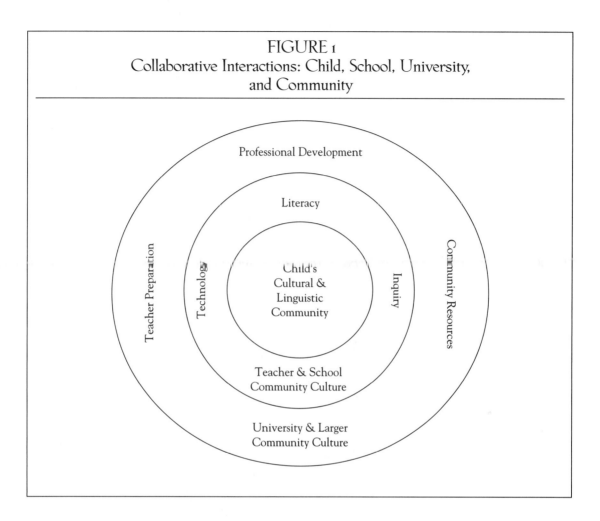

FIGURE 1
Collaborative Interactions: Child, School, University,
and Community

Professional Development

Literacy

Teacher Preparation

Technology

Child's
Cultural &
Linguistic
Community

Inquiry

Community Resources

Teacher & School
Community Culture

University & Larger
Community Culture

To initiate a discussion of possible inquiry topics, teachers drew from questions (e.g., Who painted all the pictures on these apartments?) and comments (e.g., My mom gives me mint tea when I don't feel well) they had heard children voicing. Teachers asked students to brainstorm about things they might study that were in the immediate school community. The children developed questions and surveyed all fourth- and fifth-grade children and parents about their interest in studying topics such as community practices based on herbal or folk medicine, the murals painted on the walls of the public housing project, the impact of the railroad tracks, the produce market where many residents worked, and the health clinic. Teams of students collected, analyzed, charted, and reported the results of the survey. Two topics of general interest emerged from the survey: folk medicine and the murals on the walls of the public housing development. The students and teachers chose between these topics, which resulted in one multigrade group of fourth and fifth graders with two teachers who studied folk medicine, and another multigrade group of fourth and fifth graders with the two other teachers who studied the murals. Table 1 illustrates the planning and implementation of the group that inquired into folk medicine.

Inquiry and Problem Solving

Once the inquiry topics were decided, the students brainstormed questions to investigate and ways to gather data. An important product of the collaborative inquiry study was that the children learned to plan and manage their learning by asking teachers to identify certain kinds of information, tasks, and experts that they needed to address during their collaborative inquiry. For example, early in the inquiry children asked the teacher to suggest where they could find health workers to invite to the class who could help them frame questions about the quality of herbal remedies and community health practices. The students, in consultation with their teachers, decided to form teams around the guiding questions and topics in Table 1. These questions included (a) the history of the use of herbal medicines, (b) the study of the social and cultural practices that accompany the use of herbs for medicinal purposes, (c) the survey of community sentiment and interest in folk medicine, (d) the study of the physical and chemical qualities of the herbs, and (e) the growth and care of herb gardens. There was also a technology design team and a planning team, which had to help other teams organize and document their work.

Within these teams, children focused on communicating, collaborating, researching, and documenting. They found important and authentic reasons for reading and writing. They wrote questions and interviewed specialists and community members in English and Spanish (depending on the language skills of the interviewee and

TABLE 1				
Community Connections Inquiry: Folk Medicine				
Guiding Questions	Topics/Times	Texts/Research Materials	Participation Structures and Student Engagement	Products/ Assessment
What is herbal medicine? How is it different from modern medicine?	Medicine, herbs, beliefs, healing begins study for all for 2–3 days; one team is designated as the design team.	*Green Medicine: Traditional Mexican American Herbal Remedies; Curanderos of the Southwest;* Compton CD-ROM.	Whole group takes a field trip to local public library to find additional books and references. Children paired for reading/researching basic definitions of theme/topics; whole-group sharing.	Books are checked out; students learn to use microfilm readers to conduct research; students record notes. Portfolios: each student completes a K-W-L chart and drafts a report of findings.
Who uses folk medicine? History of *curanderismo*? What do community members know about folk medicine?	Older people, tradition, beliefs, pre-modern medicine; categories of herbs, categories of uses, other objects, begins the third day; a team works on survey for 2 weeks.	Interviews of family and community members.	All students contribute questions for a questionnaire; one team constructs a survey and everyone has choice to interview family and community members to assess who uses folk medicine and attitudes toward folk medicine.	Questionnaire; data collected from questionnaire; tape-recorded interviews; parents volunteer to come to class. Teacher/student conferences with individuals and teams. HyperCard stack "What is folk medicine?" and "Who are famous *curanderos*?"

(continued)

TABLE 1 (continued) Community Connections Inquiry: Folk Medicine				
Guiding Questions	**Topics/Times**	**Texts/Research Materials**	**Participation Structures and Student Engagement**	**Products/ Assessment**
What are the tools of the trade? Can we grow our own herbs?	Herbs, food, beliefs, religious objects, messages. A team sets up visit to herb garden; all teams work on interviews; a team works on transcriptions.	Herb gardener; parents/folk medicine users; samples of herbs; *Green Medicine.*	All students interview two parents/ folk medicine healers; all students go on a field trip to an herb garden. A team works on cataloging samples of common herbs; a team researches scientific bases for claims; design team continues working.	Appointments; interviews; transcripts of interviews; cataloging of herb samples; video and photos of class on trip and of parent interviews; illustrations and descriptions for class composed book; teacher/ student conferences.
Compare cost of folk medicine and modern medicine? How does modern medicine feel about folk medicine?	Cost of herbs, cost of gardens, consultation visits, doctor's visit, medicine, one team works on cost comparison; other on gardens.	Mexican American health professional.	All students participate in interview of health professional; two teams investigate the cost of herbs and medicines for similar ailments; one team investigates the cost of an herb garden.	HyperCard stacks "Who uses folk medicine?" "What are the tools?" Portfolios: Students write self-assessment and include drafts of surveys, transcriptions, and writing for stacks. Parents/community invited for multimedia presentations; books and portfolios are exhibited.

interviewer). The children sought differing opinions and explanations, and consulted different sources for information. They were challenged by teachers, peers, and university participants to keep thinking about questions from different perspectives or disciplines (e.g., What might a chemist, historian, or community member ask about their study?). Students' comprehension of materials they read or information they gained from interviews evolved into new questions. During the weeks that followed, one team of students documented the inquiry process and planned a multimedia presentation to report their findings. They also made decisions about whom to invite to view their presentation and when and how to extend these invitations. The children, teachers, and university participants drew from their own and each other's linguistic and sociocultural knowledge and resources to assist the teams in planning, problem solving, and learning.

Literacy and Community Inquiry

Through the inquiry, students generated topics and questions that permeated literacy learning. Once the children had identified questions that interested them, they read, wrote, and problem solved as they went into the community to interview and conduct field study. The children borrowed conceptual tools such as observation, measurement, efficacy trials, and artistic expression used in different disciplines to reach conclusions and generalizations. In the context of the collaboration, they learned how to conduct an inquiry project; write plans, notes, letters, and reports; identify resources and request assistance; solve problems; and value the knowledge of peers and community members. Children used a variety of graphic organizers, such as flow charts for mapping the design of the multimedia presentation, timelines, outlines, and, in particular, K-W-L (what we *know*, *want* to know, and have *learned*) charts, which became records of the learning activities. Participants also assisted each other with explicit and implicit instruction about literacy, including the nuances of language use, spelling, vocabulary, and sentence structure.

The collaboration and inquiry did not yield only one conclusion. In fact, the inquiry fostered a further range of possible questions as

The collaboration and inquiry did not yield only one conclusion. In fact, the inquiry fostered a further range of possible questions as well as new understandings and perspectives.

well as new understandings and perspectives. The starting points and the groups' tasks were different, which required children to share knowledge and become experts. For example, the group studying the social and cultural practices of folk medicine read and reported on *curanderos'* (healers) life stories, while the group studying the growth and care of herbal gardens shared their findings about the cultivation of herbal gardens. The third column of Table 1, Participation Structures and Student Engagement, illustrates the learning activities conducted by the various groups. Through these activities, the children developed very different levels of understanding about specific aspects of the inquiry. For example, the children in the team that worked on a multimedia presentation for the culminating report developed skills related to technology and some basic knowledge about the use of herbs, but their level of knowledge about herbs was less than that of the team members who investigated the scientific bases of the healing properties of herbs.

Because the curriculum, in terms of both literacy and content learning, was developed through collaboration and inquiry rather than a predetermined body of knowledge to be mastered, children's school attendance was high—only two absences were reported during the project period—and children were motivated and actively involved. Students, teachers, and professors collected and examined a variety of products, described in column five of Table 1, to document and assess learning.

The Community Connections project continuously challenged children to use all their linguistic and literacy knowledge, in particular because some of the materials on *curanderos* was only available in Spanish and because the parent experts made their presentations in Spanish or bilingually. The children were compelled to assess their native language strengths and organize themselves in ways that valued and made use of their various linguistic repertoires. The tasks and products they developed (observation notes, books, multimedia presentations) showed dramatic differences from the ways they had previously used language and literacy.

Parents and Community

An integral part of the inquiry required tapping into the community resources or "funds of knowledge" (Moll, Vélez-Ibáñez, & Greenberg, 1990) so that parents and community members who had not been involved with the school could become interested in coming to school, sharing their knowledge, and getting involved. Seven parents and community members became very actively involved in the Community Connections collaboration—four in the inquiry project on the murals and three in the herbs and folk medicine. These parents participated as experts, sharing their knowledge of particular technical (e.g., medicinal properties of herbs, type of paint required for murals) or cultural aspects (e.g., the folk stories about *curanderos*, the symbolism of the icons on the murals). Many more parents participated by responding to the questionnaires, surveys, and interviews that the children conducted. A description of the participation of Mrs. Jurado demonstrates the benefit that the collaboration had for parents and parent-school understandings:

Mrs. Jurado, the mother of one of the fourth graders, had been trained in Mexico about the medicinal properties of plants. She and two other parents became the community experts for the inquiry dealing with the use of herbs and folk medicine. Mrs. Jurado readily acknowledged that she had received numerous invitations to get involved or to participate in school activities. She did not feel she had anything to offer. Like the mothers in the Valdés (1996) study, she believed her role was to show her children how to be *bien educados* (well mannered), and school teaching was the role of the teachers. When she heard that the fourth and fifth graders were going to conduct an inquiry into the scientific and cultural knowledge of the use of herbs in healing, she felt she had something important to share. In fact, she reported that she might have more knowledge (*quizá conosca más*) than the teachers and professors.

The following exchange between the teachers and Mrs. Jurado after her third session with the children illustrates the effect that the community connection inquiry had on parents:

Teacher: Muchisimas gracias por venir a compartir con nosotros todo
             esto que usted sabe sobre las diferentes hierbitas. [Thank you

	very much for coming to share with us all that you know about the different little herbs.]
Mrs. J.:	Gracias a usted por invitarme. Sabe, yo recibo todas estas noti-tas de la escuela que nos piden que vengamos a participar, pero yo no me he sentido a gusto en la escuela, no comprendo. Hasta cuando tratan de hablar español, nos tenemos que es-perar hasta que digan todo en inglés. Yo pensaba que yo no tenía nada que hacer en la escuela. [Thank you for inviting me. You know, I receive all these notes from the school that ask us to come and participate, but I have not felt comfort-able in the school, I do not understand. Even when they try to speak in Spanish, we have to wait until they say everything in English. I thought that I did not have anything to do in the school.]
Teacher:	¡Pero cómo! Sra. J., si el apoyo de los padres es muy impor-tante. Los padres deben venir y ayudar en la escuela. [But how, Mrs. J., the help of parents is very important. Parents should come and help in the school.]
Mrs. J.:	Sí, pero me daba vergüenza. Pero cuando Lita me hizo todas esas preguntas sobre las hierbas y como usarlas, me animé a venir a hablar con usted, yo pensé que quizás les podría ayudar. [Yes, but I was embarrassed. But when Lita asked me all those questions about herbs and how to use them, I got encouraged (motivated) to come to talk with you. I thought that maybe I could help you.]
Teacher:	Nos ayudó muchisimo, hasta las maestras y profesoras de la universidad aprendimos algo. [You helped us a lot, even the teachers and university professors learned something.]
Mrs. J.:	Me encantó poder contestar todas las preguantas de los niños y de los maestros. Hasta ni me puse nerviosa porque lo estaban grabando. [I enjoyed being able to answer all of the children's and teachers' questions. I did not even get nervous because it was being videotaped.]
Teacher:	La invitaremos a la presentación que vamos a hacer cuando terminemos la investigación. [We will invite you to the pres-entation that we will have when we finish the inquiry.]
Mrs. J.:	Muy bien, voy ha invitar a mi esposo y toda la familia. Pero sabe, ahora sí, cuando me inviten voy a venir haber en que puedo ayudar. [Very good, I will invite my husband and the whole family. But you know, now I will, when I am invited I will come to see how (in what way) I can help.]

The teacher's use of such friendly phrases as "very many thanks" (*muchisimas gracias*) and such terms as "little herbs" (*hierbitas*) in Spanish legitimizes and encourages the parents' use of Spanish. The use of the formal "you" (*usted*) by both teacher and parent shows their mutual respect and recognizes the sociocultural status of adults in this community. With the barriers reduced, Mrs. J. apparently felt good about having shared her knowledge, and she confided that she received the school communications and probably read them because the school sends bilingual notices, but has not responded in the past. Her choice of the word *me animé*, which encompasses "to feel encouraged" or "to give power or vigor to," gives a sense that because her knowledge of the use of herbs for healing was something she felt was important to pass on, she overcame any fear or misgivings she might have had about getting involved in school. Perhaps in the past she might have attended a school meeting or conference in which she did not feel welcomed or comfortable (*agusto*) and found the language translations frustrating and time consuming. It is interesting that during the three visits that Mrs. J. made to share her knowledge of herbs, she often had to wait for children to translate what she said and for the questions of English-speaking children to be translated. However, she did not express frustration at what were sometimes very cumbersome bilingual exchanges between children. Perhaps because of her role as teacher or cultural transmitter and facilitator, she did not express any language discomfort and voiced delight (*gusto*) at being able to share her cultural knowledge. The language differences were no longer a barrier to her coming to school.

Moll (1992) described how literacy tasks that build on the knowledge bases of the community can enhance the literary learning of Latino students in a school. Heath (1983) and others have documented how children can bring their knowledge of language and culture to classroom learning when teachers take the time to learn about the community. Like the Moll and Heath studies suggested, the Community Connections collaboration demonstrated how parents and children can use their community knowledge to strengthen participation and learning in the classroom.

The Community Connections collaboration became a bidirectional linguistic and sociocultural exchange that did not assume the school to be sole teacher and knowledge bearer. Thus, in Mrs. J's case, a parent reflected on her knowledge and role as a bearer of knowledge and began to imagine other possibilities in which she could play a role in school teaching and learning. What this clearly suggests is that when parents are engaged in sharing something that they know more about (e.g., the cultural or linguistic practices of the local community), their knowledge can override any reservations they may have about participating in the school environment.

Communicating, especially with language minority parents, means much more than conveying words and messages, but encompasses finding those topics that could be communicated about on an equal basis—or, better yet, where the parent can be the expert. Schools simply telling parents what to do to support school learning does not necessarily establish communication. In fact, it may just shut down communication. Valdés (1996) found that the Latino mothers in her study saw school learning and thus school-like activities as the jobs of teachers and schools. Therefore, a school that wants to engage parents in supporting school learning must first find a topic of interest to parents and in which parents may have expertise and invite them to share their knowledge with the school. Second, once communication is established, school personnel must listen to parents' expectations of teachers and schools as they engage in a frank conversation about how each sees the role of the other in learning.

> *Communicating, especially with language minority parents, means much more than conveying words and messages, but encompasses finding those topics that could be communicated about on an equal basis—or, better yet, where the parent can be the expert.*

Reassessing Community Resources

The participation by university faculty and students in the collaboration created opportunities for teachers to reflect on the progress of the inquiry, on the collaboration, and on lessons learned. During weekly sessions with the teacher education students, the elementary teachers clarified their practices, answered and posed questions, and challenged the university students' and professors' thinking. These sessions also helped to explore the teachers' and university students' views of the community and the availability of resources that might be enriching for children's learning. The university students were enrolled in a field-based methods class in which they had to identify community resources to use in the tutoring, lessons, and teaching units that were required for the class. Their participation as members of the collaborative project gave them the unique opportunity to develop a much deeper understanding of the principles taught in the class, particularly with regard to the utilization of community resources and working with parents. During a professional development session, the university students voiced typical concerns of teacher education students who are placed in urban minority schools. The following excerpt from a videotaped professional development session illustrates the views of three university students' about the community and their reflections of the teachers as they develop new understandings:

Student 1: I don't know how to say this, but when we did the assignment on community resources, I came up with very little that I thought could be used around here. I thought that the best theme for the inquiry would be something that would get the children out of this neighborhood so they could learn about things their parents cannot show them like the museum or the missions.

Mr. Cortez: Well, you know that many teachers at this school also feel that way. But we have been working this for a while now, so now what do you think? Do you see other possibilities now?

Student 2: Yes, but how did you all get to where you could see more? You know when we first came here all we could see was the railroad, the housing project. We were having a hard time seeing more.

Ms. Guerra: You have to see what people know, what they do, what they have. You can't just see the problems or the way that the media shows you the problems.

Mr. Cortez: But when we started brainstorming, it really helped; we came up with all the things that are around the school.

Ms. Guerra: We listed, for example, the restaurant Panchitos, who works there, how they order food and supplies, who does the bookkeeping; or another example is the terminal market. We came up with a pretty good list.

The professional development sessions helped the university students examine their initial negative assessment of the community and perhaps more importantly helped the teachers clarify their own assessment of the value of including community themes, resources, and parents in school learning and literacy activities. In spite of the fact that the university students had completed classes and assignments to sensitize them to issues of teaching culturally and linguistically diverse students, the students still voiced a certain pejorative assessment of the school neighborhood. Mr. Cortez acknowledged that some teachers may hold a similar assessment, but probed the student almost as if to give himself time to reassess his own as well as the students' current thinking. Ms. Guerra, who has been working with the parents on the herbal medicine theme, guided the students to refocus to see what is in the community rather than what is not there. As the dialogue continues, the first student presses the teachers, still considering that the best thing for poor minority children might be to get them out of their neighborhood:

Student 1: I just think that these children need more than what they have here in their neighborhood.

Mr. Lopez: I guess I felt like you at first, but now when I see how excited the kids are about learning and how many parents, artists, and others have gotten involved, I think they are reading and writing more. They are very excited about the technology, and the kids know they are going to share this with their families, so that motivates them even more.

Mrs. Guerra: But what surprised me was the excitement; the parents and other folks were giving us leads and materials; everyone got involved. And we are all learning the science and the culture and history of the use of herbs.

Mr. Waters: We need to do both. These children do need to learn about things beyond the neighborhood. But what we are all learning, especially me, is how easy it is to get parents involved when they get excited about sharing what they know. I think this is very important because before we have had very few parents involved.

Ms. Guerra: I bet that next time when we need some of these parents they are going to be right there. Whatever we need, we have built their confidence and gained their trust.

Student 3:   How do you know that what the parents are sharing is correct? They might be giving wrong information?

Mr. Cortez: We encourage the children to take notes and look up the information in books or in the computer. But we also encourage them to look up information that the health professional was giving them. So we want them to verify all information.

Ms. Guerra: Yes, and the children get very excited when they verify what Mrs. J. or the other parents are telling them; it increases their pride; they say things like, "Yes, Ms. G., Lita's mother knows a lot about this."

Mr. Lopez, by admitting that he also had similar thoughts about the neighborhood at first, perhaps lowered the university student's anxiety and helped her to continue in the dialogue. The teachers continued to speak with more confidence about the children's learning, and Mr. Waters addressed the need to use community resources and to help the children learn beyond their neighborhood. He and Ms. Guerra helped the university students see the benefit of the inquiry project in involving parents in school. They acknowledged the low parent participation at the school and their conviction that the parents who joined in the Community Connections will probably continue to be involved in the schooling of their children.

Another university student voiced another commonly held belief that perhaps minority parents do not have "correct information." Mr. Cortez patiently described how they are guiding the children to use good research methods to verify all information. Ms. Guerra helped the university students see the sociocultural and emotional value of the process by focusing on how "it increases the children's pride."

The Community Connections collaboration sought to examine what constitutes teachers' knowledge through partnered or participatory examinations of their work within the context of the school and community. It sought to incorporate the individual perspectives and understandings of the teachers who, in the long run, would have to carry out the very teaching practices that were being studied. Teachers were viewed as thoughtful people who made rational decisions about learning; these decisions were based on many sources of contextual information as well as on principles of learning and teaching.

Some teacher education studies argue that what teachers know about teaching is largely socially constructed out of the experiences and classrooms from which teachers have come (Bullough, 1989; Grossman, 1990). These studies report how teachers use their knowledge in highly interpretive, socially negotiated ways (Freeman & Johnson, 1998). Thus it is important for teachers and prospective teachers to be challenged to examine their own early learning experiences as well as concepts and attitudes about the diverse communities and children they will teach. Prospective teachers who will work in schools with culturally and linguistically diverse communities must develop the knowledge, skills, and attitudes to collaboratively plan, design, implement, and evaluate programs that will provide consistent, coordinated, and effective instruction in both content and language across the school curriculum.

Conclusions

In this chapter, the description of a Community Connections collaboration focused on how community resources and collaboration stimulated learning for all participants. The focus on the use of community resources and parents also showed that when these parents, such as the one quoted at the start of this chapter, were viewed as central to the children's learning, they overcame their fears of perceived barriers to school involvement. In a sustained collaboration in which all members are valued, the dynamic nature of the participation will motivate literacy and language use and cultural exchanges across time and tasks. This collaboration benefited all the participants and increased the potential for learning, particularly for children, but also for parents, administrators, professors, teachers, and future teachers.

The impact that the Community Connections experience had on the teachers and future teachers also suggests that we must continue to examine teachers' perceptions of their work and encourage collaboration. Kang (1995) argues,

> Successful collaboration involves the empowerment of teachers and other professionals to share in the decision making concerning instructional programs, curriculum, and staff development that their new roles and respon-

sibilities may entail. Though the needs of students and educational situations may differ from institution to institution, it behooves us as teachers, teacher educators, administrators, and other professionals to find the right combination and amount of structure, support, time, incentives, empowerment, and other factors to enable and encourage collaborative efforts toward effective education of students from all cultural and linguistic backgrounds. (p. 325)

By focusing learning within the context of the situated practice of the community culture and language, literacy was seen as a resource that allowed productive alternative discourses. The collaboration around situated community knowledge and literacy practices developed alternatives to the inherent conflicts, tensions, and contradictions usually experienced among school, community, and university groups. Through the use of collaboration, zones of proximal development were created where alternative knowledge and expectations could be mediated. The mediational context and tools necessary for future social and cognitive development were co-constructed through the Community Connections collaboration. Such rich contexts for learning and inclusion of diverse parents are particularly critical in a time when English-only, anti-immigrant viewpoints dominate many school policies and practices. This Community Connections collaboration inquiry provides a model for utilizing differences and diversity as resources for literacy learning.

References

Bullough, R. (1989). *First-year teacher: A case study.* New York: Teachers College Press.

Cole, M. (1996). *Cultural psychology: A once and future discipline.* Cambridge, MA: The Belknap Press of Harvard University Press.

Erickson, F.D. (1993). Transformation and school success. In E. Jacob & C. Jordan (Eds.), *Minority education: Anthropological perspectives* (pp. 27–52). Norwood, NJ: Ablex.

Freeman, D., & Johnson, K.E. (1998). Reconceptualizing the knowledge-base of language teacher education. *TESOL Quarterly, 32,* 397–417.

Grossman, P. (1990). *The making of a teacher: Teacher knowledge and teacher education.* New York: Teachers College Press.

Heath, S.B. (1983). *Ways with words: Life, language, and work in communities and classrooms.* New York: Cambridge University Press.

Kang, H. (1995). Meeting the needs of linguistically diverse students through collaboration. *The Educational Forum, 59,* 319–326.

Moll, L.C. (1992). Bilingual classrooms and community analysis: Some recent trends. *Educational Researcher, 212,* 20–24.

Moll, L.C., Vélez-Ibáñez, C.G., & Greenberg, J.B. (1990). *Community knowledge and classroom practice: Combining resources for literacy instruction.* Arlington, VA: Development Associates, Inc.

Pérez, B. (1998). Language, literacy and biliteracy. In B. Pérez & T.L. McCarty (Eds.), *Sociocultural contexts of language and literacy* (pp. 21–48). Mahwah, NJ: Erlbaum.

Schustack, M.W., King, C., Gallego, M.A., & Vasquez, O.A. (1994). A computer-oriented after-school activity: Children's learning in the fifth dimension and la clase magica. In F.A. Villarreal & R.M. Lerner (Eds.), *Promoting community-based programs for socialization and learning: New directions for child development* (pp. 35–50). San Francisco: Jossey-Bass.

Valdés, G. (1996). *Con respeto: Bridging the distances between culturally diverse families and school: An ethnographic portrait.* New York: Teachers College Press.

Vygotsky, L.S. (1978). *Mind in society: The development of higher psychological processes* (M. Cole, V. John-Steiner, S. Scribner, & E. Sauberman, Eds. and Trans.). Cambridge, MA: Harvard University Press. (Original work published 1934)

Developing Collaboration With Culturally Diverse Parents

Patricia A. Edwards and Jennifer C. Danridge

> Parent involvement is not the parents' responsibility alone. Nor is it the schools' or teachers' or community educators' responsibility alone. All groups need to work together for a sustained period of time to develop programs that will increase parents' understanding of the schools and their ability to assist their children, and that will promote student success and reduce failure at every grade level. (Epstein, 1987, p. 4)

Few would argue with Epstein's statement, but oftentimes the coordinated effort she advocates is more rhetoric than reality; we would like to increase collaborative relationships between parents, schools, and communities, yet there are very few practical examples of how to do so. The purpose of this chapter is to highlight ways that teachers can collaborate with parents from diverse backgrounds using nontraditional strategies. Toward this end, we present two examples of collaborative relationships between real teachers and parents. Pat shares the first example from her work in Donaldsonville Elementary School, and Jennifer shares the second example from her work with a first-grade teacher in Simon Community School. By offering these two examples, we hope to capture some of the struggles and triumphs that real teachers and parents have experienced as they worked to establish collaborative relationships.

Building Collaborative Relationships Using Nontraditional Strategies

> Adults who live and interact regularly with children can profoundly influence the quality and quantity of their literacy experiences. (Snow, Burns, & Griffin, 1998, p. 138)

Snow, Burns, and Griffin's words underscore the significant roles that adults in home and school environments play in children's literacy development. Literacy research has also emphasized the importance of teachers and parents. For example, Baker and her colleagues (1996) contend when the adult influences of home and school are synergistic, children are more likely to develop into engaged readers and writers. Similarly, Edwards and Pleasants (1997) assert that teachers and parents can effectively support children's literacy development by incorporating knowledge about children's home lives into curriculum and instruction.

Although the research literature strongly advocates for home-school partnerships, teachers have only had minimal success forming and maintaining these kinds of collaborative relationships, particularly with parents from diverse ethnic, racial, linguistic, and socioeconomic backgrounds (Edwards, Pleasants, & Franklin, 1999). We believe that one important reason for teachers' inability to create these collaborative relationships with parents from diverse backgrounds is their strong reliance on traditional methods of parent-teacher interactions. Open houses, parent-teacher conferences, and special school events such as plays and talent shows should not be the only ways that teachers communicate with parents from diverse backgrounds because these interactions are infrequent and superficial. Lightfoot (1978) explains,

> There are very few opportunities for parents and teachers to come together for meaningful, substantive discussion. In fact, schools organize public, ritualistic occasions that do not allow for real contact, negotiation, or

criticism between parents and teachers. Rather, they are institutionalized ways of establishing boundaries between insiders (teachers) and interlopers (parents) under the guise of polite conversation and mature cooperation. (pp. 27–29)

Lightfoot's explanation illuminates the exclusionary nature of traditional forms of interaction between teachers and parents from diverse communities. Because these forms of communication are deeply rooted in academic, middle-class discursive practices, parents from poor, minority, or immigrant communities might feel alienated and inferior (Edwards, Pleasants, & Franklin, 1999; Purcell-Gates, 1995). As a result, the ensuing frustrations, tensions, and conflicts can prevent the formation of collaborative relationships between teachers and parents from diverse backgrounds.

Moreover, conventional teacher-parent interactions might not provide access to school literacy. Many parents from diverse communities need sustained exposure to mainstream social and cultural practices in order to feel comfortable collaborating with teachers and competent working with their children (Purcell-Gates, 1995). When their contact with teachers is limited, parents from diverse communities can become discouraged and frustrated. Consequently, these parents might be wary of helping their children read and write for fear of "doing it wrong." Goldenberg (1987) provides an excellent example of a Hispanic mother who wanted to help her first-grade daughter, Violeta, learn to read. While the directive in the teacher's note had been "teach your child the consonants in the alphabet," Violeta's mother was unfamiliar with the school-based methods for doing so. Although Violeta's mother attempted to teach her daughter, she eventually stopped because she was afraid that she would confuse her child.

We suggest that teachers who want to build collaborative relationships with parents from diverse backgrounds move beyond the boundaries of traditional teacher-parent encounters. We believe that teachers who coordinate multiple encounters with culturally diverse parents need to include three critical elements in order to build collaborative relationships:

1. Establish mutual goals. It is important for teachers and parents to establish collaborative relationships around specific goals. General ideas such as "helping the child to succeed this year" or "providing a good education" can be frustrating because expectations and goals are not explicit. When this occurs, important differences between teachers' and parents' goals are not explored and negotiated, and the collaborative effort suffers (Corbett, Wilson, & Webb, 1996).

Before collaborating with parents, we suggest that teachers think about the specific goals and expectations they have for each student. It would be helpful for teachers to connect these goals and expectations to curricular and instructional practices. Moll and his colleagues (1992) assert that when cultural information (i.e., traditions, values, expectations) from the home informs classroom pedagogy, "strategic connections" (p. 132) between teachers and parents are formed. These strategic connections are integral to collaborative relationships because they foster reciprocity and establish mutual trust. Consequently, when teachers tap into parents' funds of knowledge, they can craft school-based literacy instruction that resonates with home-based literacies and cultural practices.

> *When teachers tap into parents' funds of knowledge, they can craft school-based literacy instruction that resonates with home-based literacies and cultural practices.*

2. Communicate respect for diverse worldviews. When teachers and parents from diverse backgrounds begin a collaborative effort, they must work together to deal with differences in worldviews. Teachers and parents have views of the world based on racial and ethnic heritage, socioeconomic background, gender, language experiences, and educational level (Hidalgo, 1993). In order to build collaborative relationships, teachers must interact in ways that are sensitive to and respectful of parents' worldviews.

How do teachers communicate this respect? First, teachers must acknowledge any differences between their worldviews and those held by parents. This is important because some teachers might perceive acknowledgment of differences to be racist or discriminatory. In an attempt to be fair and respectful, this type of teacher tries to be "colorblind" by overlooking or avoiding differences in worldviews. Nieto (1996) warns that this kind of colorblindness is actually disrespectful and harmful to parents from diverse backgrounds because it devalues their cultural identities and their life experiences.

Second, teachers must understand that difference does not signify deficit. When teachers perceive parents' worldviews to be "disadvantaged," they are less likely to acknowledge the intangible forms of parents' involvement in their children's education, such as creating a supportive home environment, providing an environment of high expectations and motivation, and sacrificing to help their children (Nieto, 1996). Conversely, teachers who affirm and try to understand the differences in parents' worldviews are more likely to listen to parents—an element that is critical to establishing respectful collaborative relationships between teachers and parents.

3. Support partnerships with other viable institutions. Connections among schools, families, and communities are increasingly considered to be essential to educational reform, particularly for students from diverse racial, linguistic, and socioeconomic backgrounds (Corbett, Wilson, & Webb, 1996). Collaborative relationships between teachers and parents can be reinforced and nurtured by enlisting the support of people who work in local community agencies and institutions. Community workers can act as natural go-betweens because they are nonthreatening to teachers. Corbett and his colleagues (1996) maintain that teachers can gain insights into the worldviews of parents from diverse backgrounds by talking with local community leaders. Their work illustrates how open and honest discussions between teachers and community leaders can provide a great deal of information about the social, economic, cultural, and educational needs of these communities, as well as suggestions for appropriate ways to interact with parents. Although Corbett and his colleagues do not provide specific suggestions for facilitating teacher-community partnerships, we believe that teachers can connect with community leaders by attending town meetings, community events, religious services, and other activities.

We use these three elements of transformative teacher-parent interactions to frame our discussion of two examples of real collaborative relationships between teachers and parents. Pat shares the first example from her work in Donaldsonville, Louisiana, USA.

The Donaldsonville Example

Mrs. Russell (all names that appear in this chapter are pseudonyms), a first-grade teacher at Donaldsonville Elementary School, expressed her concerns about the difficulty in attempting to collaborate with parents, especially those who have limited reading skills and are unfamiliar with school-based literacy:

> Aisha's mother is a nightmare. I can't get her to come in to see me, even though I have sent at least three notes home. She is extremely uncooperative and defensive. I encouraged her to read to her child and I even tried to tell her during our parent-teacher conference about what she could do at home to help Aisha gain more confidence in her reading and writing ability. But she didn't say, "I understand and I will try to do something about it." Instead she said nothing. It was as if she didn't hear anything I was saying to her. Nothing has worked, and I don't know what else to do.

How many times have we heard teachers say, "I don't know what else to do to collaborate with these parents"? Unfortunately, Mrs. Russell is not alone. Many teachers do not know how to reach parents who come from diverse racial, ethnic, socioeconomic, and linguistic backgrounds.

Donaldsonville Elementary School had been recognized for its good curriculum, even though teachers were disappointed with the progress of their students. Eighty percent of the students were African American and 20% were White, and most were members of low-income families. Teachers felt they were doing all they could to help these children at school. Without parental assistance at home, many children at Donaldsonville were going to fail. The teachers' solution was to expect and demand that parents be involved in their children's education by reading to them at home.

To the teachers this was not an unreasonable request. There is good evidence of positive gains made by disadvantaged elementary students when parents and children work together at home on homework and learning packets (Cummins, 1993). What teachers did not take into account was that 40% of the school's parents had limited reading skills. When the parents did not seem willing to do as the teachers asked, teachers mistook parents' unfamiliarity with the task being asked of them, coupled with low literacy skills, for lack of interest in their children's education. The continued demand that parents read to their children at home, which had a particular meaning in teachers' minds, sparked hostility and racial tensions between teachers and parents. Each group blamed the other for the children's failures; each felt victimized by the interaction. Children were caught between their most important teachers—their classroom teacher and their parents.

The principal and the teachers recognized that they had to mend the serious rift between school and home. The principal stated that she wanted to "unite the home, school, and community." Creating a process for parents to become integral and confident partners in their children's schooling was the first step. But how? Should the process be expected to emerge from traditional—and failed—interactions between home and school?

Background of the Program

To begin the project, it seemed imperative to help teachers to understand that they needed to move from "telling" to "showing" parents what "read to your child" meant. My initial questions were based on the notion that kindergarten and first-grade teachers have assumed that parents have a clear understanding of the skills needed to participate in an effective book-reading interaction with their children. The teachers had implicit knowledge of what "read to your child" really meant, but they often encountered difficulty in explaining the concept to parents. Moreover, the teachers, all of whom were from middle class backgrounds, found it difficult to single out specific skills in an organized way because they themselves used these skills so automatically and easily. Therefore, this traditional book-reading pattern led teachers to say, "Read to your child. You know, open the book and talk about the pictures." However, global statements teachers made to parents about book-reading interactions "sailed right over their heads," making it difficult for parents to translate into practice this much-requested teacher directive.

Recruiting Parents

One of the criticisms of programs designed for low-income parents, especially low-income African American parents, is that they will not participate because they are simply not interested in helping their children. This is not true. Lareau (1986) and Ogbu (1974) found that nonmainstream parents who lack knowledge about school-based literacy do not necessarily lack interest in their children's schools or in learning how to help their children.

In order to dispel this belief when implementing her program, Pat asked for community support in recruiting parents for the book-reading program. She contacted a group of community leaders who knew the parents in contexts outside of school—a bar owner, bus driver, grandmother, the ministerial alliance, and neighbors and friends of the parents.

The ministers agreed to preach from their pulpits about the importance of parents helping their children learn to read and especially the importance of parents attending the weekly book-reading sessions. After Pat's first meeting with the ministers, a priest of a predominately African American Catholic church urged parents to participate in the book-reading program, noting in a sermon that literacy was an important tool of faith and that children need to be able to read the confirmation requirements. Similar messages urging parents to attend the program and to help their children in school were delivered weekly by both Black and White ministers.

A local bar owner surfaced as a strong supporter of the program, attending all of the book-reading sessions and telling mothers who patronized his establishment that they no longer would be welcomed unless they put as much time into learning how to read to their children as they spent enjoying themselves at his bar. He also brought mothers to school to participate in the program and took them back home. He worked successfully with the social services department to secure babysitters for parents who otherwise would not have come.

Other supporters of the book-reading program included a bus driver, a grandmother, and people sitting on street corners. The bus driver offered to drive parents to the program each week; the grandmother organized a telephone campaign that involved calling program participants each week. The people sitting on the street corners began to talk about the program and encouraged all the parents they saw to attend.

The outpouring of support from the community was duplicated at Donaldsonville Elementary School, where school administrators, teachers, and the librarian staunchly supported the program. Teachers, as well as the school administrators and the librarian, enrolled in a family literacy course taught by Pat to broaden their knowledge of literacy development in different family structures. Teachers assisted in the development of the training materials designed to show parents effective book-reading behaviors, and they also agreed to observe the participating children's classroom performance in reading. The principal and assistant principal helped to publicize the program in the community, driving parents to the program each week and creating a friendly and warm environment at the school for the parents. For the first time in the school's history, parents were able to check out up to five books under their child's name. The librarian also kept a computerized list of types of books the parents were checking out. This information was shared with Pat and the children's other teachers. More importantly, the teachers, school administrators, and the librarian began to accept the parents as a useful and reliable resource.

Introducing the Book-Reading Program to Parents and Children

The book-reading sessions lasted for 2 hours once per week. The overall goal of the book-reading program was to demonstrate to parents how to read effectively with their children; this included learning specific book-reading behaviors.

In order to make the parents feel comfortable about participating in the book-reading program, Pat provided them with a wide list of materials. For example, they were informed that the "Little Books" by McCormick and Mason (1986) and a few wordless picture books and picture storybooks would be used in the initial session. As time passed, they could continue to use wordless picture books, picture storybooks, concepts books, easy-to-read books, and environmental print books. Parents were then shown the materials to use, as well as the phases of the book-reading program—Coaching, Peer Modeling, and Parent-Child Interaction. Each phase lasted for approximately 6 or 7 weeks. Parents attended the book-reading program on a weekly basis from October 1987 to May 1988. There were 23 book-reading sessions of approximately 2 hours each. (It should be noted that not all mothers attended every session.)

COACHING. During the Coaching phase, the mothers met with Pat as a group. She modeled effective book-reading behaviors and introduced a variety of teacher tapes (videotapes of teachers modeling effective book-reading practices for parents). The mothers watched, listened, waited, responded, and demonstrated what they had learned. The personal demonstrations (which were usually taped) and the teacher tapes served as a type of instructional scaffolding for them. The mothers could stay after sessions to review tapes and interact with Pat. By the end of the 6-week Coaching phase, the parents had begun to view book-reading as a routine and formatted language event between themselves and their children. They also had begun to adjust their language to their child's level of understanding and were developing an interest and sophistication in book reading. For example, they were able to label and describe pictures, vary their voices, and make motions while interacting with the texts during the sessions. More importantly, parents in their individual ways seemed to be acquiring an internal understanding of what it meant to share books with children.

PEER MODELING. In the Peer Modeling phase, parents learned to manage the book-reading sessions and strategies. This phase was based on Vygotsky's (1978) work, which suggested that the acquisition of skills progresses from a stage in which the teacher and learner jointly collaborate to perform a cognitive task (interpsychological) to a stage in which the learner has internalized and can regulate the process himself or herself (intrapsychological). During this phase, Pat assisted the mothers by (a) guiding their participation in book-reading interactions with each other, (b) finding connections between what they already knew and what they needed to learn, (c) modeling effective book-reading behaviors for them when such assistance was needed (encouraging them to review teacher tapes), and (d) providing praise and support for parents' attempts. Over the 6-week period, they shared information about the book-reading strategies and nonverbally corrected and guided each other. In addition, they provided for each other the same instructional scaffolding Pat had provided for them earlier. The mothers displayed the type of adult interactive behavior described by Morrow (1988), such as providing information about the book, relating responses to real-life experiences, inviting their peers to ask questions or comment throughout the story, answering questions and reacting to comments, and providing positive reinforcement for their peers' efforts. The mothers' storytalk increased in complexity, and their shyness about participating in the peer group decreased. Just as important, they learned to approach the book-reading sessions with confidence.

PARENT-CHILD INTERACTION. In the Parent-Child Interaction phase, Pat ceded total control to the parents and functioned primarily as a supportive and sympathetic audience, offering suggestions to the mothers about what books to use in reading interactions with their children, evaluating the parent-child book-reading interactions, and providing feedback or modeling. In this final phase, the mothers shared books with their own children and implemented book-reading strategies they learned in the Coaching and Peer Modeling phases. From these interactions, the mothers learned the importance of involving their children in a book-reading interaction, and recognized that "the parent holds the key to unlocking the meaning represented by the text" (Chapman, 1986, p. 12).

(For transcripts of the interactions during the three phases of the book-reading program—Coaching, Peer Modeling, and Parent-Child Interaction—see Edwards, 1991, and Edwards & Garcia, 1995. A fuller description of the topics covered in the book-reading sessions and sample lessons of each of the three phases are provided elsewhere [see Edwards, 1993].)

Toward Empowerment

The book-reading program highlighted in this chapter became a catalyst of hope for these African American low-income parents and children. With guidance and support during the Coaching and Peer Modeling phases, the parents were able to successfully participate in book-reading with their children. Because parents were not required to perform perfectly, they felt comfortable with their own individual way of sharing books with their children.

Parent-child book reading created a social climate that made parents feel that they were not only going to learn something that would be valuable to them and their children, but that they were true partners. The parents informed Pat that for the first time they were being invited to school not because there was a problem with their children, but to learn how to share books with their children and how to support their children's literacy growth. These parents had previously feared coming to school because of their own past experiences, but they now enjoyed coming and could actually laugh about the experiences they were encountering. Several parents said they were having the opportunity to relive in a positive way their school experiences through their children, and they were loving every moment.

The parents also shared with Pat that they were discussing what they learned in the book-reading sessions with their friends, neighbors, church members, and relatives. The program had worked itself into the daily lives of these parents and children as well as into the larger community. One parent wrote an article for the local newspaper titled "How I Can Make a Difference." An excerpt from the article follows:

> It is said that children imitate what they see, so it's up to us to show them that we, the parents, are effective teachers, in a way that provides our children with the best training possible to read. In essence, a way in which I can make a difference is by taking the time out to assure my daughter that reading is a fundamental part of our lives. (see Richardson, 1988).

The Parents as Partners in Reading program linked book reading with the contexts of their daily life. The parents became "sufficiently aware of their impact on their children's reading" (Pflaum, 1986, p. 10). The Vygotskian framework underlying the book-reading program became a program of empowerment rather than acculturation for these low-income parents and children. Through the program, low-income parents learned what was expected of their children in school. They also became aware of what their children were capable of doing with the appropriate guidance. Their own confidence in their reading abilities and opportunities to help their children with school activities increased.

The Parents as Partners in Reading program serves as a successful example of the importance of creating a structure for involving low-income parents in the schooling process and especially in their children's development as readers and writers. Epstein (1987) appropriately notes that "parent involvement is everybody's job but nobody's job until a structure is put in place to support it" (p. 10).

Pat's Donaldsonville example demonstrates how schools can create programmatic structures to support collaborative relationships with parents. We now turn to the example of Mr. Andrews, a first-grade teacher in an urban school in the Midwest, to illustrate how individual teachers can also create structures that build collaborative relationships with culturally diverse parents.

The Simon Community School Example

An Introduction to Simon Community School

Simon Community School is an elementary school located in an urban midwestern U.S. community. Locally, Simon was labeled a school that had "beaten the odds" by producing students who did well on statewide standardized testing despite the risk factors (e.g., high poverty rates, high percentages of minority students) generally associated with inner-city schools. In September 1997, the school's principal and the early elementary teachers (kindergarten through third grades) were invited to participate in a year-long study on effective literacy instruction conducted by P. David Pearson at the Center for the Improvement of Early Reading Achievement (CIERA).

As a CIERA graduate assistant, Jennifer had the opportunity to spend a substantial amount of time observing in the kindergarten, first-, second-, and third-grade classrooms. One of the teachers who intrigued her most was Mr. Andrews, a first-grade teacher who effectively taught reading in ways that valued and respected students' cultural knowledge and experiences. Mr. Andrews believed that his literacy pedagogy was effective for urban students because it centered around establishing good working relationships with culturally diverse parents. He explained,

> *"Making connections with parents is the key to effective instruction. The children have to know that their parents and I have a bond...."*

Making connections with parents is the key to effective instruction. The children have to know that their parents and I have a bond.... But making connections with inner-city parents can be difficult because sometimes they are skeptical of people in authority positions. They think that people like me will judge them. So to break down that wall, I visit them in their homes so that they will feel more comfortable coming to school.

The entire CIERA research team was interested in the idea of home visits and, by talking further with Mr. Andrews, they discovered that he was the only teacher who used this approach. Using several interview excerpts to highlight Mr. Andrews's "voice," we present this example of an urban teacher's success in using home visits as a strategy for establishing collaborative relationships with culturally diverse parents. (See also Danridge, 2000.)

A Closer Look at Mr. Andrews's Decision to Visit Homes

As a first-year teacher in an urban elementary school, Mr. Andrews experienced culture shock. Urban culture was very different from the culture of the rural town that Mr. Andrews remembered from his childhood. Much of his concern centered on working in a community that was characterized in the media as violent, dangerous, and dysfunctional. He was well aware of the urban myth that some European American teachers might believe: "If you're White and you go into a Black community that is somewhat lower on the socioeconomic scale, they are going to see you and want to take what you have."

Consequently, Mr. Andrews was uncertain about how to connect with urban families. During the first few months, he sent notes home with students as a first attempt at communication, but many parents were unresponsive. Although this was frustrating, Mr. Andrews was completely discouraged when only 2 out of 30 parents came to the first parent-teacher conference in November. He believed that urban parents cared about their children's education, but that parents might perceive conventional forms of initial contact such as notes and conferences to be confrontational, impersonal, and alienating. Similarly, Meier (1996) affirms,

> If parents' first contact with school, their first conference with a teacher or administrator, makes them feel more powerful, more useful, more knowledgeable, and better able to help their youngster, they are more likely to come back for more. If, however, coming to school is only a political act, to show the school you care, then parents with busy lives, who feel tired and defeated, find it difficult to visit the school   and each time it gets harder. (p. 134)

In order to invite parents back into the school, Mr. Andrews changed his second-year strategy for initiating contact with them. In September, he decided to visit each student's home to meet and talk with the family before parent-teacher conferences. During late August and September, Mr. Andrews made every attempt to contact parents via phone calls, relaying messages through neighbors or emergency contacts, and meeting parents when they picked up or brought their child to school.

By meeting with parents in their homes, Mr. Andrews hoped to make the initial contact with parents more relaxed and personal. He explained, "Home visits provide me with a link to the parents. It gives them direct communication with me and also puts us on familiar ground." As a result of the home visits, Mr. Andrews reported that he had "100% attendance" at his parent-teacher conferences; at least one parent or guardian attended each conference throughout the year.

During these home visits, Mr. Andrews's central goal was to informally meet parents and connect with them. He initiated the conversations by informing parents about important dates of school events such as parent-teacher conferences and open houses, and sharing general curricular and instructional goals to give parents an idea of what to expect during the upcoming year. This kind of information is particularly important for helping urban parents and other parents from diverse communities support their children's literacy learning. Goldenberg (1987) asserts that parents from diverse communities need this kind of exposure to "mainstream" literacy schooling practices in order to help them feel welcome coming into the classroom and to feel more competent working with their children at home.

Mr. Andrews spent most of the visit, however, listening to parents. Like Moll and his colleagues (1992), Mr. Andrews intended home visits to express his genuine interest in children, their families, and their cultures. Mr. Andrews encouraged parents to share important "home" information by asking open-ended, general questions such as

- ♦ What are some important traditions or customs in your family?
- ♦ What are some important things I should know about your child?
- ♦ Who are the important people in your child's life?
- ♦ What do you want your child to learn this year?

By asking these kinds of questions, Mr. Andrews initiated a parent-teacher relationship in which parents are valued as the "more knowledgeable others" (Vygotsky, 1978) about their children's early literacy and educational experiences.

Using home visits as the first contact provided the collaborative space that helped Mr. Andrews to establish collaborative relationships with urban parents in three critical ways:

1. *Home visits challenged Mr. Andrews to honestly deal with his negative perceptions of urban culture, families, and communities.* By visiting parents in their homes, he realized that many of his students and their families lived in safe, closely knit neighborhoods. Also, Mr. Andrews began to admire the hard work and investment that parents put into their children, their neighborhoods, and their communities. The positive changes in Mr. Andrews's perceptions of urban families and communities led him to genuinely respect their worldviews and cultures, fostering collaborative relationships.

2. *Home visits challenged Mr. Andrews to redefine his role as an urban teacher.* Cummins (1993) asserts that teachers who want to empower minority students, families, and communities must "personally rede-

fine" (p. 101) their roles as educators in ways that balance power and authority. Home visits provided a context for this kind of personal redefinition because teachers and parents are positioned as equally valued "knowledgeable others." Thus, Mr. Andrews did not define his role as "savior" because he realized that students and families do not need to be rescued from their urban culture and communities. Rather, Mr. Andrews defined his role as "builder" and worked to form alliances with urban parents by building on their home cultures and their desire to help their children succeed.

3. Home visits enabled Mr. Andrews to foster parents' ownership of their children's literacy development and educational lives. By entering parents' private family spaces, Mr. Andrews had to be extremely sensitive to parents' concerns because home visits can be perceived as intrusive. Consequently, Mr. Andrews offered to meet parents who were uncomfortable with the home visit in local public places, such as a library or fast food restaurant. In a further effort to be nonintrusive, Mr. Andrews generally limited the visit to 15 or 20 minutes. Although brief, Mr. Andrews' primary goal was to listen to parents in a way that affirmed their knowledge, culture, and experiences. Mr. Andrews commented, "I never want parents to interpret the home visits as trying to interfere or trying to undermine their purpose of educating and raising their child." By using these strategies, Mr. Andrews hoped to convey to parents that they were valued partners in their children's literacy development and educational lives.

Lessons Learned From Traditional and Nontraditional Strategies

We believe that it is important for teachers who want to establish collaborative relationships to move beyond traditional school strategies for interacting with diverse parents. As our examples from Donaldsonville and Simon Community School demonstrate, teachers can effectively work with parents from different racial and ethnic, socioeconomic, and linguistic backgrounds using creative, nontraditional forms of building home-school connections. In an effort to highlight the differences between traditional and nontraditional strategies, we summarize the lessons learned from Donaldsonville and Simon Community School in Table 1.

Conclusions and Recommendations

Nearly 20 years ago, Philips (1982) highlighted the fact that each culture has its own rules for what constitutes proper and respectful behavior. These rules reflect the deeply held values and beliefs of members of that culture. These rules and values make up what Philips terms *invisible culture*. The lack of awareness of each other's invisible culture often leads to miscommunications and misunderstandings between home and school.

We believe that schools will not be successful in educating all children effectively unless they become culturally sensitive to parents and their communities. Lightfoot (1978) reiterates this point by saying that "in order for schools to successfully teach black children, they will have to incorporate the cultural wisdom and experiences of black families and meaningfully collaborate with parents and community" (p. 129). Wright (1970) argues, "When schools are too largely removed from a sense of immediate responsibility to their clientele, education is in danger. The institution becomes the master rather than servant to those it teaches" (p. 270). Educators can no longer continue to think of equality in terms of "things" such as building, books, and curriculum. According to Hawkins (1970), "In all that is done in the name of equalization of opportunities, it is necessary that educators keep in mind that what is done is important, but how it is done is more important" (p. 43). The relationship between the home and the school must have depth.

This message is one that our schools should pay attention to when working to develop collaborative working relationships with parents from diverse backgrounds. For example, teachers and administrators must closely examine their school's history to determine if past policies and practices such as sending notes and fliers home and holding report card conferences have prevented them from successfully developing collaborative relationships with diverse parent populations. Epstein (1988) notes, "Schools of the same type serve different populations, have different histories of involving parents, have teachers

TABLE 1
Traditional Versus Nontraditional Strategies to Establish
Collaborative Relationships

Initiatives That Build Collaborative Relationships With Culturally Diverse Parents	Traditional Strategies	Nontraditional Strategies From Donaldsonville and Simon Community School
Inviting parents into schools	◆ Open houses ◆ Ice cream socials ◆ Parent-teacher conferences ◆ Bake sales ◆ Fundraiser events ◆ School performances	*Donaldsonville* Teachers invite parents around structured activity with children (book-reading) *Simon Community School* Teacher invites parents to school by visiting them in their homes. This might help parents to feel more comfortable coming to school.
Establishing partnerships with parents	◆ Teachers establish partnerships via school contacts ◆ Parent-teacher conferences ◆ Notes/fliers from school sent home	*Donaldsonville* Teachers establish partnerships with parents via community members. Teachers and school administrators connect with the ministerial alliance, local business owners, extended family members, and other community members in an effort to encourage parents to form collaborative relationships. *Simon Community School* Teacher establishes partnerships via home-school connections. Teacher visits students' homes to establish connections with parents. In doing so, teacher shows respect and value of parents' positions as the "more knowledgeable others" about children's early literacy experiences.
Supporting parents' ownership of their children's literacy development and educational lives	◆ Parents are generally assumed to have some school-based literacy skills	*Donaldsonville* Parents as Partners program teaches parents how to read stories in ways that mirror the curriculum. Thus, students and parents begin to "own" school-based literacy skills. *Simon Community School* Teacher supports ownership by making curricular and academic goals and expectations explicit to parents. Also, teacher makes connections between home-based and school-based literacy practices for students and their families.

and administrators with different philosophies, training, and skills in involving parents" (p. 58). This observation should encourage school personnel to ask themselves a number of questions: (1) What is our school's history of collaborating with diverse parent populations? (2) What is our school's philosophy regarding diverse parent populations in home-school collaborations? and (3) What training and skills do we need to develop to involve diverse parent populations in home-school collaborations?

As stated earlier, schools must develop creative strategies that are culturally sensitive to parents. We believe that the key to successful home-school collaborations is to know the parents as individuals, with varying experiences, situations, and backgrounds. They differ in their relationships with their own children and in their feelings about school. Some have a high regard for education, and for others their children's schooling is a relived struggle amidst more pressing concerns (Edwards, 1991). The goals and values of individual families will vary and may differ from those of the teacher and school. This individuality that parents bring to home-school collaborations challenges today's educators. When home-school collaborations ignore these important variations, the efforts can be disappointing. However, when schools acknowledge the range in dispositions, backgrounds, experiences, and strengths among families, efforts to establish sound home-school collaborations are more successful.

> *We believe that the key to successful home-school collaborations is to know the parents as individuals, with varying experiences, situations, and backgrounds.*

ACKNOWLEDGMENTS

The authors gratefully acknowledge the support of the research reported in this paper from the Center for the Improvement of Early Reading Achievement (CIERA), under the Educational Research and Development Centers Program, PR/Award Number R305R70004, administered by the Office of Educational Research and Improvement, U.S. Department of Education, and from the Spencer Foundation Small Grant Program.

References

Baker, L., Allen, J., Shockley, B., Pelligrini, A.D., Galda, L., & Stahl, S. (1996). Connecting school and home: Constructing partnerships to foster reading development. In L. Baker, P. Afflerbach, & D. Reinking (Eds.), *Developing engaged readers in school and home communities* (pp. 21–42). Mahwah, NJ: Erlbaum.

Chapman, D.L. (1986). Let's read another one. In D.R. Tovey & J.E. Kerber (Eds.), *Roles in literacy learning: A new perspective* (pp. 10–25). Newark, DE: International Reading Association.

Corbett, H.D., Wilson, B., & Webb, J. (1996). Visible differences and unseen commonalties: Viewing students as the connections between schools and communities. In J.G. Cibulka & W.J. Kritek (Eds.), *Coordination among schools, families, and communities: Prospects for educational reform* (pp. 27–48). Albany, NY: State University of New York Press.

Cummins, J. (1993). Empowering minority students: A framework for intervention. In L. Weiss & M. Fine (Eds.), *Beyond silenced voices: Class, race, and gender in United States schools* (pp. 101–118). Albany, NY: State University of New York Press.

Danridge, J.C. (2000). *In the trenches and between the borders: Border pedagogy in an urban first-grade classroom.* Unpublished paper presented at Michigan State University, East Lansing.

Edwards, P.A. (1991, April). *Differentiated parenting or parentally appropriate: The missing link in efforts to develop a structure for parent involvement in schools.* Paper presented at the Third Annual Roundtable on Home-School-Community Partnerships, Chicago, IL.

Edwards, P.A. (1991). Fostering early literacy through parent coaching. In E. Hiebert (Ed.), *Literacy for a diverse society: Perspectives, programs, and policies* (pp. 240–256). New York: Teachers College Press.

Edwards, P.A. (1993). *Parents as partners in reading: A family literacy training program.* Chicago: Children's Press.

Edwards, P.A., & Garcia, G.E. (1995). The implications of Vygotskian theory for the development of home-school programs: A focus on storybook reading. In V. John-Steiner, C. Panofsky, & L. Smith (Eds.), *Interactionist approaches to language and literacy* (pp. 243–264). New York: Cambridge University Press.

Edwards, P.A., & Pleasants, H.M. (1997). Uncloseting home literacy environments: Issues raised through the telling of parent stories. *Early Child Development and Care, 127–128,* 27–46.

Edwards, P.A., Pleasants, H.M., & Franklin, S.H. (1999). *A path to follow: Learning to listen to parents.* Portsmouth, NH: Heinemann.

Epstein, J.L. (1987). Parent involvement: State education agencies should lead the way. *Community Education Journal, 14*(4), 4–10.

Epstein, J.L. (1988). How do we improve programs for parent involvement? *Educational Horizons, 66*(2), 58–59.

Goldenberg, C.N. (1987). Low-income Hispanic parents' contributions to their first-grade children's word-recognition skills. *Anthropology & Education Quarterly, 18*(3), 149–179.

Hawkins, L. (1970). Urban schoolteaching: The personal touch. In N. Wright, Jr. (Ed.), *What Black educators are saying* (pp. 43–47). New York: Hawthorn Books.

Hidalgo, N.M. (1993). Multicultural teacher introspection. In T. Perry & J.W. Fraser (Eds.), *Freedom's plow: Teaching in the multicultural classroom* (pp. 99–108). New York: Routledge.

Lareau, A. (1986). *Social class differences in family-school relationships: The importance of cultural capital.* Unpublished manuscript, Department of Sociology, Stanford University, Stanford, CA.

Lightfoot, S.L. (1978). *Worlds apart: Relationships between families and schools.* New York: Basic Books.

McCormick, C., & Mason, J.M. (1986). Intervention procedures for increasing preschool children's interest in and knowledge about reading. In W. Teale & E. Sulzby (Eds.), *Emergent literacy: Writing and reading* (pp. 90–115). Norwood, NJ: Ablex.

Meier, D. (1996). Transforming schools into powerful communities. In W. Ayers & P. Ford (Eds.), *City kids, city teachers: Reports from the front row* (pp. 131–136). New York: The New Press.

Moll, L.C., Amanti, C., Neff, D., & Gonzalez, N. (1992). Funds of knowledge for teaching: Using a qualitative approach to connect homes and classrooms. *Theory Into Practice, 31*(2), 132–141.

Morrow, L.M. (1988). Young children's responses to one-to-one story readings in school settings. *Reading Research Quarterly, 23*, 89–107.

Nieto, S. (1996). *Affirming diversity: The sociopolitical context of multicultural education* (2nd ed.). White Plains, NY: Longman.

Ogbu, J. (1974). *The next generation.* New York: Academic Press.

Pflaum, S.W. (1986). *The development of language and literacy in young children* (3rd ed.). Columbus, OH: Charles E. Merrill.

Philips, S.U. (1982). *The invisible culture: Communication in classroom and community on the Warm Springs Indian Reservation.* New York: Longman.

Purcell-Gates, V. (1995). *Other people's words: The cycle of low literacy.* Cambridge, MA: Harvard University Press.

Richardson, J. (1988). How can I make a difference? *The Donaldsonville Chief,* p. 6.

Snow, C.E., Burns, M.S., & Griffin, P. (Eds.). (1998). *Preventing reading difficulties in young children.* Washington, DC: National Academy Press.

Wright, N. Jr. (1970). Our schools. In N. Wright, Jr. (Ed.), *What Black educators are saying* (pp. 269–271). New York: Hawthorn.

Vygotsky, L.S. (1978). *Mind in society: The development of higher psychological processes* (M. Cole, V. John-Steiner, S. Scribner, & E. Sauberman, Eds. and Trans.). Cambridge, MA: Harvard University Press. (Original work published 1934)

CHAPTER 15

HOME-SCHOOL CONNECTIONS IN A COMMUNITY WHERE ENGLISH IS THE SECOND LANGUAGE: Project FLAME

Flora V. Rodríguez-Brown

> As any parent, I always thought learning should come to our children from teachers at school, the same as religion is taught by the priest at church. But participation in Project FLAME makes you aware how important it is to participate with the teachers in our children's education and be responsible at least for 50% of their learning because we are their first teachers. In my case I have learned to communicate better with my husband and my daughter, but as a parent trainer I have also learned to communicate with the community.
>
> —Juanita, a Project FLAME parent

In 1989, when my colleagues and I started working with recent immigrant parents in a Hispanic community in Chicago, we never dreamed that parents would so eloquently describe their role as literacy teachers. Previously, when we talked to parents about their involvement in their children's learning, they explained that they could not do it because they did not know English or because they lacked formal schooling. Besides, they saw themselves at a lower intellectual level than the teachers and the school and, as such, they felt the school would not approve of them as teachers for their children.

Within their own cultural framework, parents saw it as their role to educate (*educar*) their children while it was the role of the school to teach (*enseñar*) their children. In the Spanish language, the term *educar* relates more to education in manners, values, and morals, whereas the term *enseñar* means teaching related to school subjects including reading and writing. You are educated at home and you are taught at school. Also, out of *respeto* (respect) to the school and the teachers, Hispanic parents did not want to interfere with the role of the school. This *respeto* for the school would not allow them to become more involved in their children's learning and preparedness for school.

Project FLAME: A Family Literacy Project

Research has shown that Hispanic parents have definite theories about schooling and their role in their children's education (Delgado-Gaitan, 1990, 1991, 1992). The concept of *familia* in cultural descriptions of Hispanics (Abi-Nader, 1991) supports the view that meeting the needs of the family is one of the greatest motivations for success and achievement within the Hispanic community. For this reason, in 1989 we developed Project FLAME (Family Literacy: Aprendiendo, Mejorando, Educando [Learning, Improving, Educating]) in collaboration with the University of Illinois at Chicago, the Hispanic community, and schools. Our goal then and now is to educate and support limited English proficient (LEP) Hispanic parents in order to change attitudes and improve their ability to influence their children's cognitive development, literacy learning, and academic achievement in school (Shanahan, Mulhern, & Rodríguez-Brown, 1995; Shanahan & Rodríguez-Brown, 1993).

U.S. national statistics show that Americans of Hispanic origin are the fastest growing ethnic group in public schools (Sable & Stennett, 1998). In Chicago alone, one third of the school population is Hispanic, and nationally the number of Hispanics is growing five times as fast as that of non-Hispanics (National Council of La Raza, 1990). Furthermore, in terms of illiteracy (defined as completion of less than 5 years of schooling), 12.2% of Hispanics 25 years or older were not literate in 1989, in comparison to 2% and 4.8% for the White and Black populations, respectively (National Council of La Raza, 1990). Also, according to Applebee, Langer, and Mullis (1987), Hispanics at all grade levels lag behind their "Anglo" peers in reading and writing achievement, although according to Sable and Stennett (1998), some of these gaps have narrowed over time.

Based on these disturbing statistics and because of the parents' negative self-perceptions, there was a clear need in these communities for a program that would encourage parental involvement in children's learning. Research shows that it is important for parents to be partners with the schools in their children's literacy learning in order to support higher achievement levels for their children (Epstein, 1990, 1991). Differences in communication styles, views of literacy, and the nature of literacy interactions between the home and the school can limit literacy learning (Heath, 1987). By increasing the opportunities to learn and use literacy outside the schools, particularly at home, the incongruency between home and school literacy can be decreased (Moll, Amanti, Neff, & Gonzalez, 1992; Moll & Greenberg, 1991; Vélez-Ibáñez & Greenberg, 1989).

Program Assumptions and Design

Project FLAME is a community project, based in the schools, administered by the university under the leadership of people who know and are part of the community. Our goals are to improve and increase parents' ability to

- provide literacy opportunities for their children (literacy opportunity);
- act as positive literacy models (literacy modeling);
- initiate, encourage, and extend their children's literacy learning (literacy interaction); and
- relate well with the school (home-school connections).

Parents attend two types of classes: Parents as Teachers and Parents as Learners (which will be discussed later in this chapter). Parents as Teachers sessions are held twice a month, when parents discuss topics such as choosing books for their children, using the library, developing a home literacy center, and using the community to learn literacy skills. Parents learn to share books with their children; play with rhymes and language games; teach letters, sounds, and words; and encourage emergent writing. They also visit classrooms and talk with their children's teachers. Parents as Teachers sessions incorporate components of literacy opportunity, literacy modeling, literacy interaction, and home-school connection.

> *Parents learn to share books with their children; play with rhymes and language games; teach letters, sounds, and words; and encourage emergent writing.*

LITERACY OPPORTUNITY. Project FLAME teaches parents how a supportive home environment provides children with the opportunity to use literacy. The provision of such opportunities at home is a powerful stimulus to literacy learning (Wheeler, 1971). To this end, parents go to the local library to learn how to locate and select appropriate books for their children. Furthermore, Project FLAME sponsors a Children's Book Fair and provides parents with scrip money to buy books as an incentive for attending the Parents as Teachers sessions. Project FLAME gives all participating families a Home Literacy Box, which is filled with literacy materials such as pencils, crayons, paper, glue, a ruler, and scissors. Parents generate ways to use the materials with their children, to make the box available to their children, and to keep the box supplied with literacy materials.

LITERACY MODELING. Children who see their mothers and fathers reading and writing do best in school achievement (Metritech, 1987). When mothers develop strategies for reading to children, the literacy learning among both Hispanic children and other low socioeconomic status (SES) children improves (Edwards, 1988, 1999; Gallimore & Goldenberg, 1989; Goldenberg, 1993, 1987; Goldenberg & Gallimore, 1991). Also, several studies have shown that parents are more effective as literacy models when they see themselves as effective learners (National Center for Family Literacy, 1991; Nickse, Speicher, & Buchek, 1988; Van Fossen & Sticht, 1991).

Unfortunately, Gallimore and Goldenberg (1989) found that limited English proficient (LEP) parents often do not share their English literacy with their children because of their limited literacy skills or their limited literacy in English. However, Heath (1987) describes LEP parents who, in their zeal for their children to learn English, do not provide a rich, active language environment because they try to speak to children in English when they still do not know English well. As a result, children lack good language models.

The primary vehicle for helping parents become positive models of literacy learners and users for their children are the Parents as Learners sessions, which include either English as a second language or general education diploma classes twice a week. Selected parents also participate in a Training of Trainers component. These parents are invited to participate in a 2-year program to take a leadership role in the Parents as Teachers sessions.

LITERACY INTERACTION. Direct interactions between parents and children have a positive influence on children's learning (Paratore, 1994; Paratore, Melzi, & Krol-Sinclair, 1999; Tobin, 1981). This includes formal direct instruction as well as less formal activities such as reading to children or encouraging them to pretend to read and write. Children who are read to often are more successful in school than those who do not have such experiences (Feitelson & Goldstein, 1986). These types of reading activities acquaint children with story structures and literacy conventions (Teale, 1984). Through Project FLAME, parents participate in activities that help them prepare for reading to their children more effectively. They also learn how to talk with their children about books. Parents learn to use songs, games, and other activities to increase their children's phonemic awareness. The parents learn about community resources through field trips that they attend with their children. Past field trips have been taken to libraries; art, natural history, science, and various children's museums; the botanical gardens; and the zoo.

HOME-SCHOOL CONNECTION. The home-school connection addresses the need for parents to understand what the children's teachers are trying to accomplish. Conversely, school teachers also need to understand parents' concerns and aspirations for their children. According to Goldenberg (1987), Hispanic children's literacy knowledge is highest in situations in which teachers and parents maintain frequent contact with each other. Similarly, Silvern (1988) found that cultural and social discontinuity between home and school interferes with literacy learning. These discontinuities are more likely to exist for the LEP child. Through Project FLAME, parents develop ways to improve early communication about literacy learning and home-school cooperation with their children's teachers. Improved home-school connections and mutual respect between parents and teachers develop by visiting classrooms and talking with teachers.

Most recently, we have developed Parents as Classroom Volunteers. In response to a teacher's request, FLAME parents prepare for a specific teaching role in a classroom. Parents requested this element to help them make the most of their volunteer work in classrooms.

FLAME Effectiveness: What Is Known

Through the years, we have been providing Project FLAME activities at eight sites in Chicago. Three of the sites have participated since 1989. We have an evaluation component and collect data from parents and children on a yearly basis.

Analysis of parent reports about uses of and attitudes toward literacy at home show significant changes in the areas of literacy interaction and literacy opportunity after participating in Project FLAME. These changes appear to impact children's school performance. The children, from 3 to 6 years old, are pre- and posttested to determine if our work with the parents has an effect on the children's learning and their preparedness for school. For this purpose, children are given a letter recognition test, a test of print awareness (Clay, 1993), and the Boehm Test of Basic Concepts (The Psychological Corporation, 1986). The tests are administered in either Spanish or English, depending on the children's proficiency in those languages. Statistical analyses (e.g., t-tests) show significant gains (less than .001) from pre- to posttest results in all areas tested.

FLAME researchers have also conducted a comparative study. During the third year of the project, we compared the performance of a group of 3- to 5-year-olds whose parents participated in Project FLAME to a class of non-FLAME preschoolers (3- to 5-year-olds). Because there were pretest differences between the groups (for instance the FLAME group scored significantly lower on the test of print awareness [p less than .02] and lowercase letters [p less than .0001]), analysis of covariance was used to control for pretest differences. The results indicate that no significant differences existed between the two groups by the end of the school year. We can conclude that, although Project FLAME children lagged behind the comparison children in several areas related to literacy on the pretest, their performance became similar to that of their non-FLAME peers during the months their families participated in the program.

Clearly, the FLAME children acquired additional skills. This occurred even though the children experienced no direct intervention. Project FLAME intervention was aimed at the parents—individuals who typically have very limited literacy skills themselves, limited experience with school, and limited English proficiency.

Parents' Perceptions About FLAME Effectiveness

Through the years, we have been collecting anecdotal data from writings produced by parents during ESL lessons, as well as from open-answer questionnaires. Most of the answers were written in Spanish in 1995 during a group's second year of participation in the program. Many of the parents whose voices appear here initially did not see themselves helping their children at home because of lack of English proficiency and lack of schooling. The answers were translated into English and here are organized by topic.

Parents Teaching at Home

Project FLAME validates Hispanic parents' home language. Parents work at home with their children in the language they know best. They learn that what they teach in their native language will help their children in school. This is supported by the work of Cummins (1986) and Fillmore (1990). In relation to a question on the role of parents helping their children to read, Isabel wrote,

> They (the parents) ought to be teachers and friends so that children don't look at reading as a chore, but as FUN. Parents should take kids to the library; and share books with the family. Parents ought to help kids to write (and themselves write) to help the reading process; make pictures, work together.

Irma, writing on the same topic, said, "Parents should show them the letters of their name, read them stories with big letters, draw and write with the children and play games with them." It is clear from these responses and similar ones from other parents that they clearly saw their role as *teachers* regardless of the language they used when teaching.

When parents were asked about whether children should learn to read at home, at school, or both, Margarita answered,

> In both, because they will learn much faster in school if we teach them a bit at home. What he learns in school won't go over his head as much if he already knows a bit. It's like climbing a ladder. If they know how or have an idea of how to climb, they'll climb it quicker. If they've never climbed a ladder they won't climb it as fast.

Irma replied,

> Both. We have the responsibility to teach them to read and most of all to facilitate the comprehension of what they read, because we know our children. We can inspire them by giving life to books.

These parents see themselves as partners with the school in developing literacy and a love for books.

Regarding the frequency of reading or sharing books with their children, the following three examples show the FLAME parents' views about ways to enhance interest in literacy at home. Leticia reported,

I try to read to them as often as I can. I read to them before they go to sleep. My son likes to hear the same story more than once and I like to do this because then I feel good when he tries to read it and has memorized parts of it. My husband and their grandparents also read to them. Usually it's my son who is after us to read to him.

Isabel explained home literacy use and routines she had already developed:

[We read] Everyday—in the living room, in the afternoon. I read short children's stories from the library, our own (over and over). We read round robin, and even though Ruben doesn't read, he "reads" from pictures and memory and imagination. My husband reads, too. I initiate—we have a regular schedule. We ask predictive questions and comprehension questions. We sometimes don't read the conclusion until we all imagine and tell our own.

Margarita explains how her love for reading has impacted literacy at home in the following statement:

I read with them everyday because I enjoy it. However, my children look through and "read" their books all day long. Sometimes we sit on the floor, sometimes on the sofa. We don't have a specific time, usually when I finish my housework or early in the morning. They like to look at the books they chose at the book fair and they're always after me to read with them. We talk about the pictures in the books and they always ask a lot of questions, too many, I would say.

Changes in the Family

Project FLAME validates parents' knowledge. Parents realize that not all knowledge comes from schooling and that they have a lot of knowledge to share with their children. This perspective is supported by the funds of knowledge work as described by Vélez-Ibáñez and Greenberg (1989) and Moll et al. (1992). When asked what were the three most important things the families have gained through participation in Project FLAME, Isabel wrote,

I can help my children with their schoolwork, even in English. I am more confident of myself as a helpful mother. I have lost my fear of speaking English in public. I have learned ideas from classmates and teachers and it

has opened my mind. We feel powerful when we come to school meetings. We sit together and we feel useful. People ask me for help and I can
help them. I can get what I want to achieve and participate more.

Margarita explains how her participation in the program has
changed communication and life at home:

My family has become more united as a result. My husband has witnessed
what a change spending more time with his children can do. He has
changed and really enjoys his sons more now. I have learned how valuable it is to share ideas and be part of a group. My children now have a
more responsive father who is more interested in what they learn, in what
I learn.

Leticia explains the impact of the program:

The most important thing is that I have learned so much that I can now
help my children to do better and understand them better. My children
have learned how to use books, how to handle them and they have learned
more English not only from the books we've gotten, but because I know
more English now. My children have learned more by doing the activities
I've learned to do with them and I've learned how much I can do with
them. Also, my children have learned much from the activity books given
to us.

Changes in the Schools

Project FLAME enables parents, many of whom are new immigrants,
to develop a network with other parents who share their knowledge
and interest in the education of their children. These social networks
are very important for parents because they allow parents to share
their knowledge and acknowledge their cultural assets as resources
in support of their work with their children at home and in school
(Moll et al., 1992). Teachers notice that Project FLAME parents are
more active in the school. They participate in school events and
several have become members of local school councils. FLAME parents who become candidates for the local school councils in their
children's schools run their own campaigns and have been elected
by public vote. Clearly, they are more confident in voicing their own
views about their children's education.

Some Characteristics That Have Made FLAME a Successful Family Literacy Model

A few years ago, Project FLAME was reviewed for its effectiveness by the Illinois Board of Education and, upon their recommendation, it became an Academic Excellence model through the Office of Bilingual Education and Minority Language Affairs (OBEMLA-USDE).

Project FLAME enables parents, many of whom are new immigrants, to develop a network with other parents who share their knowledge and interest in the education of their children. These social networks...allow parents to share their knowledge and acknowledge their cultural assets as resources in support of their work with their children at home and in school (Moll et al., 1992).

The first factor in Project FLAME's success is *flexibility*. Although we have a basic organization for the workshops (presentation of the topic, discussion, hands-on demonstrations, and follow-up activities), we adapt our Parents as Teachers sessions to the needs of the specific group we are serving. Each session has a specific set of objectives, but the activities are planned in a way that encourages sharing knowledge. The parents who are learning to be Parents as Trainers and other parents usually have a lot to contribute to a topic and the design of activities. This makes the sessions more relevant to them and appropriate for the children in the specific school and community.

The second factor is the *powerful social networks* that develop among FLAME parents (as described previously). This was an outcome we originally had not anticipated, but it became apparent when parents talked about what they had learned not only from FLAME teachers but also from other parents and children. One mother said that the program opened her mind as she learned ideas from other FLAME parents and teachers. Maria explained, "I liked what we learned and the strength of the enthusiasm of the teachers. Being able to interact with the other students and learn from them." Lorena said, "I liked the patience that the teachers had in explaining things and the companionship between the teacher and the students." Parents were able to build friendships, share ideas, and collaborate with school personnel.

A third factor that contributes to program effectiveness is the *format and delivery of Parents as Learners ESL classes*. Project FLAME's family literacy and ESL classes are based on a participatory and functional model. From the beginning we follow the notion of an emergent curriculum (Auerbach, 1992). Functional literacy in the context of our project is related to what the parents feel is necessary in order to facilitate daily oral and written communication in English and Spanish. This includes increasing their ability to negotiate their daily worlds: communicating with medical personnel, meeting with teachers, helping their own children, and applying for jobs.

Mothers may initially focus on improving their oral English in order to assist their children with homework, yet they soon realize they need to improve their basic literacy and computational skills in order to do this or meet other English language needs. According to Freire and Macedo (1987), "Literacy becomes a meaningful construct to the degree it is viewed as a set of practices that functions to either empower or disempower people" (p. 141).

In Project FLAME, parents' learning is not limited to increasing their skills, although this in itself is empowering. Rather, writing and speaking about their experiences have led to changes in their relationships with the wider society. In other words, functional literacy developed into a set of cultural practices that promoted emancipatory changes in their lives (Freire, 1970). The ESL lessons, then, are participatory in nature and are based on communicative competence rather than a formal perspective in language learning. Our purpose is to make FLAME participants feel they can talk and write in English. At the appropriate point, we know that the formal aspects of English will become relevant to the parents, and we will teach them.

A fourth factor that leads to Project FLAME's success with participants stems from *a context of collaboration*. Participant parents have a voice in the planning of both the Parents as Teachers and Parents as Learners (ESL) sessions. Project FLAME parents are not interested in giving up their own traditions, language, and values, yet they realize that they cannot negotiate the dominant culture without learning about it. We do not want them to forget their own culture; we simply try to add new knowledge to their cultural repertoire. We encourage discussion among parents about the effects that changing routines

> *Project FLAME parents are not interested in giving up their own traditions, language, and values, yet they realize that they cannot negotiate the dominant culture without learning about it.*

and activities have in their families and in their own lives (Freire, 1970).

A fifth factor is *assessment*. The data collected provides project organizers with information about possible participants in the program, their interests, needs and life patterns. This allows us to offer what is relevant to them and to modify program activities. Also, it is important when planning a family literacy program to integrate activities for the whole family. Although most of Project FLAME activities occur during the day and are mostly attended by mothers, we expect that fathers and older school children participate in some activities such as book fairs, field trips, and homework. This requires planning flexible activities for every member of the family.

Sixth, several *additional services* support the success of Project FLAME. We offer free transportation to and from school if needed. We also offer childcare, because some activities are not intergenerational and do not require that the children and parents stay together. Also, in order to keep high attendance, we employ community liaisons that remind families of program activities and visit or call the families if their attendance lags.

Finally, *capacity building* within the communities and schools where Project FLAME takes place is very important. Although FLAME as a university-family-school partnership has been offered for 11 years, we know that at some point the university component will have to leave. The Training of Trainers component is, in our view, a way to develop capacity among people in the community to offer the program once the university services are not available.

Conclusion

Home-school collaborations such as Project FLAME bring together parents, schools, and communities. Parents become more involved in their children's education. Most want to help their children and are an excellent resource that schools and teachers do not fully utilize (Delgado-Gaitan, 1990, 1991; Epstein, 1990, 1991; Goldenberg, 1987, 1993). Schools benefit by welcoming parents who then take active roles as volunteers. Parents feel respected when schools and teachers see them as teaching partners. Limited English proficient parents develop self-efficiency as their children's first and most important literacy teachers when they know that they can teach their children in the language they know best.

Finally, through FLAME, parents have found a program that supports the whole family—a program that takes into account their concept of *familia* and that is culturally congruent with their way of teaching and learning. Project FLAME provides a collaborative family literacy program to facilitate families' participation and understanding of their new community and schools (Rodríguez-Brown & Meehan, 1998; Rodríguez-Brown & Mulhern, 1993).

References

Abi-Nader, J. (1991). *Family values and the motivation of Hispanic youth.* Paper presented at the annual meeting of the American Educational Research Association, Chicago, IL.

Applebee, A., Langer, J.A., & Mullis, I. (1987). *Learning to be literate in America.* Princeton, NJ: National Assessment of Educational Progress.

Auerbach, E.R. (1992). *Making meaning making change: Participatory curriculum development for adult ESL literacy.* McHenry, IL: Delta Systems.

Clay, M.M. (1993). *Stones—The concepts about print test.* Auckland, New Zealand: Heinemann.

Cummins, J. (1986). Empowering minority students: A framework for intervention. *Harvard Educational Review, 56,* 18–36.

Delgado-Gaitan, C. (1990). *Literacy for empowerment: The role of parents in children's education.* Philadelphia: Falmer Press.

Delgado-Gaitan, C. (1991). Involving parents in schools: A process of empowerment. *American Journal of Education, 100,* 20–41.

Delgado-Gaitan, C. (1992). School matters in the Mexican-American home: Socializing children to education. *American Educational Research Journal, 29,* 495–513.

Edwards, P.A. (1988). *Lower SES mothers' learning of book reading strategies.* Paper presented at the annual meeting of the National Reading Conference, Tucson, AZ.

Edwards, P.A. (1999). *A path to follow: Learning to listen to parents.* Portsmouth, NH: Heinemann.

Epstein, J.L. (1990). School and family connections: Theory, research, and implications for integrating sociologies of education and family. In D. Unger & M. Sussman (Eds.), *Families in community settings: Interdisciplinary perspectives* (pp. 99–126). New York: Haworth Press.

Epstein, J.L. (1991). Effects on student achievement of teachers' practices of parent involvement. In S. Silvern (Ed.), *Advances in reading/language research*. Greenwich, CT: JAI Press.

Feitelson, D., & Goldstein, Z. (1986). Patterns of book ownership and reading to young children in Israeli school-oriented and non-school-oriented families. *The Reading Teacher, 39*, 924–930.

Fillmore, L.W. (1990). Latino families and the schools. *California Perspectives, 1*, 30–37.

Freire, P. (1970). *Pedagogy of the oppressed*. New York: Seabury Press

Freire, P., & Macedo, D. (1987). *Literacy: Reading the word and the world*. South Hadley, MA: Bergin and Garvey.

Gallimore, R., & Goldenberg, C.N. (1989). *School effects on emergent literacy experiences in families of Spanish-speaking children*. Paper presented at the annual meeting of the American Educational Research Association, San Francisco, CA.

Goldenberg, C.N. (1987). Low-income Hispanic parents' contributions to their first-grade children's word recognition skills. *Anthropology and Education Quarterly, 18*, 149–179.

Goldenberg, C.N. (1993). The home-school connection in bilingual education. In M.B. Arias & U. Casanova (Eds.), *Bilingual education: Politics, practice, and research* (pp. 225–250). Chicago: University of Chicago Press.

Goldenberg, C.N., & Gallimore, R. (1991). Local knowledge, research knowledge, and educational change: A case study of early Spanish reading improvement. *Educational Researcher, 20* (November), 2–14.

Heath, S.B. (1987). Sociocultural context of language development. In California State Department of Education Bilingual Education Office, *Beyond language: Social and cultural factors in schooling language minority students* (pp. 143–186). Los Angeles: Evaluation, Dissemination and Assessment Center.

Metritech. (1987). *The Illinois reading assessment project: Literacy survey*. Champaign, IL: Author.

Moll, L.C., Amanti, C., Neff, D., & Gonzalez, N. (1992). Funds of knowledge for teaching using a qualitative approach to connect homes and classrooms. *Theory Into Practice, 31*(1), 132–141.

Moll, L.C., & Greenberg, J.B. (1991). Creating zones of possibilities: Combining social contexts for instruction. In L.C. Moll (Ed.), *Vygotsky and education*. New York: Cambridge University Press.

National Center for Family Literacy. (1991). *The effects of participation in family literacy programs*. Louisville, KY: National Center for Family Literacy.

National Council of La Raza. (1990). *Hispanic education: A statistical portrait 1990*. Washington, DC: Author.

Nickse, R., Speicher, A.M., & Buchek, P.C. (1988). An intergenerational adult literacy project: A family intervention/prevention model. *Journal of Reading, 31*, 634–642.

Paratore, J.R. (1994). Parents and children sharing literacy. In D. Lancy (Ed.), *Emergent literacy: From research to practice* (pp. 193–216). New York: Praeger.

Paratore, J.R., Melzi, G., & Krol-Sinclair, B. (1999). *What should we expect of family literacy? Experiences of Latino children whose parents participate in an intergenerational literacy project.* Newark, DE: International Reading Association.

Psychological Corporation, The. (1986). *Boehm-R—Test of Basic Concepts* (Rev.). San Antonio, TX: Harcourt Brace Jovanovich.

Rodríguez-Brown, F.V., & Meehan, M.A. (1998). Family literacy and adult education: Project FLAME. In C. Smith (Ed.), *Literacy for the twenty-first century* (pp. 176–193). Westport, CT: Praeger.

Rodríguez-Brown, F.V., & Mulhern, M. (1993). Fostering critical literacy through family literacy: A study of families in a Mexican-immigrant community. *Bilingual Research Journal, 17,* 1–16.

Sable, J., & Stennett, J. (1998). The educational progress of Hispanic students. In National Center for Education Statistics, *The condition of education 1998* (pp. 11–19). Washington, DC: U.S. Department of Education.

Shanahan, T., Mulhern, M., & Rodríguez-Brown, F.V. (1995). Project FLAME: Lessons learned from a family literacy program for linguistic minority students. *The Reading Teacher, 48*(7), 2–9.

Shanahan, T., & Rodríguez-Brown, F.V. (1993, April). *The theory and structure of a family literacy program for the Latino community.* Paper presented at the annual meeting of the American Educational Research Association, Atlanta, GA.

Silvern, S. (1988). Continuity/discontinuity between home and early childhood education environments. *The Elementary School Journal, 89,* 147–160.

Teale, W.H. (1984). Reading to young children: Its significance for literacy development. In H. Goelman, A. Oberg, & F. Smith (Eds.), *Awakening to literacy* (pp. 110–121). Portsmouth, NH: Heinemann.

Tobin, A.W. (1981). *A multiple discriminant cross validation of the factors associated with the development of precocious reading achievement.* Unpublished doctoral dissertation, University of Delaware, Newark, DE.

Van Fossen, S., & Sticht, T.G. (1991). *Teach the mother and reach the child: Results of the intergenerational literacy action research project.* Washington, DC: Wider Opportunities for Women.

Vélez-Ibáñez, C.G., & Greenberg, J.B. (1989). *Formation and transformation of funds of knowledge among U.S. Mexican households in the context of the borderlands.* Paper presented at the annual meeting of the American Anthropological Association, Washington, DC.

Wheeler, M.E. (1971). *Untutored acquisition of writing skill.* Unpublished doctoral dissertation, Cornell University, Ithaca, NY.

Reading at Home, Reading at School
Conflict, Communication, and Collaboration When School and Home Cultures Are Different

Gisela Ernst-Slavit, Jofen Wu Han, and Kerri J. Wenger

When Tong-bing's parents received a newsletter from his teacher, Ms. Allen, announcing the launching of the first-grade Read-at-Home Project, they were amazed—and more than a little confused—by the teacher's request for parents to read daily to their children. Tong-bing's mother and father each held postsecondary degrees; they had been successful students in their homeland, China. They expected Tong-bing to succeed in his new U.S. school as well. But not once, as Tong-bing's puzzled mother reflected, had a Chinese teacher encouraged parents to spend study time at home reading stories to children!

Tong-bing's mother and father were not the only parents in his community who felt confused, challenged, and even a bit irritated by the proposed Read-at-Home Project. Some parents of limited English proficient (LEP) students felt that the teacher was asking too much of parents—and perhaps even shirking her own responsibility to teach her students to read in English. For the most part, Chinese parents in Tong-bing's community were not aware of the correlation between reading to children and children's literacy development (Han, 1996). Reading aloud to children is a literacy practice unknown to Chinese families; similarly, it is a practice unknown to families from many other linguistic and cultural backgrounds (Faltis, 1996; Valdés, 1996). Parents of many LEP students believe that school is supposed to take care of children's literacy learning.

> *Reading aloud to children is a literacy practice...unknown to families from many other linguistic and cultural backgrounds (Faltis, 1996; Valdés, 1996). Parents of many LEP students believe that school is supposed to take care of children's literacy learning.*

How can Tong-bing's teacher communicate to his parents the importance of reading at home? How can she help build a bridge between Tong-bing's parents' beliefs about literacy and schooling and the literacy practices she encourages in her first-grade classroom? In this chapter, we will address these and other questions raised by teachers and parents of LEP students. First, we briefly review the importance of parent involvement for all children—especially for LEP students. This review will serve as a backdrop for a discussion of Ms. Allen's first-grade classroom—a literacy community (Han, 1996; Han & Ernst-Slavit, 1999). Tong-bing's parents' reactions to both Ms. Allen's literacy practices and general educational practices in the United States will aid our understanding about the tensions that can emerge when teachers and parents have very different ideas about the goals of education and the roles of schooling. We then discuss Tong-bing's participation in selected activities in his first-grade classroom to illustrate how teachers' efforts to involve parents can enhance or hinder the successful participation of LEP students in classrooms. We conclude with a brief summary of this work, with suggestions for improving the development of collaborative literacy communities in classrooms for children of all linguistic backgrounds.

Importance of Parental Involvement in Literacy Instruction

Parental involvement is an essential part of educational equity for all groups. It is particularly important for LEP students precisely because of potential differences in values and beliefs about the role of teachers, literacy, education, and schools held by parents and educators. But truly effective parent involvement is not complete unless it is a two-way street (Ernst, 1994). Only when communication is systematically established and maintained between parents and teachers can we say that the school and the home work in a collaborative manner. The school may have the main responsibility for the formal education of children, but the home makes a significant contribution, because parents are the first teachers of their own children (Henry, 1996; de Santiago, 1991).

Research indicates the need for parent involvement to promote children's success in school (see Faltis, 1996; Trueba, 1987). Parents of ethnically and linguistically diverse students often fail to participate in the schools in numbers comparable to other majority group parents (Delgado-Gaitan, 1991). An increasing number of anthropology-based researchers have concluded that the culture of the school differs from that of the home in important ways for many language minority students (Ernst-Slavit, 1997; Heath, 1983; Philips, 1993; Trueba, 1987). When a student like Tong-bing enters a school in the United States, schooling becomes a discontinuous process for both the child and his or her parents, thanks to differences in languages, cultures, values, and literacy practices.

In the past few decades, researchers and educators have focused on parent involvement in schools (Delgado-Gaitan, 1991; Henry, 1996; Sarason, 1995), and one can find lengthy lists of recommendations for fostering home-school collaboration (see, for example, Garcia, 1999; Soto, 1996). However, few studies have documented specific steps monolingual teachers follow in order to collaborate with parents of LEP students. This chapter will focus on the efforts of one first-grade teacher—a native English speaker in her fifties with more than 15 years of first-grade teaching experience—to connect with parents of her LEP students and encourage their involvement in their students' English literacy learning. In the fall of 1995, Ms. Allen discovered that her class of 25 first graders included 6 LEP students, 4 of whom spoke Chinese. One of these students was Tong-bing. In the next section, we shadow Tong-bing's journey into a new world of literacy practices and English language learning in Ms. Allen's classroom.

Tong-bing's Journey: A Few Months of English, Kindergarten to First Grade

Tong-bing's first-grade classroom is in College Hill, a rural university town in the northwestern United States. Mountainview Elementary School is one of three elementary schools in the district. It is a Title I school with a K–5 student body of approximately 300 students. Students attending Mountainview are children of faculty and staff employed by the local university, business community, or international students. In any given year, approximately 10 to 20 different countries are represented in the student population of the elementary school.

During the 1994–1995 school year, six Chinese-speaking children entered kindergarten at Mountainview. Four children came from China, and two came from Taiwan. All of their parents were students in the state university. All spoke Chinese as their primary language. Tong-bing joined the kindergarten class in late March when the rest of the Chinese-speaking children had experienced almost 7 months of an enriched kindergarten curriculum and were functioning quite well in both regular and ESL classes. Tong-bing, however, from his entrance into kindergarten seemed to be a "silent stranger" in the classroom. When the school year came to an end, most of the Chinese-speaking children had developed strong English skills and seemed to be adapting quite successfully to their new school—all, in fact, except Tong-bing.

Interviews with the parents of the six kindergarten "graduates" revealed that language socialization at home during the summer vacation before first grade was predominantly in Chinese; in other words, during the summer, these children had few opportunities to practice their newly acquired English skills. During the 1995–1996 school year, the children were assigned to two different first-grade classes. Tong-bing, Pei-wen, Guan-lin, and Shao-min were assigned to Ms. Allen's class. Pei-wen, Shao-min, and Guan-lin adapted very well in the first-grade class in spite of limited practice in English over the summer. They joined happily in most activities from the beginning of the school year and communicated well with Ms. Allen and their peers. Tong-bing, however, did not.

Ms. Allen noted that all four of her Chinese-speaking students were doing well in mathematics, but she was concerned about Tong-bing's progress in reading and writing. Shao-min, Guan-lin, and Pei-wen were all reading at grade level after only a few months in the classroom. Wanting to help Tong-bing, Ms. Allen diligently tried to devise strategies for his success, both in her own classroom and at home with his parents.

Ms. Allen's First-Grade Classroom: A Literacy Community

Ms. Allen worked to scaffold reading opportunities for her students in both the physical makeup of the classroom and in the ways she organized her literacy instruction. Her room was filled with print. Arranged in a small lofted area in the classroom were several bins filled with books ranging from wordless picture books to informational books. There were three shelves of books located in different areas of the classroom, including advanced chapter books for the most proficient readers. Whenever students found themselves with free time (for example, during a few minutes' wait while others accomplished group activities), they were encouraged to select books to read, and to write or draw about them. Without doubt, students in Ms. Allen's class had a great deal of exposure to all kinds of children's books.

Ms. Allen made special efforts to include the entire school community in her first graders' developing literacy skills. For example, every Thursday afternoon, "reading buddies" from the fourth grade came to read to the first graders. During this time, children and their buddies scattered around the classroom. The fourth graders read stories to the first graders, who listened eagerly, offering comments and reactions to the books. Talk and laughter buzzed around the classroom. The cross-age, interactive reading period was a highlight of the week.

Just as Ms. Allen worked to include the school community into her reading instruction, so she encouraged the wider community to take part in her students' literacy learning. A crucial element in her reading instruction was the Read-at-Home Project, which typically began in early October. All children participated in a nightly reading program by selecting books from Ms. Allen's extensive class library to read at home. Students were expected to read and record a minimum of 10 books per month.

Ms. Allen summarizes her beliefs about literacy: "I believe in doing it [literacy] and doing it a lot." She explained that quality literature is important, but significant exposure to any kind of reading and a large amount of writing is important for developing readers. Many of her daily instructional activities focused around literacy. For example, her daily "centers," scheduled as part of an 80-minute block organized around group activities, mainly revolved around reading and writing practices across content areas. During their centers, students wrote in journals, read together and alone, practiced penmanship, and listened to stories.

Ms. Allen's Efforts to Foster Parent Involvement

As the early months of the school year passed, Ms. Allen became very concerned about Tong-bing's literacy development. He participated in center activities reluctantly, seemed obsessed with his handwriting, rarely selected books on his own, and wrote very little in his journal. In fact, the only literacy activities he seemed to enjoy were penmanship practice and drawing elaborate pictures for his journal. Worried about Tong-bing's progress, Ms. Allen hoped to enlist his family's support in encouraging his second language and literacy development. She reviewed her customary efforts to communicate, collaborate with, and involve parents. She also enlisted the help of the second author of this chapter, a researcher and native Chinese-speaking parent herself, to function as a parent liaison. During structured interviews in their home, the liaison systematically requested information from Tong-bing's parents about his language, culture, and literacy experiences, and their educational expectations. With the help of the parent liaison, Ms. Allen was able to review her communication and collaboration strategies and convey her pedagogical goals and practices to parents. Together they looked at her strategies, which included the following:

1. Handbook for parents. At the beginning of the school year Ms. Allen gave every parent a handbook with information on her first-grade curriculum and ensuing activities. The handbook contained one-year goals for each of the content area subjects (i.e., reading and writing, spelling, mathematics, science and health, and social studies). For example, a summary of the goals for reading and writing reads, "In reading, students will participate in daily large- and small-group instruction including: children's literature, big books, daily free reading to and with adults and peers, books on tape, language experience stories, and writing." Writing activities include journals, response writing, stories, and writers' workshop. In addition, Ms. Allen explained the main thrust of a unique program called the Read-at-Home Project.

2. The Read-at-Home Project. On October 2, 1995, Ms. Allen sent home with each student the first take-home book and a newsletter explaining the purpose of the Read-at-Home Project:

> Dear Parents,
>
> Today your child is bringing home her first Read-at-Home book. This is a very important component of first grade in my classroom. Because independent reading of moderately easy materials is so important to the development of reading, I believe it is important for young children to practice reading every day....
>
> In the front of the Record Book you will find suggestions for reading with your child. I appreciate your assistance in the important process of educating your child.

Some of the suggestions for parents included how to read a book to their child, how to read with their child, how to record information about the material read in the record book, and suggestions for the number of books a child should read every month.

3. Notes to parents at the beginning of a project or unit. Every time she and her students started a new area of thematic study or began a new phase of literacy instruction, Ms. Allen let parents know what was coming up for her students. For example, early in the year, Ms. Allen sent home a sheet titled "Topics for my Journal" for parents to fill out. The purpose was for parents to discuss with their children possible topics of interest. Children brought lists with topics such as family, friends, pets, hobbies, trips, games, special people, and memories. The completed list was stapled on the first page of the journals so students could consult the list when selecting a topic to write about in their journals.

    4. Structured and open invitations for parent visits and volunteerism. Other activities used by Ms. Allen to build bridges with her students' parents included the traditional parent-teacher conferences, monthly newsletters featuring students and classroom events, invitations to parents to volunteer or be guest speakers in the classroom, and school spaghetti nights. Parents were welcome at any time in her classroom, and Ms. Allen informed parents of many ways in which they might share their expertise with students.

Tong-bing's Parents' Reactions to Ms. Allen's Literacy Practices

While Ms. Allen thought about other ways she could enlist and encourage Tong-bing's family to help him, his parents were doing some thinking of their own about the strange school their son had entered. When Tong-bing's parents received the notice and the first book Tong-bing checked out from the classroom, they were amazed by the fact that parents apparently needed to read to their children. Even with their high educational backgrounds, reading to children was something they had never done before. Interviews with Tong-bing's parents shed some light about why they were so surprised about the need to take an active role in the literacy education of their child (see Han, 1996; Han & Ernst-Slavit, 1999). These reasons included the following:

    1. Lack of awareness of the benefits of reading to children. In general, Chinese parents are not aware of the correlation between reading to children and children's literacy development. Reading aloud to children is simply not practiced in Chinese families. Chinese parents believe that school is responsible for children's literacy learning. If parents provide books for their children to read, children are supposed to read those by themselves.

2. *Lack of reading materials.* Frugality is a very common trait among immigrant families. For example, at the time of this study, Tong-bing's family was living on his mother's salary as a doctoral research assistant. Their small income, in addition to their lack of awareness about the value of providing many authentic reading materials in English for a beginning reader, meant that they did not buy books for Tong-bing; they also did not take him to borrow English books from the city library. They believed that memorizing vocabulary words would be the best way for Tong-bing to learn English. The only English book that Tong-bing had at home was an illustrated children's dictionary. Most of his Chinese books were textbooks.

3. *Lack of confidence in reading to children in English.* At first, Tong-bing's parents had no difficulty in reading the simple books he brought home. Later, as he became more confident, Tong-bing brought home some science books. His mother felt that this was a very challenging task for her. "There are many terms I do not even know how to pronounce. But his appetite for reading is becoming bigger and bigger," she stated.

Tong-bing's Parents' Concerns About Educational Practices in the United States

Once they discussed the challenges involved in meeting the Read-at-Home Project goals with the Chinese-speaking parent liaison, Tong-bing's parents felt freer to articulate some unsettling concerns they harbored about U.S. schooling practices. These concerns ranged from surprise at the "open" educational atmosphere at Mountainview Elementary to a desire for their children to participate in more rigorous subject area lessons. Ms. Allen realized that Tong-bing's parents were concerned about much more than the act of reading at home to their son.

First, they saw Mountainview as "a freer educational environment." As opposed to the Chinese schooling system, which emphasizes rote learning and discipline of students by giving absolute power and authority to the teacher, the U.S. educational system seems to be a "paradise" for Asian students. Tong-bing's parents were amazed by how the value of freedom is revealed in the schooling system. In particular they were concerned about how classrooms are organized, the amount of homework, and the length of the school day. Tong-bing's parents noticed that classrooms in the United States "let us feel that this is a freer environment." Tong-bing's mother continued to elaborate on this point: "In China, we don't have...centers. We are supposed to sit in rows and everyone listens and looks at the teacher."

Another aspect that surprised Tong-bing's parents was the amount of homework assigned. "I used to hear that many children who had studied in the U.S. for a few years did not want to go back to their home countries. No wonder. Here the teacher does not give too much homework," said Tong-bing's father. Tong-bing's mother added, "In China, starting in first grade, children are supposed to do homework every night. On the average, it takes 2 hours to finish their homework." The length of the school day was another aspect that surprised Tong-bing's parents. They felt that for children to go home at 3:00 causes some inconveniences for parents. Thus, they, like other Chinese parents in the community, do not have a choice but to send their children to an after-school program until 5:00 or 6:00.

The lack of emphasis on subject matter was another concern voiced by Tong-bing's mother. She added, "This is especially reflected in the instruction of mathematics." Both parents were concerned about the slow pace of math in the first-grade classroom. While the teacher was working on one-digit addition and subtraction at school, Tong-bing's parents made him repeatedly practice two- and three-digit operations at home. As Tong-bing's mother said about the importance of math, "To succeed in America, I believe we need to be very strong in technical fields. We are non-native speakers. Any American in the street speaks better English than us. I know Tong-bing will definitely speak better English than my husband and me. But being good at mathematics will equip him with better opportunities in the future." The value placed on math is very common among first-generation Asian immigrants. In a study comparing Korean students living in Japan or the United States, Joann Fang Jean Lee (1991) points out that family and peer group factors interact to motivate Korean students to concentrate on mathematics or technical fields.

Tong-Bing's parents also voiced that they wanted Tong-bing to be "perfectly bilingual." In his autobiography *Hunger of Memory* (1982), Richard Rodriguez states that he needs to forget Spanish and his old identity to think of himself as an American. Tong-bing's parents think differently. "I want Tong-bing to be perfectly bilingual. Being able to speak perfect English plus knowing Chinese will make him a well-rounded professional in the future," said Tong-bing's mother. That is why Tong-bing was encouraged to spend his evenings and weekends learning Chinese.

Because Chinese logographs number in the thousands and are complex regarding spatial configuration, language instruction in the primary grades in China has focused on practicing Chinese characters. In China, daily homework assignments for first- and second-graders emphasize the writing of Chinese characters, in part because a character has to fit in one small square. With the belief that "practice makes perfect," Tong-bing's parents required him to practice five characters and to read aloud a three- to four-sentence-long passage from a Chinese textbook every evening. The emphasis on reading Chinese characters and the attention to penmanship became evident in how Tong-bing participated in the literacy practices in the classroom, discussed in the next section of this chapter.

Tong-bing's Participation in Classroom Literacy Activities

After observing Tong-bing's progress in school and becoming aware of his parents' concerns about U.S. literacy instruction, Ms. Allen realized that she would need to focus her attention on explaining the literacy practices that were important to student success in her classroom. Ms. Allen worked to increase Tong-bing's parents' participation in the Read-at-Home Project by more clearly articulating what she expected from Tong-bing. During school hours, she resolved to help Tong-bing become successful at two literacy practices in particular: journal writing and writers' workshop.

After observing Tong-bing's progress in school and becoming aware of his parents' concerns about U.S. literacy instruction, Ms. Allen realized that she would need to focus her attention on explaining the literacy practices that were important to student success in her classroom.

Tong-bing's Participation in the Read-at-Home Project

On the first day of the project, Tong-bing brought home his first Read-at-Home book and a beautifully covered record book with his name. The record book is used as a checklist where children are to write the titles of the books they read, which should then be signed by the parent. Tong-bing's parents misunderstood the instructions and asked Tong-bing to copy the whole book, word by word, on the record book.

The next day, when Ms. Allen noticed that Tong-bing had copied the whole book, she wrote in the record book, "Only titles, please." While a very simple instruction, this specific written request enabled Tong-bing to meet both his teacher's (keeping a record of books read) and his parents' (practicing his writing) requirements for homework. As Ms. Allen requested, he wrote only titles of his books in his school record book. Because Tong-bing's parents believed that copying the texts was beneficial for Tong-bing's knowledge of English and penmanship, they prepared another notebook for him to use at home, in which he copied the whole text from each Read-at-Home book he brought home.

As time went on, Ms. Allen continued to send brief notes and words of encouragement to Tong-bing and his parents. While his father still asked that Tong-bing copy each book he brought home and to memorize the spelling of each English word, he and Tong-bing also began to read aloud to each other at home in English.

Tong-bing's Participation in Journal Writing

The three other Chinese children, Pei-wen, Guan-lin, and Shao-min, who unlike Tong-bing had a whole year of kindergarten, did not seem to have any problems with journal writing. They could easily produce several meaningful sentences. What distinguished these three Chinese children from Tong-bing was that they were already very familiar with the particular literacy culture of "journaling"—writing down their ideas—even though they were not sure about correct spellings. Better control and knowledge of English made this adaptation possible. Moreover, these three children could easily interact with others and were aware of sources available for finding words, ideas for writings, or suggestions for spelling. For example, Pei-wen would discuss with her neighbors what to write if she could not come up with a topic for her journal. For spellings, she would look through several books or find environmental print for accuracy. One time, during the first week of December, Pei-wen was asked to write about Christmas. She searched through all the print displayed on the walls of her classroom until she found the word "Christmas" on a book cover.

Unlike his peers, Tong-bing felt very intimidated during journal writing, because he neither knew he needed to write something in his journal nor could never imagine what he might write and did not seem to feel comfortable asking his peers. Together, Ms. Allen, Tong-bing, and the second author of this chapter discovered that his difficulties arose from several problems:

1. Not knowing the nature and purpose of journal writing. The first thing that puzzled Tong-Bing was that he did not know what a journal was. He asked several times in Chinese, "What's journal?" Sometimes he even asked, "Do I have to write?" Ms. Allen would ask children to read to her what they wrote in the journal, so Tong-bing knew he needed to produce something on the paper in order to have something to read to the teacher. But not having control over much English vocabulary made him very hesitant to write any word about whose meaning he was not sure.

2. Not knowing how to "invent" spelling. Although Ms. Allen stated very clearly that children could use temporary spelling as long as they could sound out letters and write sentences that made sense, Tong-bing did not know how to sound out letters and tried to use words for which he knew the correct spelling.

3. Family influence: "I have to spell everything right." The clash between the home and school cultures became evident when literacy practices were compared. For example, every day Tong-bing's parents asked him to memorize several words from his illustrated English dictionary and asked him to copy the words in a notebook. Thus, although at home the emphasis was on memorizing words and perfect spelling, at school the focus was on writing out ideas and using invented spelling. Therefore, if Tong-bing had an idea but did not know how to spell it correctly, he would ask before trying to spell it on his own.

Tong-bing's first journal entries did not include words, only pictures. However, with the passage of time and the support of his teacher, Tong-bing developed some strategies in order to "survive" journal writing. These strategies included using the vocabulary memorized at home (e.g., for 3 weeks Tong-bing wrote about animals because he had memorized a list of animals in alphabetical order), using environmental print on hand (e.g., when writing about the colors of the animals, Tong-bing picked up the crayons and copied the words from the crayon wrappers), becoming familiar with classroom routines (e.g., using invented spelling), and learning more English. The more he wrote and read, the better his English became.

Tong-bing's Participation in Writers' Workshop

Out of all the literacy practices encouraged in and out of her classroom, Ms. Allen felt that Tong-bing made the most progress during the writers' workshop. The workshop structure and format gave Tong-bing two important things: the time he needed to immerse himself in his new language and a risk-free environment in which to write and speak in English, revise his work, and learn new vocabulary and spelling in English.

DRAFTING. The first story Tong-bing wrote was "Dad and Baby." During this stage, Tong-bing did not interact with other children and wrote quietly. When he did not know the spelling for his story's key word, *baby*, he looked it up in the B section of his list of words frequently used by first graders, compiled by Ms. Allen. After finding the word, he first said the whole sentence before writing it down on paper. It took him a one-hour session of the writers' workshop to finish the draft (see Figure 1).

CONFERENCING. On the next Tuesday afternoon, Tong-bing had a conference with the teacher. Ms. Allen congratulated him on writing a very interesting story. She suggested that he change the tense of the story: "When you are writing a story which happened in the past, you need to use past tense." As she pointed to "going to shopping," Ms. Allen said, "Let's change this to 'went shopping.'" Tong-bing agreed and murmured, "Went shopping." Then Ms. Allen wrote a note on the margin of his paper, "change verbs as needed," intended for the adult typist.

FIGURE 1
Tong-bing's First Draft of "Dad and Baby"

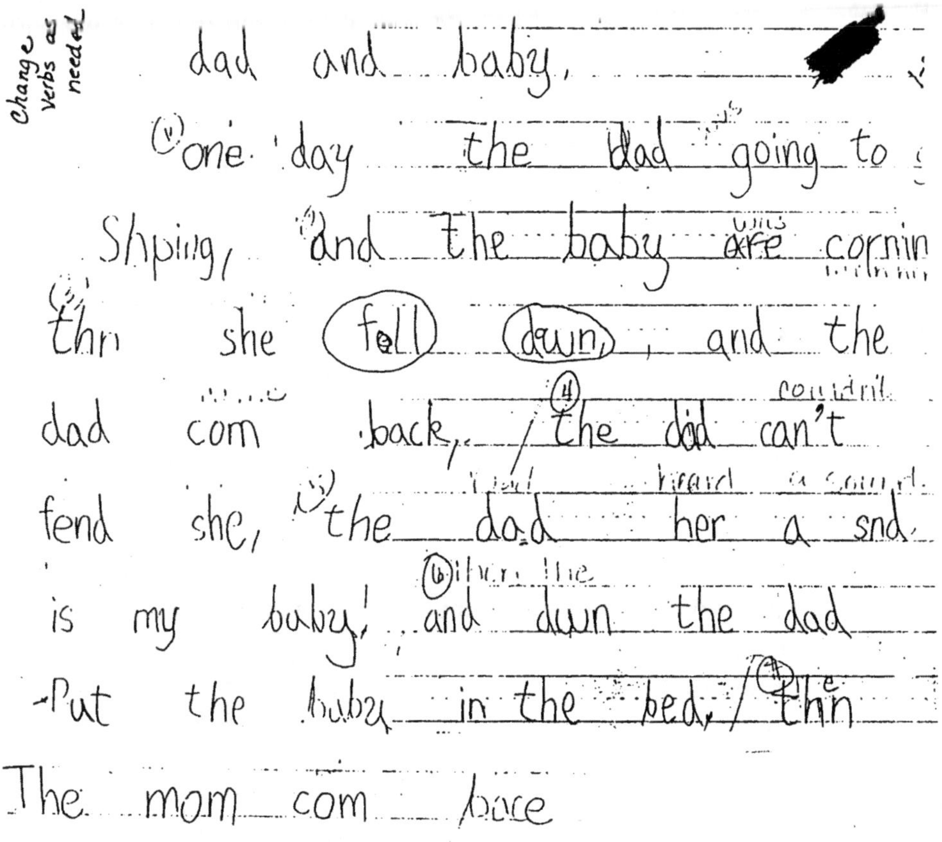

EDITING. Once the draft was revised by the teacher, each author read his or her story to the adult typist (a parent volunteer). As his story was being typed, Tong-bing mentioned that verbs needed to be changed to past tense. After the final changes were made, he read the story to the typist and a copy was immediately printed out.

LAYOUT AND ILLUSTRATION. Tong-bing carefully cut each sentence and pasted it on his book. Because Ms. Allen had emphasized the importance of illustrations, Tong-bing, who was a very dedicated artist, spent a whole hour on his illustrations.

AUTHOR'S CHAIR. Reading their stories to the whole class was an exciting event for the students and represented the end of the publishing process. Every week, during the last 5 minutes of the writers' workshop, students read their stories according to the order in which they were "published." It was during the fifth writers' workshop that Tong-bing sat in the author's chair. He read his book in a loud voice and proudly showed illustrations to the whole class. Figure 2 shows Tong-bing's first story.

The plot of Tong-bing's writing was not as sophisticated as that of other children's published work. However, during the writers' workshop Tong-bing was able to work at his own pace and to produce work he was proud to share with others. In particular, he had the opportunity to talk with the teacher and receive suggestions and attention. During the conference regarding the story of "Dad and Baby," Tong-bing came to understand the correct use of the simple past tense in English. When starting his second story, "A Greedy Cat," Tong-bing wrote, "One day mama went shopping." His correct use of the simple past tense in a different story context clearly shows that Tong-bing had benefited from his one-on-one conference with his teacher—an opportunity regularly afforded during writers' workshop.

The writers' workshop, which is organized around individual work and interpersonal interaction, provided LEP students in Ms. Allen's classroom with authentic opportunities to develop as writers. LEP students could work at their own pace and obtain individualized assistance from adults and more capable peers.

FIGURE 2
Tong-bing's Published Story

Dad and Baby

One day the dad went shopping.

The baby was crying.

The baby fell down and the dad came back.

The dad couldn't find her.

The dad heard a sound. He said, "It is my baby!"

Then the dad put the baby in the bed.

The mom came back.

Summary

According to Frank Smith (1988), learning is primarily a social rather than an individual accomplishment: "We learn from other people, not so much through conscious emulation as by 'joining the club' of people we see ourselves being like, and by being helped to engage in their activities" (p. vii). According to Smith, literacy learning occurs in the literacy club when the language and its use are meaningful, useful, continuous and effortless, incidental, collaborative, vicarious, and risk free.

The description and analysis of Tong-bing's participation in Ms. Allen's first-grade classroom illustrates how an authentic "literacy club" and community may unintentionally constitute a particularly challenging environment for LEP children—especially at the beginning stages of language and literacy development.

The description and analysis of Tong-bing's participation in Ms. Allen's first-grade classroom illustrates how an authentic "literacy club" and community may unintentionally constitute a particularly challenging environment for LEP children—especially at the beginning stages of language and literacy development. This is because many LEP children have not yet acquired a certain repertoire of words, sentence patterns, and especially certain "cultural knowledge," which keeps them from participating freely in the classroom. This is not to suggest that holistic teaching is not suitable for LEP children; in fact, we have seen how Tong-bing benefited from this kind of experience as well. At issue here is the challenge of helping newly arrived children to get support from their home so they can become active participants in their new literacy environment. Ms. Allen made a special effort to keep parents informed of goals, expectations, and activities. But collaboration and communication between the home and the school is not complete unless it is a two-way street (Ernst, 1994). Ms. Allen, who already had an understanding of the differential values and beliefs different cultures placed on schooling and literacy practices, was able to learn more about her Chinese-speaking children by working with a parent liaison. Furthermore, as a result of the knowledge gained via the parent liaison, Ms. Allen modified her communication strategies and instructional practices accordingly to enhance Tong-bing's literacy learning both at home and at school.

The challenges Tong-bing faced in Ms. Allen's classroom were not only due to his developing knowledge of English. Tong-bing's difficulties early on were partly caused by the differences between the literacy practices at home and school. Interviews with Tong-bing's parents revealed that the literacy practices at home were deeply influenced by Chinese ways of teaching and learning literacy skills. Believing that "practice makes perfect," Tong-bing's parents required him to practice five to six characters, some pages of math problems, and to read aloud a three- or four-sentence passage from a Chinese textbook every evening. The emphasis on reading Chinese characters and the attention to penmanship are reflected in the way Tong-bing participated in the literacy practices in the classroom—especially in his journal writing. He only attempted to write words he was sure of spelling, and he paid great attention to his handwriting.

Over time during the first-grade school year, Ms. Allen was able to provide the communication and support Tong-bing's parents needed to help him succeed at school practices in English. By the end of the school year, Tong-bing was not only reading at grade level but he finished among the top-third students in Ms. Allen's first-grade classroom. This success can be explained by the varied strategies used by Ms. Allen to foster home-school collaboration, which included (1) a two-way communication approach with teachers gaining as much information from parents as possible; (2) a handbook for parents outlining her first-grade curriculum and practices; (3) the Read-at-Home Project, which required parents to read to and with their children; (4) a variety of notes to parents at the beginning of projects and units; (5) structured and open invitations for parent visits and volunteerism; (6) working with a parent liaison who can understand and communicate both home and school perspectives; (7) integrating the wisdom and knowledge of the cultural groups of her students; and (8) systematically learning about her students' parents' concerns and adapting her strategies accordingly.

Although every situation for teachers is slightly different as new children speaking new languages enter their classrooms, Ms. Allen's strategies shed some light on how mainstream teachers can help students improve their literacy skills in a second language. It is important to underscore that Ms. Allen felt that knowing more about the

Chinese-speaking parents' concerns—many of which she had not encountered before—helped her explain her goals and instructional practices more clearly. Finding ways to communicate with parents in a risk-free situation in their own homes (as the parent liaison was able to do) proved very beneficial for Ms. Allen. Although Chinese-speaking parents continued to view some traditional first-grade activities as frivolous and undemanding (such as being asked to create or provide Halloween costumes, or helping children decide on journal topics), parents of LEP students were happy to receive explicit communication and instructions about how to help their children complete English literacy assignments. Like Tong-bing's parents, they worked hard at home to assist their children in adopting literacy practices advocated at school, without abandoning conventional Chinese literacy learning practices. When teachers like Ms. Allen, LEP students, and parents work together to identify and resolve misunderstandings, to foster literacy practices from diverse cultures, and to involve parents in student success at school, true collaboration is achieved.

References

Delgado-Gaitan, C. (1991). Involving parents in the school. A process of empowerment. *American Journal of Education, 100*(1), 20–46.

de Santiago, R.A. (1991). Parental involvement in bilingual education—A matter of attitude. *NABE News*, pp. 17, 22.

Ernst, G. (1994). Beyond language: The many dimensions of an ESL program. *Anthropology & Education Quarterly, 25*(3), 317–335.

Ernst-Slavit, G. (1997). Different words, different worlds: Language use, power and authorized language in a bilingual classroom. *Linguistics and Education, 9*, 25–48.

Faltis, C.J. (1996). *Joinfostering: Adapting teaching for the multilingual classroom.* Englewood Cliffs, NJ: Prentice Hall.

Garcia, E. (1999). *Student cultural diversity: Understanding and meeting the challenge.* Boston: Houghton Mifflin.

Han, J.W. (1996). *Crossing border: Literacy learning of a newly arrived Chinese child at home and at school.* Unpublished doctoral dissertation, Washington State University, Pullman.

Han, J.W., & Ernst-Slavit, G. (1999). Come join the literacy club: One Chinese ESL child's literacy experience in a 1st-grade classroom. *Journal of Research in Childhood Education, 13*(2), 144–154.

Heath, S.B. (1983). *Ways with words.* New York: Cambridge University Press.

Henry, M. (1996). *Parents: The forgotten educators.* New York: State University of New York Press.

Lee, J.F.J. (1991). *Asian American experiences in the United States: Oral histories of first to fourth generation Americans from China, the Philippines, and Japan.* Jefferson, NC: McFarland & Company.

Philips, S.U. (1993). *The invisible culture: Communication in classroom and community on the Warm Springs Indian Reservation.* Prospect Heights, IL: Waveland Press.

Rodriguez, R. (1982). *Hunger of memory: The education of Richard Rodriguez.* New York: Bantam Books.

Sarason, S.B. (1995). *Parental involvement and the political principle: Why the existing governance structure of schools should be abolished.* San Francisco: Jossey-Bass.

Smith, F. (1988). *Joining the literacy club.* Portsmouth, NH: Heinemann.

Soto, L.D. (1996). *Language, culture, and power: Bilingual families and the struggle for quality education.* New York: State University of New York Press.

Trueba, H.T. (Ed.). (1987). *Success or failure? Learning and the language minority student.* New York: Newbury House.

Valdés, G. (1996). *Con respeto: Bridging the distances between culturally diverse families and schools: An ethnographic portrait.* New York: Teachers College Press.

17

Collaboration Across Language, Age, and Geographic Borders

Teresa J. Kennedy and George F. Canney

It is March and the year is flying by! Mrs. Monroe, in her seventh year as the technology specialist at a rural midwestern U.S. middle school with a diverse student population, greets her eighth graders as they pour into the lab. They are chattering excitedly about communicating with their project partners throughout South America. Mrs. Monroe's preservice intern, Bob Ashley, is pulling together some easier reading materials on weather for two mainstreamed students.

Each computer monitor displays the GLOBE (Global Learning and Observations to Benefit the Environment) homepage. On the overhead is an outline of the period reminding them of the scheduled Web chat in Spanish at 10:43. Three Hispanic students, Luis, Soledad, and Andrea, who are in charge of preparing the chat questions, double check with their group members about the relevance and accuracy of their questions regarding the weather system La Niña.

These eighth graders are more than ready to participate online because of the ongoing collaboration among several middle school teachers—Shirley Monroe and her colleagues Bob Stewart, math; Alison Freitas, science; Seichi Taka, social studies; and Isabel Pareño, Spanish. What makes this day so special is that Dr. Postawko, a prominent U.S. meteorologist, and Drs. Arguillo and Padilla, atmospheric specialists in Mexico City, Mexico, will be discussing La Niña and its impact on global weather patterns. All the students are engaged; they are using their developing Spanish competence to communicate with international partners about the science, math, and social studies concepts presented in their other classes. More significantly, they are starting to examine authentic phenomena as scientists, mathematicians, and geographers while making cultural comparisons with other linguistic communities. As Lacey states when presenting their project to the local school board meeting, "What's so exciting about our classes is that we get to actually do stuff instead of just reading it out of a book. We get to work with real scientists." Her teachers and parents agree. This classroom of diverse learners is an example of the tremendous potential collaboration, positive teamwork, and interdisciplinary study have for helping limited English proficiency students participate in the regular class curriculum while developing their English literacy skills and assisting their monolingual peers to acquire skills in a second language.

I n every region of the United States, urban and rural, classrooms are becoming increasingly diverse ethnically and linguistically; almost 42% of the students in public schools represent minority populations (National Center for Education Statistics, 1993). School achievement tests in English indicate that students with limited proficiency in English must overcome enormous equity gaps in their struggle for academic achievement and success in our competitive society (Thomas & Collier, 1997/1998). The two most common educational options for these students are variations of transitional bilingual education and English as a Second Language (ESL) pull-out programs.

One ESL transitional model, the 50-50 model, offers a two-way, integrated bilingual setting for both native English-speaking students and limited English proficient (LEP) students. These groups stay together throughout the entire school day, during which approximately half the time is allocated to instruction in each language. Most 50-50 models found in the United States utilize Spanish as the second language in the classroom, because approximately 75% of the language-minority students in the U.S. education system are Hispanic (Padilla et al., 1991). Typically, program goals include students becoming functionally proficient in both English and the other language, acquiring the subject content taught in both languages, and developing an understanding and appreciation of other cultures (Thomas & Collier, 1997/1998). The 50-50 bilingual model has been successful in schools when there is a near equal student representation of both languages in every classroom and the teachers are bilingual themselves. Consequently, it is not a viable option in most schools.

In classrooms where a student minority speaks a heritage language other than English, pull-out programs are common. However, these instructional programs for LEP students have not been especially successful. Too often LEP students have been treated as remedial learners, or have been grouped separately from their English-speaking peers within the classroom. As a result, these LEP students are labeled as academic failures and given limited access to the standard grade-level curriculum afforded their native English-speaking peers.

> *Too often LEP students have been treated as remedial learners, or have been grouped separately from their English-speaking peers within the classroom.*

In the final analysis, the academic benefits of the 50-50 and pull-out models have been limited; frequently these programs lack clearly defined goals and the procedures vary dramatically among locations. Because most LEP students are assigned to regular classrooms taught by teachers with limited knowledge of ESL methodologies (Spangenberg-Urbschat & Pritchard, 1994), new approaches are needed to serve both LEP students and native speaking students.

A first step is for the teachers to realize that LEP students in the regular classroom offer their English-speaking peers exciting learning opportunities. Their presence in a classroom provides every student a chance for greater understanding of and appreciation for our pluralistic society. Students often develop more positive attitudes toward the countries whose language and customs they have studied or have been exposed to (Graham, 1988; Kennedy, Nelson, Odell, & Austin, 2000). Altwerger and Ivener (1994) confirm that learners bring a wealth of knowledge about oral and written language to the classroom; that the culture of the home, the community, and the society at large influences learners' language and literacy knowledge; that self-esteem and language are nurtured by the support and encouragement learners receive from the significant people in their lives; and that learners play an active and collaborative role in their learning environment. Although monolingualism can be a serious barrier to basic understanding among various ethnic groups, having majority language students (English-speaking students) and minority language students collaborate helps all students to grow academically, linguistically, and socially.

It is appropriate to hold all students to the same high academic standards, and an integrated, collaborative ESL model immerses the LEP student completely into all classroom activities. It highlights collaboration between home, school, and community; promotes respect for the background and perspective of the LEP student; and provides equal access to subject matter.

GLOBE and Content-Based Foreign Language Programs: Models for Promoting Collaboration and Second Language Acquisition

Global Learning and Observations to Benefit the Environment (GLOBE) plus content-based secondary foreign language or foreign language elementary school (FLES) programs integrate the basic areas of science, math, technology, social studies, and second language learning, as well as promote collaboration in the classroom. Content-based foreign language programs introduce students to second languages other than English; language content must overlap with the grade-level subject material. The content-based instruction (CBI) approach to learning languages gives students a more integrated view of their own learning, enabling them to see the interconnection between the various subjects they study (Brumen, 2000). This same philosophy can easily be carried into the regular classroom when working with LEP students. Studies have indicated that students involved in CBI make language gains equal or superior to those of students in traditional language classrooms, learn large amounts of subject matter, develop more positive attitudes toward the target language, show increased self-confidence in their ability to use the target language, and express an interest in pursuing its study (Dupuy, 2000). The GLOBE Program combined with CBI helps LEP students acquire English literacy skills in the regular classroom while learning the curriculum outlined for their grade level. (Acquisition of a language means to pick it up at a gradual pace, gaining the ability to communicate in the language without necessarily being able to articulate the rules [Felder & Henriques, 1995].)

The GLOBE Program combined with CBI helps LEP students acquire English literacy skills in the regular classroom while learning the curriculum outlined for their grade level.

GLOBE encourages students to behave as scientists and mathematicians; students must work collaboratively to collect, analyze, and report data. Since its inception in 1995, GLOBE has expanded into a worldwide network of Grade K–16 students and teachers in over 10,000 schools in more than 95 countries. GLOBE teachers enable their students to network with scientists, students in other countries, and community agencies while collecting atmospheric, hydrologic, geologic, and biometric data from their school's 90-by-90-meter study site. On October 13, 1999, seventh graders in a geography classroom at Walnut Ridge Middle School in Arkansas, USA, submitted the four-millionth GLOBE measurement. These data collected by students all over the world to monitor the earth are reported via the Internet to scientists connected with GLOBE, NASA (National Aeronautics and Space Administration), and NOAA (National Oceanic and Atmospheric Administration). Students extend their knowledge of math, science, social studies, and technology while they measure, calculate, report, and enter data on the Internet. GLOBE provides a creative way to integrate other subject areas into reading and writing. Consequently, teachers can explore more topics authentically and in less time. Integrating GLOBE into the curriculum enables teachers to meet high education standards in an inquiry-based and integrated fashion.

Because GLOBE is a worldwide program, materials are currently available in all six United Nations languages (English, Spanish, French, Russian, Mandarin, and Arabic), plus German, and more languages are becoming available all the time. GLOBE students are introduced to other languages and cultures as they engage in authentic projects and meaningful discussions with classmates, students in other countries, and world experts in the disciplines they are studying (Kennedy, 1999). LEP students in these classrooms are using GLOBE materials in English and are helping their classmates understand the same GLOBE content written in the LEP students' home languages. Where there is GLOBE plus FLES or other content-based foreign language programs, the learning environment is characteristically collaborative, respectful of each person's background, and all students have full access to the content material appropriate for their grade level.

The GLOBE program is a means of bringing virtually every classroom in the school together to work on the same mission with other students and scientists all over the world. Students build weather stations in their industrial technology classrooms and study different countries involved in the program as part of their geography and social studies classes. Foreign language classrooms are provided with authentic opportunities for communication through GLOBE-Mail, which connects every GLOBE classroom around the world. Students concentrate on protocols in their science and math classrooms when learning research methodologies and manipulating data sets. Students in the technology classroom use their own data sets to create elaborate charts and graphs to compare their findings with other areas around the world. The GLOBE program also supports the multicultural study of geography by providing students with hands-on experience with basic geographic skills such as understanding latitude, longitude, scale, map elements, and spatial analysis. Because GLOBE links teachers and students around the world, it fosters alliances among students and increases not only their environmental awareness but also their understanding of other cultures and their sense of a global community. GLOBE allows teachers to put the concepts of authentic learning, student-scientist partnership, and inquiry-based pedagogy into practice on an unprecedented scale.

Literacy Skill Development

Many innovative activities appropriate for LEP students integrate GLOBE into the regular math and science curriculum. Literacy skill development can be enhanced using storybooks that highlight scientific protocol areas (see Primarily GLOBE at http://www.globe.fsu.edu) and integrate grade-appropriate, inquiry-based science activities into school curricula. Many teachers are incorporating GLOBE activities into projects that require independent research and report writing, critical thinking, problem solving, and data collection. Students can simply read a book or they can combine reading with hands-on, minds-on investigation and really gain an understanding of the literature. For example, reading about water quality may not hit home until students have the chance to visit the riverbank, perform tests on the water, and record data in their field notebooks. Creative writing activities such as Haiku, a Japanese form of poetry, can be used later in the classroom to describe students' findings and to explore new vocabulary.

Second Language Acquisition

GLOBE plus content-based foreign language programs encourage LEP students to assume active roles in the classroom by facilitating cultural understanding and teaching their native languages to their monolingual peers. When paired with FLES or any secondary foreign language program, GLOBE helps students learn a second language by incorporating all five features of the National Standards in Foreign Language Education Project (1996)—communication, cultures, connections, comparisons, and communities. Following the standards allows teachers to move beyond language- and skills-based curricula, ultimately introducing as well as reinforcing other disciplines and communities. As the opening vignette of this chapter reveals, the energy and enthusiasm generated in this type of collaborative, authentic learning environment are impressive.

Meeting Diverse Student Needs

The GLOBE program has been implemented at the K–16 level to meet the diverse student needs found in each school. Students at McDonald Elementary in Moscow, Idaho, USA, for example, have been utilizing a combination of GLOBE with FLES to create an enrichment program that actively includes the Hispanic student population in the school while enhancing the academic achievements of the entire student body. This partnership includes the Moscow School District and the University of Idaho's Foreign Language Department; Institute for Mathematics, Instructional Technology, and Science (IMITS); and College of Education. School district teachers and administrators, community volunteers, and university faculty collaboratively plan the content-based foreign language curriculum. Native speakers from Spain, Mexico, Guatemala, Costa Rica, Colombia, Ecuador, Argentina, and other Spanish-speaking countries studying at the University of Idaho collaborate with elementary and secondary science, math, and Spanish language preservice teachers. Referred to as the "language experts," the native-speaking students receive a modest stipend from the Idaho Space Grant Consortium for their classroom assistance. These teaching teams provide instruction in Spanish to first- through sixth-grade elementary students for 30-minute periods, three times each week. The teaching strategies encourage collaborative and interdisciplinary activities (Kennedy, Odell, Jensen, & Austin, 1998). Preservice teachers at the university study pedagogy in their science, mathematics, and foreign language methods courses before entering the classrooms. They then introduce the required GLOBE protocols to conduct the investigations and present, in Spanish, key concepts related to science, math, social studies, and technology. Native Spanish-speaking community volunteers also assist by working directly with classroom students as well as the preservice teachers during instruction. This program provides a vehicle for the LEP students to learn content (math, science, and social studies) in their native language while developing their English skills. It also allows them to assume leadership positions in their classrooms when the discussions and Internet exchanges occur with groups from other Spanish-speaking countries. (For more information about this and similar programs in Idaho, visit http://ivc.uidaho.edu/fles or http://globe.ed.uidaho.edu/globe.)

Another example of the collaborative nature of the GLOBE program can be found at Quaker Valley Middle School in Sewickley, Pennsylvania, USA. Students in this school have been using GLOBE materials to study South America in their social studies classroom. They exchange information with South American GLOBE schools using parallel GLOBE materials written in English. The Quaker Valley sixth-grade students compose e-mail bulletins in Spanish and weekly videos that report weather data to their South American partners. This program allows all students to contribute to the classroom learning community, including LEP students who share their heritage language and culture with the class.

California's Kingsbury High School students and their classroom teacher have implemented an exemplary model of cross-age collaboration. Because of Kingsbury's early involvement with GLOBE, as well as the initiative taken by the Kingsbury GLOBE team collecting data year round, Kingsbury High School has contributed more data than any other GLOBE school in the world. The Kingsbury GLOBE team has also tutored GLOBE students in two Kingsbury GLOBE elementary schools. This cross-age tutoring has encouraged schoolwide collaboration, respect for the backgrounds and perspectives of all students, and enhanced content learning and cooperation.

Another cross-age example can be seen with eighth-grade GLOBE students at Nolan Middle School in Killeen, Texas, USA, who are involved in a number of collaborations. They communicate and conduct research projects through GLOBE-Mail with GLOBE students at Belton Junior High in Belton, Texas, USA, and have provided biometric information for a student at Tabor Academy in Marion, Massachusetts, USA. They are also comparing their data with GLOBE schools in Australia.

The increased "time on task" afforded by cross-age collaboration improves the rate of acquisition of reading skills for students who have fallen behind their instructional group. Multiage learning has traditionally been a feature of urban and suburban districts alike. These environments must be closely monitored in respect to instructional organization and curriculum development in order to maximize cooperative and self-directed student learning. Utilizing GLOBE, instructional organization and curriculum development to support cross-age collaboration are simplified through the pre-made lesson plans and established protocols employed by all GLOBE students.

In other countries where students are required to learn English as their second language, schools are using GLOBE materials written in

English. The country coordinator for GLOBE Greece shared that

> the students are excited about having the real opportunity to practice their English through communications with GLOBE scientists and students in other countries. Participating in the GLOBE Web chats is particularly exciting as it requires the students to quickly read and respond to messages in English. ("GLOBE Offers," 1998)

Students can easily gather information about different countries from books and from the Internet, but GLOBE-Mail connects them with students their same age in schools around the world. A teacher in Arizona explains,

> They write and edit very carefully when they know their message is going to another country, when someone other than me is going to be reading it. There is often a lot of back and forth between the students as they explain different hobbies and customs. It provides a huge incentive to go into more depth, and there's a lot of research, reading, and writing involved. ("GLOBE Aids," 2000)

Research has also shown that the electronic versions of dialogue journals have a significantly positive effect on the amount of language generated by students, and they improve students' attitudes toward learning and practicing the target language (González-Bueno & Pérez, 2000).

A unique program housed at the Mississippi School for the Deaf in Jackson, Mississippi, USA, uses GLOBE to teach English to students who are deaf or hard of hearing. During the summer of 1998, the students presented their research projects on El Niño at the GLOBE International Learning Expedition in Helsinki, Finland. They also taught key GLOBE terms and phrases in American Sign Language (ASL). These students' first language is ASL, but through GLOBE they switch to English text to read and write—the knowledge required to participate in online chats and GLOBE-Mail. Ongoing projects include regular correspondence with students from the Pennsylvania School for the Deaf regarding daily weather conditions, which allows students from both schools to compare temperature differences be-

> *Students can easily gather information about different countries from books and from the Internet, but GLOBE-Mail connects them with students their same age in schools around the world.*

tween a northern state and a southern state. GLOBE is a collaborative tool that facilitates learning in an inclusive classroom consisting of students with a broad range of abilities, learning styles, and special needs. The hands-on, minds-on nature of GLOBE activities provides life-centered curricula that have helped many special education students in Alabama achieve success in the classroom for the first time ("GLOBE Community," 1999). Minor adaptations to GLOBE activities allow the program to work successfully with the entire classroom without using "watered down" curriculum or untested programs.

Teachers work every day in inclusive classroom situations where students with a broad range of abilities and learning styles are provided with authentic educational experiences that foster collaboration and community building. The academic benefits of student participation in this interdisciplinary program are currently being documented as formal evaluations of the GLOBE program are under way. All indications to date are that GLOBE science and educational activities assist students in reaching higher levels of achievement in science and math, and improve ability to implement sampling, data collection, and interpretation procedures (Finarelli, 1998). Based on a survey of 344 teachers who implemented the program in elementary, middle/junior high, and high schools, students learned better observational and measurement skills, collaborated well in small groups, and employed technology effectively (Center for Technology in Learning, 1997, 1998). Leon Lederman, awarded the Nobel Prize in Physics in 1988, praised GLOBE as the "quintessentially ideal program for involving kids in science" in a November 30, 1999, address to teachers at the Fermi National Accelerator Laboratory in Batavia, Illinois, USA. Students have also indicated in surveys that they believe their work with GLOBE is important to the scientific community and that the GLOBE program helps them to better understand the Earth. Motivation to learn peaks when students are given a sense of meaningfulness in regard to their studies. Because it is linked with the goals of most second language programs, GLOBE is an effective vehicle for meeting the needs of LEP students and challenging other students to explore a second language. (For information about how your school can join the GLOBE program, see the GLOBE homepage at http://www.globe.gov.)

Where programs such as FLES and GLOBE are not available, strategies and methods can be incorporated easily into the regular classroom to address the needs and interests of every student and the required grade-level content. The remaining portion of this chapter will address other examples that provide ample opportunities for collaboration, especially for schools without adequate ESL services.

Collaborative Instructional Practices for LEP Students in the Traditional Classroom Setting

Given the wide range of literacy abilities within a classroom, students cannot be expected to excel at the same rate or be on the same reading level. Nevertheless, the same literacy teaching strategies used with English-speaking students can be adapted to teach LEP students (Canney, Kennedy, Schroeder, & Miles, 1999). Helping LEP students to share personal stories, special events, and their own languages and customs breaks down barriers to learning by alleviating the fear students feel when they cannot understand what is being said or expected of them (Morison, 1990). Sometimes LEP students struggle with English phonemes that do not exist in their heritage language. They may also transfer the syntactic patterns of their own language into English. For example, many Asian students are apt to omit inflectional endings such as *s, d, ing, er,* and *est* from both written and spoken English because there is no equivalent form in their heritage language. Spanish speakers tend to have difficulty adjusting to the English vowel system because Spanish vowels have five distinguishable sounds that rarely change.

Helping LEP students to share personal stories, special events, and their own languages and customs breaks down barriers to learning by alleviating the fear students feel when they cannot understand what is being said or expected of them (Morison, 1990).

The most natural learning sequence for language acquisition and successful literacy skill development provides opportunities for LEP students to work cooperatively with English-speaking students. Through daily conversations in the classroom and on the playground, the listening and speaking skills of LEP students emerge, providing a basis on which to build reading and writing proficiency.

The value of oral communication in the classroom for second language learning is well established (Asher, 1993). Asher's Total Physical Response (TPR) method helps students acquire vocabulary in a manner similar to how a child learns his or her first language—by immersion in a language-rich environment and by collaboration with other students to produce and practice vocabulary. As well, with TPR, LEP students learn to respond to commands without formal grammar lessons or rules (Celestino, 1993). LEP students learn English through creative activities such as games, songs, rhymes, dances, acting, and role play. The Gouin series in language instruction (Grittner, described in Curtain & Pesola, 1994) has the teacher pantomime the actions of a series of oral statements. The class responds through pantomime, first as a group and then individually. This method promotes recall by utilizing multiple meaning reinforcers such as physical action; visuals and props; logical sequence; beginning, middle, and end scenarios; and multiple sensory features. A related practice, Total Physical Response Storytelling (TPRS), provides students with listening and speaking practice, and enables them to add humor, creativity, and originality to their stories (Ray & Seely, 1997). These strategies help teachers tailor instruction for all students in a class, including LEP students.

Adding visualization and hands-on features to instruction that pairs students and engages them in active collaboration requiring them to use language enhances learning for both LEP and English-speaking students. Slides, transparencies, videos, pictures, real objects, models, and foods evoke two or more of the senses (Healey, 1990). Advance organizers (Omaggio-Hadley, 1993) and short video excerpts preceding a lesson or discussion provide and activate valuable background information for all students (Hanley, Herron, & Cole, 1995; Tierney & Readence, 2000).

Another key benefit of collaboration in the regular classroom is that the environment feels safer. LEP students are helped by their peers to explore English expressions without the fear of sounding odd or speaking and writing incorrectly. Dialogue among students encourages linguistic approximations and extended conversations about meaningful topics and texts (Swiderek, 1996). Reading and writing assignments can be completed by small groups of students and buddy teams so that the LEP student has ongoing encouragement and support to reflect, plan responses, and engage in higher order thinking in English (Hayes & Schrier, 2000). To foster collaboration between LEP students and native English speakers, the teacher might address the class as a whole, then adjust assignments for students of differing language competencies and background knowledge. The use of tiered assignments, paired or buddy learning, flexible groupings, student teams, and continual assessments make it feasible to instruct the LEP student in the regular classroom.

Content texts in the upper grades are often incomprehensible to one third or more of English-speaking students and nearly all LEP students. Consequently, the informed teacher will address the same content in lecture, video, class activities, and discussion. The class can be divided into smaller working groups arranged by English language proficiency, reading level, interests, and level of student self-directedness. In these groups, students are encouraged to assist one another on assignments appropriately tiered, or adjusted, to their needs and interests. For example, a small midwestern U.S. school district was faced with converting to a middle school plan, in which every teacher would be responsible for helping all students read. The students neither liked the text nor comprehended it well, and the teachers were unsure what to do about the situation. The model offered to them involved "slicing"—a procedure employing both flexible grouping, student collaboration, and content modification.

In a chapter on fossils, two key concepts were located that all the students—regardless of background, interest in science, language proficiency, or reading ability—ought to know: (1) paleontologists draw inferences from fossilized artifacts to infer how prehistoric life forms might have looked and behaved, and (2) paleontologists must apply their knowledge of the anatomy and behavior patterns of living animals to formulate inferences about ancient life forms. Learning these two concepts became the central purpose for assigning this text to the class.

An interesting prereading nonprint activity was created to assess, activate, and expand English-speaking and LEP students' prior knowledge about the topic. Magazine pictures of animals were cut into puzzle pieces and placed in coded envelopes. Students formed heterogeneous groups of three to piece the animal puzzles back to-gether. To approximate the conditions under which paleontologists work, some puzzle pieces were omitted and a few pieces from unre-lated pictures of other animals were added.

As the students worked cooperatively, the teacher moved among them asking what they were doing to identify their animals. They mentioned using shape, color, texture (evidenced in the print, such as a feather), and their knowledge of animals today as clues. These fea-tures, which the teacher wrote on the board, were also the ones men-tioned in the text as sources of evidence used by paleontologists to identify prehistoric life forms and potential behaviors.

Next, a list of key vocabulary was placed on the overhead, with a reference to page and column in the science text. The students helped one another locate each new word in the text and discussed what they thought the words meant. For reinforcement and to promote deeper understanding, students worked with an assigned partner to complete a word search puzzle that contained some, but not all, of the new words. Students had to first match a subset of the key terms listed to their printed definitions to know which words were in the puzzle.

To this point, the activities had not been differentiated according to individual student needs, especially different language needs, al-though three grouping formations had been employed: random peer groups, student pairs (predetermined), and whole class. Now it was time to "slice" off those students motivated and capable of handling the chapter independently. Using previous information about stu-dents' reading levels, heritage language, previous content learning ex-periences, and interest in science, the class was separated into three groups. The most self-directed, motivated, and capable readers of science texts read the chapter with a partner and completed the ac-tivities outlined in a process guide. The guide reminded them to read the thought questions at the end of the chapter first, then as they were reading to note specific statements in the text that might be un-clear or questionable. After reading the selection, students chose miniresearch projects provided by the teacher. Their findings were re-ported to the whole class when they next convened as a group 2 days later.

The remaining students, most of whom could read the text once they had identified clear purposes and acquired additional background information, stayed with the teacher. They discussed a film showing paleontologists at work, discovering that what the class did in the puzzle activity coincided with procedures typically employed by paleontologists. After discussion, the students capable of reading the text were given an expectation outline as a study guide. The outline listed some main ideas and details, with other information omitted. Two thought-provoking questions stated at the beginning of the guide helped reiterate the purposes for reading. From this point, these students worked independently to read the text, then consulted reference materials to answer the questions about how fossils are located, preserved, and analyzed. Anyone who finished early joined other miniresearch groups and helped with their projects.

Both English-speaking and LEP students who were still struggling with the science concepts and had difficulty reading the science text independently worked directly with the teacher. They explored newspaper articles, magazine features, and models of fossils. They examined a cat skeleton to determine a cat's method of locomotion, eating preferences, and likely habits. With the teacher leading, this group also examined the science text illustrations, discussed the headings and key concepts, and either listened to the teacher read or read chorally key portions of the text related to important chapter details.

On day three, the whole class reconvened to discuss what they had learned through their group efforts. The students reaffirmed the two basic concepts of how paleontologists infer so much about prehistoric animals. Their semantic web included information about the topic, famous paleontologists, prehistoric animals that possibly lived on the very site on which they were now standing, and details about particular prehistoric life forms.

Flexible grouping practices, collaborative work efforts, and tiered assignments enhanced the literacy skills and language development of LEP students and students at various reading levels, and addressed the subject material expected of that grade.

Flexible grouping practices, collaborative work efforts, and tiered assignments enhanced the literacy skills and language development of LEP students and students at various reading levels, and addressed the subject material expected of that grade. These factors promoted collaboration on tasks suitable for students' reading abilities and language proficiency, and included adequate teacher assistance. The division of effort and assignment enabled all students to access grade-appropriate science information.

The method of slicing students into temporary learning groups provides opportunities for students of differing linguistic levels and content knowledge to collaborate. It also supports explicit teacher instruction when warranted. A collaborative approach accommodates three important components of the reading process: text difficulty, the literacy and language skills of readers/audience/learners, and the context within which literacy occurs. Arens and Swafar (2000) explain that utilizing these three components during instruction allows students to comprehend what a text can "mean." This approach also avoids labeling students by assigning them to one learning group based solely on an estimate of their overall reading level. Instead, it is an economical way to allocate teacher time for instruction and promote individual student initiative through collaboration. English-speaking and LEP students learn from one another and, in the process, discover there is strength in diversity of experience, interest, viewpoint, and purpose.

Summary

The chapter began with a description of teachers, students, and scientists communicating in first and second languages to accomplish authentic science, mathematics, and social studies projects via the Internet. It emphasized collaboration among diverse learners, especially when some of those learners have heritage languages other than English. An additional bonus was that the English-speaking students were also learning a second language, creating among the students a level of interdependence not characteristic of less diverse settings.

ESL communities are wonderful resources for the regular classroom teacher when cultural and linguistic differences are brought into the curriculum. Because cross-cultural contact is at an all-time high in human history, teachers must develop collaborative relationships with other educators, parents, and their communities that benefit all their students as well as further the linguistic, social, and cultural aspects of the literacy practices employed in our schools. Classroom models that encourage dual language learning, tiered assignments, and flexible grouping are effective forms of mainstream education. So, too, are instructional practices sensitized to the diverse backgrounds, abilities, and needs of all students.

References

Altwerger, B., & Ivener, B.L. (1994). Self-esteem: Access to literacy in multicultural and multilingual classrooms. In K. Spangenberg-Urbschat & R. Pritchard (Eds.), *Kids come in all languages: Reading instruction for ESL students* (pp. 61–81). Newark, DE: International Reading Association.

Arens, K., & Swafar, J. (2000). Reading goals and the standards for foreign language learning. *Foreign Language Annals, 33*(1), 104–120.

Asher, J.J. (1993). *Learning another language through actions* (4th ed.). Los Gatos, CA: Sky Oaks Productions.

Brumen, M. (2000). Content-based language learning—why and how? *Learning Languages, 5*(2), 10–16.

Canney, G.F., Kennedy, T.J., Schroeder, M., & Miles, S. (1999). Instructional strategies for K–12 limited English proficiency (LEP) students in the regular classroom. *The Reading Teacher, 52*(5), 540–544.

Celestino, W.J. (1993, December). Total physical response: Commands, not control. *Hispania, 76*(4), 902–903.

Center for Technology in Learning. (1997, December). *GLOBE year 2 evaluation: Implementation and progress* (SRI Project 6992). Menlo Park, CA: SRI International.

Center for Technology in Learning. (1998, December). *GLOBE year 3 evaluation: Implementation and progress* (SRI Project 6992). Menlo Park, CA: SRI International.

Curtain, H., & Pesola, C. (1994). *Languages and children—Making the match.* Reading, MA: Addison-Wesley.

Dupuy, B.C. (2000). Content-based instruction: Can it help ease the transition from beginning to advanced foreign language classes? *Foreign Language Annals, 33*(2), 205–223.

Felder, R., & Henriques, E. (1995) Learning and teaching styles in foreign and second language education. *Foreign Language Annals, 28*(1), 21–31.

Finarelli, M.G. (1998). GLOBE: A worldwide environmental science and education partnership. *Journal of Science Education and Technology, 7*(1), 77–84.

GLOBE aids in teaching reading. (2000, Spring). *GLOBE—Off Line.* Also available: http://www.globe.gov/fsl/html/templ_newsletter.cgi?spring_2000_page 7&lang=en&nav=1.

GLOBE community: Meeting the special needs of all students. (1999, Fall). *GLOBE—Off Line*. Also available: http://www.globe.gov/fsl/html/templ_newsletter.cgi?fall_1999_page3&lang=en&nav=1.

GLOBE offers lessons in language. (1998, Spring). *GLOBE—Off Line*. Also available: http://www.globe.gov/fsl/html/templ_newsletter.cgi?nlspring1998_page7&lang=en&nav=1.

Graham, C.R. (1988). Assimilative motivation and the development of second languages in children. In R. Benya (Ed.), *Children and language: Research, practice, and rationale for the early grades* (pp. 72–77). New York: National Council on Foreign Language and International Studies.

González-Bueno, M., & Pérez, L. (2000). Electonic mail in foreign language writing: A study of grammatical and lexical accuracy, and quantity of language. *Foreign Language Annals, 33*(2), 189–198.

Hanley, J.E.B., Herron, C.A., & Cole, S.P. (1995). Using video as an advance organizer to a written passage in the FLES classroom. *The Modern Language Journal, 79*(1), 57–66.

Hayes, N., & Schrier, L. (2000). Encouraging second language literacy in the early grades. *Hispania, 83*(2), 286–296.

Healey, J.M. (1990). *Endangered minds*. New York: Simon & Schuster.

Kennedy, T.J. (1999, Spring). GLOBE integrates mathematics, science, social studies, and technology into the foreign language classroom. *Learning Languages, 4*(3), 23–25.

Kennedy, T.J., Nelson, J., Odell, M.R.L., & Austin, L.K. (2000). The FLES attitudinal inventory. *Foreign Language Annals, 33*(3), 278–289.

Kennedy, T.J., Odell, M.R.L., Jensen, F., & Austin, L.K. (1998). A content-based, hands-on program: Idaho FLES. *Hispania, 81*(4), 933–940.

Morison, S.H. (1990). A Spanish-English dual language program in New York City. In C.B. Cazden & C.E. Snow (Eds.), *English plus: Issues in bilingual education* (pp. 160–169). *The Annals of the American Academy of Political and Social Sciences* (Vol. 508). Newbury Park, CA: Sage.

National Center for Education Statistics. (1993). *The condition of education*. Washington, DC: U.S. Department of Education, Office of Educational Research and Improvement.

National Standards in Foreign Language Education Project. (1996). *Standards for foreign language learning: Preparing for the 21st century*. Yonkers, NY: Author. ERIC Document Reproduction Services No. ED 394 279.

Omaggio-Hadley, A. (1993). *Teaching language in context* (pp. 10–12). Boston: Heinle & Heinle.

Padilla, A.M., Lindholm, K.J., Chen, A., Durán, R., Hakuta, K., Lambert, W., & Tucker, G.R. (1991, February). The English-only movement: Myths, reality, and implications for psychology. *American Psychologist, 46*(2), 120–130.

Ray, B., & Seely, C. (1997). *Fluency through TPR storytelling: Achieving real language acquisition in school*. Berkeley, CA: Command Performance Language Institute.

Spangenberg-Urbschat, K., & Pritchard, R. (1994). *Kids come in all languages: Reading instruction for ESL students*. Newark, DE: International Reading Association.

Swiderek, B. (1996, February). Metacognition. *Journal of Adolescent & Adult Literacy, 39*(5), 418–419.

Thomas, W.P., & Collier, V.P. (1997/1998). Two languages are better than one. *Educational Leadership, 55*(4), 23–26.

Tierney, R.J., & Readence, J.E. (2000). *Reading strategies and practices* (4th ed.). Boston: Allyn & Bacon.

A School-University Project on Collaboration and Consultation

Susan S. Osborne and Ann C. Schulte

Adele Peyton had been teaching public elementary school for 29 years when we approached her about participating in a university-public school collaboration experiment. This project was funded by the Office of Special Education Programs to investigate ways to include students with mild disabilities more fully in regular education classes. At the time we contacted Mrs. Peyton, she was planning her last year of public school teaching before retiring and beginning a second career of service to children through tutoring and volunteer work. Mrs. Peyton was an outstanding teacher who had received awards for her teaching both at school and district levels. She was looking forward to making her last year her best year ever for her students and herself, and we were at her classroom door, asking her to join us in what at the time was a new and untried endeavor.

Understandably, Mrs. Peyton was skeptical. Share her classroom—that very personal space—with a special education teacher—a complete stranger, at that? Revise her class schedule to meet the needs of an itinerant teacher? Change the teaching techniques she had developed and refined over 29 years to fit with those of another teacher? Put yourself in Mrs. Peyton's place. What decision would you have made?

After thinking over our proposal and talking to some trusted colleagues, she agreed to join us on what turned out to be an important initiative that has changed education for thousands of students and teachers. Mrs. Peyton did leave her school and her school district a remarkable legacy: She pioneered in developing a model for regular and special education teachers to work together to better meet the needs of students with learning disabilities and other students at risk for school failure. Her willingness to share her initial misgivings and her later enthusiasm for the model made her an effective spokesperson for collaboration. In this chapter we will share the perspectives of Mrs. Peyton and other teachers who participated in the project. We will also share some of our own insights regarding the nature of general education–special education collaboration.

The Need for Teacher Collaboration

Until recently, teachers generally have worked in relative isolation from other professionals. This isolation is surprising because what draws most teachers to the profession is their interest in people and their desire to share their love of learning. Teachers participate in a community of scholars who share their knowledge and their excitement in learning, whether they plan to teach young children to read, adolescents to use calculus, or students with disabilities to make the most of their potential. However, in many schools, teachers have been encouraged to go into their classrooms, close the doors, teach, and solve their own instructional and management problems.

As classrooms have become more diverse by including more students with academic and social skill needs, regular education teachers have faced increasingly greater numbers of students who do not respond successfully to traditional methods of instruction. Beginning in the mid 1970s, students who often had been excluded from schools because they were difficult to teach were guaranteed a place in the school community. In 1975, Public Law 94-142, the Education for All Handicapped Children Act, guaranteed that all students were entitled to a free and appropriate public education. Special education programs increased and most students who qualified for special education services spent most of their school days in the "mainstream" education program and were pulled out for specialized instruction from a special education teacher in a resource program.

A chief component of this federal law, reauthorized in 1997 as the Individuals with Disabilities Education Act (IDEA), is the right to an appropriate education in the *least restrictive environment* in which those educational services can be provided. This does not mean that all students should or can be taught in regular education classrooms all the time. It does mean however, that we cannot simply remove students from the regular education program when they prove difficult to teach or manage.

Concerns About Pull-Out Programs

Parents and educators have long recognized limitations of pull-out programs. Too often students placed in such programs never learn the skills and concepts they need to exit special education. Many times, students who spend parts of their days in a separate special education program miss out on important instruction that takes place in regular education. Sometimes students with academic learning problems return to the regular education classroom to find that they are responsible for class work that was taught while they were attending the resource room. If they are lucky, they may get some one-on-one instructional time with the teacher to learn the new material. Often, however, they must try to make up the work with minimal instruction from the teacher or help from a paraprofessional, volunteer, or parent. Furthermore, important instructional time inevitably gets lost in transition between the regular education classroom and the resource room—often the very students who have the greatest difficulty refocusing after a transition are those who make the most frequent transitions to special programs.

Teachers and parents also have been concerned about the possible stigma children face when they spend time in special education classes. When students experience such stigma, their self-esteem and self-confidence about learning may be hurt in ways that make learning even more difficult. This occurs when students see themselves as incompetent and begin to avoid academic instruction and practice.

In traditionally organized schools, regular and special education teachers typically have little or no opportunity to plan or consult together. As a result, students who already experience academic learning problems receive fragmented instructional programs that cannot provide the intense, carefully sequenced instruction with adequate opportunities for practice and corrective feedback that they require to learn successfully. Clearly, regular and special educators have needed to find ways to coordinate instruction for those students who most required excellent, intense, well-planned instruction in order to succeed.

Concerns about the limitations of pull-out programs led the Office of Special Education Programs of the U.S. Department of Education to provide grant funding for a series of projects in 1987 to develop and test programs to provide special education support in regular education programs to students with mild disabilities. We were fortunate to receive one of these grants to collaborate with a large and diverse school district in implementing two models for teaching students with disabilities without having to remove them from the regular education program.

Teacher Collaboration Theory and Research

We had approached the director of special education programs for this school district just as special programs administrators were searching for ways to better integrate students with learning disabilities and other special needs into the fabric of regular education. District administrators worked closely with us to develop a plan to provide collaboration and consultation services to a sample of students with learning disabilities and to compare their academic outcomes with students who continued to receive traditional resource room services for one or two periods each day.

Our project hired three masters-level special education teachers whom we trained to provide consultation and collaboration services to the sample of students who participated in our experiment. These teachers worked with regular education teachers to support students in the classroom. Of course, we included parents, teachers, and school administrators in each decision to change special education services for a student.

We compared student outcomes from these programs to student outcomes in traditional one- and two-period per day resource programs. We selected teacher consultation and teacher collaboration as possible ways for teachers to work together to address needs of students with learning disabilities in regular education classes.

We based our programs for teacher consultation and teacher collaboration on a four-stage behavioral consultation model developed by Bergan (Bergan, 1977; Bergan & Kratochwill, 1990). The stages or problem-solving steps in Bergan's model—problem identification, problem analysis, plan implementation, and plan evaluation—are depicted in Figure 1.

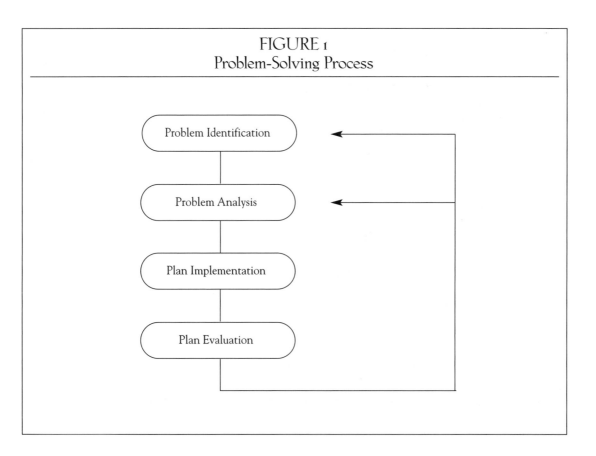

FIGURE 1
Problem-Solving Process

Special and regular education teachers serving target students followed all four steps. However, in the collaboration model, the special education teacher actually shared responsibility for teaching with the regular educator in her classroom, while in the consultation model, the special educator provided help with developing an intervention but did not actually co-teach.

PROBLEM IDENTIFICATION. Earlier research suggests that the first step toward successful problem solving is defining the problem in observable, measurable terms, or pinpointing the problem (Tombari & Bergan, 1978). For example, if two teachers discuss a student's poor oral reading skills, simply saying, "Greg is a poor reader" does not help them devise a good instructional program for Greg. The teachers need to know exactly what Greg can and cannot do and what skills are needed in the regular education classroom. Does Greg know the sounds most commonly associated with letters? Can he say them quickly? Can Greg blend sounds together to form words? How does his reading rate (correctly read words per minute) compare with typically achieving students in his class? Can Greg answer literal questions about a paragraph he has just read? Can Greg paraphrase a simple story he has read? Can he identify the most important concepts in a chapter from his social studies text? The more time teachers spend describing the problem in precise terms, the greater their chances of solving the problem. In our project, at the first stage, teachers worked together to identify the academic or social problems students with learning disabilities were facing in their regular education classrooms.

PROBLEM ANALYSIS. The next step in problem solving is to further analyze the problem and identify possible solutions. We asked teachers to try to figure out why the problem was occurring and to brainstorm possible instructional or management techniques. The special education teachers especially asked regular education teachers about any approaches they had tried in the past that had been successful in similar cases. We also asked about interventions teachers had read or heard about. The project's special education teachers had considerable experience in addressing both academic and behavior problems and had several research-based options to offer, as well.

PLAN IMPLEMENTATION. During the implementation stage, the teachers discussed the merits and limitations of possible teaching strategies and decided to try a particular approach that they believed would be successful in the regular teacher's classroom. They also decided how to apportion responsibility for carrying out the intervention procedure. For example, the special education teacher might take responsibility for modifying materials or securing alternative materials. In collaboration, the teachers might plan to co-teach the lesson and take turns presenting and monitoring and reteaching as necessary. The special education teacher might take responsibility for conducting a series of direct, intense lessons to teach and solidify particular skills. The regular education teacher might take responsibility for breaking down her goals into smaller steps to reteach the skill or concept. The teachers then would implement their intervention plans.

PLAN EVALUATION. In the final stage, teachers together determined whether their instruction and management strategies were successful in resolving the problem they had pinpointed. Collaborating teachers asked themselves whether the target student(s) met the instructional or behavioral goals. If so, they congratulated each other and planned steps to maintain or further improve student performance. If not, they returned to the problem analysis stage, asking themselves the following questions: Did I carry out my obligations in the implementation plan? Did we break the goal into small enough steps for the students to grasp and practice? Did we give enough positive feedback so that the students knew exactly what we wanted them to do? Were there other factors that could have influenced the students' performance?

One of the best ways to monitor student progress in achieving important instructional goals is to conduct frequent, brief evaluations called *probes* of exactly the skills you want students to master. Collecting frequent probes allows teachers to evaluate student learning and to revise ineffective strategies quickly (Fuchs, Fuchs,

Hamlett, & Stecker, 1991). Collaborating special education teachers collected probes on skills such as correctly read words per minute in the basal series used by the district, tasks completed during independent work periods, and on-task and disruptive behavior. Using simple graphs to record and display student performance over time allowed the teachers to evaluate the success of any particular intervention plan and make revisions as necessary. (You may want to review some of the extensive literature on curriculum-based measurement to learn how it can help teachers make instructional decisions, communicate with other professionals and parents efficiently, and provide a record of teacher accountability [Hasbrouck, Woldbeck, Ihnot, & Parker, 1999]).

Collaboration Results for Students and Teachers

When we began implementing collaborative consultation for students with mild to moderate learning disabilities in 12 randomly selected elementary schools, students with learning disabilities were enrolled in resource programs that they attended for one or two periods each day. We randomly assigned these students to one of four treatment settings: (1) one period a day of resource work with the school's resource teacher, (2) two periods a day with the school's resource teacher, (3) consultation, or (4) collaboration. Project teachers working with the child's regular education teacher provided special education services in the consultation and collaboration settings. In the consultation classes, the project special education and regular education teacher followed the four stages of problem solving described above except that the regular education teacher was responsible for implementing the intervention. The special education teacher helped with planning, securing teaching resources, demonstrating techniques, and evaluating student progress but did not take a weekly role in delivering instruction. In the collaborative consultation classrooms, the special education teacher did the same things but also had an instructional role in the classroom so that both teachers were responsible for teaching students.

At the beginning and again at end of the year, we assessed student performance on a variety of academic measures and found that all groups of students made academic gains during the year. However, we found a slight but significant advantage for students in the collaboration classrooms (Schulte, Osborne, & McKinney, 1990).

We also asked the regular education teachers who collaborated with us during the project about their experiences with consultation and collaboration (Schulte, Osborne, & Kauffman, 1993). Teachers tended to prefer the collaboration program to the consultation program. A number of teachers reported that they were concerned that students who did not receive regular direct services from a special education teacher might not be getting the assistance they needed. Teachers also expressed concern that consultation alone would not provide appropriate services for students with severe or multiple problems.

Overall, teachers who collaborated with the special educator in the classroom on an ongoing basis were very positive about the model. They reported reduced professional isolation, more opportunities to learn and advance their own teaching skills ("I haven't learned so much since my first year teaching or enjoyed it so much," Mrs. Peyton told us), and positive effects on students' learning and self-esteem. Another teacher got a frantic call from a mother whose son had proudly announced that he was no longer in special education. This mother had agreed to the student's change from part-time resource to full-time regular education with support from our collaborating teacher, but she did not expect special education services to become "invisible" to her son and other students.

> *"I haven't learned so much since my first year teaching or enjoyed it so much."*

Even teachers who were highly supportive of the collaboration program did report some difficulties, however. Teachers reported that scheduling was often difficult because the special education teacher had to be in so many other classrooms each day. Sometimes lack of space posed problems for two professionals working together in the same room. In response to our question about how collaborating was going, one regular education teacher said, "Great—except for the space. A single-wide [trailer] just isn't big enough for two teachers, a teaching assistant, and 27 kids. We're always falling over each other." Finding time for the collaborating teachers to plan together also proved difficult with many, if not most, pairs of teachers. Collaborating special and regular education teachers often turned to meetings before or after school when they could squeeze them in among grade team meetings, assistance team meetings, meetings with parents, and other noninstructional duties required of teachers. One of the collaborating teachers regularly brought bagels for classroom teachers who skipped breakfast in order to meet with her before school.

Lessons We Learned

When we began implementing teacher consultation and collaboration, we discovered that it took more than special training and support for the special education teachers and good will from all participating teachers and administrators. Regular and special educators found that collaboration took extra time. While all participating teachers had committed to spending at least 20 minutes per week planning with the special education teacher, the more serious academic and social problems of students required considerably more time, especially in the early stages.

Communication Skills for Collaboration

We quickly found that communication skills are critical to collaboration. Successful collaboration requires that teachers spend time getting to know and trust each other. In our project, we taught the special education teachers to use active listening and to watch body language for cues to possible resistance or concerns about the collaboration. We also encouraged the special educators to take the lead in addressing tensions or concerns. Often they were able to open communication by expressing their own concerns about sharing another teacher's turf, about changing the way they taught, and about scheduling. Communication skills that our participating teachers found important were using active listening to clarify the intent of the message, sharing experiences using self-disclosure, and managing conflict and resistance to collaboration by addressing it tactfully but directly.

Project special education teachers also discussed professional confidentiality early in their work with collaborating teachers, making it clear they were in the classroom to co-teach—not to evaluate the classroom teacher. Information shared in collaborative relationships should be kept confidential except in the unusual case in which a child's or teacher's physical or psychological welfare is at stake. Each pair of teachers had to find a style of communication that addressed the needs of the target students and that was comfortable for both teachers. We encouraged teachers to keep the focus on solving problems exhibited by students and to avoid personalizing difficulties or assigning blame for problems in the collaborative relationship. By focusing on the shared goal of improving student performance, teachers were usually able to work through significant differences in teaching philosophy and style. As teachers developed greater professional respect for each other, they became more open to trying new approaches and taking some risks.

> *Information shared in collaborative relationships should be kept confidential except in the unusual case in which a child's or teacher's physical or psychological welfare is at stake.*

Teachers must also consider the possibility that they will find themselves paired with another teacher whose instructional philosophy and teaching style are so different that they cannot set mutual priorities for instruction or work together in the same classroom. Some teachers resent being pushed into collaborative settings and find they cannot collaborate effectively. Fortunately, in our experience, this has been a rare situation. Nonetheless, when it does occur, the target students will suffer, and trying to maintain the fiction of collaboration does no one any good. Teachers must be able to disengage from collaboration without penalty when they are unable to provide effective instructional support for the students and collaboration becomes an unproductive use of teacher time. Teachers will be more likely to leave the door open for future collaboration when a classroom teacher says something like, "I know you have a really hectic schedule—maybe this is not a good time to start a new program," rather than, "No wonder collaboration isn't working. You're never here on time. I'm halfway through language arts before you ever get in the door!" Of course, one would hope that the teachers will make good-faith efforts to work out scheduling problems before things get out of hand. Placing blame and making accusations will only decrease the likelihood that future attempts at collaboration will be successful and will make sharing other school duties awkward.

As a result of effective communication and growing respect and trust, teachers' collaborative styles evolved over the year. In some classrooms, the special educator took primary responsibility for teaching a reading group that included the target student and others who were having difficulty learning to read. In other classes, the two teachers team taught. Sometimes one teacher took primary responsibility for teaching the whole group for part of the lesson while the other focused student attention, monitored student progress, and elaborated on the instruction as necessary. Other times teachers team taught when they shared instruction by taking turns "thinking out loud" as they worked through new material or alternated presenting main ideas and filling in details. Teachers team taught when one demonstrated a procedure while the other explained and presented commentary, or when they role played an event or situation. Still others collaborated to develop instructional centers and shared responsibility for teaching small groups and supervising center activities that included target students. The special education teachers who each worked with several regular educators reported that each collaborative relationship was different. Special and regular educators alike agreed that developing some level of flexibility was important for successful collaboration.

Preparing Teachers to Collaborate

After the initial year of our collaboration experiment, we developed and implemented a teacher collaboration preparation program in the same school district. The collaborating special education teachers worked with us to disseminate the results of our project to interested teachers and schools. For our first teacher preparation effort, we invited the schools that had participated in the experiment to join us for a series of workshops designed to help school-based teachers continue teacher collaboration in their own schools after our project was concluded. We encouraged pairs or groups of teachers, including regular and special education personnel from each school, to attend the workshops together. Our rationale for training teachers in pairs was to place a functioning team of collaborators in each school that chose to participate. By training teachers in pairs throughout the semester, we provided them with a set of shared expectations, procedures, and skills. In addition each team began to practice collaboration with the support of their colleagues and project personnel. We felt that training only half the team—just the special educators, for example—and expecting them to recruit and train their colleagues would place an unrealistic burden on teachers. In fact, over the years, many teachers have reported great frustration in trying to initiate collaboration with colleagues who are poorly prepared or even resist collaborating.

Because communication skills are so important to the process, we believe that teachers will be best served when they learn and practice those skills together in a supportive and safe environment. When teachers are required to collaborate without first building a strong foundation of professional respect and communication, opportunities for misunderstanding and mistrust abound.

In our project, teachers attended a series of monthly workshops that ran throughout the spring semester. In the workshops, we taught teachers to use the approach to collaborative problem solving described earlier in this chapter. At each meeting, we provided an overview, description, and rationale for the component of problem solving we were teaching. Then we demonstrated the process using real examples. Finally, teachers practiced by role-playing the scenarios we provided, some of which included problematic relationships between teachers. For homework, the pairs of teachers in each school selected a target student and began the problem identification and problem analysis processes. When teachers had difficulty or questions, they contacted the collaborating special education teachers from the project for advice or support. At each workshop meeting, we took time for "show and tell" when the participants reported back on their collaboration activities. By the end of the school year, each participating school had begun the process of instituting collaborative programs with teachers who had had training and supervised practice in collaboration. Teachers began planning collaborative activities for the next school year by identifying likely candidates for collaborative services, scheduling students into appropriate classrooms, and contacting parents.

We learned that collaboration is not a simple skill that can be fully addressed in a half-day mandatory workshop or a single book chapter. We have found that guided practice in developing collaboration skills will increase the likelihood that teachers will be able to address and solve problems together. Based on our experience, we have concluded that collaboration training is most successful when

- both members of the collaborating dyad are good teachers,
- regular and special education teachers prepare for collaboration together,
- teachers learn and practice a problem-solving approach to identify and address student needs,
- both members of dyads are invested in the practice of collaborating and are interested in extending their teaching skills,
- participants learn to identify and discuss tensions that arise in collaborating relationships,
- both teachers are committed to finding time to plan together, and
- teachers have support personnel available to help them resolve problems.

Barriers to Effective Collaboration

Even pairs of teachers who want to collaborate and have had good preparation training sometimes run into difficulties. The collaborating special education teachers in our project identified several barriers that can make collaboration almost impossible. Sometimes these are beyond the immediate control of the teachers.

One potential barrier is lack of active administrative support. A building administrator who gives only lip service to collaboration among the staff will make collaboration difficult. Collaborating teachers need resources in order to be successful. Teachers have repeatedly told us that the scarcest—but most important—resource is time to plan together. Without adequate scheduled time to problem solve and plan instruction, teachers often try to do it "on the fly." Catching the occasional 5 minutes in the hall, the workroom, or the women's lavatory simply is not adequate. Effective school administrators who want to make teacher collaboration a priority *must* provide time for co-planning.

> *Teachers have repeatedly told us that the scarcest—but most important—resource is time to plan together.*

Another important administrative responsibility is providing instructional leadership in the school by assuring that teachers provide high quality instruction to their students. Occasionally a school administrator will expect a collaborating teacher to coach a weak colleague. Collaboration is designed to develop *shared* instructional responsibility between two or more skilled professionals; although many regular and special educators have told us they learned a great deal from collaborating with a colleague, collaboration is not a remedial program for poor teachers. Supervising instruction is an administrative responsibility.

Another common barrier to successful collaboration is the size of teachers' caseloads. In some states, special education teachers are expected to provide individualized, effective instruction to as many as 50 students each day. Collaborating teachers cannot plan and collaborate with 10 teachers a day. Even teachers must obey laws of physics that allow them to be in only one place at a time.

Assigning large numbers of students with learning or behavior problems to a few classrooms to facilitate collaboration can defeat the goal of integrating students with special needs into the regular education program if these classrooms are simply reconstituted, segregated special education classes. The challenge to teachers and administrators in these schools is ensuring that students receive a high quality education that meets their needs no matter where it is delivered. Many experienced collaboration teams have found that five or six students with disabilities is the maximum that can be effectively integrated into one classroom. For some common potential trouble spots and possible solutions for collaboration, see Table 1.

Establishing a collaboration program to serve students with special education needs is not an easier or less expensive way to provide instruction. Collaboration will not allow teachers to "cover" more students. When Mrs. Peyton talked to other teachers and school administrators about her experiences, she said, "I've never worked so hard in my life—or enjoyed it more." A school district administrator pointed out that adopting the collaboration model required considerable financial commitment from the district. However, collaboration can be a highly effective way to serve a significant number of students when there are sufficient numbers of well-trained teachers to

TABLE 1
Trouble Spots and Solutions for Collaboration

Potential Trouble Spots in Collaboration	Solutions
Merging management styles	Discuss class rules and behavior management responsibilities *before* collaborating.
Mistakes during teaching	Discuss how each team member should handle mistakes in front of the class (e.g., one teacher inadvertently uses wrong name for character when discussing a book chapter).
Difference of opinion regarding adequacy of student response	Discuss how to suggest alternative responses (e.g., there is more than one correct answer or answer is open to interpretation). Plan procedure for demonstrating tactful negotiation of issue.
Special education teacher seems to be functioning as a teachers' assistant rather than full partner	Discuss need for full partnership and how this will be achieved before beginning collaboration. Agree to "check in" about the partnership on a regular basis during the semester.
One or both teachers too busy to plan on a regular basis	Set up a specific time to plan at the beginning of the semester. If possible, school could hire a floating substitute teacher who rotates among classes to allow teams to have hour-long blocks for long-term planning each month.
Last-minute schedule changes	Discuss how scheduling "glitches" should be handled, such as classroom teacher running late on earlier lesson, or special education teacher late because of a meeting.

provide high-quality instruction. Despite potential barriers, teachers, parents, administrators, and students found teacher collaboration to be an effective and professionally gratifying approach to service delivery. Parents whose children participated in the program were enthusiastic and strongly encouraged the school district to extend the program to all of the more than 100 elementary and middle schools in the district.

At the conclusion of the federally funded experiment, the school district committed to continuing and expanding the program. In addition to funding additional teachers, the district hired two collaborating teachers to serve as part-time collaboration consultants who provide teacher preparation and support for collaboration throughout the district. While all who were engaged in the collaboration experiment found it to be an exciting and challenging project, for us the real excitement has been the acceptance of collaboration as an important service delivery option and the transfer of ownership of our model to the public schools.

Summary

Through our partnership with a public school district, we found that collaboration can be rewarding for teachers and students alike. However, it is not a panacea. No single approach will ever solve the complex problems we face in education. It is important to remember that no placement decision is permanent. If collaborating teachers find that a student is not performing adequately, they may be able to refine their instruction to make it more effective. Occasionally, they may need to ask the individual education plan committee to help them revisit the placement decision. It is important to remember that some students' needs may require intensive individualized instruction that is more likely provided in a resource room setting, but even these students benefit when instructional approaches are conducted across settings.

Although we have relatively little research that addresses the long-term effects of teacher collaboration or the components of collaboration that are most important for its success, we know a great deal about effective instruction. High quality instruction (intense, well-sequenced instruction that targets students' needs) is more effective than poor quality or too diffuse instruction in any setting. We urge you not to let controversies about the place of instruction overshadow issues of quality of instruction. A key question to ask yourself as you work with a collaboration partner is how the presence of two teachers can be used to alter key dimensions of instruction such as student time on task, corrective feedback to students, or differentiation of instruction. We urge you not to let the unanswered questions about collaboration keep you from reaching out to your colleagues and working together to solve your students' instructional problems and enrich your own professional lives.

Wherever we serve students, we must seek to improve performance for the large numbers of students with disabilities and for those who are at risk for academic failure. Strong and effective education provides the best, and sometimes only, opportunity for many children to live productive and satisfying lives. Without highly skilled teachers who can work together to share expertise in educating our children, many children will be doomed to second-class status or worse for their entire lives.

NOTE

The research project described in this chapter was supported by funds from the U.S. Department of Education through Grant No. G008730258, Evaluation of Models for Educating Learning Disabled and Other Mildly Handicapped Students in General Education Classrooms.

The authors additionally thank Sherrill Miller, Kristen Anderson, and Karen Schinke-Akers, who provided all the collaborating and consulting special education services during this project and who assisted in training collaborating teams of teachers during the final year of the project.

References

Bergan, J.R. (1977). *Behavioral consultation*. Upper Saddle River, NJ: Merrill/Prentice Hall.

Bergan, J.R., & Kratochwill, T.R. (1990). *Behavioral consultation and therapy*. New York: Plenum.

Fuchs, L.S., Fuchs, D., Hamlett, C.L., & Stecker, P.M. (1991). Effects of curriculum-based measurement and consultation on teacher planning and student achievement in mathematical operations. *American Educational Research Journal, 28*, 617–641.

Hasbrouck, J.E., Woldbeck, T., Ihnot, C., & Parker, R.I. (1999). One teacher's use of curriculum-based measurement: A changed opinion. *Learning Disabilities Research and Practice, 14*, 118–126.

Schulte, A.C., Osborne, S.S., & Kauffman, J.M. (1993). Teacher responses to two types of consultative special education services. *Journal of Educational and Psychological Consultation, 4*(1), 1–27.

Schulte, A.C., Osborne, S.S., & McKinney, J.D. (1990). Academic outcomes for students with learning disabilities in consultation and resource programs. *Exceptional Children, 57*, 162–172.

Tombari, M.L., & Bergan, J.R. (1978). Consultant cues and teacher verbalizations, judgments, and expectancies concerning children's adjustment problems. *Journal of School Psychology, 16*, 212–219.

CHAPTER 19

Classroom Teachers and Reading Specialists Working Together to Improve Student Achievement

Rita M. Bean

Yvonne, the classroom teacher, and John, the reading specialist intern, have observed that their students need opportunities to respond to reading and to practice their expressive language skills. John suggests that *The True Story of the 3 Little Pigs! By A. Wolf* (Scieszka, 1989), would be "just the thing." John (who has a tremendous sense of dramatics) reads the story to the children. After discussing the story and the merits of the wolf's tale, John and Yvonne suggest to the children that they put on a play in which the wolf is taken to court where a judge and jury will decide his fate. Together they help children decide on the actors that are needed and make suggestions about which children might play which parts. John works with the small group of actors while Yvonne works with the jury so that they understand their role. Yvonne and John help students write letters of invitation to their parents and the students in the other third-grade classroom.

Yvonne and John, who teach in a school with a large number of students identified as eligible for Title I services, enjoy collaborating to plan literacy instruction for the third graders they call "their" students. They believe that the collaborative program in which they are involved has enabled them to implement an effective program for all students in the classroom. At the same time, Yvonne and John state emphatically, "We feed off each other; each one of us brings unique ideas to the planning."

Concern about the lack of achievement of struggling readers led leadership in this school to think about new and different ways to use the talents of the reading specialists assigned to teach them. Although reading specialists have functioned in schools for many decades, over time their role has changed. Researchers who have written about the role of the reading specialist have highlighted the many roles specialists assume, including diagnostician, instructor, and consultant or resource to teachers (see Barclay & Thistlethwaite, 1992; Bean, 1979; Bean, Cooley, Eichelberger, Lazar, & Zigmond, 1991; Bean, Knaub, & Swan, 2000; Hamilton, 1993; Robinson, 1967; Stauffer, 1967; Tancock, 1995). Much of the research has focused on ways in which reading specialists work in reading programs funded by Title I programs because Title I provides resources for a large percentage of the reading specialists who work in U.S. schools.

Criticism about the success of Title I (Puma & Jones, 1993; Slavin, 1987) as well as overall concern about the large numbers of students who are not reading successfully in our schools have led to efforts to rethink and reconceptualize the ways in which reading instruction is delivered. In *Preventing Reading Difficulties in Young Children* (Snow, Burns, & Griffin, 1998), a report of the National Research Council, two recommendations are made that are pertinent to this chapter: (1) provide appropriate staff development opportunities for teachers so that they have the expertise and competence needed to teach reading, and (2) make reading specialists available in the schools to provide support in classroom instruction.

The challenges of today's classrooms are many—children come to school with diverse needs and experiences, and our modern technological society demands high levels of literacy. There is a great need for a highly competent teacher workforce prepared to address these issues (National Commission on Teaching and America's Future, 1996; National Reading Panel, 2000). Indeed, teachers themselves believe there is a need for appropriate professional development. In a U.S.

national survey (National Center for Education Statistics, 1999), only 20% of the teachers surveyed felt confident using modern technology or working with students with diverse backgrounds. These teachers gave "low marks" to the professional development they had received. They criticized the "one shot" sessions that were often provided. Yet teachers reported that they valued frequent planning and collaboration with other teachers as a means of professional development. Indeed, research over the past 20 years has consistently shown that teachers learn best by observing, practicing, obtaining feedback, and working with other teachers (Miller, 1995). Researchers such as McLaughlin and Talbert (1993), Little (1993), and Borko, Elliot, and Uchiyama (1999) call for the development of strong professional communities in which teachers talk to each other about their work and about school reform.

At the same time, there are demands for changing the role of the reading specialist to one that directly supports the work of the classroom teacher (Snow et al., 1998). Such a demand has led to new and different roles for the reading specialist. No longer does the reading specialist work in isolation, providing "remedial" instruction for students; rather the reading specialist more frequently collaborates with classroom teachers in planning and implementing effective reading instruction for students and engages in in-class instruction.

No longer does the reading specialist work in isolation, providing "remedial" instruction for students; rather the reading specialist more frequently collaborates with classroom teachers in planning and implementing effective reading instruction for students and engages in in-class instruction.

This collaborative approach provides unique opportunities for both classroom teachers and reading specialists. They can learn from each other, try new techniques, and reflect on their effectiveness in improving students' reading performance. Such an approach, however, creates a need for institutions that prepare reading specialists by providing experiences that will help them function in this new collaborative role. Indeed, both reading specialists and classroom teachers must learn to work in new and different ways as members of a learning community (Allington & Baker, 1999; Little, 1993; McLaughlin & Talbert, 1993).

This chapter describes a project in which candidates for reading specialist certification work collaboratively with K–6 classroom teachers as part of a year-long intern program. This chapter details how these interns are prepared for their role as collaborator and how partners collaborate to provide effective instruction for students. It also discusses benefits of such collaboration as well as problems or dilemmas that need to be resolved. Results of interviews of specialist candidates, teachers, and students are used to highlight the potential of such collaborative efforts and to provide implications for professional development programs.

The Program

During the past 5 years, I have directed a collaborative program between the University of Pittsburgh (Pittsburgh, Pennsylvania, USA), and several local school districts in which candidates for reading specialist certification spend 3 hours each morning, 5 days a week, in several primary classrooms for the entire school year. This reading specialist intern is assigned to work in two or more classrooms during the week. Because the program is supported by Title I funds, the emphasis is placed on working with students who have been identified as struggling readers. However, the program in each school is somewhat different, given site needs and structures. For example, the Title I program in several schools is a schoolwide program; therefore, reading specialist interns work with all students in the school. (Schools can be designated as having schoolwide programs if a large number of their students come from high poverty backgrounds.) In other schools, specific students have been identified as eligible for Title I services. Regardless of setting, however, reading specialist interns have opportunities to work with individuals, small groups, or with the entire class. Most frequently, these reading specialist interns work within the classroom, although they may at times function away from the classroom because of purpose (e.g., preparing a play for the other students), specific needs of a child, or space problems. Regardless of where the instruction occurs, collaborative planning with the classroom teacher is a critical element of the program.

As part of this experience, the reading specialist interns, who are certified teachers working on their reading specialist certificate, receive a stipend. They also receive tuition credit for courses that they take as part of the program. The reading specialist interns are supervised at each school by university personnel who meet with them and the classroom teachers.

Components of a Professional Development Program

Our professional development program involves the following elements and procedures: written materials, support personnel, planning time, group interaction, and leadership meetings.

Written Material

All participants expressed a need for written material that would provide guidelines for program policy and procedures. In addition, teachers and interns wanted to read how others were implementing programs that required collaborative teaching.

MANUAL OF PROCEDURES AND PRACTICES. A manual, developed after the first year of the program, has been revised each year. This manual is given to all interns, classroom teachers, and administrators in participating districts. Each year, the district personnel and university staff meet to discuss its contents and the changes that need to be made. The manual includes both procedural and substantive sections. In the procedural section, various rules and regulations are discussed (e.g., attendance, roles, responsibilities). In the second section, the purpose of the intern program is discussed and the three goals of the program are described: (1) enhancing reading instruction for students, (2) providing teaching experiences for reading specialist interns, and (3) providing opportunities for classroom teachers to work collaboratively, learn from the interns, and at the same time become role models for these beginning reading specialists. The manual also describes various models of collaboration (discussed in the next section of this chapter), and gives reasons for using such approaches.

PROFESSIONAL LITERATURE. Interns are given and asked to read articles that build understanding about collaborative teaching. These articles are then discussed in class. We use as one primary reference the monograph *Effecting Change in School Reading Programs: The Resource Role* (Bean & Wilson, 1981). Other readings come from both the literacy and special education field (such as Bean, Trovato, & Hamilton, 1995; Cook & Friend, 1995; O'Connor, Jenkins, & Leicester, 1992).

Support Personnel

This project relies on support personnel from the university and the school district who are available to listen to both teachers and interns, provide feedback, and serve as a resource for professional development.

SITE LIAISON. Each school is assigned an individual from the university who has several responsibilities, such as serving as a resource to interns and teachers, providing feedback to interns and teachers, and assisting the school in developing the program so that it enhances the reading achievement of all children. The site liaison who goes to the school each week to observe and confer with interns also meets with individuals or groups of teachers to obtain feedback about the program or to respond to their requests. The site liaison participates in classroom activities or teaches demonstration or teamed lessons. The site liaison shares findings and makes recommendations to the individual at the school who is directly responsible for the program. In some schools, this is an identified reading specialist; in others, it is the elementary supervisor or coordinator of federal programs.

SCHOOL AND UNIVERSITY LEADERS. The identified program leader at the school has a major role to play in helping interns and teachers develop an effective collaborative program. This individual works directly with the site liaison to work with both interns and teachers. The school leader communicates with the university site liaison on a regular basis, meets with interns and teachers, and in general supports the ongoing efforts of all involved.

As the university leader, I interact with university site liaisons and school leaders on a regular basis. I meet with site liaisons at least once a month to discuss the weekly reports they generate, the progress of the interns, and any problems that need to be addressed at the site (e.g., the intern is experiencing difficulty with classroom management or has a style different from that of the classroom teacher). I meet with school leaders in a formal group at least twice a year, when we discuss common issues and generate ideas that are useful across sites. In addition, I visit each school to observe in the classrooms, talk with teachers and with interns, and I generally meet with the individual at the school responsible for the program. I am in touch with school leaders by telephone or e-mail frequently to address questions or issues that arise. Because I also teach one of the courses in the reading specialist sequence, I meet with interns each week to discuss their field experiences. As part of the course, interns keep a journal about their experiences at the school, which is used as a basis for discussion, feedback, and support.

Planning Time

Although each site does it differently, collaborative planning is a requirement for the program. At one site, a substitute teacher takes over the classroom for a half-hour every other week so that interns and teachers have a formal meeting time. In most schools, interns and their partner teachers have a designated time for meeting and planning, either before school begins in the morning or on a designated day of the week. In many schools, planning also occurs "on the fly" as teachers and interns interact informally in the halls, the classrooms, and even the cafeterias.

Group Interaction

INTERNS. Interns meet as a group before school begins and are introduced to various techniques for collaborative teaching. Also, they function as a cohort group during the first semester. Thus, in one of their courses they spend time on a regular basis discussing various problems and how they might address them. In one of the first sessions, I present a sample problem (e.g., teacher tends to view intern as an aide), and the group discusses various solutions to this problem. In subsequent sessions, problems or issues from each school are identified, and again the group discusses how the problems might be solved. In another course, specialists are given opportunities to think about the roles of specialists; special attention is given to leadership, communication, and interpersonal skills. Specialists read sections of texts that focus on the role of specialist as resource (Bean, Knaub, & Swan, 2000; Bean & Wilson, 1981; Radencich, 1995).

TEACHERS. Because interns are certified teachers, they can assume classroom responsibilities, which gives teachers opportunities for professional or curriculum development or other important activities. At one school, the primary teachers meet as a group on a regular basis to develop various assessment or instructional strategies to improve reading instruction while the interns teach. At other schools, this type of meeting is scheduled as needed, often as a means for the site liaison to interact with a group of teachers. More frequently, while the intern is teaching, the university site liaison meets with an individual teacher to discuss the collaborative teaching and whether it is meeting the needs of students in the classroom. These short meetings, often 10 to 15 minutes in length, are important for establishing rapport, common goals, and a collaborative partnership between the teachers and the university site liaison.

TEACHERS AND INTERNS. Although we value the opportunity to have all teachers and interns meet as a group, this is the most difficult type of meeting to schedule. Thus, this sort of meeting happens at the beginning of the year during the orientation meetings and when the school district schedules a professional development day. Both teachers and interns have told us that these meetings provide wonderful opportunities for both professional and social interactions.

Although it is difficult to schedule group meetings of teachers and interns, individual interns and their partner teachers interact frequently and systematically before and after school, during planning periods, and even via telephone. Discussions range from the philosophical (beliefs about reading instruction, learning, or children) to the personal. Many interns and teachers become close colleagues who keep in touch with each other even after the intern has completed the program. The teachers frequently support interns for teaching positions in their school.

Leadership Meetings

The collaborative efforts of the leaders of this program are essential to professional development and important for program success. Written reports from the university site liaison are sent to both the school leader and to me for review. We also confer via telephone or e-mail about various dimensions of the program, from ongoing progress reports about its implementation to issues about the school reading program itself. We also meet at least twice a year to discuss the overall impact of the program, its strengths, and problems that must be addressed. At these meetings, the group reviews the manual and discusses ways in which it can be improved.

These efforts to continuously improve what we are doing to implement this program are time consuming. At the same time, these professional development efforts have served to create a program that makes a difference for children, not only because they receive additional instructional support, but because their teachers are learning and improving how and what they teach.

Models of Collaboration

This section discusses five models of collaboration used by reading specialist interns and teachers and provides specific examples of successful efforts, benefits of the approach, and potential pitfalls. The models came from a review of literature (see Bean, Trovato, & Hamilton, 1995; Cook & Friend, 1995; Hamilton, 1993; Meyers, Gelzheiser, & Yelich, 1991; O'Connor et al., 1992) and from our own observations in the schools (see Bean, Grumet, & Bulazo, 1999). Because we are supervising and supporting the program in the schools during the entire year, we are able to observe how the teams of reading specialists and teachers actually function. These models of collaboration provide a set of labels or language that our specialists and classroom teachers now use to discuss how they can work together. These models also serve as a foundation for building a relationship. Some of these models require in-class teaching while others might occur either in class or away from the classroom; however, all require collaborative planning between the reading specialist and the classroom teacher. Table 1 provides a summary of the models.

Station or Center Teaching

In this model, the teacher and reading specialist assess students' strengths and needs to decide what activities, concepts, or skills they wish to develop into learning centers. The partners divide the tasks and develop the necessary materials and activities for their assigned centers. Students then rotate through the centers, having an opportunity to work with each teacher. Most often centers are used once

TABLE 1
Models of Collaboration

Model	Advantages	Potential Problems/Dilemmas	Location
Station or Center Teaching	Students have opportunity to work with both teachers Attention to individual/group needs or interests Small-group work Teachers have some choice (use teacher strengths and interests) Teachers share responsibility for developing and teaching	Time-consuming to develop Noise level in classroom Organizational factors Management factors	In-class
Support Teaching	Focuses on individual or group needs Small-group instruction Specialized instruction Uses talents of teachers to meet needs of students	Know both classroom reading program and specialized approaches Rigid grouping	Either in-class or pull-out
Parallel Instruction	Pacing/approach can vary Small-group instruction Same standards/expectations for all students Small-group instruction Easier to handle class	May not meet needs of students Noise level	Generally in-class (can be pull-out)
Teacher and Monitor	Same standards/expectations for all students Immediate reinforcement or help from monitor Opportunity to do kidwatching (assessment) Teachers can learn from each other (demonstration)	One teacher may become an "aide" Lack of attention to specific needs of children	In-class
Team Teaching	Same standards/expectations for all students Uses strengths of both teachers Teachers share responsibility Students have opportunity to work with both teachers Attention to individual/group needs or interests Small-group work	Lack of common philosophy or approach to instruction	Generally in-class

or twice a week as a means of reviewing skills, rereading texts, building fluency, and providing opportunity for small-group work. In one second-grade classroom, the reading specialist is always assigned the writing center because teaching writing is a particular strength of hers. She also develops the listening center, and students function there independently, using the earphones and tapes of books she provides. The classroom teacher also works with students on a game activity to review concepts, vocabulary, decoding, or other targeted areas. The other center is the computer center where students work independently using a software package that provides various reading opportunities.

Center teaching provides many benefits for students because of its focus on small-group work with greater attention to student needs and the opportunity for students to work with both teachers. At the same time, it enables teachers to share responsibilities, permitting each to develop fully one or two centers.

Feedback from teachers and interns indicates that materials or activities are time consuming to develop, but that they can be revised, thus allowing their use in different classrooms or at different times. Reading specialist interns and teachers also have to teach children to work in centers, encouraging them to use "soft" voices and to move efficiently from center to center.

Support Teaching

Support teaching enables one of the teachers, generally the reading specialist intern, to develop and teach lessons that will help students who experience difficulty with some aspect of classroom instruction or with reading in general. For example, students who need additional phonemic awareness instruction may be grouped together to meet with the reading specialist while the classroom teacher works with the other students, perhaps monitoring their journal writing or helping them with independent work. Students may be placed in a "temporary" group that meets once or twice. However, the specialist and the teacher may also decide that for an extended period of time the reading specialist will work with a small group of children who need additional help with reading (reviewing their vocabulary words, helping them with prior concepts that have not been developed). This model may be used in class or the reading specialist may take the students to another room. The decision as to where instruction occurs should be based on many different factors, such as needs and learning styles of all students, and instruction occurring for other students.

Support teaching requires teachers and specialists to have an in-depth knowledge of the needs and strengths of each child so that grouping will be appropriate and effective. It also requires that partners interact on a frequent basis so that there is flexibility in the grouping. The reading specialist, of course, must be knowledgeable about the classroom instructional program and have an excellent understanding of more specialized ways to reach children who struggle with specific aspects of the reading process. Students benefit because their individual strengths and needs are provided for; at the same time, the small-group instruction offers time for more in-depth attention to each child. Certainly the time for collaborative planning is crucial for developing knowledge and decision making.

Parallel Instruction

With this model, both the classroom teacher and the reading specialist teach, with the same materials and with the same objectives. For example, both teach a guided reading activity using the story *Jamaica's Find* (Havill, 1986). The classroom teacher may lead a literacy group in which two thirds of the students read and discuss the story. The reading specialist, who works with the remaining students who are identified as struggling readers, may read the story to the children; this is followed by rereading with the students. Additional books that follow the same theme may be used to build fluency. Because the reading specialist has fewer students in her group, she can help them more readily and can vary her instruction to meet their needs. At the same time, all students are expected to work with material designated as appropriate for that grade level; thus, standards or expectations are similar for all students.

As mentioned, with this model teachers have smaller groups with which to work and can work with their assigned students much more effectively. At the same time, the distraction caused by two teachers working within the same classroom must be addressed. Students and teachers need to learn to work comfortably in this sort of situation, "tuning out" the other group. Parallel instruction can also be problematic when struggling readers are continuously pushed through the classroom curriculum with no attention paid to addressing specific needs that they have. For example, third-grade students who are told to read a third-grade anthology but read at a first- or second-grade level may need to receive some specialized instruction that focuses on specific strategies for reading (e.g., rereading, decoding, concept development) in addition to what they receive as part of the third-grade curriculum. Again, this model allows for in-class instruction but, in some situations, students may be taught in a different setting.

Teacher and Monitor

In this model, one teacher implements the lesson while the other teacher monitors the work of the children, especially those who may be experiencing some difficulty in following directions or maintaining the pace needed to move with the group. The classroom teacher may teach while the reading specialist intern monitors and assists those children who have been identified as needing special assistance. The reading specialist intern helps the child find the correct page, identifies words that may be problematic, makes certain the child is attending, or provides words of reassurance.

At times the reading specialist teaches the whole class while the teacher monitors. For example, when primary children are doing various word-building activities, necessitating movement of letter cards, the classroom teacher moves around the room, helping children to follow directions and complete the task successfully. It is amazing how well such teaching promotes excellent classroom management and student participation. I have seen intern and teacher maintain student attention and enthusiasm in many different ways (say "If you're listening, do what we do!" [then blink or scratch an arm], or explain "I'm looking for the table that is working well together"). This is helpful with young children who are easily distracted.

There are a number of strengths in this approach. One teacher may know or understand a specific strategy better than the other teacher. Not only do the children benefit, but the lesson becomes an opportunity for the demonstration of new strategies to the other professional. Further, all students are provided with experiences necessary for their particular grade level, and students who have special needs receive immediate reinforcement or help when needed. This approach also enables one of the teachers to "kidwatch," which provides extensive opportunity to observe how a particular child handles a specific task or problem.

There are also some potential difficulties or problems with this model. If used too often, individual differences of children may be ignored and whole-class teaching may become the norm. Further, the reading specialist, who comes into the classroom of another teacher, may find herself or himself in the position of "aide." This can easily happen because of the longstanding nature of our educational workplace, which reinforces the belief that classroom teachers in their isolated classrooms have the sole responsibility for the instruction of their students. With collaborative planning and some switching of roles, changes in belief and behavior can occur.

One other helpful approach is to build into the program the adjustment that small-group instruction or workshop type experiences must occur at least two or three times during the week, thus reducing the tendency for whole-class teaching as the only approach. Our schools have encouraged teachers to use flexible grouping as part of their instructional program. This approach, of course, takes place in the classroom.

Team Teaching

In team teaching, both teachers plan together and divide the responsibility of a lesson or unit. Both are responsible for implementing some portion of the lesson with the children. The following scenario and the one at the beginning of the chapter provide two illustrations of team teaching:

> To help students develop their writing abilities, Lou, the classroom teacher, and Martina, the reading specialist, decide to have students write informational passages about various animals that can be found in the desert, the focus of their science unit. Students, who are excited about this assignment, have decided that they would like to construct a book of their work. Lou, who had been teaching the science unit in class, introduces the lesson and helps children decide on their animals and what they might include in the passage (prewriting). As children write, Lou and Martina walk around helping and encouraging students. The next day, Martina conducts a lesson on revising and peer editing. Then students share papers with each other, revise, and edit while Lou and Martina again provide the necessary support. Individual conferences to discuss writing with either Lou or Martina are scheduled for each child during this period. On the third day, students rewrite their papers and begin organizing their classbook.

This scenario is only one example of the many ways in which teachers, who enjoy working together and who appreciate the learning that comes from collaboration, can design lessons. The strengths of both teachers are used; teachers share responsibility, making a task that might be formidable for one doable and enjoyable. Students, too, benefit from the enthusiasm that generally comes from such instruction. Here Sara, one of the interns, describes her version of team teaching:

> June and I do more team teaching in this class. We usually split the class and then I teach a strategy and June does the same and we switch the children. This works well with this group of children. Last week at the end of the story "Gloria, Who Might be My Best Friend," we had the children make wishing kites. This was something the characters in the story made. They had a lot of fun and we had a chance to talk about the events in the story again, and if their predictions were right from the beginning of the story.

Team teaching works successfully only if the two participants can work together collaboratively. If they have different approaches to instruction or lack a common philosophy about how and what to teach, they must discuss their views and recognize what each has to offer. Otherwise, team teaching will be difficult to achieve. One of our reading specialist interns team taught with one of her partner teachers, but never achieved a level of full collaboration with the second teacher. Yet the reading specialist intern and the second teacher worked comfortably, using several other models, including parallel instruction and support teaching. Team teaching will occur most often in the classroom; however, there are times when a small group of children may be removed from the classroom to work on a special project with one of the teachers.

What Have We Learned About Collaboration?

We have learned a great deal about the benefits of collaboration over the past 5 years from reading specialist interns, classroom teachers, and from students themselves. First and foremost, students benefit as they experience the shared expertise of both teachers. The smaller student-teacher ratio provides more opportunities for meeting the needs of students with diverse backgrounds. Both teachers can share what they have learned about the student and contribute to instructional decision making. The reading specialist interns often attend pupil personnel or instructional support team meetings with the classroom teacher because the two of them jointly have been able to carefully analyze the needs of and potential solutions for various students. With two teachers, classroom management becomes easier, and teachers find that they have some additional time for creating new materials or trying different approaches, given the smaller numbers and the division of responsibilities.

Students also seem to enjoy having two teachers in the classroom. When we interviewed primary students as to what they thought about having two teachers, all of them were positive about the experience (Bean, Armitage, & Kephart, 1995). They realized that they were getting more help and thus could learn more: "You can do more work and get help...get better in reading." One second grader described the reading specialist as "an expert in reading." Students also indicated that when there were two teachers in the classroom, learning was "fun." And as one child astutely commented, "Both of them help students, and both can tell you to sit down and be quiet."

Teachers and reading specialists also believe that they learn much from working with another teacher. Each brings various talents and ideas for instruction or for classroom management that may be new to the other. The reading specialist may implement think-alouds, for example, that are new to the classroom teacher. At the same time, the classroom teacher has some remarkable reinforcement strategies for motivating children to learn, which he or she shares with the reading specialist. Most of all, teachers and reading specialist interns who have had successful experiences tell us that the collaboration increases enthusiasm for teaching. One intern, Kevin, described his experiences with a classroom teacher:

> Please don't think I am crazy, but I ask the class to read the directions for the page with a Southern accent. It really breaks the monotony of the day, and we all get a good laugh. I credit Pam [the teacher] for this crazy sense of humor. It works! One day I walked into her classroom and she had on a pirate hat and a patch over her eye. I laughed so hard when she told me that is how she introduced -ar words. I think that in order for a teacher to keep her sanity, some silliness must get them through each day!

Students certainly benefit when teachers enjoy and are passionate about their teaching. As one teacher said, "When something funny happens in the classroom, it's really great to have another adult there to enjoy it with you!" An idea developed by one of the teachers may spawn two more by the partner teacher. And as one reading specialist commented, "One of us can have a bad day, and our partner can pull us through." The isolation of the classroom is gone, and teachers can talk as professionals about a particular child and the best way to approach his or her instructional needs. In one of our schools, the intern and teacher developed a proposal and received funding for a program to increase student interest in reading.

The isolation of the classroom is gone, and teachers can talk as professionals about a particular child and the best way to approach his or her instructional needs.

The bottom line for educators is, of course, improvement in student reading achievement. Anecdotal evidence from teachers and parents is positive about the effects of our efforts to provide additional support in the schools. School administrators report to us that they have also seen improvement in test scores of students, generally. Models of collaboration in which reading specialists and classroom teachers work together certainly facilitate implementing programs that reflect research evidence that supports smaller class size as a means of improving achievement.

Further, collaborative teaching such as that described in this chapter seems to be an excellent means of professional development. As schools change and as teachers are asked to change what they teach and the way they teach it, the old "training models" for professional development will no longer suffice (Little, 1993). As Little states, "A new kind of structure and culture is required, compatible with the image of teacher as intellectual rather than technician" (p. 109). Meeting, talking, and reflecting with another colleague about students' strengths and needs—and how to address those—is a form of professional development that requires teachers to engage in everyday inquiry and problem solving. And as teachers think about what they do and why, there is the expectation that change in actual practice will occur.

Potential Problems to Be Resolved

It would be unrealistic to say that these collaborative models typically are successful in all instances—they are not! Some are more successful than others. This section discusses various problems and ways in which such problems can be resolved.

Preparation for Collaborative Teaching

One problem is that not all teachers or reading specialists have been prepared to function collaboratively. Such a change in the workplace requires extensive professional development for both teachers and specialists. By providing participants with models of how they can function and providing them with field experiences, you give them a better understanding of what is required. At the same time, participants need ongoing opportunities to discuss what works and what does not work for them. Collaborative planning time, support personnel who will listen and provide feedback, written materials, and time to reflect are important dimensions of such professional development support.

Planning Time

For collaboration to function effectively, participants need planning time. Teachers can be prepared to collaborate, but true collaboration cannot occur unless teachers talk about students, provide instruction that will achieve objectives, and reflect on the outcomes of their instruction. The most important dimension of collaborative teaching is that collaborative planning time must be allocated for such work.

Change Takes Time

Those involved in either directing or implementing collaborative models of instruction must be prepared to give them time to develop and evolve. Teachers need the flexibility to develop their own model of collaboration, one that provides appropriate experience for their students. A single approach to collaboration mandated by school administrators reduces chances that teachers will develop a sense of ownership, and a willingness to make such adaptations.

Summary

The collaborative models described in this chapter illustrate some of the diverse ways reading specialists and classroom teachers can collaborate to develop and implement appropriate and effective literacy instruction for students. Such instruction can exist when responsible educators communicate and collaborate as they plan appropriately for students. The models also provide for alternative means of collaboration, respecting and appreciating the differences that exist in how educators approach the instructional task. At the same time, the goal of these models is the same: to provide a thoughtfully developed and effective program for students. These models necessitate rethinking the roles of classroom teachers and reading specialists. They require the sharing of knowledge and responsibilities through ongoing communication and planning. When collaboration occurs in an environment that provides professional development and ongoing support, the advantages are many. Foremost, students in these programs will receive the instruction they need to become effective readers.

References

Allington, R.L., & Baker, K. (1999). Best practices in literacy instruction for children with special needs. In L.B. Gambrell, L.M. Morrow, D.S. Strickland, L.C. Wilkinson, S.B. Neuman, & M. Pressley (Eds.), *Best practices in literacy instruction* (pp. 292–310). New York: Guilford.

Barclay, K.D., & Thistlethwaite, L. (1992). Reading specialists of the 90's: Who are they and what do they want? *Reading Research and Instruction, 32*(1), 87–96.

Bean, R.M. (1979). Role of the reading specialist: A multifaceted dilemma. *The Reading Teacher, 32*, 409–413.

Bean, R.M., Armitage, C., & Kephart, K. (1995). *Two teachers in the classroom: Students' perspectives and performance.* Paper presented at the annual meeting of the American Educational Research Association, San Francisco, CA.

Bean, R.M., Cooley, W., Eichelberger, R.T., Lazar, M., & Zigmond, N. (1991). Inclass or pullout: Effects of setting on the remedial reading program. *Journal of Reading Behavior, 23*(4), 445–464.

Bean, R.M., Grumet, J.V., & Bulazo, J. (1999). Learning from each other: Collaboration between classroom teachers and reading specialist interns. *Reading Research and Instruction, 38*(4), 273–287.

Bean, R.M., Knaub, R., & Swan, A. (2000). *Reading specialists in leadership roles.* Paper presented at the annual meeting of the American Educational Research Association, New Orleans, LA.

Bean, R.M., Trovato, C.A., & Hamilton, R.L. (1995). Focus on Chapter 1 reading programs: Views of reading specialists, classroom teachers, and principals. *Reading Research and Instruction, 34*(3), 204–221.

Bean, R.M., & Wilson, R.M. (1981). *Effecting change in school reading programs: The resource role.* Newark, DE: International Reading Association.

Borko, H., Elliot, R., & Uchiyama, K. (1999). *Professional development: A key to Kentucky's reform movement* (CSE Technical Report 512). Los Angeles: Center for the Study of Evaluation.

Cook, L., & Friend, M. (1995). Co-teaching: Guidelines for creating effective practices. *Exceptional Children, 28*(3), 1–16.

Hamilton, R.L. (1993). *Chapter 1 reading instruction: Exemplary reading specialists in an inclass model.* Unpublished dissertation, University of Pittsburgh, Pittsburgh, PA.

Havill, J. (1986). *Jamaica's find.* New York: Scholastic.

Little, J. (1993). Teachers professional development in climate of educational reform. *Educational Evaluation and Policy Analysis, 15*(2), 129–151.

McLaughlin, M., & Talbert, J. (1993). *Contexts that matter for teaching and learning.* (ERIC Document Reproduction Services No. ED 357 023).

Meyers, J., Gelzheiser, L.M., & Yelich, G. (1991). Do pull-in programs foster teacher collaboration? *Remedial and Special Education, 12*(2), 7–15.

Miller, E. (January/February, 1995). The old model of staff development survives in a world where everything else has changed. *The Harvard Education Letter, XI*(1), 1–3.

National Center for Education Statistics (1999). *Teacher Quality: A report on the preparation and qualifications of public school teachers.* Washington, DC: U.S. Department of Education.

National Commission on Teaching and America's Future (1996). *What matters most: Teaching for America's future.* New York: Teachers College Press.

National Reading Panel. (2000). *Teaching children to read: An evidence-based assessment of the scientific research literature on reading and its implications for reading instruction.* Washington, DC: National Institute of Child Health and Human Development.

O'Connor, R.E., Jenkins, J.R., & Leicester, N. (1992). *Collaboration among general and special educators: The influence teachers exert on the process.* Paper presented at the annual meeting of the American Educational Research Association, San Francisco, CA.

Puma, M., & Jones, C. (1993). *Prospects: The Congressionally mandated study of educational growth and opportunity—Interim report.* Bethesda, MD: Abt Associates.

Radencich, M.C. (1995). *Administration and supervision of the reading/writing program.* Boston: Allyn & Bacon.

Robinson, H.A. (1967). The reading consultant of the past, present, and possible future. *The Reading Teacher, 20,* 475–482.

Scieszka, J. (1989). *The true story of the 3 little pigs! By A. Wolf.* New York: Viking Penguin.

Slavin, R.E. (1987). Making Chapter 1 make a difference. *Phi Delta Kappan, 69*(2), 110–119.

Snow, C., Burns, S., & Griffin, P. (Eds.). (1998). *Preventing reading difficulties in young children.* Washington, DC: National Academy Press.

Stauffer, R.G. (1967). Change, BUT - . *The Reading Teacher, 20,* 474, 499.

Tancock, S. (1995). Classroom teachers and reading specialists examine their Chapter 1 reading programs. *Journal of Reading Behavior, 27*(3), 315–335.

Establishing Effective Collaboration for Knowledge Building With Technology Supports

Sean P. Brophy

Professor Jack Brennon taught a course on cognition and instruction to undergraduate prospective teachers at a private teachers college. He was having a difficult time helping these future teachers reach beyond their own traditional educational experiences and adopt additional perspectives. One day he posed a hypothetical situation to the students about another professor, Michele Lee, who was having trouble connecting with her undergraduate students. She felt they were not trying hard enough. The students thought she was too demanding and required too much reading of material that did not seem relevant to their careers as classroom teachers. Jack asked his class to write tabout the situation. Students willingly shared their ideas, empathizing with Michele's students. They asked questions about the kind of work Michele expected and the students' workload from other courses.

Jack then had his students watch a 3-minute video about Michele's life growing up during the Cultural Revolution in China. Her family had been driven from their home and she was not allowed to go to school. However, her parents and siblings tutored her because of the value they placed on education. The students in Jack's class were again asked to write about the situation. At this point, the students shifted their interest and empathy to Michele, realizing that her cultural background could impact her expectations. This helped them understand a new dimension of the situation—that the teacher's and students' values and experiences when not shared can interfere with communication.

Attuning to others' perspectives is a valuable and necessary skill in collaborating and learning from others. Prospective teachers must be prepared to face situations similar to the one Michele faced in the opening vignette, because it is probable that their expectations for their students' learning and in-class participation will at times differ greatly from those of the students. To avoid the pitfalls of mismatches in personal knowledge between teachers and students, prospective teachers have to be open to seeking different perspectives and to learning from their students, each other, and other professionals. As teachers, they will encounter many challenges such as integrating new literacy programs and assessments into their instruction, meeting curriculum requirements, and accommodating special literacy needs of their students. They may not be able to efficiently find solutions on their own, and they will need to work with and learn from their colleagues who are dealing with similar challenges. Prospective teachers who learn to collaborate with their peers during teacher preparation will be more likely to use collaboration strategies as valuable assets throughout their professional careers.

Technology can be used to create collaborative environments in teacher education classrooms. This chapter presents several ways that technology tools can be used to support collaboration. These tools, used in the teacher education program at Vanderbilt University, Nashville, Tennessee, USA, can be adapted by future teachers to support students' learning in their own classrooms. Additionally, this chapter provides examples to illustrate how technology is used to support K–12 collaboration and literacy learning. I start by exploring various dimensions of how collaboration can build knowledge of both the group and individuals. Then I compare technology solutions for sustaining a collaborative dialogue among teachers, prospective teachers, and K–12 students.

Establishing a Collaborative Community That Leads to Knowledge Building

Effective learning environments contain a strong sense of community for prospective teachers enrolled in undergraduate courses. Establishing a community of learners means creating an atmosphere where students want and value the opportunity to work together in collaborative efforts. Collaboration goes beyond getting along with each other and sharing the same classroom and teacher. Collaboration is much more than a sum of individual perspectives. Instead, the potential for learning is greatly enhanced when the learners exchange and test their ideas with each other and build shared understandings that are inclusive and broadly constructed. Therefore, collaboration that supports learning occurs when the participants interact with each other to define something new—to build knowledge that they all share.

> *Collaboration that supports learning occurs when the participants interact with each other to define something new—to build knowledge that they all share.*

Prospective teachers, with their own experiences and views of schools, begin to expand their understanding as they compare and contrast their ideas with others. As in Michele's case in the opening vignette, often there are multiple perspectives in any situation based on individuals' own experiences. Without this contrast, prospective teachers' misconceptions, or lack of conception, continue and their ability to refine their thinking does not develop. Without this opportunity to develop a collaborative community, no new thoughts are brought into the classroom except for those presented by the teacher and/or textbook author.

The challenge for the teacher educator is creating a community that optimizes the learning potential for everyone. Open classroom discussions provide one method for students to share and debate ideas. For example, a literacy professor could pose a question such as, "What potential barriers might you expect in trying to encourage your class to discuss an assigned reading?" Starting with a simple topic may improve the likelihood that everyone has something to contribute. Guided by the professor, a classroom discussion can review multiple dimensions of a particular topic. Jack, in the opening vignette, uses an interesting method to get the prospective teachers to reflect on their own viewpoints. He begins by asking them to articulate what they think about a situation and then he provides new information, encouraging the students to revisit their initial thoughts and to share with others how and why their thinking is changing.

However, in class discussions some prospective teachers are reticent to share ideas for a variety of reasons. They may not think of something to contribute or they miss an opportunity to share it before the discussion moves in a different direction. Someone may dominate the conversation making it difficult for others to contribute. Discussions limited by the available class time may terminate without adequate closure, leading to confusion or even frustration by students. To address these potential limitations, teacher educators at Vanderbilt University use technological methods that

- allow for individuality,
- extend discussions beyond the designated class time, and
- support the prospective teachers' inquiry process while they gather information and build knowledge.

Technology Tools for Sustaining Extended Collaboration

Technology can be used to establish a collaborative environment for educating prospective teachers and K–12 students. This section discusses the strengths and weaknesses of three technologies: (1) online discussion forums, (2) Knowledge Forum, and (3) Knowledge Mining Process. Each tool provides a mechanism for students to write their ideas and post them to a central area for everyone to see. In an instructional setting these tools provide a method for groups to engage in a shared inquiry in which together they can build their understanding of a topic. One major difference between these tools is in how they structure and represent the dialogue between all the participants in a discussion. Another difference is how they help to synthesize the information shared by the group.

General-Purpose Online Discussion Forum

Many researchers and teachers are exploring the potential of using online (i.e., Web-based) discussion areas to extend a community's inquiry beyond the time constraints of face-to-face meetings and to expose students to multiple perspectives of a community. For example, students—including prospective teachers—communicate with book authors or write to pen pals online (Bielaczyc & Collins, 1999; Neely, 1999). These common online discussion forums allow participants to share ideas and debate positions by typing in messages that are "posted" on a central computing system for everyone to read. These discussions organize messages around specific "threads," or topics, and use a hierarchical outline method to display the sequence of replies to the original topic of discussion.

In a general-purpose online discussion forum, each new thread is represented as a major topic in the outline. The subtopics are replies to the original thread topic posted. Therefore, each major thread can have several subdiscussions occurring simultaneously. For example, a multiculturalism rhetorics course for prospective teachers and master's-level teachers used a threaded discussion area to have an extended discussion on a multiculturalism article written by Gordon Gee (see Figure 1).

The professor, Peter Sloan, started a thread titled "1.16 A Discussion Starter," in which he gave a brief description to focus students' attention on specific issues Gee raises about discourse and rhetoric. Linda, a student, began a new thread titled "Two Gee Whiz Questions," where she asked for clarification on several points. In her message she quoted sections of the article and posed related questions:

> Question 1...Why did the discourse of literary criticism "conflict less with other discourses of white middleclass men" than with the other discourses of women?

> Question 2...The example of beginning readers seems inappropriate. The simplest forms (EX. See Jane run.) would seem to have universal meaning. If texts or ages of the students were given, I might be more willing to accept his ideas. Is his point that we all interpret text differently? On a more experienced reading level, ok. When does this interpretation really begin?

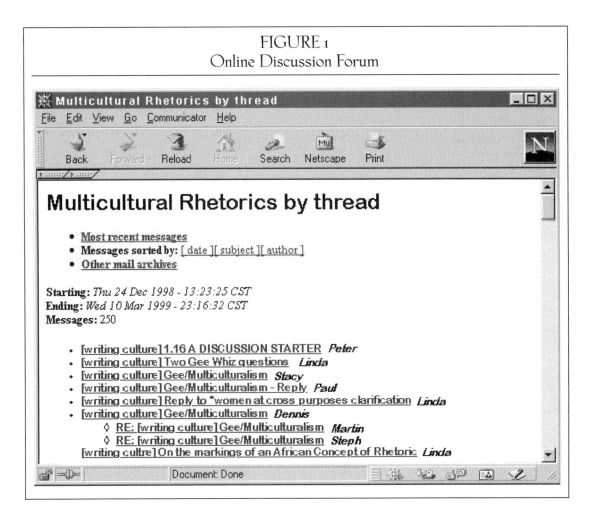

FIGURE 1
Online Discussion Forum

These entries initiated a chain of replies in a thread called "Gee/Multiculturalism." Several of Linda's peers expressed their interpretation of the passage and raised questions of their own. For example, Stacy joined the conversation with,

> What is implied for multiculturalism from the Gee article is that in order to criticize the dominant discourse, one has to have the same set of values and viewpoints in speaking and acting as the dominant group. And doing so, one will have greater power in society. Persons from the dominant group acquire the dominant discourse but persons from the non dominant group acquire their own discourse and must learn the dominant discourse if they want to be involved....

Stacy continued with a response to one of Linda's questions and raised another question of her own. This new question led to a new discussion thread on the differences between "discourse" and "rhetoric." Paul picked up on Stacy's comment about the role of a dominant groups and provided his own comments:

> Yeah, I think Stacy is right on track here. The discourse of literacy criticism is aggressive, distributive—its traits are very unlike those that early feminists found when they studied what women valued in communications. To the extent that most institutional, dominant-culture discourses exhibit what have been called "masculine discourse traits," women, in order to succeed in dominant culture institutions, have had to **learn** aspects of discourses that men have **acquired**.

Within the same thread that Linda started, the conversation continued to explore issues of how discourse is formed, how people participate in discourse, and how people with different viewpoints can truly understand the discourse of others. One aspect of this online discussion is the effect on participants' own understanding as illustrated by Linda's later comment:

> Stacy and Paul have set me straight...for the moment :) ...I wasn't thinking of discourse of literacy criticism as particularly aggressive, or disruptive (disruptive to whom, by the way)....

Another aspect of this online discussion forum is the level of participation of the individual group members during the online conversation. Just like a classroom discussion, participants take on various roles related to what and when they contribute to the conversation. For example, a participant can start out at a *low level of participation by "listening in"* on what others are talking about without making contributions to the conversation. Alternatively, one could participate at a *moderate level by initiating a thread of discussion* to ask a question or to pose a problem and request help. In response, others in the group can share their insights or opinions to help that individual. Finally, there are members of the discussion who have a high level of engagement during the conversations. These members become "key contributors" by initiating conversations and helping new members become part of the discussion (Shafer, 2000). These *high-*

level contributors can be highly productive members who help sustain the community and build knowledge around a specific topic.

Given the strengths of this forum for dialogue, there are also several challenges to using the general-purpose online discussion forum. For example, discussion histories (i.e., a hierarchical outline of the threaded discussions shown in Figure 1) can increase quickly with multiple replies to a message within a thread, and with new threads of discussion created by participants. This growth of text messages makes it difficult for any new members to pick up on all the threads of discussion. Many ideas are expressed but not all of them are pursued. For example, Linda's second question was never pursued. This could simply be because Linda chose to put two issues into one message. The most interesting question to the group was explored first, leaving the second to be forgotten. To use these systems effectively, participants must first learn certain protocols. Had Linda started two threads of discussion, one for each question, the group might have returned to the second question and explored it in parallel with the first question or at a later time.

An instructor who uses discussion as a learning tool, both in class and online, must define a method that leads to a point where ideas are synthesized. Typical online discussion areas are designed only to gather and organize messages from the participants. There is neither a specific termination of a conversation nor a built-in mechanism to have a group focus attention on achieving a specific goal. Therefore, the instructor must define a mechanism to ensure that students achieve closure on their discussion. Otherwise, the students will perceive their collaborative efforts as a waste of time and lose the learning opportunity of establishing links between their ideas.

An instructor who uses discussion as a learning tool, both in class and online, must define a method that leads to a point where ideas are synthesized.

One method to obtain closure of a discussion is to appoint a moderator or host. This host could maintain a conversation over a long period of time. The host may try to summarize the conversation from time to time to help the group refocus the discussion and help newcomers understand the main focus of the conversation. This mediation keeps the discussion from quickly splintering into many different foci, never reaching closure on any of them. Also, without a synthesis of ideas over time the main points of interest can be buried in all the text that appears on the screen. The next section presents other tools that can be used to help with focusing inquiry on a specific topic and organizing this information synthesis process.

In summary, online discussion forums provide several new dimensions to sustaining a dialogue between members of a group collaborating to build shared knowledge about a topic. These added dimensions include

- creating opportunities for sustained conversation (beyond face-to-face interaction time),
- creating a permanent record of conversation and structure using a hierarchical outline, and
- encouraging reflection on one's own thoughts.

However, these new capabilities come at a price. New challenges occur such as increases in volume of messages to process and many discussion threads to be explored (potentially detracting from the original focus or goal of the discussion). Also, for the purpose of learning, there needs to be closure and synthesis of the ideas.

Structured Communications Tools to Facilitate Inquiry

Many teachers have used the general-purpose online discussion forum effectively for instruction, but have had to deal with challenges of managing its complexity. Newer technology tools have been created to foster effective communication and aid in knowledge building and productive collaboration. This section describes two such tools: Knowledge Forum (previously known as CSILE [Computer Support for Intentional Learning Environment]) (Scardamalia, Bereiter, McLean, Swallow, & Woodrull, 1989) and Knowledge Mining Process (KMP) (Brophy, Clark, Bransford, & CTGV, 1998).

KNOWLEDGE FORUM. Knowledge Forum is designed around an inquiry model of investigation to help a group build knowledge around a topic. Therefore, each message a student posts is categorized with a keyword such as "My theory," "New information," or "Evidence," to name a few. Knowledge Forum also allows students to make links between ideas and organizes these ideas into clusters or categories. For example, a professor of early literacy development may pose the questions "How can reading literacy be assessed? What would you want to measure?" Now, the prospective teachers in the course can link their ideas to this question with their own theories, questions, and possible solutions. Figure 2 illustrates how the discussion structure has moved from a hierarchical outline of a threaded discussion (see Figure 1) to a visual map of the ideas generated by the prospective teachers. This arrangement is similar to putting ideas on index cards, arranging them on a table, then using string to make links between relevant cards.

In Figure 2, one prospective teacher (Sarah) makes the point that we need to distinguish between (a) reading comprehension and (b) fluency. She argues that comprehension and fluency are not always good measures of each other. As evidence for this argument she cites Yuill and Oakhill (1991), who mention that some students read fluently but still have trouble comprehending stories while other children who comprehend stories well may not be fluent readers. Another teacher, Susan, asks, "How often do I need to test?" Through the posting and linking of questions and ideas the prospective teachers engage in a process of inquiry. As a group they are building a shared knowledge about this domain. They are sharing and refining their individual thoughts and ideas. The technology-based "note-card" tool gives them a method to arrange and rearrange their ideas as they make sense of the issues. And, they have a useful method to create a report that synthesizes their inquiry around this issue of assessing literacy.

Prospective teachers can use a similar approach when they have their own classrooms. For example, Jim Michaels is a language arts teacher who team-teaches with Sarah Parks, a middle school science teacher. Sarah is conducting a life science unit on animal habitats, and Jim is working with the students on expository writing. Figure 3 shows a challenge Sarah posed to a group of sixth-grade students: "You have just discovered that a bald eagle has been killed and four eggs are unhatched. What do you need to do?" Using Knowledge Forum, the students begin to post their theories of what should be done, such as, "Find another eagle to sit on the eggs, but don't touch

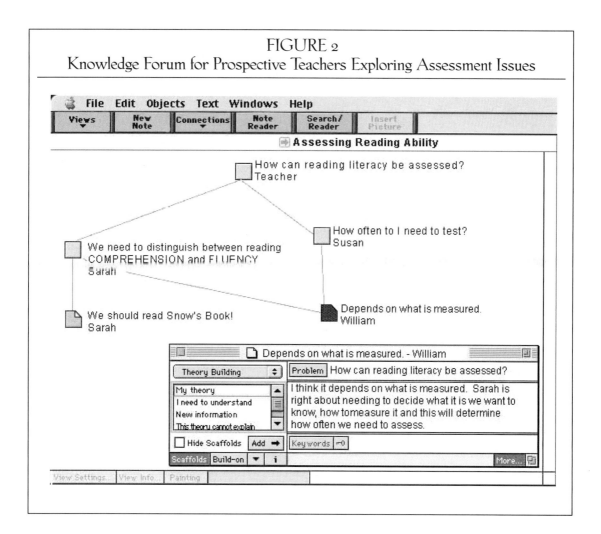

FIGURE 2
Knowledge Forum for Prospective Teachers Exploring Assessment Issues

them, because if you do, another bird can smell that a human has touched them and won't sit on the eggs." Other students can build on these ideas by offering their own "My theory" note. For example, a student may suggest, "Could we use another kind of bird? There aren't many eagles left. They are endangered." Or, students can use the "Need more Info" prompt to ask for clarification or new information like, "Do birds have a sense of smell?"

This kind of dynamic offers the opportunity for every student to participate and for teachers to trace and assess students' individual responses over time. Students can offer new theories, ask questions, and

---

FIGURE 3
Knowledge Forum for Middle School Student Exploring Animal Habitats

File   Edit   Objects   Text   Windows   Help

| Views ▼ | New Note | Connections ▼ | Note Reader | Search/ Reader | Insert Picture |

➡ Habitat

☐ Unhatched egg problem
Teacher

▨ ●Get another eagle
Susan Williams

◣ ●Do birds have a sense of smell?
Xioadong Lin

☐ Get another eagle – Susan William

Problem You have just discovered that a bald eagle has been

Find another eagle to sit on the eggs, but don't touch
them, because if you do, another bird can smell that a
human has touched them and won't sit on the eggs.

Keywords ⌐0

Scaffolds | Build-on | ▼ | i | More...

▨ ●Will another bird work?
Xioadong Lin

●Put them in the oven
Sean Brophy

☐ Will another bird work? – Xioadong Lin

| Theory Building ⬍ | Problem | You have just discovered that a bald eagle has been |

My theory
I need to understand
New Information
This theory cannot explain

Could we use another kind of bird? There aren't many
eagles left. They are endangered.

☐ Hide Scaffolds | Add ➡ | Keywords ⌐0

Scaffolds | Build-on | ▼ | i | More...

View Settings... | View Info... | Painting

---

give information based on prior experience or through their research.
Here again the visual display of index cards linked with a line provides students with a tool to sort and prioritize the information they
gather and provides the teacher with a valuable record of the students' learning. Ultimately, Sarah and Jim will work together to help
the students build their understanding of how all the information
they are gathering fits together and how to communicate this in an
expository essay.

Knowledge Forum helps students establish a dialogue with each
other much like a class discussion, but the tool also documents their

thinking. The visual metaphor of notecards and links helps remind students of previous directions, helps newcomers join in the conversation quickly, and documents conceptual change. Also, Knowledge Forum allows a teacher to listen in on and participate in several discussions at once—something that cannot be done realistically in a classroom discussion. The teacher can mediate, or guide, a discussion by asking prompting questions to increase the level of discussion between students. For example, the professor of early literacy development mentioned earlier can monitor students' submissions on a daily basis and provide comments to help them refocus or suggest where they could continue their research. When there is a decrease in the amount of submissions students make, the teacher can pose a new topic such as, "Fuchs and Maxwell report that reading fluency can be monitored using a simple curriculum-based measurement system (Fuchs, Fuchs, & Maxwell, 1988). This reference is in our course pack. What are the strengths and weaknesses of this approach for assessing reading literacy?" The teacher can spur a new direction in student inquiry and show how the readings for the course link to their inquiry. Similarly, Jim and Sarah can submit prompts or probing question to encourage their middle school students to explore new directions in their inquiry.

Programs like Knowledge Forum, and the learning activities associated with them, are designed to

- scaffold and guide inquiry by using a set of prompts (e.g., "My theory," "New information," etc.),
- organize thoughts and ideas,
- link relevant ideas using a visual metaphor, and
- manage the exponential growth of questions and ideas.

Knowledge Forum still requires the teacher to accommodate a high level of complexity—complexity associated with learning a new tool and managing the increasing volume of information the community is generating.

KNOWLEDGE MINING PROCESS. While Knowledge Forum provides a method to track the history of a conversation and trace its development, provides a mechanism to organize information, and allows newcomers to easily join the discussion, the volume of information created can still be overwhelming for students and for the teacher to moderate—both within college and K–12 classrooms. Knowledge Mining Process (KMP) (Brophy et al., 1998) is a technology tool that has been developed to quickly and efficiently gather and organize information from members of a given community. It uses a unique model of communication for refining the collective view of a group, delaying the reaction to each other's responses until all participants have had a chance to share their perspectives.

KMP most closely resembles the brainstorming phase of the problem-solving process. Brainstorming consists of listing numerous possible alternatives that could be explored as solutions to a problem, regardless of feasibility. Once the list is generated, action can be taken to review the alternatives and define a viable solution that maintains the constraints of the original problem (Bransford & Stein, 1993). For example, in the unhatched eagle egg example discussed previously, students are able to generate ideas immediately and other students can begin to expand on these ideas immediately. Therefore, some students may simply respond to others' comments rather than providing their own ideas for solving the problem. However, when a goal of the discussion is to allow everyone in the group to voice a unique perspective, everyone should participate at a high level of engagement rather than just listen or react to what others contribute. KMP allows people to share their ideas prior to diving deeper into a discussion of any one of these perspectives.

KMP begins by inviting each member of a group to share insights about a specific topic, such as, "What methods can we define to increase parent involvement in homework." This could be done through an e-mail message defining the topic and providing instructions on how to formulate a short response. Prospective teachers reflect on the topic and submit their response into a text box on a special Web site. Not until they submit their own response are the participants given a unique Web address that provides access to others' contributions. This method of "blind submission" encourages the participants to offer their thoughts about the topic, rather than only their reactions to someone else's thoughts. Figure 4 illustrates how the responses were organized by group members' names. This allows participants to quickly browse through the other responses. As participants read others' responses, they can, at any time, edit their initial response as it relates to the initial topic. *After a specific deadline the submission process is closed and an individual or small group (potentially a subgroup of the participants) synthesizes the responses into a single document.* This document becomes an object for discussion in a second round, or cycle, of KMP.

If KMP were used for the Assessing Reading Ability discussion (see Figure 2), the first cycle would begin by encouraging everyone in the group to submit ideas and issues for literacy assessment. Participants who are unable to think of a solution because they need

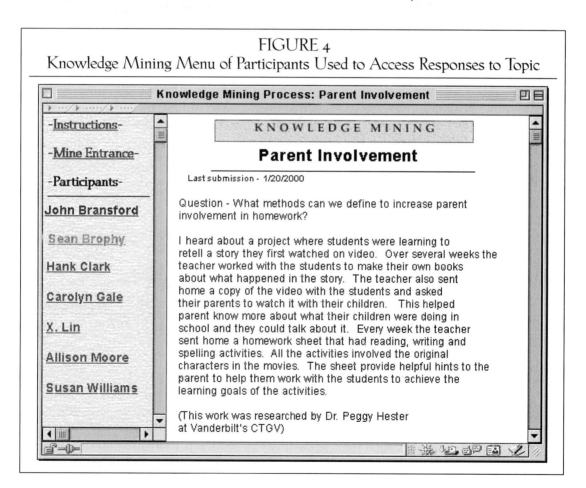

FIGURE 4
Knowledge Mining Menu of Participants Used to Access Responses to Topic

more information can respond with a question that the group should research further (e.g., What is a good measure of reading? What is the difference between reading fluency and reading comprehension?). Once everyone has contributed, the synthesis may be a simple list of the alternative solutions and questions generated by participants.

The second cycle of KMP is to expand and refine the thoughts contributed by the original participants, inviting others who would like to participate. The participants review the synthesis from the earlier cycle. Participants can respond in many ways, including clarifying their earlier position, providing new information, or sharing new insights that emerged from reflection on the synthesis document. With KMP, the amount of information is reduced to a collection of current ideas, issues, and questions a group knows about a particular topic of focus, documented in the synthesis paper. *The synthesis of each cycle provides the executive summary from which the group can build and expand ideas in future cycles.* The desired result is a refined document of the group's most current thoughts and ideas related to a specific topic. The multiple cycles produce more thoughtful and insightful responses from participants, who have been able to develop their ideas more fully by reflecting on the responses of others.

Several of the underlying characteristics of KMP, like blind submission and iterative refinement of ideas, have the potential to enhance future teachers' learning in a classroom. Professors Xiaodong Lin and John Bransford at Vanderbilt University, for example, used KMP in their course Culture and Cognition. The class was comprised of both graduate and undergraduate students from a range of disciplines including psychology, education, and general liberal arts. The professors used KMP to collect ideas for a class project on communicating what they were learning to others interested in culture and cognition. The process kicked off with an e-mail to the class outlining the general objectives and inviting the students to submit ideas for a project using the KMP Web tool. Students were given a deadline to submit their thoughts 24 hours prior to the next class meeting. After the deadline the submission process was closed, and everyone could read all the ideas contributed prior to class. This provided the students with the opportunity to read and reflect on others' contributions. Also, it helped the professors see what students were thinking prior to the class, which made it easier to anticipate what would be discussed in class. The next class meeting began with people expanding on the ideas contributed to KMP, reducing the amount of time needed to get the group talking about their ideas, giving them more time to dive deeper into the issue face to face.

Access to others' ideas before class helped the professors become aware of the range of issues about which the class was concerned. It also helped to know which direction the class discussion should take to raise awareness of alternative perspectives. Students, too, valued knowing what others thought. Lin and Bransford (personal communication, 1999) had many of their students report that they learned a lot about themselves by reflecting on others' ideas and how these ideas confront their own perspective. Overall, the professors' focus on obtaining and synthesizing the multiple perspectives of others was a positive learning experience and KMP aided in the process.

Prospective literacy teachers can use a similar approach in their own classrooms. Frank Buhler, a high school language arts teacher who co-teaches with a history teacher, spent year after year lecturing students on the events of the Great Depression, trying to help them comprehend a difficult history text. He found he could never describe how the United States might fall into another depression. When he began to use KMP, he created a report generated by the class titled "The multiple factors of Great Depression." The first cycle of KMP began with everyone contributing their theories for the Great Depression before their first meeting. Students submitted a range of ideas such as, "too many people and not enough jobs," "the banks were greedy and didn't want to give back people's money," or "we can never have another depression, because everyone is working." This provided Frank with some great topics for future classes. As part of the first class he presented a short lecture designed to target some of the issues students raised and to help identify some of their basic misconceptions about how the Great Depression began. Then the class sorted the ideas they submitted and prioritized these ideas into topics that they needed to research. Frank divided the class into several groups, which began their research.

As with the other technology tools, KMP introduces new challenges to instruction such as establishment of a safe, collaborative environment. The blind submission process can create anxiety because participants are uncertain about how their comments will be perceived; therefore, they may be unwilling to contribute. The same phenomena have been observed in traditional online discussions. Williams-Glaser (1998) reports that many users do not want to be the first to contribute, nor do they want to be the last. Often, people wait for someone to initiate the discussion or pose a question, then use others' responses as a benchmark for their own. On the other hand, some want to contribute early before someone else submits their idea. The blind submission process forces participants to contribute their own response without any benchmark or standard against which to compare quality. Therefore, this accents the need to establish this level of trust between group members during face-to-face meetings, such as class time. Another alternative is to make submission anonymous, but then participants cannot take ownership of great ideas they generate.

In summary, KMP fosters a collaborative community like the other technology tools, but it has several distinguishing characteristics including

- maintaining a focus on a single topic of discussion,
- encouraging responses from all of the members of a group,
- using blind submission to ensure a range of perspectives (i.e., restricting access to others' comments before contributing own comments),
- using a deadline for submission to ensure closure,
- synthesizing results into a single document, and
- organizing discussion through refinement of a single document rather than tracking multiple parallel paths.

Principles for Sustaining Community

These examples illustrate how technology can support the information exchange between members of a class to build new knowledge. However, if the goal is to foster collaboration between students, with or without technology, then it is the teacher's responsibility to establish an atmosphere that encourages students to freely exchange their ideas.

Creating a collaborative classroom environment requires establishing several critical conditions to reduce the anxiety of students. First, allow students to freely share their ideas without fear of criticism. Second, establish opportunities for everyone to contribute their ideas. Similarly, establish an atmosphere where everyone's contribution is valued. Third, reduce the competition for grades between the students so they are more willing to share good ideas, rather than keeping them to themselves. Fourth, create mechanisms to capture students' work to help them build on their own ideas and those of their peers. This also requires giving students time to reflect on what they have generated and how it relates to others' work. Fifth, initiate discussion with a new group by beginning with what they know. Start discussions in a way that allows students to share their perspectives. Finally, provide individualized instruction that is informed by students' contributions. Ensuring these conditions in the classroom should make it more likely that students will share what they know, and provide a record of students' performance (and teachers' instruction) over time.

One key to any successful collaborative learning environment is its ability to support diverse learners and target the multiple perspectives of a community. Exploring interesting topics as a group naturally results in accessing and acquiring a wealth of information. The level of participation can increase greatly with the assistance of a moderator (e.g., a teacher) and the continued participation of everyone in the group. Young learners develop their writing skills as they articulate their thoughts about a specific topic. They need to reason intelligently about how to make links between their thoughts and those of others. They must integrate new information they learn into what they have already discussed. These literacy skills are developed as part of a natural inquiry process. With technology, this exploration and sharing of ideas is documented, providing teachers with excellent assessment materials to monitor students' progress. With or without technology, establishing the collaborative environment to share and synthesize ideas as a group has great potential for helping students develop powerful literacy skills and learn more from others' perspectives.

Finally, creating effective learning environments that embed collaboration and technology into instruction requires learning from example. Prospective literacy teachers need to experience the instructional methods they will use later in their own classrooms. This chapter outlines several learning activities used to educate prospective teachers. Jack was able to help his students value the importance of hearing others' perspectives through a series of contrasting cases. Peter saw his students begin to identify the multiple dimensions of an assigned reading as they learned from others' comments. The early literacy professor used Knowledge Forum to help her students make links between the multiple issues associated with assessing literacy. Frank's use of KMP helped students to understand and communicate the causal factors associated with the Great Depression. Each of these examples illustrates how prospective teachers can learn from each other and build a shared understanding of the content if the right collaborative learning environment is established.

Summary

One of the main goals of this chapter was to illustrate methods for helping prospective literacy teachers and their future K–12 students to articulate their thoughts and to work with their peers to research and build knowledge. These types of activities are critical for developing the necessary literacy skills to succeed academically and can provide teachers with important assessment information. Also, extensive research (see Bielaczyc & Collins, 1999) shows that creating a collaborative learning environment provides a natural means for students to share, organize, and synthesize their ideas. Therefore, an effective learning environment for developing literacy skills—and for learning to help others develop similar skills—needs to be collaborative, use interesting challenges to engage group inquiry, and establish methods for students to generate and merge their ideas in a central place. Embedding these principles into the design of instruction, whether it is for prospective literacy teachers or for K–12 students, can lead to learners' acquiring new concepts, making links between ideas, and communicating their ideas both verbally and in their writing.

An effective learning environment for developing literacy skills—and for learning to help others develop similar skills—needs to be collaborative, use interesting challenges to engage group inquiry, and establish methods for students to generate and merge their ideas in a central place.

NOTE

I would like to thank Xiaodong Lin, Hank Clark, and Victoria J. Risko for their comments on the multiple drafts of this chapter. I would also like to acknowledge the ideas of John Bransford, Hank Clark, Allison Moore, Carolyn Gale, John Rakestraw, and Susan Williams, who helped design the Knowledge Mining Process and software tools.

Knowledge Forum is now a commercial product. For more information, see Learning in Motion's Web site (http://www.learn.motion.com/lim/kf/KF1.html).

Knowledge Mining Process is still under development at the Learning Technology Center at Vanderbilt University. For more information, visit http://canvas.ltc.vanderbilt.edu/kmine.

References

Bielaczyc, K., & Collins, A. (1999). Learning communities in classrooms: A reconceptualization of educational practice. In C.M. Reigeluth (Ed.), *Instructional-design theories and models: A new paradigm of instructional theory: Volume II*. Mahwah, NJ: Erlbaum.

Bransford, J.D., & Stein, B.S. (1993). *The ideal problem solver: A guide for improving thinking* (2nd ed.). New York: W.H. Freeman.

Brophy, S.P., Clark, H.T., Bransford, J.D., & Cognition and Technology Group at Vanderbilt (CTGV). (1998). Knowledge Mining Process [Computer program]. Nashville, TN: Vanderbilt University.

Fuchs, L.S., Fuchs, D., & Maxwell, L. (1988). The validity of information reading comprehension measures. *Remedial and Special Education, 9*(2), 20–29.

Neely, A.M. (1999). *Using technology to enhance presentation and discussion in teacher education*. Paper presented at the meeting of the American Association of Colleges of Teacher Education, Washington, DC.

Scardamalia, M., Bereiter, C., McLean, R., Swallow, J., & Woodrull, E. (1989). Computer supported intentional learning environments. *Journal of Educational Computing Research, 5*(1), 51–68.

Shafer, D. (2000, April). For whom would you design your community? *Online Community Report* [Online]. Available: http://www.onlinecommunityreport.com/features/design.

Williams-Glaser, C. (1998). *Creating new standards for higher education: Effecting pedagogical change in the undergraduate curriculum through the integration of technology*. Unpublished doctoral dissertation, Vanderbilt University, Nashville, TN.

Yuill, N., & Oakhill, J. (1991). *Children's problems in text comprehension: An experimental investigation*. New York: Cambridge University Press.

SECTION

CONCLUSIONS

COLLABORATION FOR DIVERSE LEARNERS
Reflections and Recommendations

Karen Bromley and Victoria J. Risko

> As cultural and linguistic diversity in our schools increases arithmetically,
> the challenge to education increases geometrically and possibly exponen-
> tially. (Garcia, 1999, p. 8)

We believe the challenge to education is even greater
than Garcia suggests. When differences in student
learning style, socioeconomic background, ability,
and age are added to the increased cultural and linguistic diversity
found in most classrooms today, the challenge is difficult to imagine.
We believe collaboration is one potentially powerful way to meet this
challenge. And we agree with Allington and Walmsley (1995), who
acknowledge that change is difficult but warn that literacy programs
desperately need to change to better serve all students.

There are many models of collaboration from which we can learn
to enhance literacy development and learning opportunities for the
diverse students represented in U.S. classrooms today. Indeed, a nar-
row focus on collaboration limits what we can learn from it (John-
Steiner, Weber, & Minnis, 1998). In this book we have explored
several models that fit our broad definition of collaboration—a partnership among individuals whose goal is to improve the literacy de-

velopment and learning of all students through the generation of shared decisions about curriculum and instruction. Common to such partnerships is the belief that diversity is a rich resource for all involved; thus, the participants are guided by respect for diverse capabilities, perspectives, and cultural practices.

The collaborations described in this volume represent multiple, shared perspectives on rethinking participant roles and redesigning curriculum and instruction. Our purpose has been to examine the implementation, dilemmas, and insights of classroom teachers, reading specialists, special education teachers, ESL teachers, students, parents, administrators, community members, university faculty, and other researchers as they work together. Through their voices and the stories they tell about collaboration in schools and communities around the United States, we can see what lies at the heart of the collaborative process for these participants.

Recurring Themes

In the first chapter we posed four questions that we return to now to analyze the design and implementation of projects described in this book. Here we examine how these authors provide answers and insights about those questions. We identify recurring themes in these chapters and identify possible challenges for future collaborators.

Is there meaningful improvement in the literacy development and learning opportunities for all students?

Traditionally schools have failed to provide instruction that accommodates diverse learners in ways that result in improved literacy (Allington & Cunningham, 1996; Walmsley & Allington, 1995). The aim of each of the collaborations described in this volume is enhanced literacy and learning for all students, whether they differ in language, learning style, culture, ethnicity, race, socioeconomic background, ability, or age. Chapter authors describe a wide range of students—those identified for special education services; struggling readers; ESL students; students with Asian, African American, and Hispanic backgrounds; and students in rural and inner city schools. For all these students and the wider range of diversity in today's schools, Pugach and Fitzgerald (Chapter 5) pose two questions that drive their project and that we believe should be at the heart of all collaborations: "How well are our efforts helping to improve student learning?" and "How meaningful is the curriculum?"

Projects discussed in this book demonstrate how to meet goals to improve student learning and develop meaningful curriculum. For example, instruction that is responsive to individual strengths and needs is enhanced by the teaming of classroom teachers and specialists, as described by Montague and Warger (Chapter 2), Schumm, Hughes, and Arguelles (Chapter 4), Ogle and Fogelberg (Chapter 9), Lyons (Chapter 10), Rainforth and England (Chapter 11), Osborne and Schulte (Chapter 18), Bean (Chapter 19), and Brophy (Chapter 20). As these authors discuss, these teams collaborate to provide in-class rather than pull-out literacy instruction. To achieve meaningful curriculum, these projects illustrate how to invite nontraditional interactions and support. For example, Douville and Wood (Chapter 8) focus on developing literacy through social interactions and collaborative exchanges among students who learn literacy from and with each other. In several chapters—Padak, Sapin, and Ackerman (Chapter 6), Edwards and Danridge (Chapter 14), and Rodríguez-Brown (Chapter 15)—collaborations build the literacy of both children and families. Kennedy and Canney (Chapter 17) and Brophy (Chapter 20) use technology-based collaborations to foster learning. Bean (Chapter 19) describes how prospective reading specialists collaborate with classroom teachers as they learn how to individualize classroom instruction for all students.

> *Two questions...should be at the heart of all collaborations: "How well are our efforts helping to improve student learning?" and "How meaningful is the curriculum?"*

Throughout these chapters, authors demonstrate a need for careful assessment of students' performance to document their efforts to enhance student learning. Teachers described by these authors are sensitive to the need to collect data over time and to adjust curriculum and instruction based on shared concerns and decisions. Pugach and Fitzgerald (Chapter 5), for example, align curriculum changes with daily observational data. Douville and Wood (Chapter 8) provide examples of rubrics used for student self-evaluation of collaborative team work. Osborne and Schulte (Chapter 18) describe problem solving that is assessment-based, with specialists helping teachers take on the role of individual assessment. Both Lyons (Chapter 10) and Osborne and Schulte (Chapter 18) illustrate ways to carefully monitor student development in the classroom and show how this information is used to modify instruction. Similarly, Peck (Chapter 7) and Ernst-Slavit, Han, and Wenger (Chapter 16) describe careful "kidwatching" strategies that lead to adjustments and communication with the home. Rodríguez-Brown (Chapter 15) discusses data that illustrate changes in the home as parents take more active roles as teachers of their children and changes in the school through networks of parents who participate in school programs and the school board. Finally, Brophy (Chapter 20) illustrates how to use technology to document students' participation and learning.

Authors document literacy development in additional ways. Schumm, Hughes, and Arguelles (Chapter 4) and Rainforth and England (Chapter 11) cite teacher reports of improved academic outcomes and self-esteem of students. Peck (Chapter 7) shares vignettes of literacy learning evident in student performances and joint productions. Lyons (Chapter 10) shows improvements in reading scores in one school district's lowest achieving school related to a collaborative venture. Rodríguez-Brown (Chapter 15) documents changes in children's early literacy learning through school tests and teacher and parent observations. Ernst-Slavit, Han, and Wenger (Chapter 16) show changes in student participation in reading and writing, and analyze and share student writing samples. Kennedy and Canney (Chapter 17) cite early indicators of student success in achievement and problem solving in math and science and gains in technology use and collaboration.

Does collaboration serve as a catalyst for restructuring curriculum and instruction, and as an invitation for participant involvement?

Often, changes in schools are not accompanied by changed allocations of professional resources, more professional development opportunities, or real communication among participants (Fafard,

1995). Much school restructuring in the past has resulted in superficial and temporary adjustments in routines rather than substantial redesign of curriculum and instruction (Marks & Gersten, 1998). We see curriculum and instructional change as an important theme in the projects described in this book. Many authors view curriculum as the vehicle to improve literacy, learning, and teaching. They believe that responsive and responsible collaborative curriculum development can improve the quality of classrooms and schools. They show how the day-to-day interactions in classrooms can change to provide equitable and effective instruction for all students.

Many authors describe curriculum redesign that results in schoolwide restructuring for the provision of services to students. For example, Pugach and Fitzgerald (Chapter 5), Walker, Scherry, and Gransbery (Chapter 3), Schumm, Hughes, and Arguelles (Chapter 4), Rainforth and England (Chapter 11), Osborne and Schulte (Chapter 18), and Bean (Chapter 19) describe a move away from pull-out programs and a move toward inclusion of special education students in regular education classrooms with marked changes in reading and writing instruction. Ogle and Fogelberg (Chapter 9) institute in-class reading instruction for all students and describe a classroom-based collaborative team model that replaces pull-out reading instruction for which all teachers take responsibility for the learning of all students.

Pugach and Fitzgerald (Chapter 5), Osborne and Schulte (Chapter 18), and Schmidt (Chapter 12) view culturally relevant curricula as essential to responsible teaching and perceive student differences as ways to promote learning, not as obstacles to overcome. Their restructured curriculum and classroom environments encourage students' self-directed learning and study of home and community resources. Adhering to similar goals, Kennedy and Canney (Chapter 17) call for the inclusion of language-different children in regular classrooms to provide equal access to subject matter, cross-cultural exchanges, and interdisciplinary study for LEP students using multiple forms of technology to develop literacy.

Many authors discuss additional attributes that both initiate and sustain the redesign of curriculum and instruction. Changing teacher expectations and viewing all children as capable of success is central

> *Changing teacher expectations and viewing all children as capable of success is central to long-lasting change.*

to long-lasting change, as described by most of these authors. Most also mention flexibility—described by Schumm, Hughes, and Arguelles (Chapter 4) as "elasticity" of roles—as a key to co-constructing change. Montague and Warger (Chapter 2), Schumm, Hughes, and Arguelles (Chapter 4), and Ogle and Fogelberg (Chapter 9) elaborate further when they call for changing the school's central infrastructure to allow for flexible grouping of students, flexible scheduling, planning times for teachers, flexible choice in partners, and predictable routines. These predictable routines are important for teaming with specialists who often participate in multiple classrooms. Of course, other factors are no less important. Montague and Warger (Chapter 2), Schumm, Hughes, and Arguelles (Chapter 4), Pugach and Fitzgerald (Chapter 5), and Lyons (Chapter 10) point to the importance of strong administrators who act as facilitators and advocates for their projects. Other authors echo Peck (Chapter 7) and Ogle and Fogelberg (Chapter 9), who say taking time to build trust is a common aspect of curriculum change projects.

Several authors describe how they bring multiple voices into a dialogue about curriculum and instruction and how this dialogue serves as a catalyst for change and a way to afford continuing change. Teachers establish new communication patterns with community members and parents—sometimes facilitated by home visits as described by Edwards and Danridge (Chapter 14)—and we see how the involvement of new participants results in better decisions about reshaping curriculum. Schmidt (Chapter 12) uses autobiography and biography to link home and school practices and to inform student learning activities. Pérez (Chapter 13) describes a unique, inquiry-based curriculum that changed preservice teachers' views of the community. Both Rodríguez-Brown (Chapter 15) and Ernst-Slavit, Han, and Wenger (Chapter 16) show how home-school connections are strengthened as diverse communities are represented in curricular decisions that better meet the needs of diverse students. Padak, Sapin, and Ackerman (Chapter 6) describe local and statewide family literacy programs that are successful because of the participation of many different groups and agencies. And, Osborne and Schulte (Chapter 18) and Rainforth and England (Chapter 11) bring special education and classroom teachers together to make joint decisions about instruction.

Do participants assume new roles and take ownership for their contributions, the implementation of programs, and students' literacy development and learning?

Many authors discuss new roles taken by teachers and other members of the collaborative partnerships. For example, Montague and Warger (Chapter 2), Walker, Scherry, and Gransbery (Chapter 3), Schumm, Hughes, and Arguelles (Chapter 4), Lyons (Chapter 10), Rainforth and England (Chapter 11), Osborne and Schulte (Chapter 18), and Bean (Chapter 19) involve classroom teachers and specialists in joint planning, developing shared expectations, and sharing teaching responsibilities. Padak, Sapin, and Ackerman (Chapter 6) discuss shared roles between teachers and community professionals, such as social workers, who come together to make decisions about statewide and community-based literacy projects. And Walker, Scherry, and Gransbery (Chapter 3), Pugach and Fitzgerald (Chapter 5), and Schmidt (Chapter 12) refer to decision-making roles shared by administrators and teachers in schoolwide collaboration projects.

Students assume new roles, too. Peck (Chapter 7), Schmidt (Chapter 12), and Pérez (Chapter 13) describe student questions that lead to their own investigations and instructional goal setting as students work in mixed-ability groups. Douville and Wood (Chapter 8) show how diverse students can take an active role in Readers Theatre, jigsaw groups, and collaborative strategic reading activities. Both Kennedy and Canney (Chapter 17) and Brophy (Chapter 20) show teachers and students taking on new roles as they work collaboratively to collect, analyze, and report observations.

Parents take on ownership roles in these projects as well. Schmidt (Chapter 12) and Ernst-Slavit, Han, and Wenger (Chapter 16) show parents becoming actively involved in their children's literacy. Parents begin to see themselves as "literacy teachers" in the projects described by Edwards and Danridge (Chapter 14) and Rodríguez-Brown (Chapter 15).

Does collaboration allow for continuous and dynamic interactions both inside and outside classrooms and schools?

Typically teachers have worked in isolation, segregated diverse students, ignored parents and community members, and involved only a few participants in determining appropriate programs, curriculum, and instruction (Friend & Cook, 1996; Graden & Bauer, 1992; Marks & Gersten, 1998). But, from the preceding discussion it is clear that the projects described in this book establish and respect dialogue that has not always been honored in the past. These authors write about continuous conversations in which many voices are heard. A theme we see here is the establishment of understanding and respect for the diverse capabilities, perspectives, and cultural practices of all who are involved in these collaborative ventures. These authors reaffirm the diversity not only of students, but also of parents, educators, and community members as a resource and cornerstone for collaboration and curriculum development.

In many of these chapters, intercultural and intracultural communication occurs among parents, teachers, and students within classrooms and beyond classrooms. Peck (Chapter 7), Schmidt (Chapter 12), Pérez (Chapter 13), and Brophy (Chapter 20) describe continuous communication and collaboration among diverse students and between teachers and students within classrooms as they collaborate on projects fueled by student-generated questions. Schmidt (Chapter 12) shows how these conversations extend beyond school as parents visit classrooms to tell their stories, and Pérez (Chapter 13) describes parents who teach children about herbs in her Community Connection project. Communication between home and school related to family literacy is the focus of Edwards and Danridge (Chapter 14) and Rodríguez-Brown (Chapter 15), who show how parents blend their own ways of reading to their children with teachers' demonstrations of book sharing, and then teach these literacy practices to each other.

Ernst-Slavit, Han, and Wenger (Chapter 16) explain how miscommunication between a family and teacher can be the result of different expectations for literacy curriculum and show how communication and cultural understandings are afforded slowly through the help of an interpreter or liaison. Edwards and Danridge (Chapter 14) discuss factors that can contribute to miscommunication and show how the teacher's role of listener-supporter builds over time as trust develops.

One strength of many chapters in this book is the delineation of planning and problem-solving processes that participants use. Montague and Warger (Chapter 2) and Walker, Scherry, and Gransbery (Chapter 3) discuss the dynamic and evolutionary nature of collaborative processes and remind us that collaborations differ within each school community. Walker, Scherry, and Gransbery (Chapter 3) and Osborne and Schulte (Chapter 18) explain problem-solving approaches that can support development and change in positive ways. Douville and Wood (Chapter 8) and Kennedy and Canney (Chapter 17) describe planning for collaborative literacy and problem-solving activities that require students with diverse cultural, linguistic, and academic needs to support each other's learning.

Chapter authors also identify conversations that extend collaborations beyond schools. Edwards and Danridge (Chapter 14) and Rodríguez-Brown (Chapter 15) show how developing the academic literacy of parents at home builds ownership for their children's literacy. Rainforth and England (Chapter 11) describe a clearly defined service delivery model with examples of staff scheduling and unit plans that use teaching partnerships and teams that include parents. Padak, Sapin, and Ackerman (Chapter 6) promote conversations between and among families and family literacy professionals at the local and state levels. Bean (Chapter 19) extends the collaborative conversation beyond the school to the university—as do Walker, Scherry, and Gransbery (Chapter 3), Peck (Chapter 7), and Pérez (Chapter 13)—where indeed it also belongs.

Challenges to Collaboration

As we collaborate, there are many challenges we face in order to make our work benefit the literacy and learning of all students. Here, we identify and discuss the recurring challenges our authors and their projects suggest.

Challenge #1—Keep Students at the Heart of Collaboration

Although the selected projects described in this book do keep students at the heart of collaboration and the goals of these projects are aimed at the literacy and learning of all students, collaborations can and do occur for other reasons. Some may seem to function for the purpose of professional development (John-Steiner, Weber, & Minnis, 1998), to combat teacher burnout, or to achieve higher standards. But when the literacy and learning of all students, regardless of their differences, is not at the heart of collaboration, we do a tremendous disservice to students, ourselves, our schools, and society. As we collaborate or consider undertaking collaborations, there is a danger in overlooking what should be our primary concern—student success in literacy and learning.

Although most of these ventures describe collaborations in schools, the implications for teacher education are clear. College and university students in teacher education programs also need to be at the heart of collaborative ventures so that they learn the goal of collaborative models, as Bean (Chapter 19) says, to "provide a thoughtfully developed and effective program for students" (p. 366). When preservice teacher education programs include collaborations with schools and practicing educators, the result is more effective teachers who are responsive to individual student strengths and needs and in turn stronger teacher education programs.

Challenge #2—Define, Provide, and Document "Meaningful Literacy and Learning"

Aiming for meaningful literacy and learning is not enough. Collaborators must decide what "literacy and learning" is and then carefully and consistently provide, observe, and document it. Students need to be involved in real, authentic literacy activities in which they practice the strategies and behaviors they need to learn. We must provide quality instruction and omit time spent in alternative tasks that require minimal literacy or do not engage students in the targeted literacy behaviors.

Several authors describe systematic data collection and discuss ongoing assessment that is embedded in decisions about curriculum and instruction to best meet the needs of all students. But, because much collaborative work results in nontraditional curriculum outcomes such as performances, diorama construction, autobiography writing, and complex problem solving, these curriculum changes require teachers to assess and document what happens in their classrooms in nontraditional ways. Ongoing assessment, like qualitative measures used in many of these projects—such as running records, rubrics, checklists, students' writing, portfolios, or combinations of these and other tools—will help collaborators document and understand students' development more precisely. And they will help collaborators be accountable in authentic ways for the results of their innovative work.

Technology is also viewed as valuable to support different learning processes and outcomes as described by Kennedy and Canney (Chapter 17) and Brophy (Chapter 20). We cannot overlook the promise of computer technology to both demonstrate and document student literacy and learning, as well as to provide a useful tool for communication among participants in collaboration.

Challenge #3—Keep Curriculum at the Heart of Collaborative Ventures

When we embrace students as our first priority, our conversations, goals, and decisions should revolve around curriculum and instruction. Pugach and Fitzgerald (Chapter 5) remind us that to put "deliberate decisions about curriculum at the center of collaboration redefines the goals of the joint enterprise" (p. 85). They propose that teacher collaboration is more than just working in the same room; rather, it is working together to help more students succeed through improved curriculum and instructional approaches.

Challenge # 4—Respect Diversity as an Asset in Classrooms, Schools, and Communities

This is difficult today for many educators who must adapt to swift increases in diversity that they have not experienced before. "In contrast to the racial, ethnic and linguistic diversity of U.S. students, the vast majority of teachers and administrators are white and speak English as their native- and only language" (Garcia, 1999, p. 8). But when we view differences among students, educators, parents, and communities as resources rather than deficits, we have rich capital from which to draw as we make schools and classrooms better learning places.

> *When we view differences among students, educators, parents, and communities as resources rather than deficits, we have rich capital from which to draw as we make schools and classrooms better learning places.*

Chapter authors make a case for respecting diversity. For example, Edwards and Danridge (Chapter 14) show how important it is to learn how to listen to others, which leads to sensitivity to diverse capabilities, perspectives, cultures, and languages. Knowledge and understanding of differences as assets allows us to have high expectations for all children. Every participant in the collaborative venture needs to be free of stereotypical thinking and accepting of others' differences as strengths from which to draw and build stronger collaborations.

Challenge #5—Recognize Tensions and Conflicts That Arise in Collaboration

When people with diverse voices, purposes, and roles collaborate, misunderstandings and friction often result. Clearly, safety and trust must be established among collaborators in order for them to explore tensions and conflicts (Clark, Herter, & Moss, 1998). Disharmony often results when different voices attempt to solve problems in different ways, as noted by Montague and Warger (Chapter 2), Edwards and Danridge (Chapter 14), and Ernst-Slavit, Han, and Wenger (Chapter 16), who discuss barriers to collaboration. As well, Osborne and Schulte (Chapter 18) identify lack of administrative support, lack of planning time, scheduling problems, and heavy teacher workloads in special education as barriers to effective collaboration. Many authors suggest models for problem solving that are helpful in resolving differences and dealing with these barriers. Perhaps Rainforth and England's (Chapter 11) notion of "role release" is one way to resolve tension and conflict. Further, recognizing the expertise of all members of the collaborative group can ease conflicts and tensions, and the differences of expertise and opinion can strengthen the collaboration.

Contributions Hold Promise for Building New Understandings

Several characteristics of the projects described in this text hold promise for guiding future collaborative efforts:

- Collaboration is the means to reform and not just the end product. It is sustained over time and highly dependent on *enabling the successful learning of all students*. The collaborators in these projects held *high expectations for success and were committed to understanding others' perspectives*.

- The process of collaboration is embedded in larger goals. Often these goals are *directed at curriculum and social or political reforms* that attack exclusionary practices of schools and educational practices.

- Collaborations that "work" *enrich curriculum* in multiple ways. These collaborations redesign instruction to include student-generated learning, make efforts to reach out to community and bring community resources into the curriculum, and guide instruction by careful assessments and broad/inclusionary interpretations of students' capabilities.

- Collaborations are complex entities. Most have *multiple goals addressed simultaneously* (e.g., student learning, content realignment, redesign of assessments and clarity of expectations, communication among participants).

- Collaborations are dynamic and ever-changing. They are based on project-generated goals and can (and probably should) produce *nontraditional forms of assessment and instruction* that include students' performances and productions, self-evaluation, and problem-solving tasks. Participation includes mixed-ability grouping, peer teaching, students taking roles of experts to solve problems, and parents and community leaders as teachers.

- Assessment and instruction is responsive to students. Their diverse backgrounds, interests, and capabilities are used as assets to build deep literacy learning.

Summary

Allington and Walmsley (1995) begin *No Quick Fix: Rethinking Literacy Programs in America's Elementary Schools* with four ideas that we believe are important to collaborators, whether you are new to partnerships or experienced in shared decisions. They remind us that change is not easily accomplished and, to hope for change in educational systems that are highly resistant, we must accept that

- change comes from within, not afar;
- change will not necessarily cost more money;
- there are no quick fixes; and
- there is no one best way. (p. 12)

Projects described in this book aim to enhance the literacy opportunities and learning environments for the students for which the collaborations were planned. We believe these student-centered goals and outcomes should drive all collaborative ventures. Our goals should not only be to change teacher-research relationships or improve teacher education programs (Clark, Herter, & Moss, 1998). Our goals should not only be about our own professional development, but rather focused on outcomes that translate to literacy development and learning for all students. We should aim to develop shared meanings and knowledge as we discover disagreements and alternative perspectives about students' literacy and learning. We should strive to understand and respect diversity as we engage in responsive and responsible curriculum and instructional change.

What have we learned from these projects that can help us as we engage in future collaborations? We know that we need to increase "equitable and high quality" literacy instruction (Nieto, 2000, p. 10) for students who are often marginalized or excluded from the instructional mainstream. We have learned that both novice and experienced collaborators face many challenges, including shared visions, effective communication, respect for differences, adaptability to change, flexibility in problem solving, negotiation, compromise, and scheduling. We know that as we begin to implement nontraditional curriculum and instruction, we need to explore and adopt nontraditional assessments that document the unique literacy and learning products of students.

This book provides a place to begin thinking about the issues and challenges of collaboration. Despite the successes authors share here, there is still much work to do in restructuring schools and programs to benefit the literacy and learning of all students.

References

Allington, R.L., & Cunningham, P.A. (1996). *Schools that work: Where all children read and write.* New York: HarperCollins.

Allington, R.L., & Walmsley, S.A. (1995). *No quick fix: Rethinking literacy programs in America's elementary schools.* New York: Teachers College Press; Newark, DE: International Reading Association.

Clark, C., Herter, R., & Moss, P.J. (1998). Continuing the dialogue on collaboration. *American Educational Research Journal, 35*(4), 785–791.

Fafard, M.B. (1995). Twenty years after Chapter 766: The backlash against special education in Massachusetts. *Phi Delta Kappan, 76*(7), 536–537.

Friend, M., & Cook, L. (1996). *Interactions: Collaboration skills for school professionals.* New York: Longman.

Garcia, E. (1999). *Student cultural diversity.* Boston: Houghton Mifflin.

Graden, J.L., & Bauer, A.M. (1992). Using a collaborative approach to support students and teachers in inclusive classrooms. In S. Stainback & W. Stainback (Eds.), *Curriculum considerations in inclusive classrooms: Facilitating learning for all students* (pp. 85–100). Baltimore: Paul H. Brookes.

John-Steiner, V., Weber, R.J., & Minnis, M. (1998). The challenge of studying collaboration. *American Educational Research Journal, 35*(4), 773–783.

Marks, S., & Gersten, R. (1998). Engagement and disengagement between special and general education: An application of Miles and Huberman's cross-case analysis. *Learning Disability Quarterly, 21*(1), 34–56.

Nieto, S. (2000). *Affirming diversity* (3rd ed.). New York: Longman.

Walmsley, S.A., & Allington, R.L. (1995). Redefining and reforming instructional support programs for at-risk students. In R.L. Allington & S.A. Walmsley (Eds.), *No quick fix: Rethinking literacy programs in America's elementary schools* (pp. 19–44). New York: Teachers College Press; Newark, DE: International Reading Association.

AUTHOR INDEX

Page references followed by *f* and *t* indicate figures and tables, respectively.

SUBJECT INDEX

Page references followed by *f* and *t* indicate figures and tables, respectively.